Indian Country, L.A.

Del Big Medicine (Cheyenne), Indian Awareness Week Powwow, September 28, 1986, West Hollywood Park, Los Angeles, California.

INDIAN COUNTRY, L.A.

Maintaining Ethnic Community in Complex Society

Joan Weibel-Orlando

UNIVERSITY OF ILLINOIS PRESS
Urbana and Chicago

Publication of this work was supported in part by a grant from the Division of Social Sciences at the University of Southern California.

This book is printed on acid-free paper.

Library of Congress Cataloging-in-Publication Data

Weibel-Orlando, Joan, 1938-
    Indian country, L.A. : maintaining ethnic community in complex society / Joan Weibel-Orlando.
        p.   cm.
    Includes bibliographical references and index.
    ISBN 0-252-01758-7 (cl. : acid-free paper)
    1. Indians of North America—California—Los Angeles—Urban residence. 2. Indians of North America—California—Los Angeles—Ethnic identity.   I. Title.
E78.C15W48 1991
307.76′2′08997079494—dc20   90-40682
                                                          CIP

This book is dedicated to
the American Indian people who
taught me their meaning of community.
Whether the twenty-first century finds you
on Indian lands or in urban places,
may you continue
to walk the good red road
with all your relations.
mitak' oyas'in

Contents

viii *Contents*

Preface

September 28, 1986, was another in the seemingly endless chain of hot, dry, brilliant days that typify Indian summer in Los Angeles. The sky was cloudless. It had not rained in months. Only daily irrigation sustained trees large enough to provide a dappled shade for the walkways and buildings of the West Hollywood Recreation Center. It was perfect weather for a Sunday afternoon in the park. By noon the grounds were already crowded with West-siders. Knots of young parents, having long since staked out their picnic areas, busied themselves with lighting barbecues and patting generous hamburgers onto grills. Children scrambled down slides and onto the jungle gym. Assorted urbanites of all ages lazed in the sun, read the Sunday *Times,* and tossed Frisbies to their pampered pets. Balloon sales had been good that morning, and now psychedelic green and hot pink helium-filled globes punctuated the park. Bobbing wildly as the children to whose wrists their strings had been tied dashed about from one play area or game to another, the balloons added a festive note to the cityscape. Sunday in the park—a quintessential urban recreation.

But wait . . . who is that striding in such moccasined purposefulness across the park? What can we make of the circle of brilliantly colored feathers at his waist? Is he some alien form, more bird than man? Is he from our collective past? Have we been caught up, inexplicably, in some sort of temporal black hole or time warp? He walks among us as if his beaded warrior regalia were customary and appropriate to the occasion. Is he as oblivious to our consternation and bald-faced stares as he appears? By what dramaturgical magic will he and his fellow powwowers transform an urban park into American Indian ceremonial space? Is he, in the end, merely a figment of our collective imagination, more icon than reality? What can be made of this *rara avis*, this *homo historicus*, this urban Indian in our midst?

These questions have provided the framework of my anthropological research for the last nineteen years. As incongruous as it may seem, the 1990 Census should show that decidely more American Indians in the United States live in cities than in rural and reservation areas. No longer residents of isolated, culturally conservative, ethnically homogeneous rural communities, Indians have been migrating to urban centers in increasing numbers for at least four decades. Some Indian families have children and grandchildren who were born in cities. For the most part, these second- and third-generation urbanites rarely return to their ancestral homes. When they do, it is usually for short holiday visits or during school vacations. The meaning, to individual Indians and to the development of an urban Indian community structure and a pantribal identity, of time spent in an urban setting, a mainstream education, gainful employment, and contact with other urban American Indians is an overriding theme of this book.

My research began in the spring of 1973, when I was a graduate student in the Department of Anthropology at the University of California at Los Angeles. During the next four years, while preparing my doctoral dissertation ("Native Americans in Los Angeles: A Cross-cultural Comparison of Assistance Patterns in an Urban Environment"), I had almost daily contact with American Indian individuals and organizations. Subsequent research in and publication about this community include an ethnography of urban Indian drinking behavior, an analysis of the Indian community response to abusive drinking among its members, and the study of ethnic group membership's contribution to well-being in old age. My research activities and involvement in the development of Indian community-based social services programs in Los Angeles is ongoing.

Since 1973 over three hundred Indians who lived for periods of time in Los Angeles have shared their life histories with me. These personal narratives are the vehicles by which I came to recognize and understand the interactive properties that define and sustain North America's largest urban Indian community. I owe a great debt of gratitude to these people for having responded to my inquiry with such candor, humor, and insight.

Participation in the community's institutional activities over a time span of sixteen years provided tangible evidence of continuing community process. The willingness with which the personnel of scores of Los Angeles Indian social services, recreational, spiritual, educational, and economic institutions allowed me not only to observe but also to assume functional roles in their activities can never be fully reciprocated and is very much appreciated.

My research has been supported by the Ford Foundation, the anthropology department at the University of California at Los Angeles, the anthropology department and the Division of Social Sciences at the University of Southern California, the California State Department of Alcohol and Drug Programs, the National Institute of Alcohol Abuse and Alcoholism, and the National Institute on Aging. Sylvester Whitaker, as dean of the Division of Social Sciences and Communication at USC, kindly arranged for my partial release from teaching responsibilities during the 1988–89 academic year. His generous support of the project made possible the timely completion of the manuscript.

Several people were asked to read portions of the first draft of the manuscript relevant to their own life or research experience. Their responses provided valuable early critiques of the work. I am especially thankful to the Indian community members whose life histories are summarized in section V for pointing out any inadvertent factual errors they found and for allowing me to publish personal information they shared with me. Fellow anthropologists Joan Ablon, Eugene Cooper, Shirley Fiske, Alexander Moore, John Peterson, Andrei Simić, Jack Waddell, and Walter Williams all read early drafts of portions of the manuscript. Their reactions to the material and their editorial suggestions contributed significantly to the manuscript's final structure and tone.

The powwow photographs are my own, taken in 1986 and 1987 in the context of a USC postgraduate photography class taught by Bill Aron and Diego Vigil. The seminar and practicum led to the organization of and my participation in the Ethni-City Photography Exhibit held at USC in May 1987. The Fifth Sunday Sing photographs were taken by my husband, Robert A. Orlando, and me at the April 30, 1989, sing that was hosted by the First Native American and United Methodist Church of Norwalk, California. I am grateful to the several members of the Indian community featured in the book's photographs for allowing me to reproduce their images in this way. The photograph used to illustrate the dust jacket was staged by me and taken by my husband in June 1990. The tower of Los Angeles's signature architectural icon—City Hall—provides the backdrop for the portrait of Kelly Looking Horse (Lakota), his wife, Suzanne (Pomo), and their daughters, Weyaka-win, Mauni-win, and Wichagpi-win. All the other photographs were taken at naturally occurring Indian community events. My son, William M. Weibel III, and my husband, both excellent photographers in their own right, were my original photographic mentors. With their encouragement, I eventually began to capture my perception of the Los Angeles Indian community on film. It is to them that I owe my initial and growing involvement in the problematics of visual versus written anthropological documentation.

Chase Langford, a geographer at UCLA, produced maps 2.1 and A.1. William Weibel and Alice Del Rosario produced figures 8.1, 9.1, and 9.2, which illustrate the Saturday night powwow floor plan and the urban and rural Indian church grounds, as well as figures 15.1 and 15.2, which outline two versions of a proposed urban Indian governance plan. Philip Kajszo, president of the computer consulting firm Micro-Med Enterprises, developed the software that allowed the transfer of the manuscript, prepared and stored on Alpha Micro, to disks that could be converted to the editing program used by the University of Illinois Press.

John Long, my research associate since 1978, contributed significantly to the orderly collection, maintenance, and analysis of fieldwork notes, observations, and interviews, yielding the data on which our publications have been based. His thorough and reasoned review of a second draft of this manuscript provided the invaluable third eye. His scholarship and friendship for more than a decade of joint research efforts have been rich personal resources for which I continue to be very grateful.

The book would not have been written if I had not had the loving support, technical assistance, and collegial criticism of my husband. With boundless good spirit, he took time from his busy medical practice and research to organize my collection of illustrations, maps, chapters, introductions, and reference lists into a coherent table of contents, to edit first drafts of chapters, and to construct informational tables. The grace with which he left me to my boxes of field notes and interview tapes, weekend after weekend, is a measure of his respect for the fact that, like Virginia Woolf, I need a room of my own.

Lastly, I wish to express my profound appreciation to Elizabeth G. Dulany, assistant director of the University of Illinois Press, for her initial interest in this project. Her encouragement and support during the year in which I completed the manuscript and throughout the peer review process was a model of optimum publisher and author rapport. I was greatly moved by the kindness, enthusiasm, and empathy with which she and her staff, particularly Theresa L. Sears, my editor, have treated me and the subject of my book.

INDIAN COUNTRY, L.A.

Introduction

FOR MORE than a century, Los Angeles has been a major West Coast port of entry for successive waves of Hispanic, Asian, and Pan-Pacific immigrants to the United States, the majority of whom deemed life in an American urban-industrial center preferable to the economic or political instability of their homeland. From the darkest days of the Great Depression and as a result of the disastrous Dust Bowl of the 1930s, the City of Angels also has harbored hundreds of thousands of economic refugees from the American hinterland.

Los Angeles is characterized by well-established and developing ethnic quarters or enclaves, a residential pattern shared by most great metropolitan centers that have industrialized during the twentieth century. As an ethnically diverse port of entry, the city provides a natural laboratory for the study of ethnic community development, diverse social processes, culture change, and individual adaptation.

North American Indians are among the more recently arrived culture groups to establish themselves as a community in already ethnically heterogeneous Los Angeles. Prior to World War II, there were no more than 5,000 Indians in Los Angeles County (Price 1968); by 1980 that number had increased tenfold. While the increase was dramatic, the 50,000 Indians in Los Angeles represent only a tiny fraction (0.006 percent) of the total county population and are numerically insignificant when compared to the other major ethnic and racial groups that make up Los Angeles's cultural mosaic: blacks (944,009), Asians (434,914), and Hispanics (2,065,727). Even the more recently arrived Koreans were present in greater numbers (60,618) in 1980.[1] Notwithstanding their numerical minority vis-à-vis other ethnic groups, the 50,000 American Indians in Los Angeles constitute the largest urban Indian population in the United States.

Section I of this book is a historical, demographic, and cultural profile of the Los Angeles American Indian community. Now, as in 1966 when the first comprehensive survey of the Indian population was initiated by the Department of Anthropology at UCLA,[2] the Los Angeles Indian community is characterized by extreme cultural heterogeneity, a dispersed settlement pattern, and scattered locations or nodes of symbolic and instrumental interaction. Given this diversity and attenuation of traditional social forms, one might expect a fragile (if not the absence of) social cohesion among the Indians in Los Angeles. However, continuous observation since 1973 of the county's burgeoning Indian community confirms a viability, tenacity, and political power far beyond that suggested by this loosely organized social group's small numbers, lack of geographic concentration, and cultural heterogeneity.

Longitudinal association with American Indians in Los Angeles forced me to reexamine my preconceptions about what constitutes community and its processes and how community is developed and maintained in complex society. In section II, I discuss my personal experience and biases with regard to a definition of community. These experientially determined understandings of community are compared with classic theoretical and inductively derived models of community and with my findings concerning the Los Angeles Indians' own definitions of community. Existing analytic models of community imperfectly fit the social construct American Indians in Los Angeles refer to when they invoke the term "community."

Development of an anthropological model that adequately addresses the issue of nontraditional forms of community was essential. The social entity that substantial numbers of Indians in Los Angeles think of as their community is both a cognitive construct and an interactional pattern. Community can reside in the mind, reflect a sentiment, and be the product of symbolic as well as pragmatic social interactions unrestricted by considerations of shared space. My task was to discover those social structures, symbolic and instrumental activities, and opportunities for face-to-face contact, albeit time-limited, that provide the social exchanges by which community is experienced, recognized, and defined despite, and perhaps because of, the absence of a spatial focus in the Los Angeles American Indians' residential patterns.

Curiously, though several anthropologists have worked with Indians in Los Angeles since the 1960s, no comprehensive ethnography of the Los Angeles Indian community had been published to date. In a community of this complexity, the ethnographer's task is made manageable by a reduction of scope, a honing of focus at the sacrifice of holistic perspective. Therefore, the several published articles based on early fieldwork in the Los Angeles Indian community tend to be sharply focused on anthropological theory development (Price 1968), theory testing (Fiske and Weibel 1980), ethnographic description and analysis of a single institution (Gardner 1969), social process (Weibel 1978), or social problems (Weibel-Orlando 1984). This first compilation and synthesis of my observations and the observations of others, both published and unpublished, as well as an analysis of the social trends that led to the development of the Los Angeles Indian community are my attempt to rectify this information gap.

The lack of a comprehensive ethnography of the Los Angeles Indian community after two decades of research underscores the difficulties inherent in the study of complex societies. The choice or development of appropriate observational and recording techniques, given the dispersed residence pattern and sociocultural heterogeneity of this ethnic community, is of major methodological concern. Certain generally accepted anthropological fieldwork strategies appropriate for studies and descriptions of bounded, internally consistent, small-scale societies (e.g., participant observation, the collection of life history interviews, and ritual analysis) transfer well to the urban setting. However, other theoretical and methodological tools of the ethnographer are not fully appropriate or need modification and amplification when working in dispersed urban ethnic communities or in a social field as complex as Los Angeles. Traditional mapping and census strategies, for example, would yield little ethnographically significant information because of the dispersed, mobile nature of members of the Los Angeles Indian community.

What its members mean when they intone the phrase "The Los Angeles American Indian community" reveals itself only over time and in fleetingly fragile pieces of a complex social mosaic. Continuous personal contact and involvement in the social, political, and service institutions of the Los Angeles Indian community, along with the collection of over three hundred life histories since 1973, have provided me with a holistic understanding of the ongoing interconnections of individual actors in this ethnic arena, interconnections that helped to create and sustain a sense of Los Angeles Indian ethnic corporality and community.

This ethnography addresses a number of theoretical issues. In light of the tribal diversity and increased residential dispersion of American Indians in Los Angeles, what is meant when the term "Los Angeles Indian community" is invoked? What are the sociostructural mechanisms that foster a sense of belonging and a shared identity among these people? What social phenomena provide members of particular ethnic organizations with a sense of belonging to a larger social entity that encompasses the separate institutions—that is, a Los Angeles American Indian community? How is such a social form constructed, given the divisive factors apparent in this extremely varied collection of tribal groups?

Essential to any definition of community is the location of the institutions that transcend time and individual agendas or personalities and structure the interactions of community members.[3] As demonstrated in section III, this is no simple task in the Los Angeles Indian community. More than two hundred such ethnic associations have been created, flourished, and atrophied since the 1920s, when American Indian migration to Los Angeles first occurred with some regularity. Today, the Los Angeles Indian community structure is sustained by a network of and intersecting participation in an impressive array of institutionalized political, economic, medical, religious, educational, recreational, and informational organizations, all of which are based on pragmatic but fragile constructions of ethnic unity. Distinct, often tangential, but also at times mutually exclusive special interest groups and the cooperative activities they sponsor are recognized by both members and observers as the social structures that provide a continuing sense of history, community, and ethnic identity (traditional and novel) for those Indians who have chosen to "have a foot in both worlds" and to "try making it" in the city.[4]

Institutions provide the rationale for patterned social interaction and are the contexts in which the ongoing events that constitute community process occur. These contexts provide stages on which *social drama*, in Turner's (1974) sense of the term, can be played out and validated by the witnessing community. In section IV, I describe three regularly occurring, prominent, and widely different American Indian community events, or "social arenas" (Moore 1978), where community is embodied in collective action. Infrequent to daily face-to-face interactions of individuals who perceive some common interest or bond that structures and legitimizes their interaction are the contexts in which community statuses and roles are achieved and sustained.

These arenas and the social and ritual behavior for which they are the contexts are a syncretic mix of cultural continuities and innovation. Certain patterned behaviors transcend the American Indian migration to the city. The powwows and Fifth Sunday sings, for example, have their roots in tribal rituals that predate European contact. Even the innovative Los Angeles City-County Native American Indian Commission has its structural and conceptual roots in a nineteenth-century political institution, the tribal council. In this sense, Los Angeles Indian institutional life meets the temporal criteria for community set forth by Arensberg and Kimball (1965). To demonstrate how such institutional life continues to shape and sustain Indian community life in Los Angeles, I have elected to describe the most long-lived and highly visible community institutions and calendar events.

Of equal importance is the discovery of the nexus between individual behavior and cultural context. The richness and texture of life history narratives collected over an extended period of time provide this insight. Consciously choosing to sustain their ethnic identities, a critical mass of American Indians in Los Angeles continue to interact with other Indians for both pragmatic and symbolic reasons.

Over the years, I have identified key individuals who exemplify particular Los Angeles Indian community membership types. These people fill certain recognizable statuses and associated roles in community life that often parallel historical tribal social forms. They also demonstrate, through their multilevel associations and intersecting life career paths, how the Los Angeles Indian community structure is maintained.

In section V, I describe three Los Angeles Indian community figures. Uppermost in my mind when choosing who would be the exemplars was the demonstration of how individual behavior and cognition are not only shaped by one's early enculturation and environment but also are invented, amended, elaborated, and discarded throughout life. Individuals make conscious choices, experiment, create, and don and doff ethnic stances and involvements with considerable skill and grace. The life histories presented here demonstrate how ethnic identification and involvement can be experienced and expressed differentially over a life span. For these people, ethnicity is both a constraint and a resource; they have used it for personal gain in concrete and abstract ways and have experienced the bitter reality of racial prejudice. For them, membership in and maintenance of the social entity known as the Los Angeles Indian community have both sustained and constrained their personal identity, self-worth, and well-being.

Merely cataloging the various Indian institutions in Los Angeles and presenting interesting, entertaining, and informative life histories of individuals active in Los Angeles Indian institutional life would not afford a representative ethnographic understanding of the complexities and dynamism of Los Angeles Indian life. Community is more than the sum of its institutional or individual parts—it is process, social interaction, and the dynamic intersection of its constituent parts in the face of a shared threat or toward the accomplishment of a common goal. A community crisis and the individual and collective responses to that social rupture comprise a circumstance in which community structure and process can be observed.

Such a crisis occurred in October 1986 and made Bramstedt's (1977) analytic concepts of interlocking directorates and community networks real, tangible, and describable through observed individual behavior and collective community effort. The Indian Centers, Inc. (ICI), the second oldest Indian organization in Los Angeles and the largest single employer of American Indians, was defunded. Its demise wrenched the Indian community to its core and left a gaping sociostructural void that is still being bridged. The two-year period during which the ICI closed and its human services programs were reestablished elsewhere affords an epistemological window[5] through which community dynamics and process can be observed firsthand. The deinstitutionalization of the ICI and the collective response of the Indian community to that process provide the framework for section VI, the concluding segment of the book.

The individuals whose life histories are presented in section V are among those whose community careers became enmeshed during the Los Angeles Indian community's greatest political and economic crisis. As I wrote about the events at the ICI, I became aware that my documentation of community process had taken on a narrative structure much like that of Thornton Wilder's novella, *The Bridge of San Luis Rey*. I do not mean to suggest that some metaphysical force was put inexorably into motion by the conjunction of this handful of lives at a certain point in time. Rather, economic, political, and bureaucratic supralocal forces beyond the control of the key community actors impelled the calamity that the community members seemed incapable of forestalling, though they wholeheartedly wished and worked collectively to do so. If any metaphysical forces were at work in this situation, they were the cultural notions of community and the imperative that all members of a community are responsible for its continuity.

In chapters 15 and 16, I attempt to answer a number of questions: Was the eventual demise of the ICI predictable? If so, what were the predictive sociocultural and sociopolitical markers of the impending crisis? Having been read, could interventionists have prevented the eventual loss of a major component of community structure? What positive, policy-relevant lessons are to be learned about social structure and process from this community crisis?

The larger picture is hard-won. A longitudinal perspective is essential to the construction of holistic models of ethnic community structure in complex societies. Because the modern Los Angeles Indian community is demarcated by the influx of non-Californian Indians with the initiation of the Bureau of Indian Affairs's national relocation program in 1951 and the community's struggle to maintain its economic institutions in the wake of reversed social policies during the 1980s, this ethnography covers the historical period from 1952 to 1989.

Forces both internal and external continue to shape the Los Angeles Indian community. The relative significance of particular institutions' and individuals' political and moral authority continues to shift with the vagaries of supracommunity funding policy decisions. The contributions that sociostructural and cultural analyses of these processes make to an anthropology of complex societies is the sustaining rationale of the longitudinal prospective of this study.

The ultimate lessons of my long-term, continuing fascination with the Los Angeles Indian community is an understanding of the synergistic, dynamic, and symbiotic nature of relationships between individuals and their community. A second insight is the tenacity of the idea that perpetuating a viable ethnic community is important work. All of the usual markers, the whole cloth of community (common territory, mutually intelligible language, and shared ethos) appear, at first glance, to be missing in the Los Angeles Indian community. Yet its members have created a negotiated community. Choosing to ignore or to suspend the salience of ethnic markers that would have been divisive, Los Angeles Indians underscore and make salient those notions of traditional Indian ethos and lifeways that a critical mass of its members agree are shared pantribal traits and values. Community building among the Indians in Los Angeles has been a kind of cultural patchwork, a sociostructural *bricolage*,[6] a highly creative and dynamic endeavor.

An anthropology of complex society necessitates comprehensive research designs and competencies. Urban anthropologists must also be cultural geographers, ethnohistorians, and students of bureaucratic and political processes. The fieldwork strategies, both conventional and novel, the data they produce, and the model of urban ethnic community presented here provide a set of alternative methodological and theoretical approaches to the study of ethnic group maintenance in complex societies.

The members of the Los Angeles Indian community who shared their life histories with me have given me an incalculable gift. In exchange for their generosity, this ethnography is my attempt to dispel certain ethnic stereotypes. American Indians are not necessarily urbanization's casualties. They continue to share a cultural tenacity, creativity, and strength of community spirit. The people described in this ethnographic account of community process are not shadow puppets whose functions are the exemplification and explication of social theory. Rather, they are artists at life— individuals who have created and who continue to re-create themselves and their community within the parameters of cherished cultural templates. If the Indians who have shared their roles in and conceptions of their urban community with me are made real and understandable to the reader, then I have completed a culturally appropriate exchange of gifts.

NOTES

1. The 1980 census figures have been taken from LACDRP (1981, 1983a). Most ethnic minority spokespeople and the U.S. Census Bureau itself assert that these figures probably reflect major undercounts of the populations in question and should be interpreted with caution.

2. John Price, a professor of anthropology at UCLA at the time, was the urban Indian project field director. He has written several articles and book chapters based in part on his work in the Los Angeles American Indian community of the mid-1960s (e.g., Price 1968, 1975, 1978).

3. Bramstedt (1977) is one of several early observers (see also Fiske 1979; Price 1975; Weibel 1978) to recognize the sociostructural importance of these ethnic social arenas.

4. Throughout the text, words and phrases in quotation marks are used by members of the Los Angeles Indian community with some frequency.

5. Werner and Schoepfle (1987, I:57–58) define "epistemological window" as any situation during the ethnographic process that potentially

enhances the discovery of new insights into the cultural knowledge of the people under study.

6. Lévi-Strauss (1966) uses *bricoleur,* or "jack-of-all-trades," to describe the cultural innovator who uses a fixed bag of tools, concepts, and conventions to make other things, social forms, and cultural inventions. *Bricolage* is the experimental, transformative process by which the *bricoleur* creates new constructs from recombinations of older sociocultural forms.

I

Historical, Demographic, and Cultural Profiles of the Los Angeles American Indian Community

THE UBIQUITY in the relevant urban anthropology literature of locus and quantifiable population density as prerequisites of community forced me to consider these factors as possible markers of Los Angeles Indian community and prompted the use of research strategies commonly associated with the demographer and cultural geographer. Comparisons of census data from 1950 to 1980 (see chapter 2) provide a profile of dramatic and continuing increases in the Los Angeles Indian population. Equally dramatic is the pattern of increasingly dispersed residence and centrifugal movement away from centrally located ports of entry, which is obtained by plotting relative Indian population shifts across time and geopolitical boundaries in the Los Angeles Basin. The widely dispersed community services pattern, which may be an indigenous response to perceived shifts in Indian residential concentrations, is illustrated by plotting the location of extant and inoperative Indian social services and recreational facilities (see map A.1 in the Appendix). Finally, the continuing cultural diversity of the community is illustrated by an examination of tribal representation and the proliferation of ethnic categories across time (see chapter 3).

This threefold interpretation of my findings is a product of cultural geographic and ethnohistorical perspectives. When mediated by theoretical and experiential anthropological data and analysis, these space-use patterns not only define the Los Angeles Indian community type as open, dispersed, or interactional but help to explain its possible roots in earlier, sustained Indian community cum tribal forms.

1

Historical Overview of Indian Habitation in the Los Angeles Basin

IRONICALLY, UNTIL the mid-eighteenth century the land basin we now think of as Los Angeles County was populated solely by several American Indian societies. The most prominent among these groups were the people now known as Gabrielinos (Kroeber 1967). When the basin was first colonized by Spanish missionaries in 1769, the zealous padres welcomed or coerced the seminomadic indigenous people into the Christian fold (and work force) of their agricultural, mission, and garrison complexes (Brandon 1974). Mission archivists were unnervingly painstaking in their documentation of the calamitous effects of forced sedentarization, acculturation, and Christian serfdom on the indigenous southern California population (Cook 1943). Later, under Mexican and American rules, the Indians suffered from policies that led to further loss of traditional subsistence bases and even condoned genocidal attacks (Cook 1967).

At its peak (circa 1770), the California Indian population was 133,000 strong; by 1910 only 15,000 Indians were counted in the California census (Kroeber 1967:70–74). That 90 percent reduction in the indigenous population is chilling testimony to the cultural devastation that resulted from the imposed policies. Whole Indian societies were annihilated and their languages and lifeways lost to the world (Cook 1967). The colonialization and Americanization of California are among the sorriest chapters in the history of Euro-Indian affairs. To this day, those violations of basic human rights are being addressed in scores of lawsuits on behalf of the descendants of the originally disfranchised California Indians, who seek restitution of traditional territories, cultural identification, and recognition as self-determining political and social entities by the dominant society (Olson and Wilson 1984:196).

American Indian migration into the Los Angeles basin during the mid-twentieth century is not the first culture contact of hinterland tribal groups with Coastal Californians. The seminomadic, village-dwelling Gabrielinos were not cultural isolates. Archaeological research provides rich evidence of established trade routes stretching from the southern California coastal areas to as far east as Arizona, New Mexico, and Colorado. Southern California Coastal Indians and members of Great Basin and Southwestern culture complexes regularly exchanged trade goods such as decorative marine shells, nuts, maize, turquoise, obsidian, pottery, and textiles by means of a well-developed trading system that allowed for the flow of materials and personnel (Driver 1975:214). Documented trade routes suggest continuous, regular, and symbiotic intercultural exchange among the Coastal Californian and interior peoples for at least a thousand years before European incursions into the area (Aikens 1983:177).

Prehistoric, historic, and contemporary American Indian migrations to southern California coastal areas differ, however, in scale and permanency. As late as 1890, migration of noncoastal Indians into southern California could be attributed largely to the defections of a few railroad construction workers or mining squad members. World War I, the depression of the 1930s—which stretched already precarious reservation economies to their breaking points—and enlistment in the armed services or the war machinery work force during World War II were other social forces that either pushed or pulled small numbers of Indians off ancestral lands and into urban-industrial centers in the first half of the twentieth century. Census figures indicate that between 1890 and 1950 the Indian population in California declined proportionally from 1.4 percent to 0.2 percent of the state's total population, despite its modest increase to almost 20,000 persons during the later decades of that period (Price 1968:169).

The 1950s marked a dramatic shift in American Indian residential patterns in California as well as in the nation. During that time, the Indian population in California doubled from 19,943 in 1950 to 39,014 in 1960; in Los Angeles, the Indian population kept pace with statewide increases. In 1955, for example, Los Angeles's Indian population was estimated to be 6,000; in 1960, 12,405 Indians were living in Greater Los Angeles (Price 1968:169).

The Indian population explosion in California and especially in

Los Angeles continued through the 1970s and was in large part the product of a federally sponsored program of Indian relocation. The Bureau of Indian Affairs's (BIA) urban relocation program has been linked to the general 1950s administrative and congressional drive to terminate federal responsibility for Indian welfare (Officer 1971:47). About the time Congress began to seriously consider ways to implement "termination" of the federal government's wardship over Indian tribal holdings, the BIA independently initiated a small "relocation" program on the Navajo and Hopi reservations. The program consisted of off-reservation job placements and was designed to relieve the demands on limited reservation resources by assisting Indians in resettling in the expanding urban-industrial areas of the Southwest and in California (Officer 1971:45).

Within a year of the program's inception, the BIA sought and received a small congressional appropriation to extend off-reservation placement services to Indians in other areas. By 1969 the federal government was spending more than twenty million dollars annually on Indian urban relocation (Officer 1971:53). This level of federal expenditure continued until the mid-1970s. Alice Begay,[1] a Navajo, remembered:

> [The BIA][2] would only pay me for the bus one way. . . . When I got [to L.A.] I had to find the BIA [office] downtown. And I didn't know where to go. . . . It was real scary because, the tall buildings, it was like being in a canyon. I had the directions on a piece of paper. . . . So I got off the bus [and] took a cab all the way to the BIA.
>
> I got off there and I stood there. It was early in the morning . . . seven o'clock. The [BIA office] doesn't open 'til nine o'clock. So I stood there with my suitcase and everything for two hours. And finally one of the ladies came out. "Oh, you're Indian, you come out to see the BIA, I'll take you up there." It was on the third floor. I [sat] there for a whole day. . . .
>
> Finally, they got to me before five o'clock. And they says, "We'll have to find you a place. We'll take yours [application] tomorrow." So she said, "I'm going to take you to this house where all the Indians stay and you're going to have to pay twenty dollars a week to stay there." And I told her, "I don't have any money. I don't have a dime to my name except five dollars that I've been carrying for a long time, I earned baby-sitting at Intermountain Boarding School, but that's all I have." She said, "OK, I'll give you twenty dollars for tonight. . . ." So they put me up for the night. (July 24, 1975)

As this vignette poignantly illustrates, American Indians who migrated to Los Angeles were generally ill-prepared, improbable candidates for twentieth-century city life. Simply placing them in entry-level work slots was not the avenue to hoped-for assimilation. Acquisition of marketable work skills, inculcation of the American work ethic and ethos, and basic survival and coping strategies for life in the urban world were called for. In 1956 the BIA relocation program reorganized and relocatees were placed in urban vocational training programs prior to a job search. Even with these enlightened changes, BIA officials found that large numbers of relocated Indians simply did not remain in the selected urban centers. They made frequent, extended trips back to their places of origin or simply returned home to stay (Graves 1972).

Table 1.1 illustrates the pattern of the BIA-supported migration of American Indians to Los Angeles in the twenty-five-year period from 1952 to 1976. The Direct Employment Program peaked in 1957 and experienced a rapid drop-off in the total number of participants beginning in 1958, as the Adult Vocational Training Program took effect. Participation in the vocational program peaked in 1966 and declined thereafter. Indians who came to Los Angeles alone, rather than with families, were less common under both BIA programs, although more dramatically so in the Direct Employment Program.

By the mid-1970s, it was clear to BIA officials that the relocation programs were not having the hoped-for success in relieving reservation populations and economic pressures. In the last decade, they have implemented alternative solutions to the chronic employment problems on the reservations in the form of improved vocational training at the high school level, placement in higher education facilities on or adjacent to the reservations, and self-help programs initiated by the tribal governments. These programs have stemmed the tide of federally assisted Indian migration to major urban-industrial complexes and were responsible in part for the closing of the BIA field office in Los Angeles by 1980, thus signaling the end of a historic era in federal Indian policy implementation.

In the two and a half decades of its operation in Los Angeles, the BIA's relocation program assisted 29,693 American Indians in their migration to urban Los Angeles; however, this figure masks the true size of the Indian migration to that city. In an earlier study of migration and coping strategies, it was reported that only half of a sample of Los Angeles Indians ($n = 97$) had themselves taken advantage of, or had at least one family member who had taken advantage of, the federal relocation assistance program in moving to Los Angeles (Weibel 1977). The others in the sample had migrated from their places of origin to Los Angeles on their own. Assuming that this finding can be generalized to the entire Los Angeles Indian popula-

Table 1.1 Summary of Arrivals, Adult Vocational Training and Direct Employment Service in Los Angeles

Fiscal year	Adult vocational training					Direct employment				
	Single units	Family Units	Family Persons	Total Units	Total Persons	Single units	Family Units	Family Persons	Total Units	Total Persons
1952						85	87	238	172	323
1953						142	122	412	264	554
1954						381	263	770	644	1,151
1955						380	343	1,292	723	1,672
1956						492	475	1,739	967	2,231
1957						800	574	2,400	1,374	3,200
1958	5	6	29	11	34	323	151	659	474	982
1959	76	50	175	126	251	239	111	447	350	686
1960	50	26	117	76	167	311	124	506	435	817
1961	93	46	161	139	254	286	110	382	396	668
1962	150	66	250	216	400	333	97	403	430	736
1963	180	74	260	254	440	319	128	517	447	836

1964	193	48	198	241	391	342	149	610	491	952
1965	385	135	485	520	870	272	148	593	420	865
1966	485	167	615	652	1,110	254	115	432	369	686
1967	505	133	475	638	980	258	127	486	385	744
1968	564	91	306	655	870	247	122	478	369	725
1969	393	70	240	463	633	127	77	299	204	426
1970	516	105	341	621	857	150	82	322	232	472
1971	419	119	369	538	788	138	68	263	206	401
1972	270	76	247	346	517	39	27	87	66	126
1973	179	57	176	236	355	68	43	148	111	216
1974	115	46	150	161	265	43	38	118	81	161
1975	104	39	138	143	242	51	30	106	81	157
1976[1]	151	60	177	211	328	57	35	97	92	154
Total	4,833	1,414	4,909	6,247	9,752	6,137	3,646	13,804	9,783	19,941

1. In 1975 the anniversary date of the BIA fiscal year was changed from July 1 to October 1. The fiscal year 1976, then, covers the fifteen months from July 1, 1975, to September 30, 1976.

Source: BIA 1977

tion, another 30,000 Indians may have migrated to that city unassisted by the BIA.

The post–World War II expansion and urbanization of the Indian population in California continued for the next two decades. By 1970, 76 percent of the 88,263 Indians in California lived in cities (U.S. Department of Commerce 1973a); also, the Los Angeles County Indian population had again doubled, to 24,504 (U.S. Department of Commerce 1973b). By 1980 slightly less than 200,000 American Indians, Eskimos, and Aleuts lived in California, with 80 percent of the total Indian population living in urban centers and 25 percent (48,158) residing in Los Angeles County (U.S. Department of Commerce 1983a). If urbanization of the American Indian was the goal of the federal relocation programs, in California, at least, that goal had been reached most successfully and in a relatively short period of time.

NOTES

1. Alice Begay is a pseudonym, as are a majority of the proper names of individuals in this book. I have used fictitious names to preserve the anonymity of people whose life histories were told to me in confidence and who either elected not to be identified in this book or could not be located in 1989 when the text was being readied for publication.

2. Words and phrases in brackets have been added only when speakers did not finish a sentence or when they used a pronoun rather than a name, assuming I knew who or what they were talking about.

2

Demographic Dimensions of the Los Angeles Indian Community

Population Size

THE 1980 U.S. CENSUS estimates a Los Angeles County American Indian population of 48,158, or 0.006 percent of the county's total population (LACDRP 1981:2). While numerically one of the smallest ethnic groups in the area, the Indians in Los Angeles constitute the largest and fastest-growing urban Indian population in the United States. In fact, the Indian population in Los Angeles has increased 800 percent since 1955.[1]

One of the problems inherent in making any strong assertions about the size of the Indian population in Los Angeles is that few Indian spokespeople, county officials, or, for that matter, U.S. Census Bureau agents know with certainty how many Indians live in Los Angeles County. Indian community spokespeople go so far as to suggest that the census figures for American Indians in Los Angeles systematically represent a 100 percent undercount. From the onset of my involvement with Los Angeles Indian organizations, every public statement, newspaper article, or funding grant proposal I ever read used population figures that were two to three times larger than the most current Census Bureau estimates.

Attempts to count Indians in Los Angeles are fraught with problems, as the Census Bureau is aware. In fact, Census Bureau planners had initially included an Indian component in the 1986 Los Angeles Special Census, the specific purpose of which was to devise a more effective plan for counting urban Indians in 1990. The Indian community, in turn, formed a Complete Count Committee but failed to launch comprehensive advertising and door-to-door campaigns. Due to poor initial returns of mailed questionnaires and concern with cost effectiveness, Census Bureau officials subsequently announced a 50 percent reduction in the scope of the project. The Complete Count Committee, in response to that decision, called an emergency press conference on March 27, 1986. To the assembled reporters, Bill Fredricks, a committee member and a prominent, long-standing Indian community facilitator, explained both the logistical difficulties in assessing the Los Angeles Indian population and the political and economic significance of the proposed special census count. Census figures determine the availability of government and private funds for the Indian community, he argued, and there was understandable concern that the planned reduction of effort would jeopardize any chance of developing a realistic measure of the Indian population base.

The last-ditch media event did not have the hoped-for effect. Three days after the press conference, the Census Bureau canceled its operations in the target area where Indians had established collection sites. In subsequent meetings of the Special Census Committee, members railed in frustration at the bureau's and their own cultural amnesia. "Don't the Census Bureau and the Special Count Committee members know by now that Indians don't like filling out government forms?" an unidentified member of the Indian community commented. "Why should we answer all those personal questions that are none of their business anyway? And the letters explaining the census forms probably didn't reach the people you sent them to anyway . . . [because] Indians move around a lot" (April 22, 1986). By mid-1986 some Indian community leaders had despaired of the Census Bureau's ability to produce any valid estimate about the size of the Los Angeles Indian population in 1990.

Residential mobility is a confounding factor in any attempt to count the number of Indians in Los Angeles. Those who "try making it" in Los Angeles are extremely mobile, and adults, small children, and whole families shuttle back and forth from reservation homelands to Los Angeles as family pressures, job opportunities, and illnesses necessitate. Girlfriends move in with boyfriends, grown children with parents or aunts and uncles, and grandmothers and grandfathers with adult children as layoffs, vacations, family quarrels, and love interests dictate. Not particularly concerned with informing social services agencies and other official groups of their whereabouts, Indians are best located through the "moccasin telegraph"[2] rather than through formal routes of inquiry. One's degree of Indian heritage, marriage to non-Indians, and personal decisions about ethnic identification when parents are from different ethnic groups further complicate the issue and probably result in many American Indians not identifying themselves as such in the national census.

Los Angeles Indian spokespeople and social services facilitators are convinced that for every Indian who does get included in the census equation there is another one who does not. With considerable and seasonal movement to and from the homelands, I suspect the actual number of Indians in Los Angeles at any given time is widely variable. The stable, core population lies somewhere between the 1980 official statistical model (48,158) and Indian social services administrators' politically motivated inflations (100,000) of existing census data. Given that the U.S. Census Bureau figures demonstrate 100 percent increases in the Los Angeles Indian population for each decade since 1950, and taking into account some leveling of Indian in-migration in the 1980s,[3] return migration, and the natural increase in size of the families who remained in Los Angeles to raise their children, I predict that the 1990 U.S. Census will count more than 75,000 American Indians in Los Angeles County.

Sex and Age Distribution

Overall, 52 percent of the Los Angeles County Indian population is female; however, the ratio of males to females varies inversely with age. While there are more boys (51.1 percent) than girls under the age of fourteen, the proportion of teenage boys to girls (fifteen to nineteen years of age) reverses (48 percent males and 52 percent females). The ratio of men to women further decreases with each age bracket. In fact, 62 percent of the Los Angeles American Indians who were sixty-five years of age or older when the 1980 census was taken were women (U.S. Department of Commerce 1982b).

A growing number of American Indians have members from four successive generations of their families living in Los Angeles. Those first relocatees, who migrated during and after World War II, now have children, grandchildren, and great-grandchildren who were born in Los Angeles. Not unexpectedly, then, in 1980 the American Indian population was disproportionately younger than the general Los Angeles County population. For example, 32 percent of the Indians were under the age of seventeen, while only 27 percent of the general population was (LACCDD 1982:27).

The greatest age distribution difference between Los Angeles Indians and the county's general population occurs among people over sixty-four years of age—10 percent in the general population versus 4.3 percent among Indians. Return migration accounts in part for this difference. In 1983, when I began a study of aging among Los Angeles Indians, I discovered that approximately 50 percent of the people I had interviewed who would have been at least sixty in 1983 no longer lived in Los Angeles. They had "gone home"—returned to their tribal homelands to live out their retirement years (Weibel-Orlando 1988a). This return migration pattern has served effectively to keep the proportion of elderly Indians in Los Angeles low.

The going-home phenomenon appears to have peaked, however. In 1988 and 1989, a needs assessment study of elderly Los Angeles Indians indicated that only 18 percent of those interviewed intended to return to their places of origin in the future (Weibel-Orlando 1989). Ties to friends and children, involvement in ethnic activities, and the attainment of satisfying community statuses and roles in their urban ethnic community have fostered the growth of a small but stable core of older Indians in Los Angeles.

Employment and Socioeconomic Status

As with most rural-to-urban migrants in the twentieth century, the Indians' decision to move from traditional homelands was an economic one. Post–World War II Los Angeles was an industrial boomtown. Entry-level positions in the aircraft, petroleum, construction, and manufacturing industries were plentiful. With minimal instruction (often facilitiated by the Bureau of Indian Affairs's vocational training program), young Indians could enter blue-collar positions and experience full-time, permanent employment, often for the first time in their lives.

Three decades later, the largest percentage of Los Angeles Indians remain in blue-collar employment. Commercial, public, and Indian-specific services employ the next largest percentage of Indians. A disproportionately small but growing number of Indians who have acquired training in commerce and management and/or a college education now command white-collar positions in industry and government. Although the move to the urban center has meant steady employment and relatively more income per capita than could have been expected on the reservation, there are disturbing signs that American Indians are still among the most economically disadvantaged ethnic groups in Los Angeles.

In 1980, at a time when the unemployment figure for the general population was 6 percent, American Indians (at 9.46 percent) were second only to the Los Angeles black population (at 10.38 percent) in the percentage of unemployed persons (LACDRP 1983b:3). According to 1980 socioeconomic indicators, 17 percent of the Los Angeles Indian population was below the poverty line, as opposed to 10 percent of the white population; once again, only the black population had a higher percentage of its people (23 percent) with incomes below the poverty line (U.S. Department of Commerce 1982b:6–162). For a number of Indians, urban migration has meant a grudging acceptance of plateaued careers for the sake of job security. Or else limited skills and inconsistent work habits have resulted in work careers characterized by sporadic bouts of temporary employment followed by long periods of unemployment, idleness, and dependence on the public welfare system for subsistence—the all-too-familiar reservation work patterns that, it had been hoped, would be mitigated by the move to an urban-industrial center.

Residential Dispersion

Attempts to discover the parameters of community among Los Angeles Indians is further complicated by an absence of an identifiable spatial locus. There are no Indian neighborhoods in Los Angeles, no little Window Rocks or Indian Towns. Rather, the Indians who came to Los Angeles in the 1950s and 1960s found housing where they could and where their employment dictated. The initial ports of entry were (and continue to be) poorer, transitional, central city neighborhoods where working-class white, Hispanic, Asian, and American Indian tenants have created a buffer zone between the middle-class, predominantly white suburbs and the expanding black south-central Los Angeles population. Here families with a number of small children, common among the young adult Indians who seek their futures in Los Angeles, are accepted if they are willing to pay relatively higher rents.

The American Indians who migrated to Los Angeles during the Bureau of Indian Affairs's urban relocation period were generally unprepared to assume anything but the most elementary employment. During their premigration BIA school experience, they acquired few skills that were marketable in the post–World War II Los Angeles industrial complex. Although initial employment was facilitated by BIA recruiters, Indian migrants were still among the proverbial last hired–first fired. A few months of employment at minimum wages were followed by uncertain months of layoff and job hunting. As a result, individuals moved in and out of nuclear and extended family living accommodations—at a high rate during their early years in the city—according to the current employment climate (Weibel 1977).

From its inception in 1952 until 1978, the BIA Relocation Program provided temporary rental housing for almost 50 percent of the American Indian migrants to Los Angeles (Weibel 1977). These initial orientation periods were followed by moves to more permanent rented lodgings, close to either the new employment or school sites. Often, friends and family members who earlier had made the move to Los Angeles would house the new arrivals for the initial adjustment period, and this frequently led to the location of more permanent housing in the same neighborhood. While one might expect that this strategy encouraged pockets of Indian residents, in fact no Los Angeles neighborhood has ever had large or recognizable concentrations of Indians. Only two incorporated cities (Bell Gardens and Cudahy, in southeast Los Angeles County) have ever had more than 2 percent of their residents identified as American Indians.

Table 2.1 provides information on the dispersed Indian residential pattern in Los Angeles County. The overall population increase for the county from 1970 to 1980 was 6.2 percent (LACDRP 1982:2), whereas the Los Angeles County American Indian population increased 96.5 percent during the same period. The widely varying Indian population growth patterns across the cities for which there are data suggests, however, a considerable selective residential redistribution of American Indians in the county between 1970 and 1980.

The adjoining cities of Bell Gardens and Cudahy, traditionally thought of as centers of Indian residence and activity, continue to have the largest ratios of Indian residents to total population. However, the proportional and actual sizes of their Indian populations declined 3.3 percent and 22.0 percent, respectively, between 1970 and 1980. Aside from the Indian population drift out of Bell Gardens and Cudahy, actual Indian population decreases occurred in only three other Los Angeles County cities (Artesia, Inglewood, and Compton). Compton and Inglewood have become largely black (74.8 percent and 57.3 percent, respectively) and Hispanic (21.1 percent and 19.2 percent, respectively).[4] By contrast, Artesia is largely white (58.8 percent) and Hispanic (34.7 percent). The Indian population decline in Artesia is consistent with the city's general population

Table 2.1 American Indian Population Distribution Shifts in Los Angeles County Incorporated and Unincorporated Areas, 1970–80

City/area	Native American population (%)		Number of Indians		Population growth (%)	
	1980	1970	1980	1970	City	Indian
Bell Gardens	2.2	2.6	738	762	16.4	−3.3
Cudahy	2.1	2.8	376	476	5.8	−22.0
Palmdale	1.7	0.5	208	46	44.2	352.2
Hawaiian Gardens	1.6	0.7	174	63	16.5	176.2
Industry	1.4	0.1	9	1	−6.7	800.0
Lawndale	1.4	0.8	322	199	−5.5	61.8
Bell	1.3	0.9	335	196	16.6	70.9
El Monte	1.2	0.5	978	349	13.7	181.1
Lancaster	1.2	0.3	577	138	2.1	315.8
Maywood	1.2	1.1	253	187	28.3	66.0
Norwalk	1.1	0.5	972	428	−5.5	127.1
Paramount	1.1	0.6	387	225	4.8	72.0
Baldwin Park	1.0	0.5	499	236	16.5	111.4
Irwindale	1.0	0.9	10	7	31.4	42.8
Pomona	1.0	0.4	954	388	6.1	145.9
Commerce	0.9	0.9	99	96	−1.2	3.1
Huntington Park	0.9	0.8	400	280	37.0	42.8
La Puente	0.9	0.6	268	187	−0.7	43.3
Lomita	0.9	0.2	160	40	−13.1	300.0
San Fernando[1]	0.9	0.5	154	89	7.0	73.0
Santa Fe Springs	0.9	0.2	126	30	1.3	300.0
Signal Hill	0.9	0.8	54	44	2.6	22.7
Artesia	0.8	0.9	108	133	−3.1	−18.8
Avalon[1]	0.8	0.1	16	2	32.2	700.0
Azusa	0.8	0.4	241	88	16.5	173.9
Bellflower	0.8	0.4	391	183	8.1	113.6
Carson	0.8	0.6	631	427	14.2	47.8
La Mirada	0.8	0.2	339	62	33.0	446.8
Long Beach	0.8	0.3	2,982	1,173	0.7	152.2
Redondo Beach	0.8	0.3	451	179	−0.6	152.0
Rosemead	0.8	0.5	349	192	4.0	81.7
San Gabriel	0.8	0.3	251	81	2.5	170.0
South El Monte	0.8	0.5	130	64	23.7	103.1

(*continued*)

Table 2.1 *(Continued)*

City/area	Native American population (%) 1980	1970	Number of Indians 1980	1970	Population growth (%) City	Indian
Burbank	0.7	0.4	615	355	−4.8	73.2
Downey	0.7	0.3	557	266	−6.7	109.4
El Segundo	0.7	0.3	90	47	−12.0	91.5
Hawthorne	0.7	0.5	411	267	5.9	53.9
Hermosa Beach	0.7	0.3	131	52	3.8	151.9
Lakewood	0.7	0.2	552	166	−10.1	232.5
Lynwood	0.7	0.5	329	217	12.0	51.6
Monrovia	0.7	0.2	225	61	44.4	268.9
San Dimas	0.7	0.2	165	37	53.0	345.9
South Gate	0.7	0.6	441	328	17.4	34.4
Walnut	0.7	0.3	67	19	66.5	252.6
West Covina	0.7	0.2	536	151	17.7	255.0
Unincorporated Areas[2]	0.7	0.3	6,747	2,820	—	139.3
Covina	0.6	0.2	203	61	11.0	232.8
Duarte	0.6	0.4	103	60	11.9	71.7
Glendora	0.6	0.2	232	64	20.3	262.5
La Verne	0.6	0.3	146	39	81.3	274.4
Los Angeles	0.6	0.3	16,595	9,166	5.5	81.0
Pico Rivera	0.6	0.4	315	216	11.3	45.8
Sierra Madre	0.6	0.1	66	17	−10.7	288.2
Whittier	0.6	0.3	408	188	−5.5	117.0
Alhambra	0.5	0.2	347	124	4.0	179.8
Gardena	0.5	0.3	215	123	10.1	74.8
Glendale	0.5	0.3	682	398	4.8	71.4
Inglewood	0.5	0.5	436	450	4.7	−3.1
La Habra Heights	0.5	[3]	25	[3]	—	—
Montebello	0.5	0.3	260	126	23.6	106.3
Pasadena	0.5	0.2	586	280	5.7	109.3
Torrance	0.5	0.2	648	228	−2.6	184.2
Cerritos	0.4	0.1	235	16	232.7	1,368.9
Claremont	0.4	0.2	115	50	24.9	130.0
Culver City	0.4	0.2	165	69	10.7	139.1

(continued)

Table 2.1 (*Continued*)

City/area	Native American population (%)		Number of Indians		Population growth (%)	
	1980	1970	1980	1970	City	Indian
La Canada/Flintridge	0.4	0.1	42	21	0.0	100.0
Manhattan Beach	0.4	0.2	116	71	−10.8	63.4
Monterey Park	0.4	0.1	208	73	10.5	135.0
Santa Monica	0.4	0.3	396	240	0.0	65.0
South Pasadena	0.4	0.2	89	57	−1.3	56.1
Temple City	0.4	0.2	125	52	−6.6	140.4
Arcadia	0.3	0.1	147	45	1.9	226.6
Compton	0.3	0.5	250	393	3.5	−36.4
Rancho Palos Verdes	0.3	3	93	3	—	—
Rolling Hills	0.3	0.0	6	0	0.0	N/A
Hidden Hills[1]	0.2	0.0	4	0	15.1	N/A
Rolling Hills Estates	0.2	0.0	19	0	39.7	N/A
Beverly Hills	0.1	0.04	38	33	−3.1	15.2
Palos Verdes Estates	0.1	0.03	17	4	5.5	325.0
San Marino	0.135	0.02	18	3	−6.1	500.0
County total			48,158	24,504	6.2	96.5

1. Does not appear on map 2.1.
2. All unnamed areas on map 2.1.
3. Unincorporated areas in 1970.
Source: LACDRP 1982; U.S. Department of Commerce 1973.

decline and may be attributable to the completion of the Artesia Freeway, which displaced a number of residents.

Seven other southeast Los Angeles County cities[5] surrounding Bell Gardens and Cudahy, all of which have had large numbers of Indian residents for at least fifteen years, had only modest Indian population increases (ranging from 34.4 to 72 percent) that fell far short of overall population gains and the 96.5 percent overall gain in the Los Angeles County Indian population. Once overwhelmingly white and working class, these cities are increasingly populated by ethnic minorities. For example, Spanish-speaking families from Mexico and Central America now comprise from a low of 43 percent of the population in Lynwood to a high of 81 percent of the populations of Maywood and Huntington Park. Similar shifts have occurred to the west in Carson, Hawthorne, Lawndale, and Gardena, where other pockets of Indian residence and employment exist. These southeast Los Angeles cities also tend to have lower proportions of Caucasian families than those cities with larger-than-expected Indian population growth.

The most dramatic increases in Indian population percentages in cities with at least one hundred Indian residents occurred in Los Angeles County's outer residential rim. This population shift paralleled that of white families, who have opted to live in suburbia. Indian population increases of 100–200 percent have occurred in twenty-two predominantly residential communities encircling the more highly industrialized central cities.[6] In half of these cities, the population is predominantly Anglo, while Hispanics comprise the largest ethnic group in the remaining cities. The black population is disproportionately low (under 4.5 percent) in seventeen of the twenty-two cities that had Indian population increases of over 100 percent.

Twelve cities in the Los Angeles Basin experienced increases of greater than 200 percent in their Indian populations between 1970 and 1980. These cities, located at the outer perimeter of the basin, are the least ethnically mixed and have the largest percentages of Caucasian residents (ranging from 70 to 90 percent) of those cities with similar substantial gains in Indian population. Blacks, on the average, comprise 3.3 percent of the population in these cities; Hispanics, 14.9 percent. Eight of the twelve cities straddle the San Gabriel and Antelope valleys in the northeastern quadrant of Los Angeles County.[7]

Four other areas that experienced spectacular American Indian population growth between 1970 and 1980 include the suburban working- and middle-class cities of La Mirada and Santa Fe Springs in the Whittier area of eastern Los Angeles County, Lomita in the Palos Verdes Peninsula area to the west, and Cerritos to the south. Cerritos's Indian population growth of 1,369 percent was particularly dramatic, but its import is tempered by the small numbers of residents involved.[8] La Mirada and Lomita are largely Anglo communities with tiny black populations (less than 1 percent) and a modest number of Hispanic residents (17 percent). By contrast, Santa Fe Springs is largely Hispanic (60 percent) and has only a small number of black residents (less than 0.4 percent) and American Indians (0.9 percent). Cerritos is the most ethnically mixed of the major Indian population growth areas. Predominantly Caucasian (55.4 percent), it also has significant numbers of blacks (7.9 percent), Hispanics (14.2 percent), and Asians (22.1 percent).

While these large proportional gains in Indian population in suburbia are clearly noteworthy, Indians who continue to live in Los
Angeles City, unincorporated Los Angeles County, and Long Beach
still account for over half of the total Indian population in the Los
Angeles Basin. Moreover, the nine southeast county communities
that showed modest or negative Indian population growth still have
almost as many Indian residents (3,592) as those cities with over 200
percent growth (3,959).

Residential Shift Patterns

Given certain areal discrepancies and circumstantial anomalies, a
general shift in the Los Angeles Indian population emerges from
analysis of 1970 and 1980 census data. As illustrated by map 2.1,
there has been a general movement away from the original ports of
entry in the central and southeastern cities in the Los Angeles Basin
and into largely Hispanic and Caucasian suburban communities. By
1980 the inner cities had become increasingly black and Hispanic, a
fact that coincides with a general American Indian exodus from the
areas. (Reasons for the Indian population decrease in Artesia, far to
the southeast and adjacent to Orange County, do not appear to be
associated with increases in the city's other ethnic minority populations.)

While at least 17 percent of the Indians in Los Angeles are still
economically disadvantaged even after as much as two decades of
urban living, others—and in numbers disproportionate to the overall Indian population growth in Los Angeles—appear to have realized personal goals that prompted their rural-to-urban migration.
These Indians have taken advantage of the opportunities afforded
them by the BIA Relocation Program and the largesse of family and
friends already established in the city. They have availed themselves and their children of the educational opportunities that BIA
scholarships and GI loans provide. They also have developed industrial skills, acquired service delivery expertise, and secured stable
employment. By the mid-1970s, many American Indians in Los Angeles had begun to experience upward economic mobility in public
and private industry and had created parallel employment opportunities in a comprehensive number of Indian self-help social services agencies.

Economic mobility has prompted residential mobility. Indians in
Los Angeles, in increasing numbers, have been able to accumulate
the capital necessary to move from rented accommodations in the

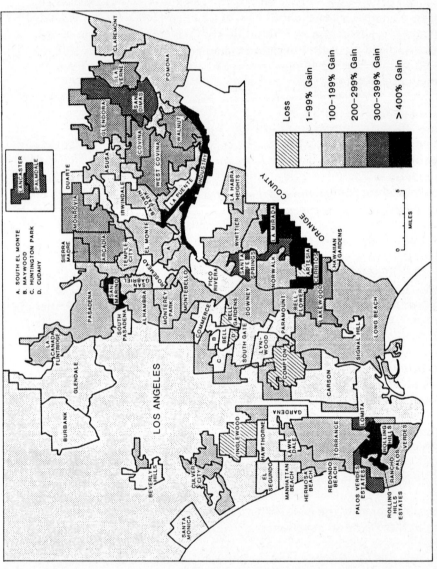

Map 2.1 American Indian Population Shifts in Los Angeles County, 1970–80 (unlabeled sections of this map are unincorporated areas of Los Angeles County)

inner city to modest, purchased homes and condominiums in "safer," "better" suburban neighborhoods. Between 1970 and 1980, Indian population increases occurred in approximately concentric rings radiating from the four core areas of decreased Indian population. The farther these communities are from the core areas, the greater the rate of their Indian population growth.

The Los Angeles Indian residential shifts in the 1970s were remarkably similar to the population shift described in the classic Chicago urban studies of the 1920s (e.g., Park, Burgess, and MacKenzie 1925). Between 1970 and 1980, the four core areas that had had substantial concentrations of American Indians began to lose their Indian and Anglo populations, becoming increasingly Hispanic and black. This residential migration pattern suggests that Indians, in increasing numbers, were choosing to live in cities with predominantly white or Hispanic populations. Residential concentrations in ethnically identified urban neighborhoods, as is the case with the more recently arrived Koreans, Thais, and Samoans in Los Angeles, seem to have been neither imposed on nor desired by American Indians.

If a dispersed residence pattern within predominantly white neighborhoods is one measure of cultural assimilation, then the Los Angeles Indian population in 1980 seemed well on its way to at least residential integration. Attaining the American dream of a home in suburbia seems to have been a major motivational force for increasing numbers of Los Angeles Indians. If shared space and residential density of a particular social group are necessary dimensions of community, then assertions that a viable Indian community exists in Los Angeles would be unsubstantiated. The entity that substantial numbers of American Indians in Los Angeles think of as their community is, however, bound by other than geopolitical dimensions or residential density.

NOTES

1. I have used the population figures cited in Price (1968).

2. The "moccasin telegraph" refers to the informal, word-of-mouth exchange of information across an extensive network of dyadic relationships.

3. In 1986 a team of statisticians in the Population Research Laboratory at the University of Southern California conducted a study that provided population estimates of several ethnic minority groups in Los Angeles. At that time, the American Indian population in Los Angeles was estimated at 64,800 (Heer and Pini 1990:5). That figure, when juxtaposed to the 1980 Los

Angeles Indian population figure of 48,158, suggests some leveling off of the population trajectory. Therefore, I estimate that the 1990 national census figure for the Los Angeles Indian population will be no more than 75,000.

4. The population percentages for all ethnic minorities have been taken from LACDRP (1981).

5. The seven cities in southeast Los Angeles County in which Indian population increases were less than 96.5 percent include Bell, Maywood, Paramount, Huntington Park, Lynwood, South Gate, and Pico Rivera.

6. The twenty-two cities in which Indian population increases ranged from 100 to 200 percent include Hawaiian Gardens, El Monte, Norwalk, Baldwin Park, Pomona, Azusa, Bellflower, Long Beach, Redondo Beach, San Gabriel, South El Monte, Downey, Hermosa Beach, Whittier, Alhambra, Montebello, Pasadena, Torrance, Claremont, Culver City, Monterey Park, and Temple City.

7. The east valley cities that had more than a 200 percent increase in their Indian populations include Covina, Glendora, La Verne, West Covina, Lancaster, Palmdale, Arcadia, and Monrovia.

8. When working with a population of 48,153 individuals dispersed across eighty-one incorporated and unincorporated urban areas, the small-numbers error has to be recognized as a general limiting factor in the interpretation of these data.

3

Dimensions of Ethnicity
in the Los Angeles
American Indian Community

Tribal Heterogeneity

E STABLISHING THE parameters of the Los Angeles Indian community's social structure is complicated by the community's extreme tribal heterogeneity. Most Indians are not indigenous to the area; in fact, a 1966 survey of 2,945 American Indians in Los Angeles identified no Gabrielinos, and only 2 percent of the sample was descended from any indigenous California culture groups (Price 1968:169). These figures are lower than those for the same culture groups in my more recent (1986) survey of tribal citations in *Talking Leaf*, the Los Angeles Indian community newspaper (see table A.1 in the Appendix). Of 481 people identified by tribe over a nine-year period (1978–86), only five were Gabrielinos and forty-three were members of indigenous California culture groups; the remaining 91 percent either migrated to Los Angeles between 1950 and 1980 or were born in Los Angeles subsequent to their parents' migration.

When Price (1968:169) conducted a survey of the Los Angeles Indian population in 1966, he and a team of UCLA graduate students identified seventy-six discrete tribal affiliations in a sample of 2,945 Indians. In a 1973 study of Los Angeles Indian drinking patterns, Burns, Daily, and Moskowitz (1974:337) created a random sample of 518 Indians representing eighty-seven discrete tribal groups from census blocks that included at least 20 resident Indians and in which Indians comprised at least 2 percent of the total population. Respondents of mixed parentage were listed by dominant tribe; or, when tribal heritage was equally represented, the respondent's father's tribe was listed. (No information is given as to the proportion of the sample affected by this paternal bias in tribal labeling.)

In my 1986 survey, I discovered 154 discrete, multiple, or subtribal specifications among 481 individuals—an increase in tribal specificity of more than 100 percent, when compared to Price's 1966 survey results. More exactly, 117 discrete tribal designations were recorded in a 1986 sample that was one-sixth the size of the 1966 sample. Although approximately the same size as the 1973 sample of Burns et al., the 1986 sample reveals a 34.5 percent increase in discrete tribal citations. I suspect that the degree to which multitribal backgrounds are mentioned in *Talking Leaf* articles about Los Angeles Indian community members is, to a large extent, an indication of the increasing propensity among Indians generally, and urban Indians especially, to choose spouses who are not members of their own tribal and ethnic groups. As table A.1 in the Appendix indicates, only one tribal affiliation was listed for each participant in the 1966 study,[1] whereas 20 percent of the participants in the 1986 survey specified multitribal affiliations.

Table 3.1 compares percentages from the 1966, 1973, and 1986 surveys for the twelve most frequently cited tribal affiliations. Because of the extreme specificity of the 1986 survey sample, I collapsed certain tribal groups into a cultural category comparable to the tribal listings of the 1966 and 1973 samples. When more than one tribal heritage was mentioned by an individual, I listed that individual under the first tribe mentioned.

A comparison of the collapsed 1986 categories indicates both change and continuity in the tribal makeup of the Los Angeles Indian community. Of the twelve tribes most heavily represented in 1966, ten are among the top twelve in 1973, and ten of the original twelve are among the most heavily represented in the 1986 survey. The Kiowas and Seminoles are not among the twelve most heavily represented tribes in 1973; however, Kiowas represent 4.8 percent of the 1986 sample and that tribe is also the seventh most frequently mentioned tribe in *Talking Leaf*. Although Los Angeles area Winnebagos are ranked twentieth in proportional size in 1966, twelfth in 1973, and thirteenth in 1986, this tribe's proportional size remains relatively stable (ranging from 1.4 to 1.9 percent of the total sample) over the three surveys.

It is noteworthy that the Iroquois tribal groups are decidedly more conspicuous in the 1986 survey than in the 1966 or the 1973 sur-

Table 3.1 A Comparison of American Indian Tribal Representation in
Los Angeles in 1966, 1973, and 1986

Tribe	% of sample			Ranking by size		
	1986	1973	1966	1986	1973	1966
Navajo	10.2	17.4	14.1	1	1	1
Sioux	10.0	12.2	12.0	2	2	2
Pueblo	7.7	2.5	5.1	3	3	5
Five Civilized Tribes	20.4	17.1	21.0			
Choctaw	7.5	6.4	4.5	4	4	6
Creek	6.7	6.4	6.0	5	4	4
Cherokee	5.8	3.5	6.3	6	7	3
Seminole	—	—	3.7	—	—	7
Chickasaw	0.4	0.8	0.5	—	—	—
Kiowa	4.8	1.4	2.9	7	33	11
Iroquois	4.7	0.2	1.4	8	19	19
Cheyenne	3.7	2.5	3.3	9	11	8
Apache	3.1	2.7	3.1	10	10	9
Chippewa	2.7	4.1	3.1	11	6	9
Papago	2.1	3.1	2.5	12	9	12
Winnebago	1.9	1.7	1.4	—	12	—
Pima	0.6	3.3	1.9	—	8	16
% of total Indian sample	71.9	68.2	71.8			

Source: Price (1966); Burns, Daily, and Moskowitz (1974); Weibel-Orlando (1986)
surveys.

veys, which may be due to the ascendancy of a small number of
Iroquois into highly visible administrative positions in the Los Angeles Indian community in the 1980s. From March 1982 until August 1986, an Iroquois was the executive director of the Indian Centers, Inc. (ICI), the administrative umbrella agency for a network of
Indian social services centers. *Talking Leaf,* one of the ICI's community services, was housed in the center's downtown headquarters,
where its staff was privy to newsworthy community services. Additionally, an Iroquois has been the ordained pastor of one of the more
successful and heavily service-oriented Indian churches in Los Angeles for the last eight years. The activities of these prominent Iroquois individuals and their families are reported on the pages of the
community newspaper, thereby exaggerating any estimate of the
actual number of Iroquois in the Los Angeles community.

California tribal groups as a whole comprise 9 percent of the
Talking Leaf citations, compared to 1.4 percent of the 1973 survey

sample and less than 1 percent of the 1966 sample. (Because no single California tribe ranks especially high, these data are not included in table 3.1). The differences may be due in part to the California Indians' successful use of the mass media. Since the late 1960s, they have initiated media events to dramatize and create general public awareness of their political and economic struggles to regain their land base. The Alcatraz Island takeover in 1969, the Chumash sit-ins at proposed nuclear energy sites in Santa Barbara, various legal disputes over land and water rights in the tiny reservations and rancherias throughout California and particularly in the Owens Valley, and reservation-based high-stakes bingo parlors—all have made headlines in national as well as Indian-run newspapers during the last two decades. While California Indians may have had overall population gains, their political actions and consciousness-raising efforts are what put them on the front pages of the Los Angeles Indian newspaper in numbers disproportionate to their local numbers.

The percentage of individuals claiming Papago tribal affiliation remains fairly constant across the three surveys, whereas the Pimans, among the most heavily represented in 1973, are less visible in both the 1966 and 1986 surveys. The relative absence of Pimans among those people mentioned in *Talking Leaf* may be the result of cyclic migration, since the Pima reservation, located immediately south of Phoenix, is within a day's drive of Los Angeles. Pimans can therefore move between Los Angeles and their family homes with relative ease.

Curiously, no Seminole citations are recorded in the 1973 and 1986 surveys, although in the 1966 survey Seminoles represent 3.7 percent of the sample and are the seventh most highly represented tribal group. I am not sure why so few Seminoles were counted in Los Angeles after 1966. There has been considerable intermarriage between Creeks and Seminoles since the latter's forced migration to Oklahoma in the 1830s and 1840s, and perhaps an idiosyncrasy of the 1966 survey resulted in people who self-identified as Creek/Seminole being designated either Creek or Seminole, to the advantage of Seminole representation. The obverse may have occurred in the 1973 and 1986 surveys.

Aside from the proportional differences just described, a major block of the tribal groups in Los Angeles exhibit little variation in proportional size across the three samples. In 1966 Navajos were the most heavily represented tribal group, followed by the Sioux; the same is true of the 1973 and 1986 surveys. Navajos comprise a low of 10.2 percent of the total sample in 1986 to a high of 17 percent of the 1973 sample. The Sioux are even more consistent: their percentage of the total sample ranges from 12 in 1966 and 1973 to 9.8 in 1986.

When combined, the Five Civilized Tribes (Cherokees, Creeks, Choctaws, Chickasaws, and Seminoles), originally from the southeastern states but removed, since 1830, to eastern Oklahoma, represented 21 percent of the Los Angeles Indian population in 1966, 17.1 percent in 1973, and 20.4 percent in 1986. Except for the Seminoles, individual tribal proportions are similar across the three surveys.

Six other tribes among the twelve most heavily represented in Los Angeles (Apaches, Cheyennes, Chippewas, Papagos, Pueblos, and Winnebagos) also have remained relatively stable in terms of the three surveys. In fact, according to the results of all three surveys, the proportional sizes of fourteen tribal groups constituting approximately two-thirds of the Los Angeles Indian population have changed only slightly between 1966 and 1986.

Twenty-nine tribes representing 5.6 percent of the sample population are included in the 1966 survey but not in the 1986 survey, while thirty-eight tribes representing 11.8 percent of the 1973 sample population are not mentioned in the 1986 study. In contrast, thirty-one (11 percent) and forty-four (18 percent) tribes identified in the 1986 survey do not appear in the 1966 and 1973 surveys, respectively. These changes are due at least in part to the continuing redefinition of outmoded tribal categories. For example, in the 1986 survey only one person was identified as being both Miwok and "Mission Indian," a label that is no longer used because of its pejorative connotations. Rather, the names "Gabrielino," "Juaneño," "Diegueño," or "Fernandeño" are used to describe the southern California Indian societies formerly lumped under "Mission Indian." The same can be said of the old category "Pueblo Indians" and the specificity with which an Indian newspaper identifies people by the particular pueblo in which they or their parents were born. Locational specificity is equally pronounced among the Sioux, who are designated individually in the 1986 survey according to seven of the eight reservations to which that tribal group was confined in the 1870s.

The importance of this level of labeling specificity is its exclusive, rather than its inclusive, function. The difficulties of attempting to build group consensus, ethnic awareness, or a sense of community among an estimated 75,000 Los Angeles Indians are magnified by the persistence of tribal and regional allegiances that fragment and divide people and often lead to clearcut animosities among the different factions. Specificity of tribal affiliation(s) when identifying oneself appears to vary widely across the 1986 survey sample. For example, no matter how many times their names appeared in *Talking Leaf*, 503 Indian community members (or 51 percent of the 1986 survey sample) are never identified by tribal affiliation. In contrast, one person's tribal affiliations included her grandmother and grandfather on both sides of the family. I suggest that how and with what specificity one identifies tribal background depends largely on one's stake in promoting a particular, rather than a global, ethnic identity and one's perception of the cultural sophistication of a particular audience. An American Indian might self-identify as simply "Indian" to a white stranger but provide exquisite genealogical detail to tribal cohorts who, it could be expected, would know the difference between a Sisseton and a Pine Ridge Sioux.

Other Salient Contrasting Social Categories

Contemporary American Indian intraethnic and extraethnic social categories can be thought of as a system of segmented but flexible social identities and allegiances that, as with the Nuer system of segmented lineages (Evans-Pritchard 1940),[2] have the relative capacity to exclude and include subsegments of the population given the social circumstances. Boundaries of contrasting social categories and the criteria by which they are defined expand and contract in response to situational factors such as social distance of the presenting enemy or stranger, political exigencies of the moment, and the history of reciprocal obligations between the interacting parties.

During World War II, American Indian servicemen were among the most decorated, valiant, and loyal defenders of our nation (Paul 1973). Indian men from scores of tribes fought side by side with Anglos and members of dozens of other ethnic American groups against the mutually hated Axis enemies. Contemporarily, the U.S. secretary of the interior, the Bureau of Indian Affairs, and the federal and state governments in general constitute extraethnic (American) sociopolitical categories that Indians "love to hate." The Indian/ non-Indian dichotomy and ethnic contrast is quite clearly and vehemently delineated.

While American Indians identify themselves as such to non-Indians, tribal identity is still strongly felt and voiced. This level of ethnic specificity is most apparent in interactions between members of different tribal groups, further underscoring the complex, situational, and political nature of ethnic categories.

In addition to national, tribal, and locational cleavages, long-standing intratribal social contrast categories exist that further divide Indian communities. "Traditionalists," the Indians' conservative faction, decry the "white ways" of "progressives." Traditionalists would have American Indians avoid westernization or modernization of Indian lands and activities as much as possible. They attempt, through exemplary personal behavior and active lobbying, to maintain their people's folkways, including perpetuation of their language and all forms of expressive culture, as well as the avoidance of non-Indian intrusion into their culture. Traditionalists work hard to enforce the notion of Indian lands or the localities of Indian activity as sacred space and to inculcate the perspective of Indian society and culture as sacred separation.

Progressives, by contrast, see the westernization and modernization of Indian culture as inevitable. Pragmatically, they view the incorporation of contemporary mainstream technology and bureaucratic structures into their lives as vital to their continuance as a sociopolitical entity. Progressives consider change and accommodation to be positive survival strategies and counsel their traditionalist detractors not to be obstructionistic. The progressives' operant philosophy appears to be, "If we can't beat them playing our game, we'd better learn to beat them at their own game."

Progressives often are labeled "apples"—that is, red on the outside, white on the inside—by their traditionalist detractors. This is considered a major ethnic slur, analogous to being called an "oreo" by black pride activists in the 1960s or a "coconut" by contemporary Chicano militants. Sensitive to the nuances of such labeling, progressives attempt to temper their political stance by extolling the ways of their forebears and sustaining some public semblance of their veneration of "Indian ways."

The political and cultural categories "traditionalist" and "progressive" are crosscut by political action groups whose profiles can be placed on a continuum from conservative to militant. The Los Angeles City-County Native American Indian Commission is a political entity within the city and county bureaucracy that was chartered to effect a liaison between the mainstream governmental infrastructure and the Indian community. It attempts to do so within the mandated legal-rational avenues of public hearings in which statements of ethnic group consensus are aired. The commission is viewed by the more militant Indian political figures in Los Angeles as conservative and demonstrating little political clout. The "young-bloods" do not look to the commission for their voice. Rather, given their self-imposed political marginality, they make their agendas known through a veritable Greek chorus of petitions, demonstrations, and sophisticated media events.

"Full-bloods" are convinced that they are intrinsically more Indian than their "mixed-blood" relatives or acquaintances. People whose parents are both full-bloods from the same tribe consider themselves intrinsically more Indian than other full-bloods whose parents are from two different tribal groups. Tribal pedigree is still highly weighted when determining who is or is not Indian, regardless of early socialization experiences that may have mitigated or ensured assumption of a tribal ethos.

Finally, formation of a pan-Indian stance as an ethnic category vis-à-vis non-Indians, and in the face of real and viable tribal differences in the urban setting, also exemplifies the elastic nature of ethnic identification.[3] After thirty years of migration to urban-industrial centers, most contemporary American Indians consider the contrast category "urban/rural-reservation Indian" to be highly salient. In 1980, for example, 53 percent of the American Indian population lived in urban centers (U.S. Department of Commerce 1983b:1–20), and rural-to-urban migration continued throughout the 1980s. I predict that the 1990 Census will reveal that more than two-thirds of the American Indian population lives in cities—a residential shift whose political and socioeconomic ramifications will be numerous and far-reaching. The continuation of a new sociocultural contrast category, "urban-rural/reservation Indian," is but one possible outcome.

Rural Indians generally distrust or attempt to exploit the sophistication and relative economic well-being of their urban kin. In contrast, Indians who have moved to urban centers deeply resent the loss of federally funded social ("community") services generally available to their reservation-based relatives. Because of their decision to seek economic independence and a higher standard of living in industrial centers, urban Indians are made to feel, by members of rural tribes and by the federal bureaus mandated to uphold treaty-directed Indian entitlements, that they have a lesser claim to the rights and privileges that tribal membership and reservation residence engender.

Figure 3.1 illustrates the major social categories currently operant in the Los Angeles Indian community—contrast categories that are

NOT AMERICAN	AMERICAN									
	NOT INDIAN	INDIAN								
		OTHER TRIBES	OUR PEOPLE (OUR TRIBE)							
			PROGRESSIVE				TRADITIONAL			
			NOT FULL-BLOOD		FULL-BLOOD		NOT FULL-BLOOD		FULL-BLOOD	
			URBAN	RURAL	URBAN	RURAL	URBAN	RURAL	URBAN	RURAL

Figure 3.1 American Indian Ethnic Categories

also salient in both rural and urban Indian communities in general. Several other contrasting sets that are evident in many urban Indian communities as well as in the Los Angeles Indian community are not included. For example, regional affiliation labels ("Northern Plains," "Southern Plains," "Southwestern," "Eastern," "Western") are regularly used in discussing behavior and worldview. Sociopolitical labels such as "Iroquois," "Pueblo," "Five Civilized Tribes," and "California Indians" are added salient dimensions of Indian ethnic categories.

Religious orientations further refine the social boundaries in the Los Angeles Indian community. People clearly recognize the distinctions between traditional spiritualists and Christian Indians and between those groups and members of the Native American church and other syncretic and religious groups that have coalesced around self-appointed charismatic spiritual guides.

Still another means of defining ethnic categories is by levels of personal involvement in community affairs. Longitudinal observations reveal four types of Los Angeles Indian community experience: (1) complete immersion in multiple community activities, or "core membership"; (2) regular, symbolic, and expressive participation in some subcomponent of Indian community life, or "selective community membership"; (3) recognition of, identification with, and occasional participation in Indian community activities or causes as a mechanism for reinforcing personal ethnic identity, or "peripheral community membership"; and (4) no identification with or an avoidance of urban Indian institutions and activities, or "nonassociation."

A small cadre of American Indians (I have documented no more than 2,000 at any given time) make up the Los Angeles Indian core community. Although core community members live in widely dispersed sections of the city, they are employed by Indian institutions, sit on multiple boards of Indian organizations, are active in many

Indian-specific leisure-time activities, and are called on by the mass media to make statements about Indian community sentiments. Core community members are completely immersed and have a vested interest in sustaining an Indian community awareness.

Regular, selective participation in some aspects of urban Indian life, or selective community participation, is a second urban Indian adaptation. Although these Los Angeles Indians constitute a much larger group than that of the core community members, I estimate that no more than 20 percent of the Indians consistently participate in and contribute to the ongoing existence of such expressive cultural events as the powwow circuit, an Indian church congregation, or Indian athletic leagues. For these people, ethnic identity is demonstrated and sustained via scheduled, repetitive, time-limited, and, more often than not, secular public ritual and performance.

Although the actual figures cannot be reliably substantiated, I estimate that the largest proportion of the Los Angeles Indian population experiences ethnic community life in a peripheral manner, that is, they occasionally attend Indian events. They may sustain inactive memberships in one or more Indian organizations, contribute to Indian causes, subscribe to Indian-focused newspapers and magazines, and publicly identify themselves as American Indians. Their daily interactions and activities are governed by panethnic work, schools, and leisure-time pursuits. For some peripheral community members, ethnicity is private, personal, and internalized. It is more historical fact and cognitive orientation than principle of social organization. For others, ethnic life is experienced most meaningfully only at the hearth, in the company of kin, or back home. The syncretic nature of urban Indian community life repels, rather than impels, such cultural purists.

For a substantial number of people who identifed as American Indian in the 1980 Census, ethnic community participation has little, no, or negative meaning. Included in this group are people with minimal amounts of American Indian heritage who may not look particularly Indian. If they so choose, they can "pass"—that is, present themselves publicly—as something other than American Indian. Or Indian people can become so completely immersed in another American subculture through marriage, school, or work experiences that they take on the attributes of that subculture. Still others, who for various reasons, usually personal, have become disenchanted with the strictures of ethnic community life, disavow such membership and actively avoid further Indian community involvements and responsibilities.

Ethnicity, the us/them distinction between groups of people who "share a history, common place of origin, language, dress, and food preferences from all those who do not" (Holzberg 1982:252), is subject to the expansions and contractions of its inclusive boundaries. Ethnic identity is situational. It is defined and functions differently at interpersonal, intercultural, intranational, and international levels of social interaction. The specificity with which American Indians identify themselves exemplifies the situational and multifunctional nature of ethnicity in contemporary American society, particularly as it is expressed in an urban environment as culturally heterogeneous as Los Angeles.

Ethnic categories that have their roots in rural and reservation life persist in the urban setting. Paradoxically, these social categories can be used both to include and exclude individuals, create and dissipate social organization, and perpetuate and prevent a sense of community. Succeeding chapters deal with how and under what circumstances American Indians who recognize these social categories situationally shift allegiances, ethnic stances, and ethnic group membership criteria for the purpose of including or excluding individuals and groups from Indian community life. Flexibility of ethnic boundaries is one mechanism by which the American Indians in Los Angeles create and sustain the ideal of pantribal accord and community.

NOTES

1. In August 1986, I asked John Price about the specificity of the eliciting questions in his 1966 survey. He thought that no participants claimed more than one tribal affiliation because: (1) they were indeed children of tribe-endogamous parents; or (2) they chose not to offer more specific background information to Anglo graduate students. With respect to the latter, Price suggested that in 1966 Indian interviewees perceived the young, white college student interviewers as not sufficiently sophisticated about Indian tribal distinctions to understand the importance of an intertribal background. Another explanation is that some tribal groups only recognize their personal tribal affiliation through their maternal or paternal lineage.

2. American Indians do not subscribe as fully to the fictive kinship ideology that links Nuer groups, although the notion of pan-Indian brotherhood (and sisterhood) is used rhetorically.

3. Ablon (1964), Gardner (1969), Hirabayashi, Willard, and Kemnitzer (1972), and Fiske (1977) are among several anthropologists who have published articles about the urban pan-Indian phenomenon.

II

Community in Complex Society: Definitions, Theoretical Models, and Methodologies

Many times in the past, we Indians were faced with conflicts from within our ranks and from outside forces. We have faced assimilation, that ever present "owl"[1] which will not leave us behind no matter how peaceful our hearts. We have and still face financial difficulties, which hamper the building blocks to an informed, cohesive community.

And yes, we face conflicts from within our own ranks. As any society with a long history will teach us, it is in overcoming these inner conflicts that brings strength, communication, understanding and continuity to that society.

Survival.

. . . Recently we faced a serious threat to a program that is essential to our people. Our strength as a community has shown its ability to overcome yet another obstacle toward servicing our people as well as our neighbors. (MB 1985:8)

Published under the dramatically metaphorical caption "Community Strength Shines through Clouds of Doubt; Programs Continue," the *Talking Leaf* article excerpted above invokes the Los Angeles Indian community as a given, a concept on which there is an a priori consensus, a social fact. Clearly, community is a viable cultural concept and social entity among these people, not simply an imposed theoretical construct. It exists as one of several dimensions of the Los Angeles Indian worldview, as such, it is invoked as a valued set of institutions by which individual and collective behavior is determined and assessed.

The phrase "Los Angeles Indian community" is commonly used among the Indian people with whom I work. Whenever they wish to validate their political or service activities, they make a point of presenting themselves as acting on behalf of and for the "good of the Indian community." I therefore was certain I was not imposing an analytically convenient metaphor that more clearly mirrored my own ethnocentric ideas about community than the actual processes by which a community consciousness had developed and is sustained among the Indians in Los Angeles.

At the onset, my task was to determine if the criteria by which I define community are shared by Indians who view themselves as living in community in Los Angeles. If my preconceptions did not parallel their criteria, then I would have to discover and describe those parameters and markers of community in the Los Angeles Indians' own terms. Finally, I needed to address the relevance of defining and providing an ethnographic description of community, as it exists and is expressed among the American Indians living in Los Angeles, to general urban anthropological theory.

These three issues prompt a number of theoretical questions, which I address in chapter 4. Is the open, dispersed, intentional, interactional configuration of informal and formal ethnic associations that, I posit, constitutes community structure for the Los Angeles Indians in fact a recurring phenomenon across complex societies? Is there some recurring, optimal associational mechanism by which humans create and experience *communitas* (Turner 1974:45) that, I suggest, is the prerequisite of community? How is Turner's (1974:201) "community of feeling" sustained in and by social structure? Is that optimal association always a subcomponent of, not antithetical to, complex society? If so, how do these community subcomponents articulate with each other in complex society? The discussion in chapter 4 of these theoretical propositions about community calls for a demonstration of the relevance of my model of community in complex society to the study of complex societies and urban anthropology in general.

Urban anthropology readers of the last two decades share a number of structural similarities. Introductory chapters outline the problems inherent in applying anthropological field methods honed in small-scale, "primitive" societies to the study of community in complex societies. According to Weaver and White (1972b:1), "One of the major problems [of urban anthropology] is whether traditional anthropological methodology, techniques, and theoretical frameworks are adequate for work in the city, or whether new approaches must be developed or borrowed from related disciplines." Some authors argue that classic ethnographic methods are largely applicable to the study of urban groups and that anthropologists, by adopting urban research strategies from other disciplines, "may be in danger of selling [their] birthright" (Spradley 1972:21). Others advocate the search for "new research tools and techniques to reshape the working styles and assumptions which have been successful in small isolated communities but which cannot span the complexities of these new disciplinary interests" (Pelto 1972:6). In chapter 5 I discuss the evolution of and rationale for my longitudinal, multidisciplinary, and multivoiced approach to an ethnography of an ethnic community in complex society.

NOTE

1. In many North American Indian societies the owl is a harbinger of death. Thus, the newspaper editor's metaphoric use of the term equates assimilation with death, or the irretrievable loss of culture and ethos.

4

Toward a Definition of Community in Complex Society

A Priori Notions of Community

SOCIETAL MODELS are shaped by our earliest and all subsequent social experiences. Ideas about what constitutes community are no exception. I am impelled, therefore, to make known my own cultural bias. I grew up in community; to be exact, in a small, southwestern Connecticut town[1] that in the 1940s boasted slightly more than four thousand inhabitants. My first notion of community structure was formed when, at the age of three, I overheard and empathized with my parents' concerns about our impending move from the center of town to my maternal grandparents' farm on the town's rural periphery, a relocation of only four miles. Listening to my mother's descriptions of what it would be like "to live out in the country again" convinced me that the move constituted a dislocation of major and terrible proportions. The distress it engendered was my first awareness, albeit at an impressionistic level, of such things as "core and peripheral social spheres" (Wolf 1966:1). Additionally, where one was located within those spheres appeared to make a difference in one's perceived quality of life. As far as my mother was concerned, the move away from the conveniences and social density of town life and back to the family farm was synonymous with orbiting out of civilization.

Starting in the first grade, I was taught and regularly reminded of the more formal parameters of community. History and civics classes stressed the ideological distinctions that splintered the tiny farming colony of Danbury within seventy-five years of first settlement of the area[2] and led to the formation of the First Ecclesiastical

Society of Bethel and, seventy-five years later, the formal, political incorporation of the Bethel township.

Since the town's creation, Bethelites have defined themselves in relation to their home community. "Being from Bethel" meant "not being from Danbury," a distinction that was made quite clear to me throughout my schooling. Intertown athletic rivalries were serious year-round affairs. A classmate who dated a Danbury boy bore the brunt of the kind of gossip engendered by extravillage assignations in a village-endogamous society. Going to Danbury for a day of shopping was exciting, a move from small-scale familiarity and boundedness to the exotic and unfamiliar heterogeneity of a perceived large-scale society.[3] My early experiences in community clearly preadapted me for easy acceptance, twenty years later, of Redfield's (1955) dichotomous model of little and great traditions.

To this day, Bethel conforms in many ways to the little, bounded communities of early, classic community studies. It certainly provides the opportunity for ongoing, face-to-face interaction with other community members, one prerequisite of early anthropological models of community (Murdock 1949). Children I met for the first time on entering grade school attended classes with me five days a week for the next twelve years. I knew the names and considerable personal history of all fifty-one students who graduated from high school with me. Small-scale, geographically demarcated, identified with an ideologically inspired origin codified by a revered creation myth, Bethel could have been Plainville (West 1945) or Tzintzuntzan (Foster 1948).

There were, however, elements of Bethel community life that even in the 1940s did not conform to Redfield's early ideas about the "little community." With only 4,100 inhabitants and encompassing no more than thirty square miles, Bethel was neither harmonious nor homogeneous. As Hannerz (1980:172) points outs, even local communities can be unmanageably complex social units. Not everyone in Bethel was involved in continuous, face-to-face interactions. Rather, one learned early on that the white-clapboard-and-green-shutter conformity of the New England community's public face masked a mosaic of at times mutually exclusive interactional groups that in some cases saw themselves in opposition to each other.

After the Civil War, small, successive waves of Irish, Italian, and Eastern European immigrants established themselves—along with a Roman Catholic parish—in the formerly all Anglo-Saxon, Protestant community of Bethel. The emergence of the hatting industry in the nineteenth century in an otherwise agricultural community allowed for the development of a three-tiered class system: a large wage-earning proletariat, a small merchant and service-providing petite bourgeoisie and dwindling landowning farming gentry, and a tiny entrepreneurial capitalist elite. Other forms of community segmentation and dynamism included political and ideological factions, an in-town/out-of-town dichotomy, and an eastside/westside neighborhood split. Finally, even when I was a preschooler, my parents' comments about certain town "characters" underscored the associational distance between the bulk of the townsfolk who were hardworking, law-abiding, "decent people" and an assortment of local marginals and ne'er-do-wells who made up Bethel's stable, if tiny, "underclass."

There were dozens of social, recreational, and civic institutions in our community with which my family and I were selectively involved. My father, a lifetime member of the Masonic Lodge, never thought to join the Rotary Club. My mother was the town's fiscal clerk for a time but declined to join the PTA. My sister was a badge-winning Campfire girl for all the years I was a violin-playing member of the high school orchestra. Although we probably would have been welcomed, none of us ever attended the Kiwanis Club's Wednesday night bingo parties or joined one of several town athletic leagues.

We were equally selective in the community roles we assumed. A well-known and universally liked town personality, my father chose the stewardship and philanthropic responsibilities of Masonic Lodge mastership over any overtures to involve him more actively in town politics. And I chose a successful bid for class valedictorian over what would probably have been an unsuccessful tryout for the high school cheerleading squad. Yet all of the institutions and social arenas in our township, together with their associated roles, were recognized almost without exception or challenge as aspects or resources to which any resident of that territorially defined community potentially had privileged rights of participation.

Given the selectivity with which Bethelites interacted with each other, there were certain locations, institutions, and civic events with which everyone identified and to which everyone had unlimited rights of participation. Doughboy Park was one such public locus. The high school gym, which doubled as the town's only secular public auditorium, was certainly another node of community interaction. Greenwood Avenue (Bethel's main street), the town offices, Parloa Field, and the public library were other places to which every community member had equal access. A yearly calendar of Memorial Day and Fourth of July parades, as well as the firemen's balls, were rites of intensification intrinsically associated with community process to which all Bethelites were privy.

Years later, having learned the lexicons of the cultural geographer, sociologist, and anthropologist, I could label what had been, up to then, an experienced but unarticulated and intuited model of community. My original conceptions of community included territorial boundedness; geopolitical definition; differences in core and peripheral population and service densities; early and sustained enculturation within a small, age-graded group of peers with whom the individual has continuous, face-to-face interaction; and a constellation of established social institutions and public events as foci of assemblage to which every community member hypothetically has equal rights of participation. Within these conventional parameters of community, I recognized the selectivity with which individuals choose to participate in the array of community arenas and events. Additionally, my personal, culture-specific community model accommodated the reality of intervening ethnic, class, and ideational differences that mitigate unlimited personal access to all community resources.

The community model derived from my childhood experiences prepared me incompletely for the complexities and ephemerality of the Los Angeles Indian community, whose "no-thereness"[4] contrasted sharply with my ideas of geographic integrity as a prerequisite of community. Bethel's settlement pattern of in-town density and out-of-town sparsity was no analogue for the Los Angeles Indian population's dispersed residential and community services patterns. Growing up in Bethel necessarily meant daily, face-to-face interaction with members of the same peer group. By contrast, Los Angeles Indians must take heroic steps to ensure a similar pattern of social interaction. When I was born, the array of social institutions to which I potentially could participate in my community were already well established, whereas the American Indians who migrated to Los Angeles had to create all the institutional mechanisms by which a community could be identified and sustained. These social processes still characterize that community.

Only the relative heterogeneity and segmentation of community life and the selectivity with which individuals shape their participation in community life are features that I recognized in both my home and the Los Angeles Indian community. Even these factors seem little more than analytic abstractions when faced with the magnitude of the Los Angeles Indian community's cultural heterogeneity. Clearly, my original community model, the result of early membership in a New England mill town, needed expansion, revision, or replacement in order to be applied realistically to the structure and quality of Los Angeles Indian community life.

Community as System and Process

The Arensberg and Kimball (1965) community model and their ideas about community as mirror and sample of the complex society in which it is embedded have provoked spirited and continuing discussion, challenge, revision,[5] replication, and defense.[6] Convinced that community is not an abstraction "in the sense of shared sentiments" (1965:ix), they take exception to "psychologistic or collective sociological definitions of community" that "appealed to the putative need of human beings to belong, or to [the belief in] the survival necessities of cooperation and solidarity, or even to consciousness of kind, or the gregarious spirit" (1965:15). However, they acknowledge the importance of common interest as a factor in establishing such loose collectives as the open or pioneer settlements as communities: "Community strength, past or present, has been built on a pattern of a community of interest which has provided the cultural integration and systems of communication permitting common agreement and concerted action" (1965:180).

Recognizing the "more limited view of the community taken by anthropologists"—that is, "an instance of settlement pattern, a subdivision of political organization, a residential setting or subsistence base for family and kinship, or a field-use system or resource pattern"—as "useful and correct," Arensberg and Kimball (1965:xi) nonetheless maintain that these markers of community are incomplete. Murdock's (1949) "settlement patterns" are, they insist, not community interactional systems but their potential cultural expression (1965:3). Instead, they propose three variables by which community can be defined. "Environment," "social form," and "patterned behavior" are understood to be "functional interdependencies." And by discovering the interconnections between such interdependencies, community as system is revealed (1965:4).

Arensberg and Kimball (1965:17–18) argue that their community model favors the study of both stability and change:

> A prime key to [community] wholeness, then, is to be found, not so
> much in the territorial separateness of the community, but . . . in-

stead in its temporal dimension. . . . Thus the unit minimum population aggregate, the community, is a structured social field of interin-
dividual relationships unfolding through time.

[Community is] where the drama of living is done by and with
culture, in a particular ethnographically differentiable human way of
life. It is a natural unit of the drama of successive repetitions of the
life of an enduring culture or society.

Assuming that community is process involving social structure
and cultural behavior, Arensberg and Kimball (1965:2) seek community continuity in "those regularities in the relationships among
individuals that are revealed in their activities with each other and
with the physical items of their environment." Thus, "social forms
congruent with one type of settlement pattern can also persist in a
new social setting, if in sufficient isolation, as exemplified by the
immigrant ghettos in large cities." The temporal and processual
nature of community as expressed in interrelated individual career
paths and life histories is a major conceptual model that has proven
extremely productive in the analysis of Los Angeles American Indian community process.

Additional conceptual innovations introduced by Arensberg and
Kimball that have proven helpful in defining the Los Angeles American Indian community include the views that community need not
be particularly heavy geographic concentrations of people and the
assertion that community members do not have to feel that they
have reached consensus on all issues. Community members, in fact,
alternate between strife and accommodation, solidarity and antago-
nism. It is by this very internal dynamic tension that community
boundaries can be defined (Arensberg and Kimball 1965:27; Talai
1988:52).

Arensberg and Kimball (1965:19) suggest that dispersed settlement patterns do not necessarily preclude community. In these
cases, community is expressed as its members cyclically come together for some expressed purpose. The open community of the Irish
countryside (Arensberg 1968[1937]) and the nineteenth-century
North American "pioneer community" (Arensberg and Kimball
1965:110), composed of little more than a few buildings at a
crossroads where scattered neighbors of a huge hinterland met at
prescribed and critical times, both constitute viable and applicable
community forms.

To the alternative open and pioneer community typologies I add
the dispersed residential patterns of prereservation and postreserva-
tion North American Indians. Arensberg's description of open com-

munity has parallels in the residential, space-use, and social interactional structures of many nineteenth-century North American Indian foraging and big game-hunting societies. Small kin-based residential band dispersals for major portions of the year, interrupted by seasonal tribal cum community (to use Leed's [1973] analogue) congregations at established encampment sites, characterized the annual community calendars of foraging Indians prior to 1870. Thereafter, the pioneer community, in both configurational and functional aspects, was replicated on Indian reservations in approximately the same historical period it was developed by non-Indians on adjacent lands. The dispersed Los Angeles Indian settlement patterns, with their established "crossroads" nodes of ethnic community interaction, may in fact represent a continuity of community form rather than an innovation imposed by the urban environment.

Community Study in Complex Society

Arensberg and Kimball's inductively derived model and my experience of community are based on observations of relatively homogeneous, bounded, small-scale social fields. These community constructs are in large part the reflection of shared professional inquiry and personal models of what constitute ideal human association. Anthropologists critical of the Arensberg (1968[1937]) model as a conceptual tool in the study of community in urban contexts point to its rural or small-scale bias and to the difficulties inherent in the claim that social macrosystems can be generalized from an analysis of microenvironmental structures (see, e.g., Weaver and White 1972b:97; Leeds 1973:16). Arensberg and Kimball (1965:110) are not unaware of these concerns: "Community structures and intentions are complicated by an urban-industrial context. Development and maintenance of community interest in such an environment is far more difficult. Institutional bridges across which communication can easily flow are imperative if community is to be sustained. The community does so by the injection of an interest that is common to all."

Arensberg and Kimball (1965:2) also concede that "communities . . . do not exist *in vacuo.*" Rather, "they exist across time, within greater societal environments, and are sensitive to technological, political, and economic change. A holistic description of community necessarily includes consideration of all those linkages between the locality and its impinging intercommunity and extracommunity institutions and resources" (1965:14).

In terms of an analysis of cultural cognition and its behavioral expression, concerns about representativeness could certainly be leveled at any attempt to equate the community consciousness of Los Angeles American Indians with a more global Los Angeles worldview. In terms of sociostructural analysis, however, the decentralized, dispersed, heterogeneous, and self-fabricating character of the Los Angeles Indian community mirrors the postmodern metropolis that is its matrix. Whether parallel economic, political, and class structures, and principles of social organization exist in the Los Angeles Indian community and its host society entails a macrocosmic level of analysis that will not be attempted here.

Arensberg and Kimball's seminal community model contributes a rich, comprehensive, and conceptually broad array of markers of community in complex society and the dimensions by which it can be measured, defined, and described at any level of population density or sociocultural complexity. Explanatory principles such as "community as system," "communication linkages," "interaction," "process," "common interest," "stage," "locus and repository of cultural life," "functional interdependencies," a "time-space configuration," and "interconnections to the larger societal whole" continue to act as catalysts to the general field of community studies. These concepts provide the structure and inspired the strategies by which I looked for, discovered, and now describe the Los Angeles Indian community experience.

Other Constructs of Community in Complex Society

Introduced by Barnes (1954), the concept and techniques of social network analysis have enjoyed increasing acceptance and application since the mid-1960s, particularly among urban anthropologists. Interest in interactional ties rather than place ties may be a way of teasing out the spatially dispersed, "non-place communities" that are common in metropolitan areas (Connell 1973). In the face of overwhelming social complexity and the loss of "natural" social boundaries, network analysis offers an alternative strategy for analyzing urban life as a social field (Hannerz 1980:172). In this way, "the city [is] not so much a conglomeration of people and institutions but . . . a multitude of social networks, overlapping, and interacting in various ways" (Craven and Wellman 1973:58).

Keefe (1980:52–53) calls the social networks she tracked "personal communities" or "the total network of primary social relationships maintained by an individual." She defends social network analysis as a research strategy because the diminishing strength of "strong neighborhood ties" in contemporary urban centers indicates that "social life in cities might be best conceptualized as interacting personal communities or networks rather than spatial communities." Rather than being anchored to a place-community, urban communities appear as networks anchored in individuals. Therefore, examination of urban life can begin with the individual.

Working with the Micmac in Boston, Guillemin (1975:72) espouses the value of social and communicational network analyses as ways of dealing with urban population dispersals:

> The idea of a network is useful in the study of tribal people for two reasons. First, it allows their forms of social organization to be compared with those of other urban people, including non-tribal ethnic groups. Second, the concept releases them and other groups from the need to have community identified with geographic stability, because the concept essentially treats patterns of communication as social structure, or at least allows [the consideration of community as] enduring patterns of culture spread over time and space.

The personal network, or personal community, construct parallels the concept "reference group" contributed by symbolic interactionists in sociology (Goffman 1959) and supplemented by the much more specific concept "identity group" introduced by anthropologists (Barth 1969). Such concepts define population units and community boundaries through analysis of the referents and identities displayed in social interaction. In contrast to an arbitrary delimitation of a social group (e.g., an organization or an incorporated township), this approach to group boundedness, whether open or closed, is expressed in terms of self-concepts and actual behavior that have reality to the participants (Weaver and White 1972a:119).

Inherent in the focus on individual behavior as a strategy for divining community, particularly in complex society, is the assumption that people are not simply passive recipients of the conditions thrust on them but act on their own behalf and volition. Individuals can and do manipulate the political situation to mobilize community action. They make choices within a structure of constraints that then modify that structure (Mullings 1987:8). The fluidity and temporal nature of community can also be seen in investigations of social life as a career over time and in role attainment, execution, and continuity among the roles assumed by an individual (Hannerz 1980:274).

Ethnicity and Community

> I encourage you all to pull together, remember, our people
> in the 1920s in Los Angeles and in 1930s who had abso-
> lutely nothing and were flagrantly discriminated by gov-
> ernments and people, stuck together. They started from
> nothing and gave us a [community] center. (Sophie Wade,
> Choctaw, longtime Los Angeles resident, letter, October
> 13, 1986)

Plotnicov (1983:145), in a five-year (1977–81) review of urban anthropology doctoral dissertations, found that, after women's stud- ies, ethnicity was the most popular dissertation topic. Why was there such concerted interest in ethnic groups in urban contexts? Arensberg and Kimball (1965:110) suggest that community in com- plex society is sustained by "injection of an interest common to all" and by building "institutional bridges across which communication can easily flow." Conventionally defined as a principle of social organization based on shared place of origin, history, and cultural norms, ethnicity may provide such a common interest and institu- tional bridge for any number of groups who live in cities.

Ethnicity can be broadly defined without reference to common ancestry, whether historical or fictive. For example, an ethnic group can be defined as "a collectivity of people who share some patterns of normative behavior and form a part of a larger population, inter- acting with people of other collectivities within the framework of a social system" (Gmelch and Zenner 1980:203). Talai's (1988:52) def- inition of ethnicity includes the notion of communality, or the "right to make moral claims upon each other in virtue of their shared ethnic identity," whereas Cohen (1980:211) emphasizes the utility of common symbols in organizing people on behalf of their common interests, in a manner that parallels the thinking of Arensberg and Kimball. In Cohen's view, ethnicity—that is, the consciousness of ethnic difference—becomes salient at the point where diverse people meet and interact. It is double-edged and can be used to isolate and disarm, as well as be emblematic of, group effort and acquisition of enhanced political status and rights vis- à-vis the larger, encompassing social entity. The expression of eth- nicity is situational, dynamic, and experienced by individuals in varying degrees of intensity across situations and the life course (Weibel-Orlando 1988a).

As Zenner (1980:203) points out, Lynch (1980) generally shares Cohen's view that ethnic groups can use the construct of a common subculture to further their ends. Building on Spradley's (1969) earlier notion of bicultural competence, Lynch has explored how and why people who have more than one identity in terms of caste, region, language, and socioeconomic class stress only certain aspects of their identity across social situations and particularly across urban microenvironments. The city, he argues, is the enabling locus for creativity and selectivity in identification and public presentation of self.

Ethnicity and Rural-to-Urban Migration

Ethnicity as a principle of community organization in rural-to-urban migration and adaptation has been widely studied across cultures.[7] Primary ties (family, kinship, and ethnic association) are important in the "urban village," which remains a place of conformity and homogeneity, a preferred way of life, through the concerted and cooperative efforts of its migrated members to reconstruct its infrastructure within the urban superstructure (Gans 1962).

Guldin (1980:244–45) makes the distinction between the "ethnic neighborhood" as locus and "ethnic community," where primary relationships, through "actions and social relations," tie the group together. He further notes that "this type of community, of course, presents far greater analytical and methodological difficulties than is the case with the spatially distinct ethnic neighborhood," and he suggests that some measure of "interactional intensity" needs to be developed so as to measure that "point [at which] ethnic interaction gives an overall ethnic flavoring to the social interaction of a specific group" (1980:245, 257). Ethnic community can be spatially dispersed yet remain as a "social construct in the minds of the city's residents" (Gordon 1964:163).

American Indians in Urban Society

The contemporary worldwide phenomenon of large-scale migration from small-scale, nonindustrial societies to industrialized urban centers has parallels in the post–World War II United States, when tens of thousands of American Indians were pushed off the reservation by endemic unemployment or family and social pressures, or were pulled to urban centers by the promise of jobs, education, and a new way of life. As a result, studies of the American Indian rural-to-urban-to-rural migration experience proliferated in the 1960s and 1970s.[8] Most of these studies are issue-oriented, with sociologists, social psychologists, and anthropologists focusing on the explication of acculturation, adaptation, and assimilation either at the individual or ethnic group level with but passing reference to the city as a system or to "the larger perspective" (Weaver and White 1972a:113).

Those concerned with holistic description and analysis tentatively have labeled the relationships they saw in urban Indian life "community." For example, Guillemin (1975:11, 20) describes the Micmac in Boston as a "kind of urban tribal community" and a "group which, like many others, has had to be perceived as a viable community." After the move to Boston, she notes, Micmacs found urban arenas in which to continue to express core values such as courage and endurance, as well as other valued cultural traits (1975:66). Ablon (1964:299), who worked with, in her words, the "Indian community" in the San Francisco Bay area in the 1960s, defines that community as "an organized, visible body of persons who interrelate with regularity in socially meaningful ways." She has looked to "the many active social, religious, and political Indian organizations of the Bay Area, rather than to any network of relationships encompassing individuals or families," for evidence of "Indian community."

Others simply assume, a priori, that the collections of Indians with whom they work in urban centers have community (e.g., Mucha 1983; Morinis 1982). Still others despair of finding any evidence, much less capturing a holistic view of ethnic community life, given the complexity of urban Indian social interactions. Rather, their work focuses on manageable microunits of interaction and analysis: case histories (Olson 1971), ethnic enclaves and social cliques (Snyder 1971), networks of interaction (Hirabayashi, Willard, and Kemnitzer 1972), social distance (Fiske 1977), and assistance patterns (Weibel 1978).

Ablon (1964:299) concedes that "the reality of an actual 'Indian community' is indeed tenuous." For example, fewer than one-sixth of the adult Indians in her study were regularly involved in the activities she considers markers of community life. Lack of authoritarian leadership, a general practice of group participation in planning, and a frequent absence of concrete pre-event duty assignment are other indicators that community, as defined by either Arensberg or Leeds, was not among the set of relationships that structured American Indian life in San Francisco as Ablon viewed it in the 1960s.

Focusing on pan-Indianism as an adaptive strategy, Ablon and her contemporaries[9] saw the phenomenon as a neo-Indian social identity. Pan-Indianism is defined as "those processes through which Indians of various cultural backgrounds identify and associate with each other" (Hirabayashi et al. 1972:77) and is said to have evolved from diverse tribal groups being labeled and treated as a discrete ethnic entity by the Bureau of Indian Affairs and non-Indian Americans in general. Some anthropologists see pan-Indianism as a defensive maneuver, a way of responding to white dominance, a parallel ethnic institution. According to James (1961:744), the "key to pan-Indianism appears to lie in social relations between Indians and Whites rather than in relations between tribes." However, Ablon sees a positive reason for the development of urban pan-Indian activities, namely, when surrounded by the white world, the self-image of Indianness stands out more sharply than at home. "Thus a neo-Indian type on a new level of self- and group identity with a pan-Indian as well as tribal orientation may be born from the necessity of mingling with members of other tribes" (Ablon 1964:303).

Pan-Indianism is fostered and shaped by the non-Indian stereotype of the High Plains warrior as the embodiment of all things Indian (Hirabayashi et al. 1972:77). Weekly Saturday night pow-wows, film and television depictions of nineteenth-century Indian life, and bumper stickers forewarning others that "Custer Died for Your Sins" all invoke Plains Indian cultural styles as models for contemporary Indian identity. Importantly, the Plains Indian ethos serves as an icon for both the non-Indian general public and a considerable number of urban Indians who are not Plains Indians. Its invocation by those Indians who wish to create and sustain an overarching mythic commonality supports a sense of a shared ethnicity cum community.

More than two decades ago, Ablon (1964:304) suggested that pan-Indianism, or at least a pan-Indian public stance vis-à-vis the non-Indian host society, could be a precursor of and prerequisite for the development of supratribal urban Indian communities. As the city is the context in which cross-ethnic interaction is a given, it is possible that pan-Indian community, as a sociocultural response, can only be born from an urban womb. The development of a pan-Indian stance and a consensus about those political issues, economic concerns, and cultural traits with which all Indians in Los Angeles can identify are therefore factors in the creative process by which an urban Indian community consciousness is instilled and sustained.

American Indian Community in Los Angeles

In searching for relevant markers of viable community among Indians in Los Angeles, I have focused on those social interactional patterns that have persisted over time as the result of an overarching principle of social organization—namely, ethnicity. In this specific case, ethnicity has come to mean a created supratribal identity and pan-Indian stance vis-à-vis the dominant society. The creation, perpetuation, and interconnectedness of an impressive array of Los Angeles-based Indian organizations reflect community process and structure. These grass roots organizations in turn provide the stage on which the drama of an Indian way of life is enacted. Participation in the numerous recurring "Indian" events reinforces and reintensifies community consciousness and connection.

Contemporary concerns about the local and supralocal linkages in complex society are well noted. Throughout the descriptive and analytic passages of this book, I am careful to consider the extracommunity influences on particular institutions, events, or decisions. Identifying the cognitive and sociostructural boundaries of this nonplace community involves looking to the peripheries of social connectedness for the point at which the context and personnel of a particular environment are no longer considered Indian or community. At this point, unlike Leeds, or for that matter Arensberg and Kimball, I am not ready to include the various federal, state, or even county organizations that interface with Los Angeles Indian program administrators as the furthest extensions of the Indian community. Rather, these organizations are seen by most Los Angeles Indians as extracommunity resources to be used for the "good of the Indian community." They are decidedly not of the Indian community.

In the case of the Indians of Los Angeles, the term "community" means something quite different from Leeds's (1973:19) conception of community as the whole network of all possible social interrelations between a locality and its supralocal hinterland. Most Indians with whom I have talked, while agreeing that there is some social entity they consider community in Los Angeles, are hard-pressed to provide its operational definition. From observations of and discussions about the nature and frequency of interactional patterns, community appears to mean all those Indians in Los Angeles who seek out other Indians with whom to associate, no matter how infrequently, for political, economic, health, religious, affectional, and recreational reasons. Furthermore, indigenous definitions of the Los Angeles Indian community are associated with the belief that Indians are entitled to the delivery of Indian-specific community services, no matter where they currently live. Finally, all Indians and their non-Indian affines in Los Angeles—those who either identify as Indian or with Indian causes—can be seen as members of a common-interest collectivity whose overarching consideration is the maintenance of ethnic group consciousness, ethos, and community.

NOTES

1. Bethel, Connecticut, located within fifty miles of New York City, is as much in a dynamic relationship with external socioeconomic and political forces as is the Los Angeles Indian community. Massive freeway construction in the late 1950s and out-migration to Bethel and the surrounding area of New York–based light and high tech industries in the 1960s and 1970s have increasingly incorporated the former hatting town into the Greater New York City hinterland. By 1980 Bethel's population had expanded to more than 17,000 and showed no signs of reaching a plateau in the next decade.

2. The first colonists in that section of southwestern Connecticut settled the town of Danbury, immediately adjacent to and northwest of Bethel, in 1684.

3. Ironically, Danbury had a population of only about thirty thousand in the 1940s. Its physical plat and plant have always been those of a small industrial city, as opposed to Bethel's more rural, nineteenth-century, small-agricultural-town configuration, an observable difference not lost on me in youth. Both towns have maintained these community styles to this day.

4. The phrase, "There is no there there," is attributed to Gertrude Stein. Although it was said originally of Oakland, California, it is easily applied to the dispersed residential and institutional patterns of Los Angeles County.

5. Leeds (1973) is among the most vociferous critics of Arensberg's community study method and his ideas about community as mirror and microcosm.

6. In *Culture and Community in Europe* (Lynch 1984), ten of Arensberg's former students demonstrate their mentor's considerable contribution to both their understanding and subsequent studies of communities in complex societies and the field of community and urban studies in general.

7. Anthologies by Gmelch and Zenner (1980), Press and Smith (1980), and Mullings (1987) are among several contemporary works that provide an overview of worldwide trends in rural-to-urban migration and urban ethnic communities research. Among the scores of ethnographic accounts of so-

ciocultural continuities stemming from such migrations are Doughty (1970) in Peru, Epstein (1972) in Brazil, Salisbury and Salisbury (1972) in Papua, New Guinea, Abu-Lughod (1961) in Egypt, and Mayer (1962) in sub-Saharan Africa.

8. Readers by Waddell and Watson (1971) and Bahr, Chadwick, and Day (1972) remain the most comprehensive, yet dated, among those that include landmark studies of American Indian in urban settings.

9. James (1961) and Price (1972) are among the other early observers of the urban, pan-Indian phenomenon.

5

The Search for Community
in Complex Society

The Urban Field Team Approach

METHODOLOGICAL CONCERNS have been a focus of the sub-discipline of urban anthropology since its inception, and urban anthropology courses have been offered as standard anthropological fare since the early 1960s. Initially, team research was proposed as one fieldwork strategy for dealing with the contextual complexities of urban life. In the mid-1960s, the anthropology department at the University of California at Los Angeles established a yearlong urban field school sequence that employed a multifocused research team approach. Each year a team of anthropology professor-mentors and graduate student fieldworkers targeted a different urban research population and each student chose a specific research focus. Operating under the assumption that the complex whole could be inductively discerned from descriptions and analyses of its more easily located and observed parts, the multifocused field team was intended to develop an urban research strategy alternative to the conventional one village-one anthropologist approach to ethnographic fieldwork.

In 1966 the UCLA field school target population was American Indians in Los Angeles. That year the urban field school enjoyed only partial success. John Price, the faculty mentor, subsequently published a number of articles dealing with the issues of tribe-specific rates of acculturation and assimilation (1968) and a stage theory of ethnic institutional development (1975). Two students published articles on their topic-specific inquiries (Gardner 1969; Bell 1979), and a summary report describing the preliminary findings of each of the student participants was deposited in the anthropology department library (Price 1966). It would seem that a holistic view of the Los Angeles Indian community was something more than could be derived from a review of its parts.

Microsystemic and Issue-oriented Urban Anthropology

In 1973, when I began to work with Indians in Los Angeles, the team approach to urban fieldwork largely had been abandoned. A student interested in urban anthropology fieldwork was encouraged to explore an issue, test a particular theoretical position or methodological approach, ask a "big question." The emphasis was on focused, structured observation, analytic rigor, and a contribution in some innovative (if circumscribed) way to the established body of knowledge. Armed with such research mandates, students were left to their own devices in the urban field.

For these reasons, my Los Angeles–based initial inquiry and research focus for the next decade was not the study of the urban macrosystem and its linkages with supralocal institutions, the macrocosmic focus advocated by Leeds (1973), Weaver and White (1972), and others. Rather, until I began to write this book in 1986, my contribution to the depiction of the American Indian experience in Los Angeles was characterized by the very narrowness of focus for which early urban anthropology is now consistently criticized (Ansari and Nas 1983; Mullings 1987).

Methodological Continuities and Innovations

Each focus and set of research questions I explored required a particular set of methodological approaches. My early interest in assistance patterns and shifts in problem-solving strategies over time prompted the use of a modified version of social network analysis, a research strategy that was decidedly in vogue at the time (Mitchell 1969; Snyder 1973; Southall 1973). Through the use of sets of questions designed to elicit information about people or agencies who assisted the interviewees in actual problem-solving situations over time, as well as the interviewees' frequency and intensity of involvement in Los Angeles Indian community organizations, events, and pancultural activities, I developed profiles of the density and cultural heterogeneity of the "personal communities" (Keefe 1980) of ninety-seven individual Indians. I found that familial, tribal, regional, subcultural, and Los Angeles Indian community memberships are important factors in determining the character of personal assistance support systems across time. Situational and opportunistic selectivity in assistance-seeking behavior are also apparent (Weibel 1977, 1978).

Validity is always an issue in the use of retrospective data, and my fieldwork was no exception, even though I asked people to recall life crisis events of such magnitude that they should have been imprinted indelibly in their memories (or so I thought). Furthermore, this research strategy was not sufficient in itself to determine fully an individual's sense of membership in Los Angeles community life. Granted, individuals could be located across organizations, events, and personal communities, but the character of these linkages, their relationship and contribution to the social entity known as "Los Angeles Indian community life," remained problematic.

If community is to be found in the ongoing interaction of individuals in collective activities, there is no substitute for direct observation of these processes. The central identifying method of anthropological inquiry, that is, participant observation, is as crucial in determining the parameters of community in complex, heterogeneous urban settings as it is in the study of bounded, isolated, relatively homogeneous societies. From its inception, my experience with the Los Angeles Indian community has been guided by this anthropological sine qua non.

Arranging to "be there" in the conventional sense of communal locality in the "quasi-thereness" of the Los Angeles Indian community posed a number of logistical and conceptual difficulties. Nodes of regularly occurring ethnic interaction had to be identified. The linkages of individual social arenas through formal and informal ties of membership, function, and collective action had to be established. And questions concerning who chose to function within these settings and in what manner had to be addressed. All of these tasks required an initial period of relatively unstructured observation and participation in the more publicly accessible Indian organizations, service delivery programs, church parishes, and regularly occurring public events that my original contacts had identified as significant community activities.

At the onset of my fieldwork, I had the romantic idea that, once I discovered where the Indian community core was (the image of Greenwood Avenue in Bethel, Connecticut, was clearly operant here), I could replicate the classical anthropological field experience (total immersion) in the urban environment. My twelve-year-old son and I would move to an American Indian neighborhood and live there for a year. Because of our proximity, we would be caught up in and thereby made familiar with the daily routine of urban Indian community life, and my relationship to and assumed role in the community would be allowed to manifest itself over time. In the best of all possible worlds, I would eventually evolve from curious cultural marginal to integrated observing participant. I would experience community as did its sustaining members. In short, I would do "real" anthropology.

The problem with all of this anthropological good intent was that my preconceptions about how Indians in Los Angeles experience community were ill founded. As in 1989, Indian Country, L.A., in 1973 was not the inescapable, daily, face-to-face interaction of most community members in a geographically defined, relatively homogeneous, small ethnic enclave. A review of the 1970 national census figures and a mapping of the Indian organizations indicate the complete absence of any discernible Indian neighborhood. There simply was and is no conventional "there" there.

In the absence of an ethnic locality in which I could immerse myself, I developed other means of identifying what I labeled the "interactional community" of the Los Angeles Indian (Weibel 1977). I combined the collection of issue-specific, semistructured interviews with observations of the interviewees' interpersonal contacts across Los Angeles Indian organizations. As people were interviewed, their names were placed on a field site observations checklist and I then noted their presence or absence and their statuses, roles, and behavior at every community site I visited. This research strategy allowed for additional insights into the nature of and mechanisms for maintaining the Los Angeles Indian community structure.

Focused observations provided partial checks on the discrepancy between self-reported social networks and involvement in Indian activities and actual interaction with other Indian community members and institutions. It was gratifying, for instance, to discover that self-reported drinking behavior, long thought to be notoriously underreported, was 80 percent consistent with observed interviewee drinking behavior in Indian bars (Weibel and Weisner 1980). Structured observations revealed the multiplicity of interlinkages between individuals, ethnic institutions and individuals, and ethnic institutions, and also provided a measure of an individual's relative interactional density and frequency both within and beyond the Indian community. Finally, structured observations afforded participants the opportunity to demonstrate the real rather than the ideal nature and quality of their reported ethnic community involvements.

Establishing Rapport in a Complex Society

To experience the Los Angeles Indian community as its core members do was more easily said than done. Although Los Angeles was where I lived, I could not expect acceptance or claim the rights, privileges, and responsibilities inherent in a shared ethnic identity. I could not be sustained, as was Myerhoff (1980a) in her work with elderly Jews in Los Angeles, by the surety that it was important for me, personally, to know something about the people with whom I was engaged because of the inevitability that one day I would become one of them. Rather, three hundred years of Anglo-Indian relations worked to this Anglo anthropologist's disadvantage in the highly politicized, informed, and vocal urban Indian community.

The four hundred or so positions of paid employment within the complex of urban Indian human services organizations were jealously guarded against non-Indian incursion. Racially toned intimations that a new employee of the Indian Free Clinic or the Indian Centers, Inc., was probably more Mexican, black, or white than Indian were early clues that I should never expect to experience total core community involvement. The "image of limited good" (Foster 1965) was clearly operant even in the 1970s heyday of relatively unlimited federal human services funding.

Over time I improvised a compromise between unrealistic expectations of total immersion in Indian activities (as a small fraction of the Indians in Los Angeles experience community) and selective involvement (the way community is experienced by a much larger percentage of the Indian populace). If I could not hope to acquire and sustain formal roles in Indian community life, I could create informal ones. Thus, I regularly volunteered my time and talents to a number of Indian human services organizations. For two years I worked at the front desk of the Indian Free Clinic on the two nights a week that it was open. I was a hymn-singing, violin-playing, churchgoing, unofficial member of the First Southern Baptist Indian Mission on Clara Street in Bell Gardens for years, as well as a regular visitor to all of the other Los Angeles Indian churches and Fifth Sunday sings, and a shawl-wearing, two-stepping participant at Saturday night powwows. For the larger portions of five years I was in daily, face-to-face contact with members of various segments of the Los Angeles Indian community, recording life histories, observing ongoing ethnic events, and, when asked, participating in collective action. At the end of each particular Indian event, my Indian co-workers and I drove our separate ways to our dispersed homes and families.

Curiously, the pattern of time-limited, intense, face-to-face interactions of a collectivity premised by shared ethnic concerns and punctuated by periods of dispersal into kin-based, residential units is not unique to urban Indians or to my fieldwork experience. This same interactional pattern characterized the community experience of most nineteenth-century Indian foraging and big game–hunting societies (Lowie 1954).

An obvious question, then, is, Why study the core and selective types of urban Indian ethnic experience when they are clearly in the minority among the Indians who live in Los Angeles? The high visibility of these people and the ease with which they can be identified were two powerful determinants of the focus of this book; a third was the desire to demonstrate the work of ethnic community maintenance, not its dissolution. The number or proportion of Indians living in an urban context who mean to sustain a sense of ethnic community is irrelevant. The fact that at least two thousand Indians in Los Angeles are committed to the concept of ethnic community and the need to carry on its work is not. Why many Indians choose not to participate in community life, or do so only in the most serendipitous way, is the subject of another book.

The associated issues of acculturation, assimilation, passing, and culture denial—the antithesis of ethnic community maintenance—are important but cannot be examined adequately within the framework and scope of this book. However, as general theoretical assumptions of the 1960s and 1970s, such issues are overdue for a thorough and revisionist critique. Although not explicitly stated herein, this book stands as a testament to the weaknesses of earlier models of inevitable cultural assimilation. Secondarily, the succeeding chapters graphically demonstrate that the idea of and structure by which ethnic community is sustained are not inoperative or devoid of cultural meaning. Rather, ethnic community tenaciously continues to exist as a valid principle of social organization.

Toward an Anthropology of Community in Complex Society: Time, Process, Continuity, and Change

In 1983 I began, with my University of Southern California colleagues Barbara Myerhoff and Andrei Simić, a three-year study of ethnicity's contribution to well-being in old age. One of the major concepts we explored was the intensity with which the ethnic experience is sustained over a lifetime. Documentation of ethnic continuities over time necessitated the collection of life histories, a fieldwork strategy that has enjoyed long and wide acceptance among anthropologists (Langness and Frank 1981; Myerhoff 1980b; Shaw 1980). At that time, I had known for more than ten years several of the Indian elders who agreed to share their life histories with me; in fact, over the years I had interviewed most of them at least once and some as many as four times. This made it possible to discern their personal and cultural continuities and life career shifts, both within and external to the Indian community, by comparing their most recently recorded life history narratives with earlier presentations of self. In doing so, I stepped beyond the anthropologist's usual penchant for synchronic description of cultural phenomena and into the diachronic worldview of the ethnohistorian or the ethnobiographer.

The follow-up study, twenty to fifty years later, of a community in which one did research early in a professional career is not new to anthropology. Mead's *New Lives for Old* (1966), which recounts her lifelong personal and professional connection to the people of Manus, and *A Weave of Time* (1986), Adair's refilming (by Susan Fanshel), forty-eight years later, of the Navajo family with whom he worked in the 1930s, are but two of a growing number of early fieldwork retrospectives. For me, comparison of sets of personal narratives across time and about different aspects of urban life facilitated the discovery of ethnic community processes as life history context. This analytic model proved to be the innovation, methodological breakthrough, and epistemological window that had eluded me, or that I had ignored, for a decade. The depiction of ethnic community as a tapestry of interwoven life histories, a metaphorical whole cloth, now seemed possible.

Community Study: A Multidisciplinary Approach

In 1986, as I began to organize ten years of field notes, interview transcriptions, photographs, film and video footage, and archival materials on the Los Angeles Indian community in preparation for writing this ethnography, I realized that the original UCLA field team model for research in complex societies had not been inappropriate, only incompletely executed. It had had two conceptual and administrative weaknesses. First, in the absence of an overarching theoretical goal and analytic orientation, the individual research reports, although accurate depictions of parts of the whole, were unrepresentative of the whole. There was no gestalt. Second, although the urban field school faculty mentors were expert, their theoretical and methodological orientations were narrowly anthropological.

A holistic ethnography of community in complex society necessitates a multidisciplinary approach. Applied anthropologists, because of their research settings and issue-specific foci, have appreciated this position for some time (Foster 1969; van Willigen 1986; Wulff and Fiske 1987). The nature of my work with alcohol abuse intervention programs and aging confirmed this position. A culturally sensitive perspective of medical explanation and practice was not sufficient to deal meaningfully with the biological and psychological aspects of either drug addiction or the aging process. My subsequent analyses would have been significantly more comprehensive had I been the beneficiary of a course in human chemistry and the psychology and pathology of addiction and aging prior to the field research experience. In the end, the search for research strategies powerful enough to elicit community processes among the Indians in Los Angeles led to disciplines other than anthropology.

The development of an urban Indian community is not unique to Los Angeles. Indians migrated in significant numbers to major urban centers across the United States. Thus, it is equally important to review the anthropological, sociological, and social psychological accounts of Indians in other urban centers to determine those processes that are unique to the Los Angeles Indian experience and those that transcend local idiosyncrasies. Cross-city commonalities may lead to the discovery of generic patterns of rural-to-urban migration, adaptation, and community development processes.

Finally, the issue of temporality, particularly when working with migrating populations, assumes an ethnohistorical depth that encompasses not only the postmigration adaptation processes but also the cultural tenets of the societies from which the new urbanites have migrated and to which they return with regularity. A review of classic ethnographies of focal tribal groups has been extremely helpful in the development of a major theoretical theme, namely, the propensity for cultural continuity in the development of an urban ethnic community.

Community as Cultural Repository and Stage

The concepts and descriptions of community institutions, roles, and processes presented in sections IV and V are clearly the products of research strategies and analytic perspectives well within the conventional definition and strictures of ethnographic inquiry. The descriptions of the three Los Angeles Indian arenas of ethnic group interaction in section IV derive from participant observations in these settings spanning fifteen years. My personal observations are buttressed by those of other social scientists in parallel cultural scenes and by ethnohistorical accounts of earlier indigenous institutional forms. Key informants played a major role in the development of these ethnographic descriptions of community interaction and ceremonial behavior. Core members of each cultural scene who acted as interpreters of ongoing social process during my field observations were enlisted as technical advisors and helped me edit first drafts of these chapters.

The life history vignettes in section V are based on numerous interviews and personal conversations over more than a decade with the people involved. Observation of the exemplars interacting with other Los Angeles Indians and representatives of supralocal institutions also contributed to the description and analysis of each person's community statuses, roles, and influence. In order to ensure factual and analytic integrity, I shared my observations with the person on whom the description is based and asked for, and responded to, their comments about my depiction of them and their roles in the Indian community.

The ethnographic descriptions and analyses of cultural scenes and associated community roles presented here represent a compromise. I could have written short synopses of twenty or thirty of the most active, longest-lived, or most influential Indian organizations in Los Angeles. By arguing that they represented the community organizations' typological range, I could have allowed description of the social field to stand for ethnographic holism. Bramstedt (1977) attempted to do just that. Notwithstanding the limited explanatory power and essentially historical contribution that his fifteen-year-old ethnographic description now offers, Bramstedt's work is essentially static. He hypothesizes that community was to be found in the interlocking memberships of the Los Angeles Indian organizations. But his interactional frequency distribution charts, while illustrating that interlocking memberships do exist, fail to demonstrate the dynamics of such social networks.

I mean to construct something more than comprehensive, synchronic description of community elements. Richly detailed "thick" descriptions and analyses of community ritual process and performance that have withstood the test of indigenous criticism provide windows of understanding as to how the Indian collectivity in Los Angeles organizes, expresses, and experiences community. I therefore describe three widely different community arenas and a status and role associated with each, and I do so in such ethnographic detail that ensuing analyses are properly and sufficiently placed in context and are supported by actual, observed behavior.

The settings described in section IV obviously do not represent the range of Los Angeles Indian community interactional arenas. They are, however, extremely salient, long-lived, and particularly influential in determining the nature of community consciousness and the pattern of social interactions among community members. Additionally, all three organizations described in section IV and the individual community members described in section V played highly visible roles in the community crisis described in section VI. I therefore describe these institutions and the key individuals associated with them for their instrumentality in demonstrating community interaction and collective action over time and in times of community crisis.

The analytic approaches to the observations of arenas of community interaction and the enactment of community-defined roles within those culture scenes address the following anthropological concerns: ritual process, ritual continuity and innovation, symbolic interaction, symbolic transformations of space, and dimensions of expressive culture. Conceptual concerns such as the cultural (cognitive) implications of public presentation of self, the correlation between space use and social distance dichotomies, markers of ethnic categories, ethnic identity, and the processes by which ethnic pluralism is sustained are also explored. These topics are of equal interest to qualitative sociologists, cross-cultural psychologists, and cognitive anthropologists.

The conceptual and methodological boundary markers that social scientists assertively erected and jealously defended as their own purview during the disciplinary border wars of the 1960s and 1970s seem extraneous when attempting to meet the challenge of doing fieldwork in a complex society. Rather, my multidisciplinary approach is driven by intellectual pragmatism: I prefer the eclecticism that allows a match between research issue and its appropriate (best-fit) research approach.

"Sophie Will Read This, You Know":
The Ethics of Writing an Ethnography of and in One's Own Culture

For two years, and in a fugue state of awful intellectual fascination and personal frustration, I observed the process by which the

Los Angeles Indian Centers, Inc., fell in on itself, followed by the efforts of community members first to save and then to resurrect the institution. Most of the time, I was sure the process I was monitoring was so important historically and anthropologically that it warranted documentation. At other times, however, I was consumed by self-doubt and convinced that my preoccupation with this particular community process bordered on intellectual ghoulishness. On a number of occasions, I remembered Nancy Scheper-Hughes's poignant disclosure of the unanticipated depth of hurt and anger with which her frank, not always complimentary ("You described every single wart") depictions of mental health in rural Ireland had been met by her key informants.[1]

What prompted me to document, submit to analysis, and make public my findings about a social process that culminated in the loss of a vital community institution and unprecedented anguish and embarrassment in the Los Angeles Indian community? The saliency of the crisis to me and to the community was one rationale. Another was that the awful inevitability of that two-year process of devolution and institutional demise provided a social drama of such intensity that formerly opaque community structures surfaced as high relief. The processes by which individuals from every segment and level of ethnic community life were made aware of the impending community crisis and variously drawn into cooperative (or competitive) action were made immediately recognizable. Lines of communication, political alliances, problem-solving strategies, muted and subtle in less threatening times, pulsated with the raw energy of unmitigated urgency and real emotional investment. The crisis at the center mobilized the Los Angeles Indians as no other community process had in the last decade. Its power to illustrate and explicate community processes, and thereby community structure, was undeniable, its documentation irresistible. For these reasons, I concluded that anthropological analysis of that process was warranted within certain self-imposed informational constraints.

Doing fieldwork in and writing about one's own society or a group of people who perceive themselves as an ethnic minority oppressed by the anthropologist's peer society is fraught with any number of ethical dilemmas. The question of anonymity is also particularly pertinent to ethnographies of segments of one's own society. Much of the ethnographic information presented here is historical record. I use the correct names of the Los Angeles Indian organizations because of their public and historic visibility and general third-party corporate status.

I decided early on to use pseudonyms for all of the individuals mentioned in this ethnography who are not well-known, immediately recognizable public figures beyond the Los Angeles Indian community, even though this standard anthropological convention has always seemed arbitrary and is an essentially artificial device when applied to the American Indian community in Los Angeles. Any core community member who reads this book will recognize immediately the persons about whom I write, pseudonyms notwithstanding. However, since I still live in the city and interact with most of the key people I mention, the issues of accountability to the described community and its individual members, in general, and the quality of my relationship to the community subsequent to the book's publication, in particular, are highly salient to me.

In what ways, then, are individual rights of privacy served by conventional anthropological strategies for ensuring subject anonymity when writing about people in one's own society? My handling of the community members' anonymity is an outcome of my policy to share their life history chapters with them prior to publication. In one case, I unexpectedly learned that, aside from a few minor historical adjustments in the narrative, the family's main concern was the inappropriateness of the pseudonym I had created to mask their identity. They suggested I use their real surname because the pseudonym I had chosen was "so common back home that it's like calling someone here John Smith." Surprised, and not a little flattered, that the family wished to be identified in the text, I wondered why I hadn't thought of this solution sooner and on my own. I subsequently asked people if they wished to be identified or if the use of a pseudonym was preferred. The result was essentially an even split between a preference for full identification and the wish to remain anonymous.

Issues of Representation and Voice

A number of anthropologists who have written about American Indians in urban society portray the Indians as victims: pawns of a more global pattern of proletarianization (Jorgensen 1971) or forced assimilation (Officer 1971), or as anomic individuals in an overwhelming, alien world (Graves 1971). Others see them inevitably moving in a unilinear, uncompromising manner toward full assimilation into a mainstream America ethos (Price 1968, 1975). In most cases, American Indians are portrayed in a unidimensional manner, either as passive reactors to a powerful, disorienting host society or as self-destructive, pathological respondents to a perceived hostile environment.

There are, however, powerful exceptions. Guillemin's (1975) beautifully written *Urban Renegades* successfully captures the grit of contemporary Micmac reservation/city life and resonates with ethnographic truth. In a sensitive portrayal of real-life, real-people situations, she strikes a magical balance between "describing every wart" and meaningful ethnographic detail. I tried to maintain that balance in this ethnography, with the help of the people about whom I write. I asked them to critique relevant chapters and tell me when ethnographic detail had slipped into pointless gossip. I am indebted to them for their counsel in these matters.

My preoccupation with documenting and understanding urban Indian life from the standpoint of individual problem-solving strategies, drinking behavior, and life histories has allowed me to know, in ways that do not mirror early urban Indian typologies, over three hundred Native Americans. As in Spradley's (1969) wonderful, collaborative effort in compiling the autobiography of the Kwakiutl biculturalist James Sewid, I have come to know core members of the Los Angeles Indian community as complex, resourceful, resilient, psychological wholes. Shaped by historical, familial, and ethnic influences, they are also products of their own creativity and misadventure. For the most part, the Indians who have shared their lives with me are not anomic and unwilling proletarians, twentieth-century cultural casualties, or spiritually superior rustics. In relation to my own life experience, they are more mirror than alternative image. They wish to improve the quality of their lives and those of their children, and they work hard to do so. They aspire, compete, and achieve. They suffer from self-doubt, pride, envy, and lack of perspective. They have, at times, aspired too high, competed too callously, and made mistakes. They are, in the end, totally and wholly human. My intent is to portray that humanity.

The community processes described in this book derive from the observed behaviors and interactions of specific individuals in the context of their reference group and represent not only my perspective but also those of the relevant actors. I ensure this stereoscopic view and stereophonic narrative voice by presenting my analyses to the people who shared with me their life stories and participation in or response to the community crisis and by including their concurring or alternative perspectives whenever offered. Finally, as much as it is possible, I try to reproduce the vitality, personal insight, humor, dialect, and cadence with which people described their personal experience through illustrative, direct quotations from their life history transcripts. The ethnographic voice, then, eschews imposed and monotonal analyses in favor of negotiated, polyphonic, if occasionally aharmonic, narrative and discourse.

NOTE

1. Scheper-Hughes spoke frankly about the ethics and aftermath of the detailed, graphic, unfiltered ethnographic description of mental illness in her book *Saints, Scholars, and Schizophrenics: Mental Illness in Rural Ireland* (1979) during a panel session at the 1981 Annual Meeting of the Society for Applied Anthropology in Edinburgh, Scotland.

III

Ethnic Institutions as Community Context

... an understanding of the social organization of urban localities must include analysis of the structure and function of local organizations and their linkages. (Jones 1987:99)

INDIGENOUS VOLUNTARY associations, self-help organizations, and all other social institutions created within a collectivity are the contexts in which a pattern of coexistences, roles, and relationships (community) are expressed. Institutions are structural indicators of community cohesiveness, completeness, and inclusiveness and are characterized by regular, repetitive, grounded activities invoked as cultural tradition. The work of grass roots community organizations transforms collective action into social process. In such collectivities, individual action is the function of community-defined statuses and roles (Arensberg and Kimball 1965; Kimball and Partridge 1979; Jones 1987).

The social mechanism that binds the otherwise heterogeneous and dispersed Los Angeles Indians into an entity they recognize as community is the regular intersection of individuals representing a variety of special interest groups across a range of ethnically inflected activities. Scores of Los Angeles Indian organizations provide the arenas in which this social integration occurs.

The existence of institutions, their intersection, and their continuity over time and beyond the life or involvement of any one individual or social group meet Arensberg's temporal criteria for community. Bramstedt (1977) and Fiske (1975) were among the first to recognize and comprehensively document the phenomenon of intersecting social fields in the Los Angeles Indian community.[1] Their accounts of the Indians' voluntary associations cover the period from 1920 to 1973, before the full effects of major federal, state, and county funding of minority social services programs were realized. Their Indian organizational typologies, as discussed in chapter 6, serve as valuable historical documents and sociostructural models for those of us who worked in the Los Angeles Indian community in the following decades, and their historical outlines provide evidence of the community's structural continuity.

Community and Temporality

Arensberg and Kimball (1965) stress the importance of documenting both community pattern shifts and continuities over time. In section III, I introduce a model that assumes ethnic institutions are the context of community structure. Further, patterns of organizational development, fluorescence, and atrophy are among the sociocultural dynamics by which community process is identified. The analytic approach is essentially ethnohistorical.

The research findings of people who worked in the Los Angeles Indian community before, during, and after my concentrated fieldwork periods provide an extremely useful running narrative of institutional development and change. I assume that the historical accounts presented in these works are accurate and thus consider them to be valid secondary data. By arranging the works chronologically and comparing the scholarly descriptions of institutional history with community history narratives of key informants, as well as my personal observations of organizational activity across time, I have constructed a longitudinal view of Los Angeles Indian institutional development. This diachronic perspective is supported by other secondary sources (organizations' annual reports, monthly meeting agendas, promotional flyers, brochures, annual calendars of events, and formal and informal correspondence).

Community institutions and grass roots organizations are not impervious to external influences. As Fiske (1979) notes, the effects of contemporary national social movements and political policy trends on the development of Indian organizations and community services have been profound. Therefore, historical accounts of Indian-Anglo relations (Officer 1971; Taylor 1986; Olson and Wilson 1984), *Talking Leaf* and *Los Angeles Times* articles, government agency reports, and analysis of mass media news coverage of Indian affairs over the past two decades constitute important secondary sources for this study. Their use establishes the linkages between the supralocal context and the Los Angeles Indian community through time and the significance of these linkages to community continuity and change.

Communities and their institutions are not immutable. Rather, they are processual in nature and are shaped and changed by internal and external forces. In chapter 7, I discuss the organizational configuration of the Los Angeles Indian community in the 1980s and compare it with Bramstedt's and Fiske's findings from earlier decades. I conclude that patterns of organizational continuity and change appear to be associated with the relative local control of resources that sustain such ethnic organizations.

In a review of the 1978–86 issues of *Talking Leaf*, I documented 135 separate Los Angeles Indian organizations or affiliate groups, not including Indian representation in national organizations, committees, and administrative bodies (see table A.2 in the Appendix). Often redundant, competitive, and conflictual, these organizations are also cooperative and mutually supportive. I initially grouped the organizations and their associated statuses and roles into seventeen discrete social categories. Subsequently, several groupings were subsumed under more-inclusive, generic institutional, status, or role categories. Reclassification resulted in eight institutional categories: political; economic and social services; healing; religious; educational; recreational; communicational; and kinship, marital, and familial. These can be compared to Bramstedt's (1977:17–18) nine discrete institutional types: tradition-oriented, tribal, service, politically oriented, athletic, youth-oriented, educational, gender-oriented, and religious.

My category "communicational institutions" is not usually included among the sociostructural components in traditional ethnographies. However, I feel it is important to recognize the network of local Indian radio and televisions shows, telephone calling systems, hearings, conferences, workshops, and the monthly Indian newspaper *Talking Leaf* as among the most important mechanisms by which community awareness is sustained. When geographical location and tribal affiliation are no longer viable markers of corporate ethnic group identity, intelligence sharing and the visual and aural evidence of shared concerns and activities that an institutionalized information dissemination system provides become increasingly important elements of community structure. Documentation and dissemination of information that provide for an awareness of a common history, shared purpose, and familiar experience are the cultural protein by which people from over one hundred fifty different tribal orientations have created and perpetuated a Los Angeles Indian community ethos.

Three of Bramstedt's nine voluntary association classifications (politically oriented, educational, and religious) correspond exactly to three of the eight categories in my institutional outline. The number and scope of organizations consistent with his service classification had proliferated to such an extent in the 1980s that I have divided them into two institutional subtypes: (1) economic and social services, and (2) healing. I have chosen to aggregate Bramstedt's tradition-oriented and athletic associations under the more-inclusive category "social and recreational," where Fiske (1975:28) and I include the so-called Indian bars. Bramstedt's institutional categories "tribal" and "gender-oriented" did not appear to be major organizing principles in the 1980s. However, male and female athletic teams and at least one gender-specific special interest group, Indian Women on the Move, were still active in the mid-1980s.

Youth-oriented groups, the ninth of Bramstedt's organizational categories, were viable in the mid-1980s. By 1986, however, those federal funds still available for Headstart and continuation school programs for ethnic minority youth were being divided among several competing urban ethnic groups due to the demise of the Indian-directed social services facilities that had administered the youth programs in the past. I grouped those youth-oriented activities that still exist under the categories "educational" (Title IV enrichment programs in the public schools), "economic and social services" (the LEAP tutorial program administered by the Southern California Indian Centers, Inc.), and "recreational" (softball and basketball teams, powwow princesses, tiny tots and junior powwow dancers, and drum groups).

Bramstedt focuses his attention on volunteer institutions as the structural units of community among the Indians in Los Angeles and therefore does not include kinship and family relations as a category in his outline of social organization principles in contemporary urban Indian life. I believe, however, that a holistic description of the social structures that provide a sense of community for Indians in Los Angeles must include the institutions of family, kinship, and marriage.

Interlocking directorates and board memberships, regular and wide-ranging use of "for-Indian" services, and personal interest and participation in a year-round calendar of Indian events provide Los Angeles Indians opportunities for full, selective, or peripheral immersion in face-to-face coethnic interactions. In an urban context characterized by residential dispersion and tribal and factional heterogeneity, regular, consistent, predictable, face-to-face interactions in the context of ethnic institutions are the mechanisms by which Indians in Los Angeles approximate traditional community structures and ethos.

NOTE

1. Despite the filing dates of their respective dissertations, Bramstedt's fieldwork (1968–71) was conducted prior to Fiske's (1971–73). The latter overlapped with the initiation of my own association with the Los Angeles Indian community.

6

A Historical Overview
of the Development of Los Angeles
American Indian Institutions

The 1920s to the 1940s

THE EARLIEST recorded attempts to organize modern pan-Indian social or special interest groups in Los Angeles occurred in the 1920s (Bramstedt 1977:81) when five Indian organizations were formed. The Teepee Order was a national fraternal, pan-Indian organization that "attempted to provide its members with a positive image of the Indian past and present" (Hertzberg 1971:225) The War Paint Club, a group of Los Angeles Indians employed by the film industry, organized to achieve fair employment practices for themselves. An Indian women's group, the Wa-Tha-Huck (Brings Light) Club, was affiliated with the General Federation of Women's Clubs. The American Indian Progressive Association was a study group whose members were interested in understanding the problems of all American Indians. The Wigwam Club dedicated itself to the betterment of Indian children. None of these organizations still existed when Hertzberg (1971:223–25) did her fieldwork in the late 1960s.

Four Los Angeles Indian organizations were begun in the 1930s. They included a group that promoted Indian land reclamation and/or compensation (the California Indian Land Rights Association); a restricted sodality of male fancy dancers and the precursor of the modern-day powwow[1] clubs in Los Angeles (the Roach Society); a nondenominational Christian church group (the American Indian Mission, established in 1936), and the Los Angeles Indian Center.

The California Indian Land Rights Association disbanded socially in 1965 and legally in 1970, while the Roach Society disbanded in the mid-1950s. Both the Los Angeles Indian Center and the American Indian Mission (which became the First American Indian Church of Los Angeles in 1959) were viable throughout Bramstedt's (1977) and my fieldwork periods. In fact, the First American Indian Church of Los Angeles is the oldest continuously operating Indian religious institution in the city.

Bramstedt (1977:93) explains that the Los Angeles Indian Center, founded in 1935, was the most widely known Indian institution in Los Angeles and "played an integral role in the formation of service organizations. In fact, if the history of [Los Angeles] Indian groups had any common thread, it was produced by this organization. Besides being the first Indian services group established locally . . . it also existed longer and was more of a focal point of sentiment among [Los Angeles] Indians than any other Indian organization, past or present." Certainly, into the 1980s the center was the nexus of ethnic community life for both the hundred or so people it employed to run its various social services programs and the hundreds of American Indians to whom it provided those services.

The period from 1937 until 1952 was quiescent for the small number of Indians in Los Angeles at that time. Neither Hertzberg nor Bramstedt could locate a single Indian organization that was formed during that fifteen-year interval.

The 1950s and the 1960s: Relocation and Reestablishment

The mid-1950s were characterized by an abrupt, dramatic resurgence and development of Los Angeles Indian organizations. Between 1952 and 1961, twenty new Indian organizations were created. Since proliferation of these ethnic social and service organizations coincided with the national initiation of the Bureau of Indian Affairs's urban relocation program and the establishment of a BIA field office in Los Angeles in 1952, it may be assumed that the accelerated development of Indian social institutions was a reflection and outcome of federal Indian policy.[2]

Five of the twenty Indian organizations initiated in the 1950s were tradition-oriented powwow groups (Bramstedt 1977:85). The American Indian Drum and Feather Club (1954), which specialized from the beginning in Southern-style drumming, the Orange County Group (1957), the Federated Indian Tribes (1958), the Singers and

Dancers of Many Trails (1959), and the American Indian Tribes, Inc. (1959), were all dedicated to the perpetuation of the Plains Indian–inspired powwow. The proliferation of these powwow organizations is evidence of the dramatic influx of Plains Indians into Los Angeles during that period.

Within three years of its creation, the Drum and Feather Club split into two groups, apparently due to regional differences in drumming and chanting style. Northern-style drummers evolved into the Sioux Singing Club and eventually provided the nucleus for the Many Trails Indian Club that formed in 1959. From its inception, the Drum and Feather Club specialized in the Southern drumming style. Some of the Southern-style drummers who lived in Orange County also left the Drum and Feather Club and formed a splinter group of their own, the Orange County Group, which eventually became the nucleus of the Orange County Indian Center (Bramstedt 1977:89). This service organization is still active and effectively provides a variety of social services for the Indian residents of that county.

The Federated Indian Tribes disbanded in the mid-1960s. The Drum and Feather Club and the American Indian Tribes, Inc., rarely show up at weekly powwows. Until June 1989, the Singers and Dancers of Many Trails was responsible for the highly successful second-Saturday-of-the-month powwow held from September through June at the Cecil B. De Mille Junior High School in Long Beach.

The Navajo Club and the Papago Club, two groups that Bramstedt (1977:91) classifies as tribal, were established in the 1950s and remained active for ten to fifteen years before disbanding. Both clubs were dedicated to the perpetuation of tribe-specific traditions, language, and worldview. Bramstedt (1977:92) cites the American Indian Missionary Society as the only new service organization developed during the 1950s. Although he indicates that AIMS was still active in 1971, no mention of it was found in community literature dating from 1978.

The most dramatic proliferation of Los Angeles Indian organizations during the 1950s occurred in the religious sector of the community. Seven new church groups were initiated between 1955 and 1959, but only the Brighter Day Indian Mission survived into the 1980s under its original name. The increase was partially the consequence of fissioning church memberships.

> Most [separatist] movements consisted largely of Oklahoma Indians who tended to have Baptist or Methodist backgrounds. Generally,

these were Creeks and Choctaws, along with some Seminoles and Cherokees. . . . Nondenominational churches were most susceptible to fission; in fact, no congregation of this type escaped it. Each such group contained one or more significant categories of members with common denominational experiences which also tended to be internally uniform in terms of tribal and geographical backgrounds. In times of major discord or disillusionment, these membership segments tended to be the principal units of common sentiment and, if it occurred, fission. (Bramstedt 1977:104–5)

A large proportion of the earliest relocatees to Los Angeles came from the eastern section of Oklahoma that had been designated as Cherokee, Choctaw, Chickasaw, Creek, and Seminole (the so-called Five Civilized Tribes) territories in an earlier federally mandated Indian relocation program. Originally from the southeastern states, these culture groups were removed forcibly from their ancestral lands in the 1830s. Each tribe was given its own territory and allowed to reestablish its cultural and institutional forms in its new Oklahoma homeland (Foreman 1934).

Chief among the social institutions at the time of the Trail of Tears were the Christian church parishes. Proselytization of the Southeastern Indians had begun in the last decade of the eighteenth century, and by the first two decades of the nineteenth century, Baptist, Presbyterian, and Methodist missionaries, especially, had insinuated themselves in significant ways into Cherokee, Creek, and Choctaw villages (Berkhofer 1972; Bowden 1981). By 1830, when the Indian Removal Project was fully initiated, Christian church membership was an established social form among all of the Five Civilized Tribes. In fact, several Anglo missionaries accompanied their Indian congregations on the Trail of Tears. From the onset, the missionaries assisted their Indian brethren in the reestablishment of their churches and church campgrounds in the Oklahoma Indian territories. A legation of Anglo-Christian church elders was the earliest appointed supervisory board of the Oklahoma Indian territories (Keller 1983).

In 1952, when the BIA Relocation Program was introduced in Oklahoma, the Indian Christian church had been an indigenous institution for over one hundred years (Prucha 1979) and had in fact become a traditional social form. A salient principle of social organization, the Indian Christian church survived the urban relocation programs. Establishing sociostructural institutions in Los Angeles that paralleled those back home was a major concern of the early relocatees from eastern Oklahoma. In the mid-1950s and to this day, the Christian Indian churches both in Oklahoma and Los Angeles continue to provide a social context in which the ethnic self can be expressed.

The earliest Indian Christian churches in Los Angeles were nondenominational and pantribal. In the first few years of urban relocation, there were simply not enough denominational and regional cohorts to warrant establishing church groups that perfectly paralleled those back home. Within a decade, however, the number of cotribespeople and codenominational church members from eastern Oklahoma (including, in some cases, people from the same parishes) had increased dramatically. Los Angeles now had critical numbers of people from all of the Five Civilized Tribes. Therefore, members of the city's nondenominational Indian church groups could revert to more traditional sacrosocial forms based on principles of tribal and denominational exclusivity. Bramstedt (1977:105–6) clearly documents this social process.

> The Brighter Day Indian Church [originally and to its end in 1990 a nondenominational institution] experienced fission in its initial year, 1959. It lost about ten to fifteen members, or about one-half of its former Baptists, who were primarily Oklahoma Choctaws, the remainder being Creeks from the same state. . . .
>
> New denominational churches also developed through fission from congregations of the same denomination. In 1961, for example, about 50 Creek and Seminole Baptists separated from the Creek-Seminole Hugo (Baptist) Mission. . . . Most of these persons, comprising about one-half of the active mission membership, came from the Sand Creek Baptist Church in Wetumka, Oklahoma. After leaving the Hugo Mission, they organized the Sand Creek Indian Mission.

Establishing social forms in the urban context that parallel familiar, viable, and significant social forms in the place of origin was a major strategy by which the relocating Indians were able to effect a sense of cultural continuity in an unfamiliar and at times forbidding social context. The fissioning of pantribal church organizations into smaller, more exclusive, more traditional alignments allowed for the proliferation of rank-enhancing community roles familiar from childhood. To this day, twelve small church groups, identified by their Christian denomination and their tribal concentrations, perpetuate earlier, culturally conservative social forms for their Los Angeles Indian members.

Proliferation of Indian organizations continued during the 1960s. Eighteen new groups formed between 1962 and 1966, including two more powwow clubs, Shooting Star Trails and the Little Big Horn

Plains Indian Club (Bramstedt 1977:85). The former was short lived; the latter, headed throughout the 1970s by Iron Eyes Cody, the redoubtable Indian film star, hosted the first-Saturday-of-the-month powwow at the Eagle Rock Recreation Center. Two tribal organizations, the Cheyenne-Arapaho Nation of California and the Kickapoo Tribe of California, were established in 1966 (Bramstedt 1977:90). Although still active in 1971, neither organization is mentioned in community publications after 1978. Two service organizations formed in the mid-1960s, the Indian Welcome Center and the Shooting Star Foundation (Bramstedt 1977:92), are also no longer active.

The major organizational thrust during this period appears to have been the formation of a variety of athletic associations, including at least six all-male, all-female, and youth basketball, softball, and bowling teams (Bramstedt 1977:96). The American Indian Athletic Association and the American Indian Bowling Association continued to provide all-Indian recreational arenas into the 1980s.

Three Indian churches, the First Southern Baptist Indian Mission, the Grace Southern Baptist Church, and the American Indian Full Gospel Mission, originated in 1964 and 1965 (Bramstedt 1977:103). The most viable of the three, the First Southern Baptist Indian Mission, is an established, autonomous church that still holds services at its Clara Street church grounds in Bell Gardens. Organized by Choctaws and Creeks, its eighty-member congregation is now pantribal and is determined to continue past the return of its originators to Oklahoma. The church tirelessly perpetuates weekly cycles of Wednesday night prayer meetings, Thursday night visitations, and all-day Sunday school, prayer meeting, potluck lunches, and evening vespers. These weekly events are enhanced by yearly cycles of Fifth Sunday sings, revival meetings, special church holiday programs, and monthly potluck feasts.

The Late 1960s and Early 1970s: Lyndon Johnson's Great Society and the Proliferation of Urban Indian Social Services Programs

The period 1967–71 was one of greatest growth among the American Indian population as well as in the number of newly organized Los Angeles Indian organizations. During this five-year interval, thirty-eight new Indian organizations surfaced in Los Angeles. Bramstedt (1977) notes that seven tribal organizations were initiated, only one of which, the San Fernando Mission Indians, is still active. Spearheaded by Rudy Ortega, the group organized in 1971. By

1975, when I first met Mr. Ortega, the group had already lobbied for and won reparations for confiscated lands in the San Fernando Valley during California's territorial period.

During the late 1960s, Los Angeles Indian-oriented and -operated human services organizations proliferated, courtesy of President Johnson's Great Society. Funds were made available, in amounts never before experienced in ethnic minority communities, for the establishment of self-help, nonprofit, social services programs. Newly mandated Comprehensive Employment and Training Assistance (CETA) funds provided paid employment during short-term training periods. Several of the Indian services agencies, the Tribal American Consulting Corporation, the Indian Centers, Inc. (ICI), and the American Indian Free Clinic, among others, applied for and received generous CETA grants during this period. These funds provided jobs for hundreds of American Indians within an evolving ethnic community social services network.

In unprecedented numbers, emerging urban Indian leaders with ten to fifteen years of urban life experience to their credit took advantage of these windfall appropriations. From 1967 to 1971, at least ten new social services organizations were established in Los Angeles (Bramstedt 1977:92). Chief among them were three organizations formed to provide social services not offered by the downtown branch of the ICI.

The United Indian Development Association (UIDA),[3] established in 1969, remains true to its mandate "to help qualified Indians start private businesses and, thereby, develop a significant body of Indian businessmen" (Bramstedt 1977:95). The American Indian Free Clinic was established in 1970 to provide a comprehensive health program for low-income Indian families. A second clinic, the Indian Free Clinic, Inc., opened in Huntington Park a year later, after a struggle for administrative control at the American Indian Free Clinic ended in a bitterly contested board of directors election. As Fiske (1975:29) observes, fissioning along factional, regional, and kinship lines, so characteristic of the early proliferation of powwow and church groups, appears to have triggered this sociostructural realignment as well: "The presence of two Indian free clinics is directly linked with factionalism. It is unusual to have any free clinics for an ethnic minority, let alone two of them! The original free clinic was directed, housed, and controlled by a prominent Indian reverend in his Southern Baptist Church. The group of dissenters who broke off and established their own clinic with separate funding were considered Pow Wow people."

The proliferation of social services institutions in the Los Angeles Indian community in the 1970s was a direct consequence of political policy developed at the federal, state, and local levels. Importantly, a number of Indians in Los Angeles had the requisite political, grant-writing, and administrative skills to (1) recognize the developmental possibilities for their ethnic community in the new federally mandated human services programs, (2) fashion requests for funding in such a way as to secure funds, and (3) administer funded programs effectively.

Several youth-oriented organizations also surfaced during this time. All were short lived, none lasting more than three years. This suggests a possible countervailing trend to the otherwise uninhibited vitality of urban Indian institutionalization in the late 1960s. By 1967 some Indian families had been in Los Angeles for ten years or more. Many had children, some in their teens, who had been born and raised there. Most of these children knew their ethnic culture only through occasional or sporadic involvements in urban Indian activities, visits to relatives on the reservation during the summer, or by word of mouth from family and friends. Culturally, these children more fully reflected the folkways and worldviews of their urban, non-Indian age peers. In most cases, ethnic continuity was not a burning issue for these second-generation urban Indians. The inability to sustain the five youth groups initiated during this period of institutional fluorescence therefore reflected a desire on the part of Indian parents to do something about ensuring cultural continuity and their children's relative lack of interest in doing so.

The period 1967–71 marked the beginning of a new type of Los Angeles Indian social organization that could be linked to national policy trends of the time. Great Society social welfare programs included generous educational grants to deserving members of ethnic minorities. The Bureau of Indian Affairs was charged with providing scholarships and various forms of financial assistance to Indians wishing to attend college. Because of these policies, hundreds of young adult Indians were, for the first time, afforded access to universities and professional schools. From 1968 to 1971, eight Indian student organizations were established on five different local college and university campuses (Bramstedt 1977:100).

Bramstedt was unable to document the formation of a single new church after 1965. However, since 1973 at least four major Los Angeles Indian religious organizations have evolved, ranging from nativistic movements to a fully institutionalized Methodist Indian church. The Four Directions Foundation is a spiritual and healing

society that is non-Christian and based on Sioux ritual. The syncretic but largely Sioux-influenced American Indian Unity Church
holds well-attended weekly meetings in Garden Grove. Both of
these organizations have coalesced around individual and charismatic middle-aged Sioux men. The membership of the homegrown,
part social, part educational, nondenominational Bible Study Group
mainly included newly arrived Navajos. In 1975, the First United
Methodist and Native American Church was established in Huntington Park.

Although the Four Directions Foundation and the Bible Study
Group welcomed all comers, their tribal orientations were clear.
The former still holds an occasional spiritual training session, while
the latter is essentially moribund. The highly successful American
Indian Unity Church and the First Native American and United
Methodist Church are pantribal, a fact that may have ensured their
continuity.

Fiske's (1975) study of Navajo cognition and behavior in Los Angeles bridges the period between Bramstedt's and my fieldwork periods. Three of the institutional categories she developed in her survey of volunteer Indian associations active between 1971 and 1973
parallel Bramstedt's (athletic, tribal, and service). Although her
catalog of organizations is less exhaustive than Bramstedt's, she
mentions three groups that he does not: the Tribal American Preschool, the Indian Lodge (an all-male alcoholism inpatient treatment program), and the White Buffalo Workshop (a theatrical training group). All three service organizations, newly initiated during
Fiske's fieldwork period, had been only in embryonic stages of development when Bramstedt finished his fieldwork. Fiske subsumes
organizations that Bramstedt and I view as political, youth-oriented,
educational, and health-related into the more inclusive category
"service organization."

Fiske expands Bramstedt's category "tradition-oriented" by including social organizations with the powwow groups. She also
makes the important point that bars in the central city area frequented with regularity by Indians are "never listed on organizational rosters, but [are] very important informal gathering places"
and should be included as social and recreational Indian institutions
(Fiske 1975:25). My Indian drinking pattern studies confirm Fiske's
earlier observation. At the time, at least six bars in downtown and
south-central Los Angeles were so consistently frequented by Indians that they were known as Indian bars (Weibel 1981:221).

In 1973, when I began my association with the Los Angeles Indian community, its social services sector was in its heyday. The Indian Center, initially located only in the central city area, had recently become incorporated. Additionally, the center's administrators had become so skillful at writing grant proposals that funds had been secured for the development of satellite centers in Huntington Park and Culver City. These centers were placed in locations known to have large concentrations of Indian families who had moved from the downtown areas in which they were initially placed by the BIA's Los Angeles–based relocation field officers.

By 1975 the grants portfolio of the Indian Centers, Inc., included approximately $1.5 million in federal, state, county, and private funds earmarked for the provision of social services to Indians in Los Angeles. The centers employed scores of mostly Indian services providers, administrators, and support staff; their purpose was to offer services ranging from emergency food vouchers, clothing, and housing to continuation schools, job training, legal assistance, and foster child care. They also provided linkages between the city's Department of Health and Human Services and needy Indian individuals. In addition, the ICI published the highly popular community newspaper *Talking Leaf*. This extremely important communications vehicle provided members of the far-flung Indian community with a sense of "being on top of things in the Indian world." At the height of its circulation, approximately 3,000 copies of *Talking Leaf* were distributed monthly.

When I first became aware of their existence, both the American Indian Free Clinic and the Indian Free Clinic, Inc., were fully established and optimistically expanding their health services. In the spring of 1973, the two clinics provided testing and referral services; nutrition vouchers for women, infants, and children; prenatal and well-baby instruction; dental services; and birth control and gynecological counseling. For nearly two years, in 1973 and 1974, I was one of several volunteer outreach workers at the Huntington Park clinic, a role well suited for an anthropology student interested in meeting Indian individuals in a dispersed community. Although the Indian Lodge was founded to treat male alcoholism, within three years it had responded to the need for substance abuse intervention programs for Indian women by establishing a separate Women's Lodge. By 1976 the American Indian Free Clinic had initiated the Main Artery, a drug and alcohol inpatient treatment center and halfway house on its Compton campus.

Sponsorship of the weekly powwows from September through June were the ongoing responsibility of four powwow organizations.

However, dozens of university student groups and political groups sponsored special powwows to raise funds for school programs, political causes, and the continuation of endangered free clinic programs; to honor an elder or a deceased community leader; or simply to have fun. Major, well-attended Indian and western arts and crafts shows were held with regularity in Santa Monica, Pasadena, and Commerce.

A dozen or more Indian churches in Los Angeles were filled on most Sunday mornings. The Indian Revival Center in Bell Gardens, for example, boasted a membership of more than two hundred fifty (Gardner 1969). Its mostly Pima, Papago, and Navajo members had erected not only a handsome church edifice and a two-story stucco classroom annex but also had purchased a fine organ and gowns for the members of their thirty-voice choir.

The 1970s was an exciting time to be a member of the Los Angeles Indian community. A heady sense of growth, vitality, and burgeoning self-determination prevailed. Ethnic group participation held the potential for community and self-improvement. Within the Indian community's social services institutional network, monies for heretofore only dreamed-of human services projects were now readily available. An easily demonstrated need, the cooperation of a skillful grantsperson, and a handful of Indian people willing to work together as an institutional governing board were sufficient to establish any number of Indian-directed social services facilities in Los Angeles.

A growing cohort of Indian administrative elites were fashioning ethnically inflected status hierarchies and personal careers for themselves through creative program development and self-promotion. Institutional expansion seemed limitless. Newly established sets of economic and service institutions paralleled those in the dominant society as well as those reservation community services lost with the move to an urban area (Bramstedt 1977:138). These institutions provided both employment and access to needed services and a novel set of arenas of honor.[4]

The 1970s was also an ideal historical period to be doing fieldwork in the Indian community, especially as I was interested in issues of social change and adaptation. The unrivaled fluorescence of special interest groups and the attempts of their organizers to gain social validity and a constituency within the Los Angeles Indian population provided unique opportunities to observe the dynamics of social construction, the processes by which community is created and sustained.

NOTES

1. The term "powwow" is a variant of the Algonquian word *pawaw*. It was originally used in reference to a healer and his/her healing ceremonies attended by large numbers of a communal group. Later, the meaning of the term was expanded to include any type of council or intertribal conclave (Kurath 1966). The contemporary powwow is thought to have its origins in the social dances held each summer during the Plains Indians tribal convocations and just before the great communal buffalo hunts (Young 1981). See chapter 8 for a detailed description of an urban powwow.

2. Urban Indian institutionalization in the 1950s was not restricted to the Los Angeles Indian population but was duplicated in dozens of urban-industrial centers throughout the United States (Ablon 1964; Garbarino 1971; Waddell and Watson 1971).

3. In 1988 the UIDA officially adopted the name National Center for Indian Enterprise to reflect its national scope.

4. Myerhoff (1980a) develops the concept "arenas of honor" in her excellent ethnography of a Venice, California, senior citizens center. Arenas of honor are sites or stages on which individuals publicly play out certain status-enhancing roles. They are places in which exemplary performances are witnessed and personal honor is awarded by a significant, validating group.

7

Los Angeles Indian Community
Institutions in the 1980s

CLASSIFICATORY SYSTEMS are, by nature, both inclusive and exclusive. At best, the criteria by which inclusion in a particular
category is determined are valid representations of indigenous
classificatory systems; at worst, they are reflections of observer bias.
I have organized the 135 Los Angeles Indian special interest groups
and corporate institutions active between 1978 and 1989 into eight
generic classifications. Of course, some of these groups and institutions do not fit neatly into only one category. The Indian Centers,
Inc., for example, was not only a social services delivery facility but
also an important Los Angeles Indian economic and political arena.
Assignment of the ICI to one category was ultimately an arbitrary
decision based on my determination of the major and formally
stated goals of the institution. The following classification system
illustrates the central focus of the identified Indian organizations
but not necessarily the scope of their activities. Where they exist, an
institution's multiple dimensions are identified in the narrative.

I have not attempted to describe fully all 135 groups nor to
chronicle their inception or incorporation into Los Angeles Indian
community life. Rather, the most influential, long-lived, or landmark institutions are described, along with those organizations that
are indicative of continuing or novel institutional trends or foci of
the Los Angeles Indian community.[1]

Political Institutions

Included in this category are politically active, largely volunteer
special interest groups, militant protest organizations, political ap-

pointees, career bureaucrats who now work within the mainstream governmental infrastructures for Indian purposes, and Indian program administrative elites. The latter two are included since people who occupy these positions usually do so because of their political acuity and because of their perceived ability to influence, shape, and carry out public policy. They fulfill role expectations of the institution, provide political leadership for their ethnic community, and serve as role models for their ethnic peers.

American Indians historically have been, and continue to be, politically heterogeneous. Litigation on behalf of Indians who perceive that their ancestors were wronged and their children disfranchised through careless, biased, and, frequently, rigged treaty negotiations is often based on the contention that those individuals who represented the affected indigenous groups at treaty meetings did not, in fact, speak for the whole community. These so-called tribal leaders, often selected by federal Indian agents, were given the authority to speak and sign for their people, not by their tribal brethren, but by federal officials eager to construct a document of title no matter how spurious the authority of the tribal signatory (Taylor 1986:53). Some American Indian ethnohistorians argue that these government representatives frequently were naive rather than duplicitous. Based on ethnocentric understandings of political conventions such as representational democracy, foreign diplomacy, and nation-states, treaty negotiators wrongly assumed analogous political processes and social structures existed among their Indian adversaries (Oswalt 1988:40). Size, perspective, and relationship to other Indian political constituencies and the Indian community as a whole are, therefore, crucial factors in determining the extent of a particular group's political influence and the extent to which it can effectively function as a liaison between Indian and non-Indian constituencies.

The issue of representation, that is, who speaks for what faction, let alone for the entire Indian community, is further complicated by the overwhelming number of culturally distinct tribal groups and political orientations in urban centers. Twentieth-century Indian spokespeople generally maintain that their espoused positions are their own and not assertions of group consensus. The multiple political factions within any concentration of American Indians usually eludes members of the dominant ethnic group. Habituated to thinking about American Indians by stereotype, the host society and, in particular, its mass media representatives continue to deal with Indians as a cohesive ethnic entity. This general lack of sensitivity to Indian political heterogeneity frustrates contemporary American Indian political figures.

On April 18, 1986, an outspoken, longtime member of a militant minority within the Los Angeles Indian community made one of his regular, for-the-media public appearances. On this occasion, his forum was the Los Angeles Press Club. Media people hoping for good copy from a clutch of pro-Khadafy activists filled the room into which Lonetalker made his entrance. A resplendent archetype in his medicine wheel, bead- and feather-bedecked braids, Lonetalker, the spiritual leader of the Four Directions Foundation, a cultural survival school, strode to the microphone. In the familiar hyperbole of the politically aroused, he intoned one of his more flagrant condemnations of the federal administration. Announcing his support of Khadafy's dream to give "liberty and freedom to his country" and branding President Reagan a "terrorist," the aging, latter-day word warrior urged Anglos and Indians alike to "wake up" to the real villainy among us. His were ringing words, a firebrand's call for his spiritual brethren to take up the good fight.[2]

Executive directors of and spokespeople for several American Indian special interest groups in Los Angeles promptly called for a second press conference at the Los Angeles Press Club. They meant to put Lonetalker's pro-Khadafy statements into perspective, given that the "overwhelming majority of Native Americans deplore the use of terrorism" (Rose and Howell 1986:4). Within two weeks of the Lonetalker press conference, several equally vocal and well-prepared members of the Indian community—organization representatives and individuals wishing solely to voice personal reactions to Lonetalker's extremism—situated themselves about the Press Club at the appointed time and, one by one, made their positions known to an accommodating crush of newspaper and television reporters. Media America was about to receive a lesson in American Indian representational democracy.

The spokesperson for the Big Mountain Support Group, a recently formed Los Angeles chapter of a national advocacy organization, provided the cultural context. The youthful activist blamed media ignorance of the Indian community for confusion over who actually speaks for Indians in Los Angeles. He explained that the Indian community is made up of "the churches, the powwow clubs, the Indian Centers, the services. Because you don't know our community, you accept one small group. Look at the community here. There are 80,000 Indians in Los Angeles, yet you focus on a small lunatic fringe" (Rose and Howell 1986:4). Lonetalker, it seemed, was a spokesman bereft of a critical community constituency. In the tradition of such diehard cultural conservatives as Geronimo, Sitting Bull, and Crazy Horse, Lonetalker deplores and rejects the compromise and constriction imposed by federal rule. Now, as then, the lonely ideological rebel enjoys spiritual communion with the few.

Lonetalker's political marginality is not unique, for there truly is no major political faction or unified Los Angeles Indian voice. Indeed, if the historical trends of the last three hundred years are predictive, there never will be an Indian consensus on anything other than the most global, focused, or time-limited political issues.

The Los Angeles City-County Native American Indian Commission (LACCNAIC) is the closest approximation of a forum in which Los Angeles Indian community consensus can be established. Mandated and funded by the county of Los Angeles in 1976, the commission continues to be the major forum for Indian political issues, grievances, and, when possible, collective opinion. (The early history and current contributions of this organization are discussed in greater detail in chapters 10 and 13, and in the introduction to section VI.) The commission is the community's moral authority and the mechanism by which a representative consensus is obtained, even though the LACCNAIC has no formal policing and limited executive powers. Its strength lies in the validating and critical authority that both the governmental agency under which it is subsumed and the Indian community, on the whole, allow it to assume and to which these constituencies agree to adhere. The commission ensures a continuing Indian voice in policy and program delivery development in the wake of the massive federal cutbacks in human services funding in the 1980s.

The Politics of Infiltration: An Indian Voice in Municipal, Regional, and State Governments

The LACCNAIC, formally instituted within the county infrastructure, is nonetheless viewed by most core ethnics in the Los Angeles Indian community as their forum. Establishing ethnic minority advocacy institutions within the framework of county government is a survival strategy that Indians in Los Angeles have used to good advantage. The association of the American Indian Council on Aging with the Los Angeles County Area Agency on Aging, the American Indian liaison officers within the mayor's and governor's offices, the Indian Alcoholism Commission of California, the Commission of American Indian Education, the American Indian Employee's Association, and LACCNAIC are all examples of successful attempts to create and preserve a forum for Indian interests within municipal, regional, and state infrastructures and at policy-making levels of influence.

Los Angeles City and County Bureaucrats Who Are Indian

Placement of qualified or qualifiable American Indians in mid-level city and county government administrative and human services posts is another infiltration strategy that the Los Angeles Indian community has used effectively. Indians now hold positions on the Los Angeles County Affirmative Action Board, the Department of Adoptions, the Department of Social Services, the Los Angeles County Human Rights Commission, the city's Department of Health Services, and the county's Department of Mental Health.

Price (1975) was among the first to predict this assimilative eventuality for urban Indian political institutions. While conceding a trend, Fiske (1979) argues that certain types of urban "Indian only" political and administrative institutions would persist. In part this continues to be true, but the shift to block grant funding initiated by the Reagan administration in the early 1980s has accelerated the infiltration of government infrastructures by effective American Indian administrative elites.

Ad Hoc Special Interest Groups

Other politically oriented Indian social arenas include the numerous special interest and lobby groups that coalesce around topical issues. Relatively more unstable than the organizations mentioned above, these vocal, volatile groups tend to surface and recede with the immediacy of a focal cause. From 1978 until 1986, at least thirty groups sought community recognition and constituencies. Their titles and proclaimed goals provide an index of urban Indian concerns in the wake of national social services program funding retrenchment in the 1980s.

The Los Angeles American Indian Council on Aging, for example, represents the health, housing, transportation, and social concerns of a growing number of Indians in the area who are approaching or are in retirement. The California Indian Legal Services evolved as a response to the preponderance of alcohol-related crime convictions and family and property contests in which the Indians involved were incapable of paying for their choice of legal representation.

Groups such as the Los Angeles American Indian Concerned Citizens Council, the American Indian Community Coalition, the Tri-

Valley Council of North Hollywood, and the Alliance of Native Americans are loose collections of people interested in addressing a broad range of urban Indian issues through discussion, consensus development, and initiation of volunteer, goal-oriented events. Their activities have ranged from fund-raising powwows for agreed-on causes (the Nighthorse Campbell political campaign and the Leonard Peltier Defense Fund)[3] to organizing an annual elders' recognition luncheon. Other special interest groups have organized around such diverse issues as the creation of an Indian culture center (the Native American Culture Center in the Santa Monica mountains) and the 1984 presidential campaign (Indians for Reagan-Bush).

Indian Women on the Move and the Los Angeles American Indian Women's Coalition are what Bramstedt (1977) would label "gender-exclusive groups." Their original purpose was to work for improvement in the quality of life for American Indian women in general, but their agendas are now much broader in scope. They have been instrumental in initiating an impressive list of goal-oriented projects. They also recognize their particular potential for political accomplishment, reasoning that if things are going to get done, as usual the women must "get the ball rolling."

Militant Activist Groups

Members of most of the special interest groups mentioned so far are people with moderate to slightly left-of-center political views. Wishing to address a particular social issue affecting Indians in Los Angeles, they call together like-minded urban Indians and mount a cooperative effort. They may provide letters of recommendation, or deliver position statements at public hearings, or mount action programs or fund-raising efforts for the initiation of such programs.

Within the Los Angeles Indian community are a small number of well left-of-center political activists. These firebrands continuously amend their grievances in response to what they view are the latest in a continuing series of violations of indigenous peoples' human rights at local, national, and international levels. Their political associations, present in Los Angeles since the mid-1960s, find little focus for their revolutionary activities in the cities. Rather, the city is the stage on which Third World issues, as experienced in American Indian reservation community life, are dramatized and find a large, responsive audience. More often than not, the mass media communications industry and philanthropic, non-Indian sympathizers are located in urban centers, and the cities therefore serve as exploitable resources rather than the sources of political issues for most Indian militant movements.

Although modest in number, the militants have been extremely successful in making their grievances against the American political system known to the general public. Declaring themselves citizens of Indian sovereignties, they claim exemption from the edicts of what they view as an oppressive and foreign enemy. Their numerous sit-ins, drum-ins, break-ins, camp-ins, and confrontations with the FBI, the National Guard, and the state militia have resulted in widespread media coverage for the last twenty years. The American Indian Movement (AIM) and the Big Mountain and Yellowthunder Camp support groups have gained considerable backing, often from non-Indians, for such nonurban issues as halting the Hopi-Navajo Relocation Project, reclamation of the Black Hills of South Dakota by the Lakota Sioux, and a retrial for Leonard Peltier, who currently stands convicted of the 1973 murders of two FBI agents in South Dakota.

Even the most vocal Los Angeles Indian political lobbyists are committed to nonviolence, to working within the current political system for Indian rights, or to creating parallel, self-determining Indian political infrastructures. As much as the U.S. Department of the Interior and the Bureau of Indian Affairs are government structures Indians "love to hate," only a handful of Indian revolutionaries throughout the nation would ever commit themselves publicly to the demise of those institutions. The BIA and the Department of the Interior are, after all, the strongest structural links Indians have been able to maintain and use to communicate their needs to federal funding sources.

Members of the groups included in this institutional subcategory may take issue with the rubric I have chosen to depict their distinctive character and political stance. The term "militant activist," however, is what most Los Angeles Indians I have interviewed over the years use to categorize the political stance of such groups as AIM and the Big Mountain, Wounded Knee, and Yellowthunder Camp support groups.

The political conservatism of Indians who migrated to the cities after World War II is understandable, given that they are economic, not political, emigrés. Their urban migration represents career choices millions of other non-Indian Americans have made since the Great Depression and the Dust Bowl catastrophes of the 1930s began to empty the Midwest of its family farmers. The promise of steady employment, a chance for their children to receive a mainstream education, and the opportunity to improve their standard of living—quality-of-life issues that defy ethnic boundaries—pulled Indians by the thousands to urban-industrial centers, where they hoped to improve their lives by accessing, not dismantling, the capitalist system.

AIM's early militancy and anti-American stance found only a small, episodic audience of supporters within the Los Angeles Indian community. In 1973 Los Angeles Indians were generally sympathetic to the plight of the cadre of Indians who, protesting continuing injustices of the federal government toward Indians, had taken over a church in Wounded Knee, South Dakota, and were then besieged by federal agents and police forces. Food, clothes, supplies, cash, personnel, and, rumor had it, arms also flowed with regularity from Los Angeles to Pine Ridge in 1973 from all over the United States, Canada, and Europe in support of the demonstrators. From interviews conducted at the time, I formed the opinion that most Indians in Los Angeles were glad to make donations to their beleaguered "bros" on the reservation, "just as long as they [didn't] try any of that strong-arm stuff in Bell Gardens," as one interviewee put it. However, subsequent killings, arrests, and imprisonment of AIM leaders, along with rumors of internecine dissension, indiscretions, disaffections, and flirtation with Third World revolutionary forces, have weakened the movement's allure to the general Indian public.

In the 1980s, Indian militancy seemed to be focused on more immediate infractions of Indian rights. Big Mountain Support Group has garnered widespread support in Los Angeles for the plight of the Navajos who were being forced off lands officially ceded to the Hopis. Anyone who has thought at all about the health effects of exposure to radioactive uranium ore can identify with the pleas of Navajos in the Four Corners area that their water be protected from unchecked uranium mine drainage. Health and human rights violations are issues with which most Indians, whether living in cities or on reservations, can empathize and take on as their own.

American Indian political militants are viewed as marginals by most Los Angeles Indians, yet they serve Indian and non-Indian audiences by dramatizing and underscoring worst-case ethnic discrimination scenarios. Their hyperbole, in fact, provides a focus for programmatic response. For example, the outcry in the late 1970s against forced sterilizations in the Indian Health Services hospitals and exposés dealing with preventable diabetes-related amputations led to major reforms in health care delivery. These militant groups thus help define current and future political climates for their less vocal, more moderate urban sympathizers. Their concern with national, not necessarily local or urban, Indian issues also underscores the urban Indians' continuing ties and identification with their homelands and the national, pantribal Indian community.

Economic and Social Services Institutions

Social Services Delivery Programs

Since Bramstedt (1977) concluded his observations of Los Angeles Indian organizations in 1971, major shifts in federal, state, county, municipal, and private funding policies have significantly influenced the development and contraction of Indian-oriented and Indian-operated social services facilities. I have organized such service structures, most of which evolved in the 1970s, into two categories: economic and social services, and healing institutions. The former includes the various branches of the Indian Centers, Inc., and their employment and training capacities, the Urban Indian Development Association, and the entertainment industry.

Critical to establishing a sense of a core ethnic community among Los Angeles Indians was the existence of the social services–oriented Indian Centers, Inc. (ICI), initiated in 1935, and its various satellite operations throughout the Los Angeles Basin. (See section VI for a discussion of the organization's contribution to community life in Los Angeles.) In the early 1980s, the ICI's central city headquarters on Washington Boulevard boasted a complex of three buildings that housed the social services offices, emergency clothing and food supply storage rooms, administrative suites, classrooms, editorial offices for the community newspaper, a graphic arts studio, and a print shop. By the mid-1980s, the ICI, perceived by its constituency and by government funding agencies as a stable, well-established, viable social services facility with a lengthy track record of administrative and executive integrity, maintained a grants portfolio that was a mix of nearly two million dollars in city, county, state, national, and privately funded social services contracts. Central High School, its continuation tutorial program, prepared high school dropouts for Graduate Equivalency Diploma exams. The Job Training and Employment Partnership Program was a re-employment conduit for hundreds of Indians in need of training in currently marketable skills. *Talking Leaf*, published monthly, provided welcome community news to an eager readership.

The highly regarded Tribal American Consulting Corporation

(TACC), with its several Indian-run preschools and day care centers, did not fare as well. Established in 1971, TACC served hundreds of Indian preschoolers for several years through its carefully programmed, experimental teaching formats (Guilmet 1976; Long, Canyon, and Churchman 1973). By 1980, however, TACC had fallen in on itself due to the sheer weight of its top-heavy, isolated, and unmonitored executive elite.

Unlike other Indian-administered service organizations that were unable to sustain themselves, the United Indian Development Association (UIDA) has continued its award-winning record of accomplishment and service to the community. UIDA (renamed the National Center for Indian Enterprise in 1988) maintains its integrity by limiting its size and growth and studiously avoiding unplanned, or fortuitous, expansion. It refused to create and staff additional positions not justified by the workload simply for the sake of "making work for another Indian" or because CETA funds were available for the asking. Moreover, UIDA always has sustained and limited itself to the goals of its original charter. In that way, expertise gained through experience in a bounded set of services is ensured to the potential client. Expertise has also been guaranteed through careful selection of staff, a third possible factor in the continuing viability of this enterprise.

Indians and the Entertainment Industry

Movie moguls at the turn of the century decided to take advantage of southern California's relatively cloudless, dry, brilliantly sunny climate and relocated their film production companies to the West Coast. Since that time, there has been a steady demand in Hollywood for "real Indian" extras and the occasional line-speaking Indian actor. Bramstedt (1977:418) notes that the first formal incorporation of American Indians involved in the entertainment industry occurred as late as 1967. At that time, Jay Silverheels (Tonto of the Lone Ranger films and television series), who was probably the most recognized, steadily employed Indian in Hollywood, established the Indian Actors Workshop to circumvent what most Indians who dreamed of film stardom saw as prejudicial Hollywood hiring practices. Silverheels meant to train aspiring Indian actors in the theater arts. In that way, they would be not only ethnically correct for certain roles but also have the requisite skills to be competitive in their chosen field.

The Indian Actors Workshop quickly became an outlet for Indian actors' and stuntmen's views. It was the voice for Indians dis gruntled and discouraged by the casting of Burt Lancaster as Jim Thorpe, the great American Indian athlete, by Jeff Chandler as Cochise, the diehard Apache warrior, and by Raquel Welch as a Crow captive and heroine. Indian actors let it be known that they wished equal consideration with the legions of hook-nosed, dark-skinned, low-voiced, Italian-American, Mexican-American, and Armenian-American actors who consistently were hired for the major film and television roles that called for an Indian character to speak on camera.

Hollywood's perception of the low "bankability" of Indian actors has not changed much since the producers of the Lone Ranger series took a chance on Silverheels back in the 1950s. At the time, "taking a chance" meant placing Silverheels, a Shakespearean-trained Iroquois, in a major film role in which his principal and weekly responsibility was to monosyllabically save the Lone Ranger's life and reputation. Since then only a few Indian actors have been given important supporting roles in major films. Most notably, Will Sampson gave a memorable performance as Chief in the Academy Award–winning film *One Flew Over the Cuckoo's Nest.* Iron Eyes Cody is known internationally as the Indian reduced to tears at the sight of a smog- and freeway-strangled Los Angeles. But even today, most Indians who work in films are cast in wordless crowd, chase, or battle scenes for visual authenticity, while non-Indians made up to look like Indians continue to verbalize and act out certain cherished Indian film stereotypes.

Members of the Los Angeles Indian community recognize a few entertainers of partial Indian ancestry who have been able to carve out careers for themselves exclusive of their identity as Indians (e.g., Jonathan Winters, Burt Reynolds, and Buffy Saint Marie). These stars have used their influence to ensure that other Indians get work as actors, stuntmen and women, musicians, writers, and technical advisors. They also have been instrumental in ensuring that the historical and cultural contexts of scripts about Indians are researched so as to provide ethnographic validity to the films. Community members point with pride at these role models and venerate them at honoring dinners and in notices of their activities in *Talking Leaf.* By and large, however, Indian actors are still not viewed as particularly bankable "properties" by the major film production companies.

More recently, organizations such as the American Indian Registry for the Performing Arts and the National American Indian Press and Broadcasting Council have been formed to promote the hiring of

Indians to do more than fall off horses or be cardboard figures against a Western horizon. Smaller independent and documentary film production companies have been more willing to mount projects about and enacted by Indians. For example, *Broken Rainbow*, a film documenting the dangers of uranium pollution in the Four Corners area of the Navajo Reservation, won the Academy Award for best documentary film in 1986.

One of the more positive developments in the last decade, and consistent with the growing impetus for self-determination, is the development of several independent, nationally endowed, all-Indian theatrical troupes. Eagle Spirit Productions and the Two Snakes Dance Ensemble are examples of Indian performance groups that determine what materials they perform and what images of the American Indian experience they will publicly present. Combining traditional Indian themes, narrative styles, and music and dance forms with contemporary and non-Indian theatrical idioms, these groups of young Indian aspirants have created a new brand of performing arts. Their delighted audiences span both cultures.

Healing Institutions
Western Medical Model Health Services

The omnibus medical care provided on reservations by the federally funded Indian Health Services was (and still is) sorely missed by urban Indians. Thus, with the initiation of President Johnson's Great Society social welfare programs, the Los Angeles Indian leadership quickly established Indian free clinics as a community service priority. The American Indian Free Clinic (1971), its satellite operations, the rival and spin-off Indian Free Clinic, Inc., in Huntington Park (1972), and the several support groups and treatment centers for Indian alcohol and drug abusers provide another constellation of social arenas in which Indians in Los Angeles interact on a regular basis and enact a variety of community-defined executive statuses and roles.

The American Indian Free Clinic in Compton provides primary diagnostic testing and referral services, nutrition programs, prenatal and well-baby education programs, and transportation services. For a few years, it also provided a hot lunch program for the elderly. In 1983 a second facility was opened just west of downtown Los Angeles on Pizarro Street. Until its funding unexpectedly ended in 1987, the Los Angeles Indian Health Center provided medical, nutritional, counseling, and referral services for the thousands of Indians living in the central city area who could not negotiate the thirty-mile round-trip to the Compton clinic.

During the 1970s, a heyday for the federally supported delivery of health and human services, frontline facilities were able to survive a certain amount of internecine conflict. Program monitoring was low key, and batteries of evaluation forms could be completed in ways that provided an optimal performance profile. Quarterly reports often masked true performance, quality, and quantity of service. Only a major political rupture, a signed petition, blatant financial indiscretion, or the demand for a third-party audit would have prompted a more thorough, on-site program evaluation. Indians had a track record of two hundred years of negotiations with federal authorities. They established contacts and successfully implemented those lobbying tactics that worked in Washington, D.C. They knew the federal territory.

The block grant system of the 1980s forced urban Indian health and human services facilities to compete for funds in another, less familiar political arena. State, county, and municipal funding agencies were not necessarily as sympathetic to Indian petitions for assistance as were the federal funding agencies that formerly had heard the Indians' pleas for help. American Indians in Los Angeles now competed with the large and vocal black, Hispanic, and Asian communities for social services funds. The local public funding agencies, in an effort to maintain control of the limited monies available and the service delivery operations, opted for greater participation in and scrutiny of the programs with which they contracted to provide services. Important in the rationalization of the new funding system was the development of an allocation-of-service-funds formula, a key element of which was the size of a particular service facility's client population. This factor in itself greatly reduced the small Los Angeles Indian population's chances for major funding consideration.

The free clinic in Huntington Park did not survive the period of localization and rationalization of social services in the early 1980s, largely because internal and external forces militated against its continuance. The 1980 Census shows no more than 50,000 Indians living in Los Angeles County, making it difficult to justify two separate Indian health care facilities in light of the health services needs of expanding black, Hispanic, and new immigrant, low-income, Southeast Asian populations. In fact, by 1980 less than half of the patient population at the Huntington Park clinic was Indian. When that statistic was combined with questions about the clinic's accountability—in part the result of continual in-house dissension and power struggles—the result was that programs funded through the clinic were not renewed when their contracts expired, and new proposals were not funded. Those Indian health care programs that did get funded were administered by the American Indian Free Clinic in Compton, which was viewed as a more stable institution with a better administrative track record.

By 1981 the Huntington Park Indian Free Clinic was in serious financial straits. Appeals for donations, volunteer medical help, and instruction from people skilled at grant writing went out to the community at powwows and in *Talking Leaf.* There was insufficient community response, however, and in 1982 the clinic's funding portfolio fell below a level sufficient to sustain a skeleton staff and minimal screening and referral services. Having lost its Indian patient load majority and thus its viability as a community resource, in mid-1982 the Huntington Park clinic, after ten stormy years as an ethnic community services institution, closed its doors. Its demise foreshadowed the fragility of ethnic institutions dependent on external funding sources for their existence.

The Indian Alcohol and Drug Abuse Intervention Network

In 1970 the Comprehensive Alcohol Abuse and Alcoholism Prevention, Treatment, and Rehabilitation Act created the National Institute on Alcohol and Alcoholism (NIAAA). Originally a treatment and research-funding agency, the NIAAA was to have a profound effect on the development of alcoholism treatment programs among American Indian populations (Vanderwagen, Mason, and Owan 1986). In 1972 an Indian desk was established at the NIAAA, and over the next six years, approximately one hundred sixty Indian alcoholism treatment programs were initiated or fell under the agency's funding apparatus. The Indian Men's Lodge, the Indian Women's Lodge, the United American Indian Involvement (UAII) open-house facility on Winston Street, and the Main Artery in Compton were all started during this period.

In 1976 Public Law 94–437, the Indian Health Care Improvement Act, was passed by the U.S. Congress. It contained the first official authorization for the Indian Health Services (IHS) to involve itself in alcoholism program activities. Partly as a result of P.L. 94–437 identifying alcohol abuse as an Indian health problem, and because initial NIAAA funding was for research and demonstration treatment projects but not for long-term treatment support, Congress directed that the 158 Indian treatment programs then under the administrative and funding umbrella of the NIAAA be transferred, in phases, to the IHS. Only mature programs (i.e., those in existence for at least six years) would be subject to transfer. The process, initiated in 1978, was completed in 1983 (Vanderwagen et al. 1986).

By 1980 the various Indian free clinics and the one alcoholism intervention program that Bramstedt (1977) and Fiske (1975) include among social services institutions had developed into a health care network of such community impact that it had its own separate, corporate identity. The Main Artery, which had expanded its substance abuse intervention program to include drug and multiple substance abusers and women, also had opened other facilities, such as halfway houses, to shelter and support the newly sober program graduates. The Indian Men's Lodge and the Indian Women's Lodge in the central city area still provided shelter and counseling for Indians hoping to break the cycle of their addiction or avoid a jail sentence for alcohol-associated crimes. The UAII's Winston Street facility provided sanctuary, a shower, a change of clothes, a mailing address, and two free meals a day for Indians living on or near skid row who would not, or could not, stay away from alcohol.

The Los Angeles Indian Alcoholism Commission (LAIAC) was created in 1977 to provide technical assistance to area alcoholism programs. The commission functions as a lobbying force at the local, state, and national levels for Los Angeles Indian alcoholism prevention and intervention institutions. LAIAC also has lobbied for liberalization or "medicalization" of existing laws that currently treat some of the illegal effects of alcoholism (e.g., vagrancy, panhandling, theft, and violence) as legal and moral, rather than medical, problems.

In 1979 a highly experimental, syncretic drug rehabilitation program called Mother Earth was established at Mount Baldy in San Bernardino County by one of the originators of the UAII skid row sanctuary. Specifically placed in a rural setting far removed from the drug-infested downtown Indian hangout areas, the program treated both southern California reservation and urban Indian drug users. The conservative, all-white, rural community in which Mother Earth found itself was unaccustomed to dealing with either drug addicts or Indians. Mother Earth's eclectic mix of conventional drug intervention protocols, Indian spiritualism, and Plains Indian ceremonialism, including the controversial ingestion of peyote during Native American church services held on campus, may have been additional factors in its brief, conflict-ridden existence.

Changes in federal administrative and funding mechanisms were instituted in 1980 that would affect the Los Angeles Indian alcoholism intervention system as dramatically as funding cutbacks and reallocations were affecting the Indian medical care system. When the Indian Lodge programs matured, for example, they were transferred to the IHS for administration, as was the Main Artery program, which matured shortly thereafter. As in the case of general health services facilities, IHS administration meant that service delivery officials had to follow an entirely new set of program parameters, evaluation measures, and reporting procedures.

The IHS, established primarily as a health services provider for Indians on reservations or in rural and traditionally Indian territories, had neither the bureaucratic apparatus nor the budget to expand its services to 50 percent of the Indian population then living in urban centers. Even though alcoholism intervention delivery funds were reallocated to the IHS from the NIAAA and a line item allocation for alcoholism intervention programs was in place, the IHS had little experience or inclination to provide substance abuse intervention in urban areas. Considered administratively and programmatically sound, the Main Artery and its ancillary programs continue to be funded by the IHS. The Indian lodges survived for a couple of years after their transfer to the IHS, but in 1985, citing underutilization of the lodges' services and the need to cut back funding, the IHS declined to renew their service contracts. The two central city inpatient programs thus were forced to close their doors.

When the lodges closed, a few determined former employees of the Indian lodges formed a self-help group, the Independent Men's Lodge. A charismatic spiritual guide and former alcoholic formed yet another outpatient self-help group, the Soaring Eagles. Both groups continue to offer treatment and social support for recovering addicts, but they maintain low community profiles. By 1986 a group of former Indian Lodge clients had regrouped and opened a second inpatient treatment facility, the Eagle Lodge, in the Long Beach area. The Eagle Lodge offers a syncretic mix of Alcoholics Anonymous philosophy and traditional curing regimens such as regular sweatlodge participation. It also provides both in- and outpatient support for Indians who wish to overcome alcoholism and/or drug addiction.

Traditional Healing Systems

The Medicine Wheel Group, which surfaced in Los Angeles in the late 1970s, holds seminars and weekend workshops two or three times a year. This group is an eclectic mix of Indian healers, Mexican *curanderos*, and Anglo acolytes who believe in the healing power of channeled good thoughts and that good health is the product of the individual being in balance with the natural forces. Employing the traditional symbolism of the Plains Indian medicine hoop (the circle of life and the good health of its four quadrants, in harmony with each other), the Medicine Wheel Group promotes homeopathic medicine and parapsychological experimentation as alternative, preferable paths to holistic health.

The Four Directions Foundation, which has been in existence since the mid-1970s, evolved from its creator's early and continuing involvement with the American Indian Movement (AIM). Lonetalker, a longtime member of the Los Angeles Indian community, underwent political and spiritual conversions around the time of the Wounded Knee, South Dakota, standoff in 1973. He took oaths of abstinence and did penance for his sins and for the good of his community by participating fully in the four-year Sioux sun dance cycle. His political conversion was so complete that in the mid-1970s he expressed his disrespect for the United States as a political power by appearing in public with an embroidered patch depicting the U.S. flag sewn upside down on his denim jacket sleeve. He also publicly berated his fellow urban Indians who worked in or administered government-funded social services programs for "tainting their hands with the white man's blood money."

AIM and most of its members (including Lonetalker) had foregone their more exaggerated militancy by the 1980s, when they came to the realization that their cadre of perhaps two hundred core activists was no match for the combined efforts of state militia, the National Guard, and the FBI. The movement redefined itself in spiritual and educational terms, as its Indian cultural survival schools began to surface in urban centers. Indian children and young adults who had spent most of their lives in urban centers were encouraged to join the AIM survival schools to ensure that Indian lore would be passed on to the next generation. The Four Directions Foundation was initiated as one of these survival schools. Lonetalker, by then a full-fledged pipe carrier and self-styled spiritual leader, and a handful of his associates provided instruction in herb collection and preparation, pipe ceremonies, sweatbath conduct, and a number of other traditional Plains ceremonial rituals. He has dedicated his life to the preservation of the traditional Sioux ethos.

Although the Medicine Wheel Group and the Four Directions Foundation maintain low profiles and are essentially marginal to core ethnic activities in Los Angeles, they nevertheless represent particular stances concerning the preservation of Indian spiritual and healing practices vis-à-vis the Western medical model. The Medicine Wheel Group tends to be inclusive. Because it hopes to spread the goodnesses of the Indian way of life to all interested parties, its instructional workshops are open to anyone willing and able to pay the registration fee. The Four Directions Foundation tends to be more exclusive. Lonetalker's power place is sacred ground, and its integrity must be maintained through sacred separation. The potentially polluting energies of the nonbeliever are jealously guarded against. Lonetalker carefully screens his potential apprentices for what he is convinced he can intuit as sincerity and goodness of heart. Not everyone is meant to experience, let alone carry, the pipe.

Going Home for a Healing

The decision to move to urban centers has not meant a total, irrevocable break with traditional and rural Indian life, for people regularly move back and forth from the city to the reservation. In addition to its function as an escape valve for urban pressures, a trip back home to the reservation can also be for the purposes of a healing. Many tribal groups still perform traditional healing ceremonies, and healing sodalities continue to exist, as do their clienteles. Gifted individuals are still sought out for their healing powers.

Going home for a healing is often reported as a last-resort attempt to obtain relief from physical or psychic pain. Scores of people have structured their accounts of indigenous healings in such similar ways as to imbue the narratives with mythic intent. The narrative outline usually takes the following form. Feeling debilitated, suffering from headaches and other unexplained maladies such as fainting spells, nausea, and stomach cramps, the afflicted person consults medical doctors in the city, to no avail. Only on taking the advice of a mother or grandmother to participate in a sing or a healing ceremony that the person's family has arranged back home is the person relieved of the symptoms of his or her particular malaise, returned to health, and made strong enough to endure another year in the city.

Important in these accounts of miraculous indigenous healings is the conjunction of the stressed individual with the healing properties of the homeland, family, and the spirits. Spiritual healings occur in sacred, not secular (or profane), realms. In a cosmology that divides the world into the sacred and the profane, reservations are clearly sacred and cities are profane. For people in need of curing, spirit power can be purely experienced only when one is removed from the polluting city.

Religious Institutions

Christian Indian Churches

Twelve Christian Indian churches in Los Angeles continue to provide contexts in which Indians can worship and commune as they did back home. A few small church groups coalesced around charismatic leaders (e.g., the Silverheels Evangelistic Ministry and the Intertribal Mission). However, church groups established in the 1950s and 1960s along regional, denominational, and/or tribal coordinates continue to provide the majority of spiritual guidance, social structure, and social arenas in which traditional and honorific religious statuses and roles can be attained and enacted.

The First Native American and United Methodist Church (FNAUMC), one of the most recently established Indian church groups in Los Angeles, had become a major religious and social force in the Indian community by the 1980s. (The early history of this organization is discussed in detail in chapter 12.) FNAUMC, which has consistently maintained a pan-Indian stance even though the original spiritual leadership and constituency were largely Eastern Oklahoman, boasts tribal affiliations from all North American culture areas in its congregation. Although tribal diversity is celebrated, identification as a Methodist takes precedent over members' tribal distinctions. Southwestern singers chant in Hopi and Eastern Oklahomans sing "Amazing Grace" in Choctaw in services that also include performances of rock gospel by the adolescent, electric guitar-wielding faithful.

By 1984 FNAUMC had moved to a large, well-appointed Methodist church complex in Norwalk, where it shares space with an aging Anglo congregation that continues to view the church complex as their own and the Indian congregation as Methodist brethren in need of their help. Needless to say, relations between the two ethnic congregations occasionally have been strained to the point of rupture. The Caring Center, one of FNAUMC's several human services programs, is located in the basement of a second Methodist church in the East Hollywood district. That location was chosen because it is an easy bus ride away for the downtown concentrations of low-income and homeless American Indians the center serves.

FNAUMC has thrived and remains a dynamic Indian subcommunity. Its Fifth Sunday sings, potluck feasts, and annual Christmas bazaars are always well attended. The congregation has enjoyed a consistent, if modest, growth rate. The church's membership ranges widely in both tribal and socioeconomic backgrounds. Homeless street people are made welcome by a congregation that includes the president of the United Indian Development Association and his family. Reverend John Goodman, the Seneca pastor of FNAUMC since 1978, in keeping with his and his church's commitment to social involvement, accepted a three-year term on the ICI board in the early 1980s.

The process by which Indian social services programs have survived by making a place for themselves within a mainstream bureaucratic infrastructure is also the strategy by which FNAUMC has been able to prosper. Maintenance of its status as an ethnically inflected institution within a supralocal administrative infrastructure works for both the First Native American and United Methodist Church and its host institution. "Helping Indians out" is mutually beneficial. It allows the ethnic institution to maintain a certain amount of internal consistency while affording the host institution the opportunity to fulfill and publicize liberal social programs as mandated by institutional policy.

Syncretic Religious Groups

I have been intrigued by Harry Janis since I first experienced his mesmerizing effect on an audience of UCLA academics in 1975. Since that time, he has transformed himself from a successful insurance salesman and part-time college instructor to a charismatic spiritual guide. When I first talked with Harry in 1978, he had been experimenting with parapsychology for some time and had returned to his Sioux roots to "get balanced" and find his mission in life. In the early 1980s, he was frequently called on to lecture about American Indian spiritualism, to offer prayers in Lakota at various ceremonial functions, and to provide psychological counseling to both Indians and non-Indians.

In 1983 Harry and his family began to hold prayer pipe ceremonies and sage smoke cleansings in his home. Interest in the prayer sessions grew so quickly that Harry was soon unable to accommodate fellow worshipers in his home. In May 1984, when I attended his public services for the first time, they were being held in a packed Garden Grove church auditorium. Approximately fifty people, mostly Plains Indians but also several Southwestern tribespeople and a few Anglos, made up the congregation.

Mr. Janis's American Indian Unity Church is his own syncretic creation. Consistent with Siouan shamanic tradition, he dreams his own rituals, which change with his dreaming. During the 1984 ceremony I observed, Mr. Janis spoke mostly in English; when in prayer, he occasionally lapsed into Lakota, a language he acquired in adulthood subsequent to embarking on his personal spiritual quest. His message is exquisite in its simplicity: We all have the possibility for goodness and change. We all are brothers, God's children, His sacred vessels. We all need to love ourselves so that we can know how to love others, and to do that we have to bring our lives into balance, into harmony with the grandfather spirits. Drugs, alcohol, money, material possessions, and life in the fast lane won't do it. Harry Janis should know. He had tried them all for most of his adult life. Bringing oneself back into balance, into harmony with the grandfather spirits, is the only way to do it.

Harry's message of personal redemption through dedication to traditional Indian beliefs and values carried great weight with the group assembled in the church auditorium. People queued up and waited patiently to fan the cleansing smoke from his sagebrush offering into their faces and to receive his benediction. Many embraced their spiritual leader and tearfully whispered their fears, concerns, pain, and joy, hanging on his Delphic words of assurance. A powerful medicine was being practiced. In the best Siouan spiritual tradition, religion and healing were two dimensions of a single process. Mr. Janis had created himself as healer in response to an observed community need in a familiar if syncretic form. The American Indian Unity Church continues to provide spiritual fellowship and a message of personal cleansing and universal love to a dedicated congregation convinced of its charismatic founder's power to lead them to that healing power in themselves.

Traditional Indian Religious Forms

Apart from Lonetalker's spiritually grounded healing apprenticeships at the Four Directions Foundation, no other formal, pre-Christian Indian religious institution is publicly recognized in Los Angeles. Instead, many people return home with regularity to attend family sings or their societies' ceremonial dance cycles. Those traditional spiritual rituals that are practiced in the city tend to be private and are dictated by personal crises. This individuation of religious practice, which is certainly consistent with traditional folk practices, eloquently expresses the internalization and privatization of core ethnic values and beliefs as a survival strategy in the urban environment.

Educational Institutions

In 1986 I found Bramstedt's (1977:100) assertion that "student associations will continue to experience the most dramatic rate of growth" particularly prophetic. Over fifty separate associations, conferences, workshops, and other educational activities were documented between 1978 and 1986, with Indian educational programs being mentioned more often in the community newspaper than any other institutional type. Indian education programs appeared to be maintaining a high community visibility and adequate funding bases while other Indian social services programs were succumbing to the budget reductions that characterized the national human services funding policies of the 1980s.

Most of the college-level Native American studies programs and Native American student organizations that Bramstedt notes as having evolved in the 1970s continued into the 1980s. The number of Indian college student and college preparatory associations attests to a continuing belief in a formal mainstream education as the way out of the economic underclass. Groups and activities such as the Billy Mills Indian Youth Leadership Program and the College Motivation Program were designed to motivate Indian youngsters toward such goals.

Other groups, such as the California Indian Education Association and the American Indian Education Advisory Council to the California State Department of Education, along with the American Indian education commissioner for the Los Angeles Unified School District, lobby at local and state levels of policy development for increased cultural awareness and sensitivity to Indian issues in school curricula. Educational Opportunity for Native Americans (EONA) has provided Indian cultural enrichment programs in Los Angeles County public schools for many years. Most recently, a number of self-help and self-improvement classes have been offered to the Indian community. These classes focus on topics such as family health, parenting skills, foster parenting, family strengthening, leadership potential, and developing a positive mental attitude.

The interest in instilling, from the onset, the value of a good education in their children was evident in the numbers of Indian parents who enrolled their offspring in the Tribal American preschools and the various Indian Headstart and preschool programs, summer youth workshops, and youth diversion programs administered by the Indian Centers, Inc. Parents also involved themselves in PTA programs in the public schools as well as at Central High School, the ICI's continuation program for dropouts. In four years of operation, the individualized tutelage and all-Indian context of the Central High School program resulted in scores of young Indian adults successfully attaining a high school graduate equivalency diploma. Yearly issues of *Talking Leaf* were devoted to exhaustive lists and photographs of eighth grade, high school, and college Indian graduates. Routinely, honoring dances are held at June powwows for recent graduates.

The Comprehensive Employment and Training Assistance program that had provided short-term training and employment for hundreds of Indians in Los Angeles beginning in the mid-1970s was dismantled in the early years of the Reagan administration. The Job Training Partnership Act (JTPA) provided alternative programs, with the goal of greater participation by the private sector in training and employing participants. The ICI quickly became an administrative agent for JTPA programs and within two years was receiving nearly two million dollars annually in JTPA funding.

Recreational Institutions

This category includes four discrete kinds of Indian social and recreational activities and the associations of people who promote such activities. Powwow and dance club participation (described in greater detail in chapters 8 and 11), athletic leagues, the Indian bar scene, and arts and craft classes provide many opportunities for Indians in Los Angeles to be involved in expressive and sociocultural aspects of contemporary urban Indian life.

Powwows and Dance Clubs

Powwows and their support clubs, drum groups, and exhibition dancers provide social arenas in which Indians and non-Indians can observe, attempt to emulate, and thereby participate in stereotypic and increasingly pantribal Indian activities. Powwows are the stages on which traditional role models are presented and certain culturally recognized honorific roles are enacted. Long-established powwow groups such as the Many Trails Indian Club, the Little Big Horn Association, and the Concerned Community Indian Movement supported weekly powwows throughout the 1980s. Additionally, several new drum and dance groups were initiated in the last decade. The All Nations Drummers, the Iroquois Social Dance Group, the Melvin Deer Singers, the Two Valley Drummers, the Whitecloud Drum Group, the Standing Arrow Singers, the Red Tepee Dancers, and the Red Nations all established their roles as cultural conservationists during this time.

The Iroquois Social Dance Group intentionally focuses on the preservation of certain elements of Iroquois expressive culture, but it does not exclude non-Iroquois from participation in group activities. The Plains powwow drum groups specialize in either Northern or Southern Plains drumming and singing styles, but their memberships include tribespeople from all culture areas. The Whitecloud Drum Group, for example, is made up almost exclusively of men from Pueblo societies. The Red Tepee Dancers is a Southern Plains family that has researched and faithfully reproduce traditional dances from a number of Plains cultures. The family's acceptance of a grant from the Los Angeles Cultural Affairs Department to present dance exhibitions in the city's public schools and parks represents the ability to work within the urban administrative infrastructure to preserve one's culture.

Youth drum groups have also organized and are encouraged to participate in the weekly Saturday night powwows. Although they present a reedy and often out-of-tune contrast to the throaty resonances of the adult singers, their performances are pointedly praised by powwow emcees. These youth groups are positive proof that this form of Indian expressive culture will survive into the next generation.

Athletic Associations

Athletic associations are among the earliest-formed and longest-lived urban Indian organizations. Los Angeles still boasts an extremely active American Indian Athletic Association as well as the Los Angeles American Indian Bowling League. No new athletic organizations, other than the ICI's Central High School softball and basketball teams and an attempt to establish an Indian lacrosse team, were initiated in the 1980s.

The annual weekend-long bowling and softball league tournaments in the summer and the Indian basketball league tournaments in the winter are well-attended events. Hundreds of Los Angeles players and their families, as well as rival teams from as far away as Arizona, Washington, and northern California, make the tournament weekends a holiday. Picnics, awards ceremonies, dances, and nightly beer bashes at the Indian bars in the Bell Gardens area where the tournaments are held contribute to the celebrational character of the annual displays of ethnic solidarity.

Indian Bars

Both Price (1975) and Fiske (1979) rightly underscore the institutional qualities of the Indian bar scene. To be an Indian bar, an establishment's clientele need not be predominantly Indian. Rather, at certain prescribed times of the week (usually Friday and Saturday nights), visible numbers of Indians should regularly frequent that bar. Price (1975) describes Indian bars as places in which Indians know they can come together, be with other Indians, and feel comfortable. These bars are identified by Indians as their own "time-out" and "partying" territory.

Several of the bars in which Indians chose to congregate in the 1950s are still considered Indian bars (e.g., The Hut and Rusty's, in the central city area; Grassy Shores, in Bell Gardens; Cross Roads Inn, in Long Beach; and the Astor,[4] on skid row). Others (e.g., The Columbine, at Third and Main) have closed permanently. Still others changed ownership, were refurbished to appeal to a particular non-Indian clientele, and, on reopening, served the targeted clientele to the exclusion of former Indian patrons. For example, the Irish Pub, which closed in 1977, reopened the next year as a salsa bar. Both the Moulin Rouge and the Pretty Girl near MacArthur Park were purchased by Koreans, redecorated, and reopened to cater to the growing Korean and Southeast Asian populations in the mid-Wilshire district.

Contrary to Price's (1975) opinion that the utility of the Indian bar as a socializing institution in the urban environment was time-limited and had probably run its course by the mid-1970s, these bars continue to be scenes of considerable social, political, and recreational activity for Los Angeles Indians. They are protected public arenas in which Indians can come together to socialize and exchange life experiences. Here, the newly arrived can locate friends and family already in the city; young adults can gossip, flirt, make friends, and negotiate romantic liaisons; and community administrative elites can form political factions, relax, and "let it all hang out." Indian bars are informal arenas in which information gets exchanged, political positions are voiced, people get hired, and alliances are formed that might not have in a more formal setting such as the ICI boardroom (Weibel and Weisner 1980; Bill Fredricks, February 24, 1979).

Indian bars are institutions in that implicit rules about comportment when drinking and the group's responsibility for its members are clearly demonstrated in patterned behavior. These bars are also nodes of interaction, consistent with other Los Angeles Indian institutions, in which sectors of the Indian community come together on a regular basis (Weibel 1981).

Arts and Crafts Associations

Indian handicrafts are still much-sought-after, marketable items. A number of beadwork, basket weaving, silversmithing, and language classes have been offered by the Indian Centers, Inc., the Natural History Museum, the Southwest Museum of Art, and by enterprising individuals. Aside from the extremely well organized, semiannual, non-Indian-run Bullock's Indian arts and trade shows in which Indians are encouraged to participate, and a couple of small Indian-run craft shops (Buzzard's Roost in Burbank and Big Bear's in Torrance), no entrepreneurial Indian group has formed to act as a broker on behalf of Indian crafters and artists.

Several Indian artists trained in traditional Indian and Western art forms have created exciting syntheses of these artistic traditions. The latest works of a few American Indian artists (e.g., R.C. Gorman, Fritz Scholder, and Amado Pena),[5] who have enjoyed phenomenal worldwide recognition, hang in trendy La Cienega Boulevard galleries. However, most Indian artists, like most artists in general, struggle for recognition and acceptance. Two attempts were made in the early 1980s to organize Indian artists for the promotion of their work. The Native American Fine Arts Society and a group with the fanciful name Continuous Journey to the Sun were active between 1981 and 1983, but they have maintained low profiles in the Indian community since that time.

Communicational Institutions

Given the dispersed nature of the Los Angeles Indian population, an efficient communications system is vital if a sense of community or common purpose is to be sustained. In many respects, the informal communications network (often referred to as the "moccasin telegraph") is the most viable and efficient vehicle for the immediate dissemination of community information. The weekly powwows are hotbeds of informal information exchange. If one attends powwows every week and make the rounds of the trade tables, dining rooms, and bleachers, one's information about Indian community doings need never be more than a week old. The same can be said for the weekly exchange of information that occurs in such diverse social settings as church potluck dinners and Indian bars.

However, not everyone in the far-flung Los Angeles Indian community attends Indian cultural and social events with any regularity. For these people, access to Indian community information is more formal. Before its demise, *Talking Leaf*, the monthly newspaper published by the Indian Centers, Inc., was an informational mainstay of the Indian community. It provided a calendar of local, state, and national Indian events, information about new programs for Indians in Los Angeles, news of employment availability, and human interest stories about the successes and hardships of Los Angeles Indians. Its community organizations directory was continually updated to reflect available resources and services for urban Indians.

In significant ways, *Talking Leaf* promoted and perpetuated the notion of an Indian community in Los Angeles. Its standardized informational sections visually outlined the ethnic community's institutional and ceremonial structure. Its editorials provided a moral stance to which individuals could and often did virulently react. Except for a story or a photographic essay about major and past local events (a memorial powwow for recently deceased community elite or a successful elders' luncheon), after 1986 the newspaper's focus became increasingly more national.

In the 1980s, three Los Angeles–based radio programs devoted to Indian affairs provided their listeners with local and national information about Indians. The "American Indian Hour," for example, aired each Saturday morning at eight o'clock since 1975. "Our American Heritage," a somewhat more politicized radio program, aired on Sunday mornings at 6:30. Early risers were apprised of the latest local, state, and federal Indian events and issues. "American Indian Airwaves" broadcast similar kinds of political interest news every other Tuesday at 3:00 P.M.[6] Importantly, these radio programs broadcast information about Indians, particularly those in Los Angeles, to a much wider, largely non-Indian audience. In this way, empathies can be developed that have the potential of broadening the Indian political base beyond the minimal clout one might expect of such a modest-sized constituency.

Indians also make good mass media human interest copy. At least four times a year, articles about American Indians appear in the *Los Angeles Times*. Interest in Indians is also generally high among the issue-hungry local television newscasters and talk show hosts.

The general newspaper and broadcast media are information-disseminating vehicles that Los Angeles Indians still underutilize. Militant activist groups have been more successful in this regard, but similar strategies have just begun to be explored by the more centrist local Indian advocacy groups.

Kinship, Marriage, and Family

The importance of kinship reckoning as a principle of social organization in tribal American cultures has been exhaustively documented.[7] Persistence of clan reckoning and inheritance rules systems among the Indians of the Northwest, the continuing power of the matriclan to order social relations across such diverse culture groups as the Navajo and the Seneca, and adherence to collateral kinship terms that label biological cousins (in mainstream American terms) as grandfathers among the Cheyenne attest to the tenacity of kinship as a viable American Indian principle of social organization.

It could be hypothesized that the importance of kinship as an organizing principle is compromised by competing forces in the urban Indian community. The value of membership in urban, pan-tribal associations and accommodating such foreign practices as antinepotism in publicly funded places of employment certainly oppose earlier understandings that one's kin make the most trustworthy work associates. Additionally, legal-rational hiring practices that place greater weight on qualifications such as previous experience, character and skill references, and proven performance, and attempt to discount or militate against such criteria as tribal, regional, and kinship commonalities, are still alienating concepts to many Indians. These kinds of associational rules undercut kinship-dictated systems of reciprocal relationships with and responsibility for clan or lineage members.

The power of kinship ties to regulate behavior does not appear to be as vulnerable to external and competing forces as one might expect. Bramstedt (1977:207) briefly mentions the role of kinship ties in establishing interlocking statuses and roles in his sociostructural model of community among the Indians in Los Angeles.

Although some voluntary associations were known to open membership only to relatives, no Indian group was of this type. Without employing descent as a formal membership criterion, however, several organizations became composed primarily, or developed around an influential or controlling core, of kinsmen. . . . It resulted usually from officers and, less often, rank and file members finding that kin bonds were the most reliable and accessible means to satisfy organizational and personal needs.

Fiske (1975:30) also acknowledges the tenacity of the notion among her Navajo informants that kin are ultimately the most trustworthy associates.

The fluorescence of individual efforts [in community organizations] is fine, but is solidified by the fact that most of the individuals are related. By "related" is meant that the kinship thread which binds them is by virtue of being cousins, siblings, or in-laws. For example, out of 14 Board members on the Indian Free Clinic Board, 10 of them are related to other people in prominent positions in the Indian community.

My initial work among the Los Angeles Indians substantiates the persistence and power of kin relations to influence behavior. Interested in problem solving and assistance seeking among the urban Indians, I found that Navajos in the city exhibit a consistent preference for the use of primary assisters (kin or friends) from among a support network predominantly composed of other Navajos in the urban environment. This pattern is impressively persistent over time and constant across several problem-solving situations (Weibel 1977:xvii).

Discussion

In a critique of John Price's "model of successive stages of urban ethnic institutions," Fiske (1979:149) stresses the often overlooked "longitudinal perspective toward group adaptations and the influence of national (supralocal) policies and institutions" on the development of such institutions. Her point is well taken. The fluorescence and subsequent atrophy of a number of Los Angeles Indian institutions in the decade since she suggested that "national policy may be more closely linked with types and development of migrant's associations than previously suspected" support her thesis. The demise of the Huntington Park Indian Free Clinic, the Indian Health Center on Pizarro Street, the Indian lodges, and ultimately the Indian Centers, Inc., in the 1980s was directly associated with a general federal retrenchment of human services funding allocations. As demonstrated in section IV, an institution whose existence is dependent on policy decision-making processes far removed from the institution's influence and control is particularly vulnerable and unstable.

In the climate of general retrenchment of public support of community services organizations in the last decade, the institutional structure of the Los Angeles Indian community has become increasingly volatile and given to disequilibrium. In the wake of Reaganomics, the vagaries of block grant funding, and increased demands for human services by new and competing special interest groups, Los Angeles American Indians have had to look elsewhere and inward for stabilizing structures. As Chapple and Coon (1942:443–46) note, "institutions do not exist in a vacuum. . . . When a change takes place in one institution, a series of compensatory changes takes place in other institutions tangent to it." The development of Indian bureaucratic statuses within the intermediary city and county governments is one such adjustment. This survival strategy is not without its risks, however. Jones (1987:101) warns that grass roots organizations that embed themselves within supralocal institutions are likely to be transformed into components of the higher-level institutions rather than function as subverting representatives of the community constituents. Much of the recent concern about the relative effectiveness of the Los Angeles City-County Native American Indian Commission relates specifically to the issue of co-optation.

Continuity of traditional institutions independent of supralocal control is a second stabilizing factor in an otherwise fairly unstable system. The inherent familiarity of traditional social forms (pow-wows, spiritual practices, and kinship ties) provides a solid social, spiritual, and enculturational matrix in which community can be located. The Arensberg and Kimball (1965) definition of community includes the existence of a comprehensive, integrated set of social institutions that transcend individual invention or leadership. The Los Angeles Indian organizational outline clearly meets this criterion. The political, economic, medical, religious, educational, recreational, aesthetic, and familial institutions of classic ethnography are all present in this urban Indian collectivity. The Arensberg and Kimball community table of organization (three generations and two sexes) is equally present. Clearly, the American Indians in Los Angeles have the structural capacity for community.

Essential to defining the American Indians in Los Angeles, or any other urban ethnic group, as a community is the manner and density with which the institutions identified by a certain locus or ethnic group intersect and their members interact. "The equilibrium of a society is itself a state of equilibrium between institutions, which are themselves in equilibrium, and which in turn are made up of the equilibria of individuals" (Chapple and Coon 1942:462). Substitute "community" for "society" in this statement and we have a model and rationale for the ensuing discussions of the interconnections between ethnic institutions as context, ethnic events as process, and ethnic statuses and roles as the vehicles by which community structure and consciousness are embodied, demonstrated, and sustained.

NOTES

1. For the locations and a complete listing of the 135 Los Angeles Indian organizations and their satellites in existence between 1978 and 1988, see map A.1 and table A.2 in the Appendix.

2. Segments from Lonetalker's speech are quoted in Rose and Howell (1986). A description of his apparel and demeanor was provided by two community leaders present at the press conference who wish to remain anonymous.

3. In 1986 Ben Nighthorse Campbell, a Democrat and a Northern Cheyenne, was elected to the U.S. House of Representatives. Although he represents Colorado's Third Congressional District (a 53,000-square-mile district in the southwestern corner of the state), his campaign was national in scope and included a successful Los Angeles–based fund-raising powwow and a series of media events arranged by southern California supporters.

Leonard Peltier, a Sioux, was among approximately 200 armed men, members and supporters of AIM, who faced off U.S. marshals, FBI agents, and BIA police at Wounded Knee, South Dakota, a small settlement of some 400 people on the Pine Ridge Reservation, in the spring of 1973. During the two-month occupation of the hamlet, two government agents were fatally shot. Based largely on circumstantial evidence and controversy-laden ballistics reports, Leonard Peltier was convicted of the crime and sentenced to double life imprisonment. His case has been given worldwide media attention. The Free Leonard Peltier Movement has major supporters in Los Angeles and throughout the United States, Canada, Europe, and the Soviet Union (Anonymous 1984:13). Its efforts have included raising funds to support the cost of an appeal and ensuring the public's awareness of what his supporters see as a terrible miscarriage of justice. As of May 1990, Leonard Peltier was still incarcerated in a top-security federal prison.

4. I have used pseudonyms for the Indian bars and obscured their locations to protect the privacy of the Indian people who still frequent them.

5. It should be understood that, although their art is well known and has a market in southern California, none of these artists is a resident of Los Angeles.

6. As of May 1990, "American Indian Airwaves," the most recently initiated Indian news program, was still broadcasting bimonthly. "Our American Heritage" aired on KLAC from 1981 to mid-1984. The station then sponsored a substitute program entitled "Conversations from Wing Spread," which went off the air in 1988. The "American Indian Hour," the longest-lived Los Angeles Indian radio program, last aired in August 1988.

7. In 1851 Lewis Henry Morgan published *The League of the Iroquois*. In 1880 Major John Wesley Powell, chief of the Bureau of American Ethnology, called *The League* the "first scientific account of an Indian tribe ever given to the world" (Powell 1880:115). Morgan's groundbreaking work contains considerable ethnographic description of Iroquois kinship terminology and was the basis of such later works on kinship as his 1859 paper "Laws of Descent of the Iroquois" and his monumental ethnological opus, *Systems of Consanguinity and Affinity of the Human Family* (1871). Morgan's early preoccupation with cross-cultural similarities and differences in kinship terminologies became the model for and a major element of subsequent ethnographic work among American Indians (Lowie 1917; Spier 1925; Swanton 1928; Spoehr 1968[1947]). Indeed, to this day kinship systems that regularly occur throughout the world are identified by the American Indian tribes (e.g., Crow, Eskimo, Iroquois, Omaha) in which the systems were first systematically documented (Nanda 1980:234–36).

IV

Ethnic Events as Community Process

The self, as that which can be an object to itself, is essentially a social structure, and it arises in social experience. (Mead 1967:140)

SOCIAL ARENAS, those central nodes of interaction "in which people can play out their lives, the circles of persons among whom their views, their actions, their reputations matter" (Moore 1978:25), are the stages on which consensus about social behavior specific to a particular culture scene can be demonstrated and learned by individuals and by the group. They are the context of community. Within social arenas, individuals and groups can engage in recognized patterns of behavior that validate and incorporate them into the larger social entity.

The concepts "role performance," "impression management," and "social status" are reified through their public execution. Hannerz (1980:207), paraphrasing Erving Goffman, points out that although "impression management [is] largely a personal activity . . . sometimes teams of people cooperate in a performance aimed at others. Successful team performance involves partners who tend to have shared access to a wider range of information concerning one or another or a combination of their selves . . . [and] have an at least tacit agreement on what information should be actively presented."

In an urban environment as complex as the Los Angeles American Indian community, the individual has an enormous range of potential social arenas from which to choose. Unlike Moore's (1978:24) Chagga village, in which personal choice of social arena participation is limited and change occurs slowly, Indians in Los Angeles can totally immerse themselves in ethnic social arenas or, with little personal penalty, forego the Indian community experience altogether. In this sense, the quality of the relationship between Los Angeles Indians and their community is as tenuous as Janowitz's (1952) "communities of limited liability" or Lewis's (1967) "part-time engagements." As Hannerz (1980:261, 273) notes, if things "are not to one's liking, one can withdraw from them," usually without penalty.

Why, given the lack of personal liability for nonparticipation in urban community affairs, do so many Indians invest time, energy, and economic resources in the perpetuation of American Indian social arenas in Los Angeles? The answer is not simple. It begins with individual social needs and motivations. Hannerz (1980:205) argues that there appears to be an inherent intent on the part of individuals to involve themselves in activities "during a period of continuous presence before some set of others [for the purpose of producing] some kind of effect on them," which Goffman (1959) describes as a "performance." By doing so, individuals make indications, to their audience and to themselves, about their own qualities. Although hardly determined wholly by contact with others, individuals' conceptions of who they are and what they are like—a central tenet of symbolic interactionism—are born in social interactions and continue to be nourished by them (Hannerz 1980:222). The development of a definite sense of self, then, is registered not in self perception or family but in more complex settings of social arena and community.

It may be that individuals, in the process of maximizing self-image, well-being, and social context, search out or create and access those social arenas in which they have already achieved a certain level of legitimacy and cultural competence. For American Indians who have sought economic sanctuary in Los Angeles, urban social arenas that allow them to display cultural competency are, in large part, those they either have invented or re-created from earlier social forms.

As demonstrated in chapters 6 and 7, American Indians have created an impressive array of familiar social arenas in Los Angeles. Although individuals have a wide selection of focal activities and cultural orientations from which to choose their particular spheres of ethnic activity, personal choices are structured by such dimensions as age, sex, tribal heritage, and early enculturation. I found, as did Guillemin (1975:67), more cultural continuities than discontinuities in the urban Indian community.

Two of the three Los Angeles Indian social arenas described in this section are faithful re-creations of rural Indian ceremonial events. The powwow and the Fifth Sunday Sing have roots extending back at least as far as the nineteenth-century ceremonial calendars of the Plains and Five Civilized Tribes cultures, respectively. In each case, the physical configuration of the social arena is as important symbolically as are the behaviors the setting engenders. The powwow concentric ring configuration structures comportment and signals a worldview in which a clear set of conceptual dichotomies (sacred/profane and Indian/non-Indian) are expressed. The powwow is the urban Indian worldview and ethnic social structure in microcosm. The Christian Indian church ground configuration re-creates the eastern Oklahoma Christian Indian campground in the urban context. That configuration, I suggest, parallels earlier community forms, namely, the pre-Christian Creek and Choctaw ceremonial villages of the eighteenth century. Rather than co-optation, the Indian Christian church community may ultimately represent a particularly subtle, yet effective, strategy of cultural survival, that is, cultural encryption.

The third urban Indian social arena, the Los Angeles City-County Native American Indian Commission, is a fascinating synthesis of contemporary mainstream bureaucratic structure and process and traditional tribal political hierarchy and function. The commission was invented as a response to the needs of an urban constituency. Its form and purpose gain legitimacy from their easy comparison to the liaison role of the nineteenth-century tribal councils and the moral authority with which they dealt with internal and external threats to the social integrity of the tribe.

In all three social arenas, individuals take on community-validated roles and perform culture-specific acts with relative competency. Their actions are observed, evaluated, and confirmed by others to whom these individuals concede the authority to do so. In all three social arenas, it is the setting-specific, culturally competent social act that signals an individual's rights to claims of community membership.

8

The Saturday Night Powwow: Ethnic Theater, Iconography, and Microcosm

Historical Antecedents of the Contemporary Powwow

Powwows, as they now are enacted in rural and urban settings throughout North America, originated as a Plains Indian cultural phenomenon. The historical antecedents of contemporary powwows were the social, spiritual, war, and healing dances held during the great summer convocations of the nomadic bands of Plains Indians (Young 1981). Sharing a common language and ancestry, band members also shared the responsibility of cooperating in their tribe's yearly, communal buffalo hunts. During the halcyon weeks of midsummer, while men hunted the buffalo and women butchered the animals, dressed the skins, and rendered the buffalo meat in preparation for the long and relatively gameless winter months ahead, evenings were spent in ceremonial ritual, secular aesthetic performance, and social exchange. With the setting of the sun, the entire camp of band clusters gathered in the open, grassy areas at the centers of the semicircular tribal encampments. Camp fires were lit, and men and women donned their finest ceremonial regalia. To the insistent beat of buffalo hide–headed drums and gourd rattles and the shrill punctuations of bone whistles and reed flutes, the people expressed their cultural unity in dance and song, sometimes into the next day.

Powwows were not only sacred but also secular cultural events. The original, primary functions of the gatherings were spiritual and ceremonial. Dances to propitiate the spirits of the buffalo were performed before and after a major hunt. Dances to honor the ancestors and departed warriors also were performed at these times. Prayers for ailing members of the tribe were offered and various life cycle markers (a child's initiation into dance traditions, entry into adulthood or a sodality, and thanks for another year of good fortune) were all integral spiritual aspects of the original communal dances and early powwow ceremony (Wissler 1916).

The great tribal convocations were also times to gossip, exchange news of the past winter and spring, arrange marriages, and, for the young, meet, flirt, sexually explore, and commit themselves to potential mates. The opportunity to socialize was an important, though secondary, aspect of the early powwows.

The Contemporary Powwow

Powwows are still very much a part of the Plains Indian summer ceremonial cycle (Young 1981). Scores of Plains Indian communities host powwows each week from June through October. Starting in the 1920s, as Plains Indians began to migrate to urban centers, they incorporated elements of the summer powwow into their new urban life-styles (Ablon 1964, 1971b; Margolies 1973). The summer powwow was modified, truncated, and restructured to accommodate certain constraints of the urban scene. Significantly, the urban powwow cycle occurs between September and June so as not to conflict with the summer rural powwow season. This arrangement allows individuals who are dedicated to a full year of powwow participation the opportunity also to be involved in powwows back home.

The original ceremonial, social, and informational functions of the nineteenth-century tribal convocations continue to be in evidence in the modern powwow. Today, however, powwows are more secular than sacred events. No longer an expression of tribal unity, powwow participation, particularly in urban centers, is increasingly intertribal and panethnic. Powwows have also become pantribal marketplaces. Increasingly, commercial elements have been introduced into powwow activities. Large portions of the public facilities in which powwows are held are designated as "traders' areas."[1] Booths display and offer for sale Indian handicrafts ranging from Southwestern jewelry, pottery, rugs, and basketry to Plains leather goods and beadwork to Woodlands quill work and birch-bark baskets. Ethnic food kitchens coexist with booths offering American standards such as Coke and Pepsi, hot dogs and hamburgers.

Powwows are public events. The institutionalized Los Angeles schedule of weekly powwows is advertised in *Talking Leaf* as a public service to the Indian community, as are the powwows hosted by colleges and special interest groups. Flyers announcing upcoming powwows are posted at the sites of various Indian social services programs throughout the city and are handed out at meetings of Indian groups and at earlier powwows. Both Indian and non-Indian powwow attendance is encouraged.

Certain sacred elements, such as the flag salute and song, the opening prayer, memorial dances, and a careful demarcation of sacred-to-secular space on the dance floor, are regular ritual features of Saturday night powwows. Three types of social, quasi-sacred, and competitive dances are performed. The social dances include free-style events, in which anyone who wishes to dance can move onto the floor and do so, and specialty dances, such as a ladies' choice and the two-step, which require some prior dance experience as well as a dance partner. Quasi-sacred dances include memorial and honoring dances, whereby the participants demonstrate their connection to or respect for a particular faction or clique within the total Indian community. Contest dances are displays of skill by exemplary performers whose virtuosity is judged and rewarded in relation to that of other competitors of comparable age, sex, and regional dance and dress style categories.

The Los Angeles Saturday Night Powwow

Every Saturday night from September to June, a powwow is held somewhere in Los Angeles or Orange County. On these occasions, three to four hundred American Indians gather in public recreation centers or high school gymnasiums to dance and socialize. Only special memorials for well-known community members or the pre-Christmas powwows, with their promise of free gifts for all of the attending children, attract a bigger crowd. Other well-attended powwows include the weekend-long "annuals," or yearly campout powwows, and contest powwows in which dance specialists compete for cash prizes.

"Powwow people" and "church people" form clearly defined ethnic subgroups within the Los Angeles Indian population. Powwow people tend not to be highly involved in the Indian church organizations, and church people tend not to go to powwows. This is particularly true of the church people who have migrated from the Choctaw, Cherokee, Creek, Chickasaw, and Seminole territories in eastern Oklahoma. Originally from farming village cultures in the southeastern United States and removed to Oklahoma in the 1830s, these people historically did not engage in the kinds of communal convocations and dance traditions that were Plains Indian precursors of the present-day powwow.[2] Their enculturation into the Christian Indian community during childhood inculcated a belief that activities such as powwow participation were tantamount to pagan abandon—a state akin to consorting with the devil (Gardner 1969; Weibel 1981).

Some Indian administrators regularly attend powwows as a form of personal recreation, to ensure their children's involvement in powwow traditions, or to "keep in touch with community needs." However, many attend powwows only occasionally and opportunistically. An Indian Commission or Indian Centers, Inc., board of directors election, the need to inform and gain community support for some Indian cause, the wish to encourage more Indians to use an agency's facilities, or the desire to advise community members of new services available to Indians in Los Angeles all bring Indian program officials to the microphone during the time most powwows set aside for public service announcements. Occasionally, activist or social services groups set up informal display tables in the traders' area to disseminate information about their cause or service.

The powwow people represent a widely diverse group of ethnic ritualists. The dancers, drummers, and singers tend to be from Plains Indian cultures. However, there are significant numbers of people from the Southwest, Northwest Coast, and Eastern Woodlands cultures for whom powwow participation began with the move to Los Angeles.

Occasionally, hobbyists (non-Indians who have studied the powwow traditions, assembled elaborate costumes, and mastered the intricacies of the various war, medicine, and contest dance steps) join the dancers circling about the central drum. Interestingly, the hobbyists are more easily accepted as powwow participants than are the presumptuous "wannabees." Hobbyists harbor no pretensions about their ethnic orientations. They easily identify as "white people" enamored of Indian folklore and folkways. Their powwow participation is strictly an act of scholarship, skill, enthusiasm for, and empathy with an appreciated cultural tradition. Most powwow regulars see the hobbyists' unabashed emulation of their ethnic displays as the sincerest form of flattery.

"Wannabee" participation in powwows, on the other hand, is resented. "Wannabee" as a label has a decidedly negative connotation and is conferred on people who claim—often based on spurious documentation—that they are part-Indian. Their motives for doing so are thought to be less than sincere and probably gratuitous. Before powwow participation can function as a rite of incorporation into the ethnic community, other membership criteria must be met.[3] Chief among these is a determination of the individual's personal motivation for seeking community incorporation. Demonstrated personal credentials such as community service, generosity, cooperativeness, and observable or verifiable Indian kin are other criteria for Indian community incorporation. People who, for economic or political reasons, suddenly opt for inclusion in Indian activities as a way of demonstrating ethnic group membership are suspect. This is especially true if they previously had preferred the company of non-Indians. "Wannabees" can expect to be treated with subtle yet complete civil inattention[4] at powwows.

Powwow participation holds special significance for "breeds" (people who have less than full to only minuscule amounts of Indian ancestry) and culturally marginal Indians (people who have been raised in urban or home environments in which Indian culture was suppressed or nonexistent) who wish to retrace and experience their Indian heritage in adulthood. For these people, the "roots phenomenon" includes learning their tribal dances, constructing dance regalia typical of their people's nineteenth-century ceremonial accoutrements, and just "hanging out" with other Indians in clubs. Often, breeds have the most-elaborate, best-researched dance regalia.

The several powwow dance and drum groups that have organized during the last three decades have evolved distinct orientations and memberships. One powwow club membership is composed primarily of people who are no more than one-quarter or one-half Indian and who are phenotypically Anglo. For many of these people, dual ethnic orientations were difficult to synthesize during their formative years. Assertion of their Indianness through powwow participation in adulthood therefore takes on added symbolic and psychological importance.

Indian college students and professionals employed in bureaucracies other than the Indian social services agencies also attend powwows with some regularity. Their attendance at these events takes on the attributes of a pilgrimage. Concerned that their higher education and professional careers may create social chasms between other less well educated Indians and themselves, upwardly mobile Indians attend powwows to symbolically demonstrate their continuing ties to their community. Powwow participation, then, becomes an emblematic act of ethnic intention. Through shawl-wrapped and

Shelah Panjwani (Navaho) joins Cher Sisto (Apache-Navaho), the 1986 Orange County Indian Center Princess, in an intertribal dance.

Ernest Big Medicine (Cheyenne-Arapaho) adjusts his nephew's (Pete Onco, Cheyenne-Arapaho) roach before entering the dance arena.

Southern drummers provide the grand entry song.

Grandpa Whitecloud (John Whitecloud Garcia, Laguna Pueblo) and his great-grandsons, Ricardo "Sha-wi" Pacheco (*middle*) and Lorenzo "Yogi" Garcia (*right*), take a much-deserved break between dances.

John Firethunder (Lakota) leads the grand entry at the Many Trails Indian Club Powwow, Cecil B. De Mille Junior High School, Long Beach, California, February 14, 1987.

Wilma Kay Big Medicine (Cheyenne-Arapaho) in a women's fancy shawl dance.

cowboy-booted dance, the bicultural competents acknowledge the importance of "remembering where [they] come from."

Powwows are hosted by various powwow clubs and special interest and action groups that have developed since the 1930s to promote tribal arts, crafts, and social activities for their members (Bramstedt 1977). Among their goals is ensuring the orderly progression of monthly powwows throughout the year. Every officer and dues-paying member of a club is given a list of powwow duties. Great effort is made to provide the quality of site, food, crafts, and security that promotes good powwow attendance by participants and spectators alike. Usually not-for-profit corporations, Indian clubs cover the costs of gym rentals, security guards, flyers, and advertisements through various money-making activities. Funds are raised by selling ethnic foods, raffling donated Indian handicrafts, renting booths to the traders, and requesting voluntary contributions at the door. Treasury surpluses are used to pay for the transportation of a visiting drum group from back home, to cover the costs of the annual powwow princess contest,[5] and to finance the club's annual three-day campout powwow.

For nearly two decades, Iron Eyes Cody's group, the Little Big Horn Association, has been the powwow host of record for the first-Saturday-of-the-month powwow.[6] This powwow is usually held at the Eagle Rock Recreation Center, a municipal park facility approximately ten miles northeast of downtown Los Angeles. During the 1980s, the Many Trails Indian Club hosted the second-Saturday-of-the-month powwow, held at the Cecil B. De Mille Junior High School gym in Long Beach, a public school facility located about fifteen miles south of downtown Los Angeles.[7] Until 1985 the third-Saturday-of-the-month powwow was the sole responsibility of the Orange County Indian Center. Currently, responsibility for the powwows on the third and fourth Saturdays is shared by the Orange County Indian Center and several community coalition groups. Chief among the grass roots advocacy groups is the Concerned Community Indian Movement. The powwows that the Orange County group sponsors are held at a public hall in Stanton, a suburban area near Disneyland, approximately thirty miles southeast of downtown Los Angeles. Depending on scheduling demands, the CCIM powwows are held at the Eagle Rock Recreation Center, Ford Park auditorium in Bell Gardens, or the Cecil B. De Mille Junior High School gym.

Further urban adaptations include the fund-raiser powwows held throughout the year by various Indian self-help and activist organizations. The Indian studies centers at the University of California at Los Angeles, California State University at Long Beach, and California State University at Northridge, as well as the Educational Opportunities for Native Americans program of the Long Beach Unified School District all sponsor yearly fund-raising and educational powwows. These events are usually held at the site of the sponsoring organization. However, some grass roots groups with no formal meeting facility rent public spaces such as the Ford Park facilities or the Whittier Narrows Park area in order to hold their powwows in spaces large enough to accommodate five hundred or more participants.

The Saturday night powwow sites are staggered so as to apportion the distances powwow people who live in outlying areas have to drive each week. Importantly, powwows occur with weekly ritual regularity. Indians who wish to express their ethnic identity and community involvement in ritual public displays of expressive culture are assured regular access to this sort of public arena. Every Saturday, starting around five in the afternoon and often continuing until midnight, the Los Angeles powwow people cognitively prepare for and organize their social interactions and activities around the ritual powwow. It is the symbolic enactment of their will to be, and to sustain their identity as, Americans Indians.

Powwows as Ethnic Theater

The Saturday night powwow incorporates several institutional elements. Powwows are educational, recreational, aesthetic, political, and quasi-sacred events. Stereotypical Indian behavior is enacted at powwows for the benefit of Indian and non-Indian participants and observers. The Saturday night powwow is ethnic theater; it is a paean to a people's dance, music, traditional dress, and food— their expressive culture. The dance area is a stage on which, in the sense that Turner (1974) uses the term, the drama of ethnic identity is performed and thereby reified.

The official, advertised Saturday night powwow starting time is usually seven o'clock; however, members of the host club arrive at the powwow site an hour beforehand. In the two hours between the time a club's powwow chairperson opens the gym to the early arrivals (club officials and craftspeople intent on securing their favorite locations in the traders' area) and eight o'clock, when the opening ceremonies take place, an urban public space is transformed into an arena for the display, enactment, and experiencing of ethnic per-

sonas by participants and spectators. For the next three hours, traditional tribal dances and honoring rituals sustain that transformation. This recasting of urban secular space into Indian ceremonial
arenas has been formulated and refined over the approximately forty
years that powwows have been held in Los Angeles. The transformational process is, in itself, another in a complex of familiar ritual
behaviors that demonstrate and sustain, through performance, a
sense of ethnic community for American Indian participants.

The Many Trails Indian Club's March 1987 powwow was archetypal. Around 7:00 P.M., the Cecil B. De Mille Junior High School
gym began to fill with the paraphernalia of American Indian expressive culture. Sacred drums were hauled in, and their positions
around the perimeter of the basketball court were staked out by
cowboy-hatted, bronze-skinned, and ponytailed male drummers and
singers. By 7:30 male dancers' Addidases had been replaced by
beaded moccasins, Esprit tank tops by buckskin shirts, and trucker's
caps by porcupine and horsehair roaches and feathered headdresses.
In the girls' locker rooms, the women dancers were exchanging
miniskirts, stone-washed jeans, and sweat clothes for beaded, elk
teeth–yoked dresses of buckskin, satin, and Pendleton wool. From
the kitchen of the adjacent cafeteria, fry bread,[8] hot from Jessie
Cruthers's skillet of boiling lard, was steaming its pungent appeal
throughout the gym. Overwhelmed by its aroma, even the most
health-conscious powwow-goers succumbed to temptation and ordered generous portions of the "Indian national food." After all, you
are what you eat.

By eight o'clock, the principal dancers were assembling at one
end of the gymnasium. At the microphone, George Beaverstail, the
powwow master of ceremonies, repeatedly implored "all dancers
[to] gather at the locker room door for the grand entry." Ankle bells
clanked with the heavy step of male fancy dancers.[9] Shawl fringes
curled about the beaded hems of the women's heirloom, white elk-
skin dresses. A red wool–sheathed, otter skin–decorated coup
stick,[10] the host club's standard, was hoisted triumphant from its
protective case. The coup stick would be carried at the head of the
dance line by Dale Featherman, that evening's honored head male
dancer.[11] At this point in the spectacle, the drum's insistent rhythm
became regularized, hypnotic. The opening chant spiraled from
Wakantankan[12] heights.

The powwow emcee admonished the spectators jammed onto the
gym bleachers and in lawn chairs surrounding the dance arena to
"all stand for the grand entry." Men in braids removed cowboy hats

and trucker's caps and clasped them respectfully at their sides. Women, momentarily discontinuing their weekly exchanges of personal and community information, lifted themselves and their lap-held children to attention. The entire assembly stood in silent, respectful deference to the sanctity of the ceremonial moment. The emcee repeated his entreaty over a worn, unmodulated public address system. His message was rendered essentially unintelligible to the uninitiated ear. No matter—everyone appeared to know the ritual invocation: "Everybody up. Everybody dance. It's Saturday night powwow time in Indian Country, L.A.!"

Powwow Participation as Ethnic Iconography

The Saturday night powwow is an arena for the establishment and perpetuation of community statuses and roles, honor and respect, and skills and knowledge. Through regularized symbol, ritual, movement, and sound, a people share salient cultural acts. Through the communal and ceremonial act, the powwow dancers also express their ideal selves to others who do not, or cannot, share the cultural act but who respect its validity as a marker of ethnic group membership. In this respect, powwow participation is iconic; it provides visual models of ideal ethnic comportment.

The consistency of the powwow structure marks it as secular and quasi-sacred ritual. The current powwow princess and the head male dancer with feathered staff in hand lead the evening's opening ceremony, the grand entry. They move with deliberate dignity at the head of a column of a hundred or more dancing kin, friends, and acquaintances. Community membership, cooperation, and the obligation of the individual to suppress personal pride on behalf of the collective good—core values that have sustained tribal life since its inception—are embodied in the swaying, bobbing, fringe-swirling phalanx of powwow dancers. Scores of dancers in full ceremonial regalia proceed in single file about the circumference of the gym—a solemn, graceful promenade of ethnic icons.

Differences in tribal and regional paraphernalia can be discerned; however, Plains ceremonial regalia predominate. Twentieth-century Pimans, Chumash, Cherokees, and Creeks indiscriminately adopt the Plains warrior bustle, bead, and roach regalia with little concern that it has no precedent in their own tribal ceremonial dress. Ironically, the stereotype of the American Indian as Plains noble warrior, a generalization that infuriates scholars who have devoted entire careers to describing the wide cultural diversity among American Indian societies, is perpetuated, indeed reified, in the pan-Indian powwow.[13]

The powwow is an arena of honor in which individuals take on highly visible, prestigious roles and display not only their knowledge of appropriate cultural behavior but also their right to assume these honorific social positions. Enactments of these roles demonstrate, through ritual behavior, a set of cultural assumptions and ethnic group core values. Chief among these roles is that of the powwow master of ceremonies. Almost exclusively male, powwow emcees are usually older, well-known, consistent contributors to the Indian community who are also respected for their organizational skills, diplomacy, and oratory. Other powwow roles (head man dancer, head woman dancer, head drummer and singer, prayer leader, arena director, and powwow princess) are sought out and proudly enacted. Special events such as honoring, veterans', and memorial dances provide ceremonial mechanisms by which individuals are acknowledged for their continuing contribution to community maintenance.

By 8:30 P.M., the emcee at the powwow I attended in March 1987 had finished his customary intoning of the names and tribal affiliations of the powwow officials. The honoring flag song had been chanted by Henry Hale, the head singer of the host drum group. At that point, the emcee summoned Grandpa Whitecloud, the evening's designated honored elder, to the microphone to lead the opening prayer. With his feather fan raised to the heavens, Grandpa Whitecloud, in a voice grown vibrant with the resonances of his tribal language, invoked the spirits' blessings. The crowd stood once more, and with heads bowed, hats and hands on hearts, showed their respect for this solemn moment and the iconic role that was being enacted for them. Chanting in a language only a handful of his audience understood, Grandpa Whitecloud embodied an ethnic ideal—the community elder as the repository of spiritual lore and the locus of spiritual leadership.

At the prayer's end, Grandpa Whitecloud returned to his seat in the dancers' circle and prepared himself for an evening of dancing. The head male dancer and his attendants placed the host club's banner, the American flag, and the feathered staff at the speaker's podium. These acts symbolically marked the completion of the ritual prologue and the beginning of the dance program proper.

For the next three hours, more than three hundred urban powwow people participated in a continuous round of social and ceremonial dances. Everyone in attendance was encouraged to dance, whether or not they were outfitted in ceremonial regalia, and most of them did so at some point in the evening's program. Pow-wows are family affairs. Entire kindreds, occasionally four generations strong, attend and participate in powwows en masse. Such corporate family participation dramatically underscores the importance of kin-based, self-help networks as the basic, abiding social institutions of American Indian life. There are no restrictions as to age, sex, or ethnicity of the dancers. Infants imprinted the rhythms and movement of the dance as they were carried about the dance hall in their mothers' arms. Toddlers padded onto the dance floor, tiny fancy dance bustles bobbing precariously atop their bulging disposable diapers. Grandmothers promenaded at discreet but watchful distances behind their grandchildren and great-grandchildren, monitoring their tiny charges' uncertain steps. Stolid, leather-jacketed teenagers, who twenty minutes earlier had disappeared with battered suitcases into the locker rooms, now appeared as splendid man-birds and elegant towers of totemic womanhood. Lumbering gaits lightened into graceful prancing. Slouched shoulders straightened into regal carriage. Ungainly inner city school dropouts leapt and whirled in impressive displays of cultural competence and aesthetic accomplishment. Encircling the host drum in slow, solemn steps, the dancers were transformed into a collective ethnic display, a demonstrative act of community incorporation and solidarity.

The Saturday night powwow is a rite of intensification, a regularly practiced communal ritual that exemplifies core community values and ideal in-group behavior. Rites of intensification allow individuals to express, in a public arena, their membership in a larger human corpus that shares and endorses certain cultural activities and perspectives. Powwow participation allows individuals, through shared ritual dress, dance, song, food, and ceremonial behavior, to demonstrate to an audience that is wider than their immediate or extended family their continuing adherence to and appreciation of a valued cultural heritage.

In most small-scale societies in which rites of intensification have been studied with thoroughness, the audience is composed of like-minded, culture-sharing individuals. Significantly, the Saturday night powwow incorporates not only Indians but also non-Indians. The audience members can be placed on a spectrum from culturally aware and sympathetic to totally uninformed about Indian folkways and worldview. In this respect, the urban Saturday night powwow takes on additional educational functions. First, the youngest Los Angeles Indians learn the elements of ideal public Indian behavior. Second, the powwow exemplifies what Indians would like non-Indians to know about their life-style prior to Western European contact and their contemporary ties to, as well as their ways of expressing, that valued cultural heritage.

The dancing at a powwow is occasionally interrupted for quasi-sacred rites of incorporation. The ceremonial giveaway is the most spectacular of the Saturday night incorporating and validating ceremonies. This is a ritualized gift-giving ceremony in which a family honors major participants in the powwow and friends to whom they owe a debt of gratitude, to whom they wish to express their love, respect, and allegiance, or with whom they wish to establish an exchange relationship. The rationale for a giveaway may be the occasion on which a child initiates formal entrance into the dance traditions, the return of a veteran, the successful completion of one's education, a memorial for a deceased family member, a celebration for the winner of a powwow princess contest, or dozens of other community-recognized status passages.

The giving of gifts (handmade dance shawls, lawn chairs, water jugs, lanterns, camp stoves, cartons of cigarettes, blankets, sewing materials, handmade men's shirts, and dozens of other articles of clothing and housewares) takes considerable preparation on the part of the donor family. Some giveaways include hundreds of gifts worth thousands of dollars; as such, they are corporate family enterprises. Families may spend a year or more gathering gifts earmarked for certain people. Some of these gifts are customized, handmade items of dance regalia and usually go to favorite friends or relatives. For many families, hosting a giveaway constitutes major executive and financial commitment.

Generosity—a willingness to share one's material wealth with kin, friends, and strangers—is among the most highly regarded cultural traits expressed in the ritual giveaway. Indians are expected to give ritually, generously, and throughout their lives to the communal good. In the act of giving to others, they most approximate an Indian ideal type. To be Indian is to recognize and demonstrate one's interconnection to family and community. The ritual giveaway dramatically delineates the giver's place in a personal network of significant others. To be of good heart means that one gives willingly, repeatedly, and without comment or expectation of praise. The importance of the giveaway in establishing the legitimacy of an individual's membership in the community is evidence of the continuing strength of the core value—generosity—in Indian society.

People chosen to assume honorific powwow roles are the generous-hearted community members who can be depended on to make fry bread, set up trading booths, sell raffle tickets, or lead the dancing on Saturday nights while their peers watch TV, "cruise the streets," or "party."

Viable ethnic group membership demands high involvement in community activities. Weekly attendance at and participation in powwows exemplify that cultural tenet. The primacy of the collective good over the ambitions and needs of the individual characterizes tribal life historically as well as contemporarily.

The Powwow as a Microcosm of Ethnic Community Structure

The powwow dance arena is a cognitive map of or metaphorical paradigm for an urban Indian worldview and ethnic community boundaries. As figure 8.1 illustrates, it is demarcated by a set of concentric rings or areas of diminishing sacredness (Weibel 1981). Behavior appropriate to each zone is governed by recognized rules of comportment. The most sacred area of the powwow arena is its core, the very center of the dance floor. The host drum is placed at the core and the dancers file around it.[14] The drum is referred to as the heart of the powwow, its beat synonymous with the body's life-affirming pulse. It is both the vehicle by which the powwow's energy is created and the symbol for the continuing vitality of Indian ethnic life in the urban environment. Eating and drinking, especially alcoholic beverages, are highly improper in the center of the dance floor as they are considered impure, secular activities, while the drum and its immediate radius are sacred areas.

The next concentric ring radiates from the drum circle to the dancers' sitting area. In this space, usually about twenty feet in diameter, the dancers, both Indian and non-Indian, move about the drum. Since the dancers have more opportunity to interact with the non-Indian spectators and the occasional non-Indian dancers than do the drummers, the dance area is a less sacred space than is the drum circle. Conversely, because the dancers have a greater potential for interacting with the spiritual center of the powwow than do the spectators, the dance arena is more sacred than the area in which the spectators sit, on the bleachers or in lawn chairs.

To legitimize one's presence in the dance arena and to ensure its relative sanctity, dancers observe certain prohibitions and prescriptions. Women, as an act of respect, should wear at least a dance

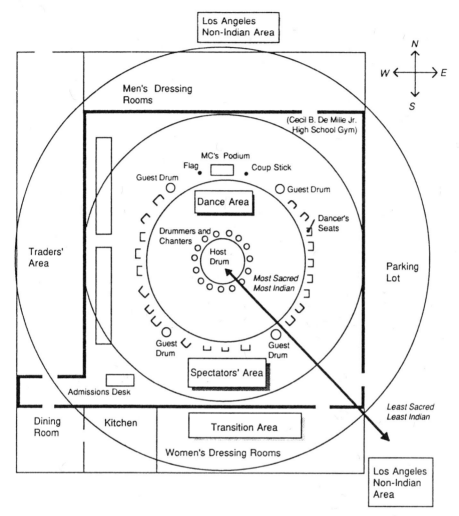

Figure 8.1 Symbolic Use of Space in Urban Powwows: Concentric Rings of Most- to Least-sacred and Indian Space

shawl over their shoulders as they move around the drum. Moccasins are preferable to standard shoes and high heels. The more elaborately outfitted dancers take great ritualistic care in the systematic assembly of their regalia. It is also a matter of personal pride that, even after three hours of strenuous dancing, no item becomes dislodged from its proper place in a dancer's ordered ceremonial adornments. A feather that falls from a bustle or hairpiece onto the dance floor is cause for the dancing to cease until a powwow ritual-ist[15] can be brought forward to examine the offending ornament. The ritual specialist (often the evening's prayer leader) carefully examines the desecrated spot for oracular signs, while the owner of the feather is identified and admonished to exercise more diligence in the arrangement of his or her ceremonial attire. Satisfied that the dancer understands the seriousness of the offense, the spiritual lead-er intones a cleansing prayer over both the spot on which the item landed and the feckless dancer who dropped it. Having done so, the rip in the ritual fabric is repaired. Dancing can be renewed, safe from the contaminating influences of impaired performance.

Strong prohibitions about drinking and dancing while intoxicated apply in the dance arena, and food is also forbidden in that area. Understanding and complying with these dance participation rules underscore an individual's cultural competence and ethnic group membership. Breaking or ignoring these rules marks the individu-al's marginality to the group.

Beyond the dance arena is a third, narrow concentric ring in which the most active powwow participants (the ceremonially garbed dancers, their families, and guest drum clubs) sit. This is a transitional zone where the sacred and secular elements of the pow-wow intersect.

The fourth concentric ring is also fairly narrow, about twenty feet wide, yet it is occupied by approximately 75 percent of the powwow attendees. The spectator area is decidedly more secular than sacred. Observers can choose to sit and passively watch the ongoing specta-cle. Or they can largely ignore the ongoing ritual in favor of informal socializing with their bleacher neighbors and promenading friends. Or they can rise occasionally from their seats and enter the dance arena as active participants in the ethnic theater.

Spectators are predominantly Indian, although a few Anglo and Hispanic spouses and friends accompany their mates and children to powwows. Troops of non-Indian boy scouts or elementary or church school classes on a field trip also occasionally attend powwows. Overwhelmingly, however, the spectators are organized in pantribal clusters of Indian families and friends.

The commercial zones, located beyond the spectator zone, are usually outside the dance auditorium proper. These areas are highly secular in nature and are not governed by the prohibitive sanctions that restrict behavior in the dance arena. The kitchen in which the fry bread, chili, and Navajo tacos are created may also contain tables from which coffee, soda pop, and the host club's memorabilia are sold. Here, eager customers sit and eat their weekly ration of symbolically Indian food. Another room adjacent to the auditorium may house from six to ten tables or booths from which Indian craftspeople sell their ethnic wares. Community services programs establish booths in these areas for the dissemination of information about ongoing services or recent innovations in services. Socializing and exchanges of secular information are expected behavior in the commercial zones. Oral accounts of Indian events, announcements of personal life events, and gossip about other Indians—the types of informational exchanges that sustain community consciousness—are shared in these places.

The locker rooms, which on powwow night serve as dressing rooms, are adjacent to the commercial zones and the gymnasium but out of sight of most of the casual spectators. Here, the major dance figures transform themselves from twentieth-century urban dwellers into ethnic icons. The dressing rooms constitute primary transitional zones, or ethnic thresholds. Behind closed doors and separated by sex, the dancers relinquish the trappings of their blue-collar urban lives and become buckskinned and feathered latter-day ceremonial dignitaries.

Although the most obvious symbolic transformations occur in dressing rooms, ingestion of ethnic foods in the kitchen or purchase of ethnic markers such as beadwork jewelry, ribbon shirts, and lavishly fringed dance shawls in the traders' area also constitute transformational processes. Ethnic transformations can be internal (you are what you eat) and external (you are how you dress). In these transitional zones, and through ingestion and acquisition of ethnic symbols, individuals symbolically gird and mark themselves for fuller participation rights in and identification with the ethnic community activities in the dance sphere proper.

The final and most secular of rings occurs at the periphery of the commercial and transformational zones. Beyond the confines of the public facility, in the parking lot, in their cars, trucks, and vans, and in the open-air recreation fields beyond the parking lot, adults who view the powwow as primarily an occasion for social interaction sit and talk, smoke cigarettes, and drink beer. Children play catch, tag, and hide-and-seek. Adolescents flirt, laugh, fight, make dates, and fall in love. Occasionally, the dancers undergo their personal transformations in the privacy of their vans. More regularly, however, they leave and reenter this most secular, non-Indian zone in their secular, urban-dweller personas. This is the zone of departure from and return to the workaday reality of urban secular life.

Discussion

The spatial division of powwow activities according to their sacred-to-secular dimensions parallels Lévi-Strauss's (1963:135) structural model of social organization as concentric dualities. That is, areas of human habitation and use are symbolically divided into sacred and profane space—those places inhabited, on the one hand, by humans, our people, the tamed, and characterized by society; and, on the other, those places inhabited by nonhumans, strangers, the wild, and characterized by anarchy. The Winnebago village plan as described to Radin (1949) is among the ethnographic examples Lévi-Strauss uses to illustrate the underlying, cross-cultural binary oppositions in the concentric structuring of human community. In his analysis of aboriginal village configurations, he concludes that a "complex system of oppositions between sacred and profane, raw and cooked, celibacy and marriage, male and female, central and peripheral" exists in village configurations across cultures (1963:137). For example, "the analogy with the concentric structure of the Winnebago village is striking, especially because the Winnebago informants spontaneously introduced into their descriptions ecological characteristics which serve . . . to conceptualize this opposition. Here the built-up village area [sacred] is opposed to the peripheral ring, or cleared ground, which is in turn opposed to the encircling forest [profane]" (1963:139).

Lévi-Strauss (1963:136) deplores "Malinowski's indifference to problems" and claims that Malinowski "sketched all too briefly a highly significant structure [of an Omarakana village in Melanesia], the further analysis of which would have been richly rewarding." Rather than a simple dichotomy of sacred and profane, Lévi-Strauss (1970:93) argues, "the mythical system and the modes of representation it employs serve to establish homologies between natural and social conditions or, more accurately, it makes it possible to equate significant contrasts found on different planes: the geographical, meteorological, zoological, botanical, technical, economic, social, ritual, religious, and philosophical."

The concentric structure of the powwow symbolizes something more than dichotomous sacred and profane spaces. It is also an analogue for the us/them dichotomy of ethnic space and social distance as experienced by American Indians and particularly by urban American Indians vis-à-vis their non-Indian social context. The sacred, ceremonial center of the powwow dance arena, marked by the host drum, is the equivalent of ethnic purity on the Indian-to-non-

Indian continuum. The farther one moves away from the drum, the less sacred, pure, ceremonial, and Indian is the inhabited social space and, by association, its inhabitants.

Lévi-Strauss (1963:135) would argue that the dual organization I have identified in the contemporary powwow abounded in pre-Western European contact American Indian social structure. As such, the powwow takes on an additional historical dimension. Its spatial arrangement is the analogue for the nineteenth-century mid-summer tribal encampment. Dance and ceremonial events re-create the annual rites of tribal intensification held before and subsequent to the communal hunt. The great tribal encampments have become the archaic totems of American Indian life as it was experienced in its most unmitigated and encompassing form. The symbolic re-creation of the tribal encampment in the physical, social, and se-mantic constructions of the contemporary powwow therefore ex-presses an ethnic archetype and provides a model for ethnic unity for the benefit of its participants and its Indian and non-Indian ob-servers.

In the sense that Turner (1974) uses the terms, the powwow is the microcosmic field and metaphor for Indian ethnic identity vis-à-vis their urban, non-Indian social environment. The closer to the cen-tral core of ethnic expression, symbolized in the powwow by the host drum in the middle of the dance area, the more sacred and pure (Indian) the cultural experience. As one moves away from the cen-tral ethnic icon (the host drum), the more diluted and impure (non-Indian) one's ethnic experience becomes. As one moves beyond the periphery of the ritual zone of purest ethnic expression, one be-comes transformed, changed, less obviously ethnic in demeanor and consciousness. Psychic and spiritual losses are thought to character-ize the non-Indian, secular, profane urban world, and it is thus im-portant to endure or resist the culture-threatening elements of the secular domain and ensure one's sense of ethnic integrity. Indian individuals reinforce their connection to the sacred domains of core ethnic experience through weekly powwow participation.

NOTES

I am extremely grateful for the editorial and technical assistance of the Many Trails Indian Club in the preparation of this chapter. Eva Northrup (Hopi/Cherokee), a regular Los Angeles powwow-goer and the director of the Long Beach Unified School District's Educational Opportunity for Na-tive Americans program, was most helpful in the assembly of the ethnohistorical materials and the identification of particular subgroups discussed in this chapter.

1. The term "traders' area" probably has its antecedents in the nineteenth-century Indian trading post phenomenon. Today, the term refers to the area adjacent to the powwow dance arena in which craftspeople offer their wares for sale.

2. There is considerable seventeenth- and eighteenth-century evidence of dance ritual among the horticultural Indians of the Southeast. Swanton (1918:69) describes scalp dances performed in the seventeenth century among the Choctaw. Creek and Cherokee stomp dances first observed by Western Europeans in the eighteenth century (Adair 1968[1775]: 17) survive to this day (Young 1981:155). With the incursion of Protestant missionaries into Southeast Indian societies in the first decades of the nineteenth century, dogmatic condemnation of these pagan rituals was such that Christian Indians felt themselves in violation of their newfound faith if they attended the old dances (Bowden 1981). The social and ideological dichotomy between powwow people and church Indians is clearly drawn in contemporary rural and urban Indian communities. These social categories take on the attributes of a worldview that recognizes and operates from notions of secular versus sacred ethnic domains.

3. Van Gennep (1960) introduced the term *rite de passage* into the anthropological lexicon. It is his thesis that major status passages in a person's life are marked by ritual to which the community is witness. His model of ritual structure includes three phases: separation, transition, and reincorporation. The individual must first be ritually separated from the previous social status. This is followed by a transitional or liminal stage in which the individual is taught what must be known to successfully take on the new status. When the individual is properly and completely trained for the new social status, the community acknowledges the person's right to embody that new social state through ritual incorporation or reincorporation of the individual into the community in the newly acquired status.

4. "Civil inattention" is a term Goffman (1963) coined to describe avoidance behavior in public places. In the case of American Indian interaction in Los Angeles public places, civil inattention can be manifested by avoidance of eye contact and no attempt to speak to or interact with the offending individual, but no overt attempt to sanction the offending behavior in any way.

5. "Powwow princess" is an honorary status and title conferred by competitive contest on a young female member of the Indian community. Powwow clubs and other Indian organizations that sponsor powwows hold yearly contests in which they chose their respective princesses. The winner maintains the title for one year and is responsible for a number of ceremonial duties during that time, including leading her sponsor's powwow grand entry and subsequent dances. For a full discussion of the iconic quality of powwow princesses, see Weibel-Orlando (1988b).

6. Since 1987, the Future Generations powwows have been held on the first Saturday night of the month at the Cecil B. De Mille Junior High School in Long Beach. Iron Eyes Cody, advanced in years and in failing health, has sponsored increasingly fewer of the Eagle Rock powwows since the mid-1980s.

7. At their May 1988 monthly meeting, several members of the Many Trails Indian Club voiced their wish to be relieved of their responsibility for hosting the second-Saturday-of-the-month powwow. They announced that decision publicly at their annual campout powwow in September 1989. During the 1989–90 urban powwow season, a number of newly organized culture conservationist groups vied for the honor of hosting the second-Saturday-of-the-month powwow. The competing groups included the Alliance of Native Americans, the Community Concerned Indians Movement, the Urban Indian Consortium, and the Red Nations.

8. Fry bread is bread dough that has been pounded into a thin circle, approximately four to six inches in diameter. It is dropped into boiling oil or lard and quickly fried. Fry bread can be eaten without garnish, with honey, sugar, and jam, or topped with refried beans, lettuce, cheese, and onions (a Navajo taco). It is served as an ethnic food throughout the country and is jokingly called the "national Indian dish" by its sellers and eaters.

9. "Fancy dancing" refers to the most flamboyant of the Plains Indian dance traditions. Largely a Southern Plains-inspired male dance tradition, it is marked by the spectacular double bustle, roach, and beaded dance regalia and the execution of intricate, fast-paced dance-step patterns.

10. When the Plains Indians still led a nomadic, buffalo-hunting lifestyle, men acquired enhanced social prestige by besting their enemies in battle. To be able to enter into the fray armed only with a long, crooked pole with which to strike, but not take the life of, your enemy was a sign of great personal valor. These instruments by which personal bravery was demonstrated were called "coup sticks," or hitting sticks, by early nineteenth-century French trappers who followed the High Plains rivers into buffalo-hunting tribal territories.

11. In Southern Plains–style powwows, "head male dancer" and "head female dancer" are two other honorific titles and powwow statuses. Head dancers have the responsibility for initiating and leading the nightly round of dances. Unlike the powwow princess, head dancers can change monthly.

12. *Wakantanka* is the Lakota Sioux term for the "great sacredness." Composed of sixteen elements, it is the sum of all natural resources. Wakantanka resides on high and can be called forth to aid humankind in times of pitiable need. Powers (1977) provides an excellent depiction of the concept in *Oglala Religion*.

13. For a detailed discussion of the Plains American Indian stereotype, see Ewers (1964).

14. A drum, drummers, and singers in the center of the dance arena and the dance floor configuration described in this chapter are Southern Plains

powwow traditions. Until the mid-1980s, the Southern Plains–style pow-wow protocol predominated in Los Angeles. Since that time, there has been a resurgence of Northern Plains powwow protocol and "traditional" dance regalia and style in southern California. During the 1989–90 powwow season, a Northern-style powwow was held at least once a month in Los Angeles.

15. The origins of the fallen feather ritual is unclear. It may, in fact, be a modern innovation designed to underscore the seriousness of the powwow ceremony to Indian and non-Indian spectators who might otherwise treat the powwow only as entertaining secular performance.

9

Fifth Sunday Sings:
Indian Community Continuities
in Los Angeles

Ceremonial Structure and Process

DURING ANY given year, three or four months will have five Sundays, which by tradition are the occasions for special daylong gatherings of all the eastern Oklahoma Christian Indian church parishes in the region. These convocations, appropriately called Fifth Sunday sings, are well-established ceremonial traditions (McKee and Schlenker 1980:191). The eastern Oklahoma Indians who migrated to Los Angeles in the 1950s have perpetuated this ceremonial tradition in the urban setting.

The Christian Indians who first invited me to attend a Fifth Sunday Sing assured me that I would never "see anything to beat it" and "wouldn't soon forget" the potluck dinner that the women of the First Southern Baptist Indian Mission[1] on Clara Street in Bell Gardens were "fixing to feed all the folks who will join us after their church's Sunday services are over." Their enthusiasm persuaded me that the Fifth Sunday Sing is more than the ceremonial sum of its participating churches. Plainly, participation in a singing carried great symbolic, sociocultural, and psychological weight for those who urged my attendance.

I had been in the field only two months when I attended a Fifth Sunday Sing for the first time. I arrived at the Bell Gardens First Southern Baptist Indian Mission church ground on the morning of the fifth Sunday in April 1973, in time for the nine o'clock Sunday school class and the weekly church service at 10:30. Located on

Clara Street, one of the major east-west streets transecting this low-income, largely Hispanic neighborhood, the Indian Mission church ground is surprisingly large. In fact, it extends across two of the oversized city lots that characterize this section of southeastern Los Angeles County.[2] The church is a modest (approximately twenty by forty feet) one-story, one-room, wood-frame building. Signs on the rooftop and lawn announce not only the mission's formal title but also its presiding pastor and weekly ritual schedule. Attendance at the morning service appeared to be good. I could not find a curbside parking space on the streets immediately surrounding the church ground, so I followed the example of people who drove up at the same time I did. That is, I pulled into the unpaved driveway between the church building and the church ground's west fence and parked on the spacious, well-kept lawn.

Three smaller wood-frame buildings on the grounds are set back about thirty feet from the church. The largest of the three, originally a four-room residential bungalow, had been converted into a cookhouse that now includes an ample kitchen, a small dining area, a pantry, a storage room, a nursery, and a classroom. The other two outlying buildings are smaller affairs, not more than two- and three-room cabins. They appear to have been motel bungalows or transient farm worker housing built during the 1920s and 1930s to accommodate immigrant casualties of the Dust Bowl. Originally converted into church offices and Sunday school classrooms, these buildings have, on occasion, housed indigent church members for limited periods of time.

I was impressed with the orderliness and care with which the church ground and building complex were maintained. The buildings, though simple and essentially unadorned, were in good repair. The expansive lawn was mowed and devoid of the garbage that befouled the residential areas surrounding the church. The irreverent graffiti scrawled on fences on either side of the church ground were respectfully absent from all of the church buildings. This was, after all, sanctified space, the model for which can be found in early forms of Muskogean ceremonial spatial arrangements (Spoehr 1968[1947]: 211).

After parking my car, I walked into the church and joined the Sunday school lesson already in progress. The sanctuary, which at most accommodates a congregation of a hundred, was less than half full. Curiously, those in attendance were mostly men and children, in marked contrast to the predominance of women in church gatherings I had attended previously. The parish women, consistent with

Fifth Sunday Sing tradition, were in the cookhouse preparing the noontime feast.

Having grown up in a small New England Methodist church community, I found the tiny sanctuary's spare appointments and the morning's biblical instruction and congregational worship familiar ritual context and structure. Eleven pairs of wooden, cushionless pews along a center aisle faced a simple wooden pulpit. Altarless, the raised dias was adorned only by two bulletin boards that offered weekly attendance and collection statistics; a handmade poster heralding a week-long revival meeting the church had sponsored two years earlier; a roughly hewn wooden cross; and a worn upright piano. There was no hint of Roman Catholic baroque here, only Puritan austerity and spiritual zeal.

I spent the first hour with the members of the adult Bible class. We discussed the significance of Job's seemingly unearned sufferings for our lives and generally agreed that Job's constancy was an inspiration and model for us all. Submission to the will of God, no matter what our life circumstances, it was concluded, was the kind of faith Christian Indians needed to "get through the hard times." Four Bible study groups categorized by age clustered at various places in the church building. The members of each group shared their interpretations of the morning's scriptural lesson for approximately an hour.

At 10:30 A.M., Billy James, the lay preacher, called the Bible study groups together for the morning worship service. A full-blood Choctaw man in his early forties and a charter member of the mission, Mr. James has since gone on to a full-time career as a missionary to Indian communities in the Southwest. The mission's service included ceremonial features consistent with most contemporary Fundamentalist Protestant worship services. Some preliminary, piano-accompanied congregational singing was followed by an opening prayer in English. Another set of congregational hymn singing was followed by church announcements, a collection and offertory, and a couple of voice and guitar "specials"[3] by a middle-aged Choctaw man whose country and western–style solos and accent suggested not only the down-home influence of Hank Williams or Bob Wills but also this man's own eastern Oklahoma origins.

Third and fourth sets of congregational hymns bracketed the lay preacher's morning message. The sermon was forty minutes of theological meanderings based loosely on that morning's Bible lesson. Mr. James's homily was liberally spiced with what, after only two months' attendance at Indian church services, had already become familiar admonishments about backsliding, or the lack of Christian commitment and the consequences of an unsaved life.

Billy James is a natural charismatic spiritual leader. His booming baritone, husky good looks, and positive good humor had earned him not only a civil service position in the Los Angeles city bureaucracy but also the unanimous and loving support of his congregation. He laced the usual admonishments of Christian Fundamentalism with pithy Oklahoma localisms and personal stories of deliverance. In his case, the demons were not the usual Indian fates (alcoholism, depression, job failure, urban anomie, or loss of mate) but gambling. With obvious personal satisfaction, he graphically described the depths to which his "affliction" had drawn him and the heights to which his trust in Jesus had "lifted [him] up." Repeatedly, he denied a personal role in his deliverance, stressing that only through faith in Jesus do such miracles occur. It was a message of hope to which most of the men in the congregation could append their own personal histories of demon-wrestling and by which they could measure the strength of their own faith and deliverance.

Mr. James ended his homily with an earnest call to those parishioners who were "troubled and lost" to come to the altar to be "prayed over" and to experience the "embracing arms of the everlasting Lord." The pianist softly accompanied him with arpeggioed choruses of "Just As I Am." Mr. James also entreated the assembled faithful to bow their heads and pray along with him for all the Indian afflicted. Intoning the unfailing generosity of Jesus' love, the inherent danger of Christian backsliding, and the personal joy associated with Christian rebirth, he badgered the congregation for approximately ten minutes before determining that no one would be coming forward that morning for "a healing." Reluctantly, he asked the congregation to sing one last verse of "Just As I Am" before offering the final amen that signals the end of the morning service.

The congregation gathered that morning agreed that the preacher's talk had been a fine one; fine enough, in fact, to have evoked a rededication or two "if the need had been there." However, none of the assembled Christian Indians had felt sufficiently lost to seek salvation through public rededication to the Faith. Parishioners agreed that if Mr. James were to deliver that same talk at the afternoon service or at that summer's week-long camp revival meeting, he would certainly "have them standing in the aisles."[4]

The morning service ended around noon. Ambling out onto the church ground, parishioners talked of family and the about-to-be-relished food. A dozen large, butcher paper–covered picnic tables

Norma Sam (Choctaw), one of the piano-playing Fifth Sunday Sing "regulars."

Geraldine White (Choctaw) and her granddaughter, Melissa Sanchez (Choctaw-Mexican), join the congregation in singing three verses of "Victory in Jesus."

Members of the Brighter Day Indian Mission (Los Angeles), the First Southern Baptist Indian Church (Bell Gardens), and the First Native American and United Methodist Church (Norwalk) sing a "special" in Choctaw.

Song leaders Hanson Wade (*left*) and Ireta Hudson (both Choctaws) encourage the congregation to "make a joyful noise unto the Lord."

A typical Fifth Sunday Sing food line.

Left to right: Ila Dunzweiler (Quechan), Lucy Wilson (Choctaw), and Melba Abrams (Caucasian) were among the cooks at the April 30, 1989, Fifth Sunday Sing hosted by the First Native American and United Methodist Church in Norwalk, California.

graced the lawns immediately adjacent to the cookhouse. People were beginning to queue up in front of two serving tables that groaned from the weight of their savory offerings. The hyperbole with which the Fifth Sunday Sing feast had been described to me was justified. The hot foods table barely accommodated the six or seven different chicken dishes, vats of mustard greens, chili, a half dozen bean, pea, and corn soups, and platters piled high with generous slabs of roast pork, barbecued pork, and ham hocks. The second serving table held the side dishes and sweets: two or three jello, fruit, and vegetable concoctions, green salads, carrot salads, fruit salads, cakes, pies, and peach cobblers.

No Fifth Sunday Sing feast would have been ritually correct without the inclusion of one or more traditional and now ceremonial Southeastern Indian foods. Since the host church membership on this particular Sunday was largely Choctaw and Creek, their ritual participation in the singing included providing a sampling of "their people's food." Sour corn bread, *tash-lubona* (a hominy corn and pork or, less commonly, beef stew), and *banaha* (a cornmeal ball wrapped with corn husks and boiled—the Southeastern Indians' version of the tamale) were prominently placed on the hot foods table and were quickly consumed.

The Southeastern Choctaws and Creeks, for a millennium prior to Western European contact, had thrived on the American Indian horticultural corn-bean-pumpkin triad (Swanton 1931). Originally staples of their diet, this modest fare is as much ceremonial Indian food to these descendants of the Southeastern horticultural culture area as buffalo meat is to the contemporary descendants of the Plains big game–hunting cultural complex, as mutton stew is to the pastoral Navajo, and as fry bread is to pantribal Indian assemblies everywhere.

The women of the mission had been planning this meal for the past three months. After the last Fifth Sunday Sing, when it was decided that their church would host the next singing, the women held several organizational meetings to plan buying, cooking, serving, and cleanup assignments. Food preparation occupied their energies for the week preceding the singing, and the result of this collective effort was impressive. The spread that afternoon was at once formidable, expected, appropriate, and traditional. Eating the foods that are so carefully planned and prepared constitutes a licit revel, for any guilt associated with the consumption of such rich fare is absolved for having done so in the company and praise of one's Christian brothers and sisters.

From noon until about one o'clock, the church ground filled with the cars of Fifth Sunday Sing participants from the other Christian Indian churches in Los Angeles. Having finished their own morning worship services, the guests looked forward to the midday meal and an afternoon of music and communion. They prefaced taking their places on the food line by fifteen or twenty minutes of greetings and friendly exchanges with those already assembled. For many Los Angeles Christian Indians, quarterly Fifth Sunday sings provide their only contact with Indians other than members of their own congregation. Exchanges of personal and community information commanded the better part of the sing's midday feast. Conversations among friends who share both the urban migration experience and ideological orientation were animated, positive, and incorporating.

By 1:00 P.M., the eager buzz of dinner conversation had quieted as feasters, fighting off the midday drowsiness that accompanies such a bounteous meal and precludes late afternoon attention to ritual, strolled about the church ground in groups of two and three. Reluctant to submit themselves to the sweltering afternoon closeness of the church building, they took their time entering the sanctuary. Many lingered in the shade of the cookhouse's lanai, talking of leaky carburetors and annual summer trips "back home to see the folks."

Around 1:30 the cooks (always the last to eat) were finishing up the remains of the lemon pudding cake and peach cobbler, draining the bowl of Hawaiian Punch and the coffee urn of their now-tepid offerings, and comparing notes about how "their spread stacked up" against feasts at other sings. A percussive rendition of "Victory in Jesus"[5] pulsed forth from the sanctuary's most precious ritual object, the vintage upright piano. Percy Bokchito, a perennial favorite from among the several Los Angeles Christian Indians who play a form of gospel piano accompaniment known as Stamps Quartet style,[6] was warming up. His muscle-flexing arpeggios and driving rhythms heralded the formal opening of that spring's sing. By 1:45, well within the limits of both "white man's time"[7] and "Indian time," the interdenominational portion of the Fifth Sunday Sing was about to start in earnest.

The ritual structure of the afternoon communal sing has remained virtually unchanged over the last fifteen years I have attended Fifth Sunday sings. The service opened with the sing master of ceremonies leading the congregation in fifteen or twenty minutes of unabated gospel hymn singing. This was followed by approximately fifteen minutes of specials, with each participating church choir performing a set of hymns as its contribution. Several smaller groups of people who sing together regularly and specialize in three- and four-part harmonization also performed during the first specials segment.

Every sing has a set of tribal language specials. At the first sing I attended, this segment of the ceremony was initiated by the emcee coaxing all Cherokees in the congregation to "come forward" and sing a special in their language. That tribe-specific performance was followed by all the attending Creeks singing a song in their language. The call for all Choctaws to come forward to sing a hymn in their language was met with noisy confusion and knowing laughter, for the Choctaws regularly outnumber the other tribal groups at sings. Broad jokes about "more people at the lectern than in the congregation" and cries of, "Aren't some of you really Cherokees? You can't all be Choctaws," underscored the primacy of Choctaw participation in the perpetuation of the Christian Indian sing tradition in Los Angeles.

At the sing I attended in April 1973, popular Protestant hymns that have been translated into the indigenous languages were offered. "Amazing Grace," for example, was sung in Cherokee, Choctaw, and Creek. Two of the specials consisted of Creek and Choctaw chants whose origins predate early nineteenth-century Christian incursions. In these cases, Christian lyrics had been superimposed on tribal cadences. Most of the specials involved soloists or small groups of singers (purely instrumental solos or large group performances are rare). More often than not, the singers were accompanied by guitar and piano. As I had played the violin in previous church services, I was called forward to give my renditions of "Amazing Grace" and "The Church's One Foundation."

After about an hour and a half of steady congregational singing, interrupted only by an occasional group of specials, the emcee initiated a ceremonial shift by calling for community announcements. Members of the congregation were encouraged to come forward and talk about special upcoming events (revival meetings, the arrival of a popular singing group from back home, bazaars, special memorial services) at their churches. Leaders from secular Indian organizations also came forward to invite people to a public hearing about various Indian health or political issues, an open house at their facility, or to announce the availability of new social services at the Indian Free Clinic. The head cook and her assistants were brought forward during this time and their hard work was acknowledged by the congregation's round of applause and the master of ceremony's teasing asides. This segment of the sing also included an offertory hymn, a collection, and the election of the sponsor of the next Fifth Sunday Sing.

Apparently, there was a time when sing sponsorship was a hotly contested honor. In 1973 and again in 1974, I witnessed congregational votes in order to decide which of two church groups who had assertively pursued the next sing sponsorship would be granted the honor. More recently, however, sing sponsorship is coaxed rather than contested. At the sing I attended in April 1973, the master of ceremonies initiated the election by asking representatives from the various churches to stand and let the congregation know if their group was willing to sponsor the next sing. This invitation was met with obligatory silence, for petitioning churches should not appear too eager to acquire the honor and privilege of sing sponsorship. Indeed, asking to sponsor a sing too frequently is derided as "hogging the limelight" and is said to be done "for all the wrong reasons."

After a moment or two of disquieting demurral, the master of ceremonies began to call the names of the five churches that traditionally sponsor sings in Los Angeles. As each name was called, a representative from that church stood and either offered to sponsor the next sing "if nobody else wants to take it, because somebody's got to do it," or demurred by variously explaining that the group had not really discussed the issue or that it could not make that decision in the absence of a quorum. One church group apparently had already decided not to sponsor the next sing because, when called on, its representative stood and emphatically announced, "We pass." Within ten minutes, all of the churches had been polled and the issue of ritual continuity had been decided. The Brighter Day Indian Mission, the group willing to host the next Fifth Sunday Sing if no one else wanted to, was cajoled into accepting the responsibility for the July 1973 sing.

The singing resumed around four o'clock, even as the congregation—which peaked at about one hundred fifty at three o'clock—began to thin out. (Because of the general flux of people during the day, total attendance figures at this or any sing can only be estimated.) The master of ceremonies again skillfully coordinated periods of general singing, directed by male and female song leaders he called forth from the congregation, and sets of specials. The thirty or forty people still singing when the evening supper was announced at about five o'clock were the perennial core sing leaders and sing die-hards. Some of them continued their informal singing throughout supper and, I was told, until ten o'clock that night. After supper singing is a sure sign that a sing has been a good one and that "the Spirit had really been with us at that singing."

Fifth Sunday Sing Membership

Sings are sponsored by only five of the dozen Indian churches in Los Angeles, but all Indians are welcome to attend, whether or not they are Christians or from Eastern Oklahoman tribal groups. As Gardner (1969) points out, Los Angeles Indian churches are pan-Indian institutions. The Assembly of God congregation in which he made extensive observations, for example, boasted a membership of 250 people representing more than twenty different tribal groups. There are, however, distinct regional and even tribal concentrations within individual Los Angeles Indian churches and particular denominations. These associations are outcomes of nineteenth-century denomination-specific missionary incursions into the culture areas most heavily represented in the contemporary Los Angeles Christian Indian congregations.[8] Even though the Fifth Sunday sings in Los Angeles are pantribal, Choctaw, Creek, Seminole, Cherokee, and Chickasaw Baptists, Presbyterians, and Methodists predominate, in that order.

Sing congregations are almost exclusively Indian, although a few Christian Indians are married to Anglo or Hispanic spouses who accompany them to sings. It is a major happening when Sister Martha, a black lay missionary and occasional member of the Brighter Day Indian Mission congregation, attends a sing. Her no-holds-barred black gospel singing style and occasional lapses into tongues are welcome, if raucous, counterpoints to the afternoon's otherwise low-affect Indian gospel singing style. In general, however, unlike at powwows, non-Indian attendance at sings is not particularly encouraged.

Sings are not for the passive spectator. Their function lies in the inclusive power of group participation and personal identification with the activity. In this respect, sings are rites of intensification for the already incorporated. This is not to say that the occasion for a rite of incorporation or reincorporation is not possible at a sing. Indeed, they are hoped-for events. Most Indians who attend sings are practicing Christians, although an occasional non-Christian or Christian backslider does participate. As with the Old Testament's prodigal son, these people engender considerable congregational interest and attention. A "saving"—that is, a profession of personal commitment or recommitment to the Christian faith—and "giving testimony"—publicly proclaiming one's wrongdoings or travails and God's hand in one's saving or transformation—are rare but validating sing events. According to Cushman (1972[1899]: 102), these "savings are rooted in earliest missionary conversional efforts among the Southeastern Indians."

In 1978 the Native American Ministries (later renamed the First Native American and United Methodist Church), then located in the Pico-Union area, about a mile from the skid row district of Los Angeles, began a missionary outreach to homeless Indians on skid row. Every Sunday morning, three or four of them could be found tentatively fingering Methodist hymnals in the back pews of the Fourteenth Street sanctuary. The regular members of the congregation made heroic efforts to get their afflicted brethren to the sings, and six or so members of the skid row Indian subculture did attend sings with some regularity.

Occasionally, sing visitors from skid row preface their specials with personal testimony about how Jesus is working in their lives to deliver them from temptation.[9] These public announcements of re-birth and rededication to the Christian life are the occasion for moving displays of Christian community. The saved soul is quickly surrounded by an embracing, equally tearful, congratulatory community of well-wishers whose willingness to accept that person so unquestioningly into their fold is not without secondary gain. Each saving constitutes a public demonstration of the congregation's faith and its spiritual power to move others to Christian commitment. For small, insular, self-limiting religious associations, the rare conversion is an affirmation of their own continuing viability and growth as a Christian community. The unsaved guest, non-Christian, or backslider, then, embodies the potential for dramatic, group-intensifying, and often spontaneous rites of incorporation.

People who attend powwows occasionally also attend sings, but they are in the minority. Overwhelmingly, sings are attended by members of the Five Civilized Tribes of eastern Oklahoma, the tribal groups who created the Fifth Sunday Sing and brought it to the urban setting almost without structural alteration. Like pow-wows, sings are family affairs. Everyone, from infants to great-grandparents, is expected to attend church services that day, and the children are expected to attend morning Bible classes. Parents are pleased if their children are interested enough in the congregational ritual to sit through the worship service; however, it is common for children to wander in and out of the sanctuary at will. The church courtyards and lawns are all large enough to accommodate the children's play when they grow tired of the music and the sacred ritual. In fact, it is not unusual to see a ball game in progress on the church ground during the afternoon singing.

All of the host church's members are expected to attend their sings. These people tend to arrive at the church early on the morning of the sing, usually a few minutes before the nine o'clock Sunday school service begins. Depending on their roles in that day's sing, they may remain on the church ground until nine or ten that night. Less-committed members of the host church join the day's activities at will. Members of the other Indian churches in Los Angeles begin to arrive around noon and may stay for only an hour or two, or for as long as there are still people and piano players who want to "raise a joyful noise to our Lord."

Status, Role, and Community Prestige in Sing Participation

Shared sing sponsorship incorporates the several small Los Angeles Indian church congregations into a larger subcultural community. Sponsoring a sing entails providing a facility large enough to hold a hundred or more participants. The sponsoring church should also advertise the event sufficiently to ensure a good turnout. Sing committees are responsible for selecting a qualified master of ceremonies and song leaders. Food committees arrange for the provision of large enough amounts of food to ensure that the huge midday feast can be followed by the traditional post-sing supper around six o'clock in the evening.

Food preparation is the responsibility of the women members of the sponsoring church, a division of labor consistent with early social forms (Swanton 1931:139). "Head cook" is an important, high-ranking status, and women interested in establishing themselves as church elders lobby for the privilege of executing the duties of a sing head cook. Upon her selection, the head cook chooses the assistant cooks and cleanup squad. The head cook and her assistants are responsible for cooking the large meat dishes that, consistent with contemporary Southeastern Indian culinary traditions, are usually made from chicken and pork. Sometimes, when the sponsoring church's budget can withstand the extra cost or the head cook decrees it, an entire pig is roasted for the occasion.

All female members of the sponsoring church, whether or not they have been recruited to kitchen or sing duty, are counted on to bring a covered dish to supplement the food that is officially provided. Regular sing participants from other churches also exhibit good form by bringing a food item for the feast. Guests who are unfamiliar with sing etiquette are not expected to contribute to the communal potluck meal. Rather, they should assume the role of appreciative recipient of the host church's largesse. Finally, because the cookhouse is a strictly female domain, men are not involved in the preparation of food, only in its consumption.

Conversation on the food line frequently entails determining the creators of specific dishes. Certain women are renowned for their preparation of particular Indian ceremonial food, and their dishes are admired almost to the point of having their own ceremonial import. It is a Los Angeles Christian Indian church tradition to have Sara Williams, a tiny, ancient sparrow of a Choctaw woman, provide the sing's *banaha*. Alice Homans, a Creek woman who was in her eighties when she finally left Los Angeles to return home to Creek Territory in Oklahoma, was equally encouraged to make a batch of her sour corn bread for the sings she attended. Anna Monroe's mustard greens are particularly prized for their tanginess, while one can always expect Rosie Miller's *walakshi*, a sweet grape pudding and dumpling concoction, to be whipped to syrupy perfection. Familiar, traditional foods, the continued participation of the person with whom the food is associated in community life, and one's ingestion of the ceremonial dish become ritual exchange, a symbolic act of ethnic and spiritual unity.

To underscore the ritual importance of the sing feast, Indian church cookhouses usually include a larder, a well-outfitted kitchen, and a supply of eating utensils, dinner plates, and serving ware. Great soup vats, roasting pans, mixing bowls, carving utensils, and meat platters are as much a part of the Christian Indian church material culture as are offertory plates and hymnals. The degree to which the sponsoring church provides a conspicuous surplus of food is an indication of its commitment to sustaining the Fifth Sunday Sing tradition, its viability as a functioning institution in the Christian Indian church subculture, and its adherence to the Christian Indian tenets of generosity, good will toward all, and inclusiveness.

The sing program provides participants with a number of additional highly ranked community statuses and roles to which they may aspire. As in the powwow, "master of ceremonies" is the most prestigious sing status, and there are other parallels as well. The sing master of ceremonies is usually an older, high-ranking male member of the host church; however, high-ranking female host church members, particularly Choctaw women, assume this status on occasion. Verbal and organizational skills, an ability to lead and command authority, knowledge of sing ritual structure, familiarity with the song favorites, and humor are qualities the sponsoring churches seek in their masters of ceremonies.

Sing emcees should be skilled orators who are comfortable speaking to as many as one hundred sing participants. The afternoon announcement period is usually prefaced by the master of ceremonies's welcoming speech, and oratorical skills are crucial to this segment of the ceremony. These expected talks often take the form of discursive, reflexive, and essentially personal statements about the importance of continuing the sing tradition, admonishments about Christian backsliding and forgetting "who we are," and personal testimony about "what singings mean to me." Congregations kindly, if bemusedly, endure the more rambling discourses of unskilled talkers. Occasionally, emcees publicly admit their oratorical limitations by inviting more proficient speakers in the congregation to "come up and give us a few good words." The skilled talker can, with homely humor, personal asides, and heartfelt verbiage, make the welcoming speech meaningful ethnic allegory, as illustrated by this speech, delivered on October 31, 1976, at the Brighter Day Indian Mission by Buck Jones, a fifty-four-year-old Choctaw man:

We hope to create more interest of more people who are interested in trying to hold their culture of their people, of their children of the younger generation, and to better communicate with our fellow men in this particular thing. I think that this is beautiful. That we are all aware of the fact that on the other side of town that we have many different types of people that are doing their thing. Well, you can say that we are more or less doing our thing here today. The Mexican type of people have their church, their singing, their communication, their talking, their language. The Italian people have theirs, the German people have theirs, the French people have theirs, and so forth. And this is one beautiful thing that we are aware of today—that we type of people have our communication, our association right here.

A lot of us are aware of the fact that we have had a Choctaw class going in the process of teaching the Choctaw language, the culture, to keep the interest in our younger generation. Now may I say this openly, that I like to believe it is a true fact that most of your younger children are just like us. That when we get out on the job, we have to do what these people do. We have to pick up their ways in order to make it easier for ourselves. When our children go to school, they associate with the majority—colored people, white people, Mexican people. If there's any other language (like there's an awful lot of Mexican talk in the state of California), they automatically grab this—which is good—in order to comprehend something else. Although we don't want them to lose our own culture.

So I'd like to express my feeling about—I know that we have a tight schedule in life in order to keep our nose above the water today; I know that we all have got our movement in our everyday pattern of living—but I hope that we might keep in our minds that somewhere along the way that we might allow ourselves to not forget our culture. To hang on to what we have and to be proud that we have this thing, that we are able to hang onto it and to put forth a little bit of effort in order to come to these things and to associate and let our children know that we are interested in hanging on to what we had.

Chosen from the congregation because he "always has a lot to say," this keen observer of social process spoke eloquently to the sociocultural significance of that afternoon of singing. His understanding of the power of expressive culture in sustaining a valued ethnic identity was abundantly clear to the approximately sixty members of the Los Angeles Christian Indian community still assembled in the sanctuary of the Brighter Day Indian Mission. Caught up by his thoughts about culture conservation, Mr. Jones quickly diverged into philosophical discourse on the importance of indigenous language, ritual association, and enculturation of the younger generations into such ethnic activities as the maintenance of ethnic group. Nodding to each other, the congregation agreed that it had been a good talk. He, indeed, had had "a lot to say."

The master of ceremonies at a Fifth Sunday Sing is also responsible for contacting and encouraging well-known musicians in the Indian church community to attend the next sing and be prepared to perform one or more specials. Organization of the afternoon congregational singing and the specials performance schedule, and the enlistment of song and prayer leaders as ritual assistants, are other functions of the sing emcee.

Song leaders are usually core members, both men and women, of the various churches represented at the sing. Song leader selection criteria include longtime, highly active participation in one's church, group recognition of one's good singing voice, and group song leadership abilities. Song leaders choose the next set of three or four gospel songs to be sung by the congregation from the several hymnals on hand; announce which of the several printed verses will be sung and who in the congregation is to sing them; choose the accompanist from among the half dozen or so pianists in the congregation; and, from the front of the sanctuary, goad and admonish the congregation into communal song.

A good emcee will try to have enough specials lined up ahead of time to ensure no lulls in the day's program. However, who gets to perform specials is often serendipitous. Friends and family groups who sing together may be visiting sing participants, and their unexpected presence is reason enough to coax them forward to show "how they do their singing back home" in Oklahoma or Arizona. A favorite, multilingual, itinerant lay preacher and former Los Angeles resident may appear and be prepared to lead the Cherokee-, Choctaw-, and Creek-speaking segments of the congregation in some hymns, chants, or prayers in their own languages. Local family groups scheduled for a particular slot in the afternoon's events may, for sundry reasons, not show up and extemporaneous groups are quickly formed to fill the ceremonial void.

Importantly, the skilled sing emcee attempts to give everyone who wishes to contribute to the afternoon's activities a chance to do so. Some performances are polished, familiar, and eagerly anticipated; others are painfully unrehearsed and sorely executed. Aesthetic excellence is not at issue in sings; rather, most performances go equally applauded regardless of their relative aesthetic quality. The value of a special is in that person's or group's willingness to perform. It is the act of performing that is emblematic of the individual's continuing inclusion in and contribution to the ethnic group's collective good.

The seasoned master of ceremonies is sensitive to the mood of the congregation. Specials segments should not go on indefinitely. Sing regulars are quick to criticize both the emcee and the sing itself if specials predominate, with condemnations such as, "That's not how singings used to be" and "I came here to sing, not to listen. I could do that at home watching TV. I don't have to come all the way out here to do that." Such comments suggest the participatory rather than passive, observatory, and performance nature of a good Fifth Sunday Sing. The Christian Indians are there, after all, to contribute to and experience the bonding and incorporative power of a community voice raised in song.

Fifth Sunday Sings as the Context of Indian Community Continuities

Curiously, sings are not particularly sacred or religious events. Although all of the music pieces are hymns, the lyrics of which are filled with appeals for God's help, mercy, and forgiveness, or His promise of a better, safer, happier afterlife, the general mood of sings is more social than solemn, more self-fulfilling than penitent, more interactive than contemplative. There are always several points in the sing at which the officiating or an occasional visiting minister or lay preacher will be asked to pray over the food, bless the offering, lead the congregation in prayer for afflicted loved ones, call forth the newly saved, and offer the benediction. The attending spiritual leaders may, in fact, be asked to come forward during the announcement period to say a few words to the group—invitations that sometimes prompt short homilies.

People who perform specials often preface them with short personal testimonies or explanations as to why the hymn they are about to sing is so special to them. Public announcement of an earlier saving or current personal crisis is often followed by an appeal for the congregation's prayers for the singer and his or her family. At times the officiating ministers or lay preachers may be asked to pray for a healing. These appeals and the self-announced savings are the most solemn and religious events in a sing. They are, however, peripheral to the sing's ritual intent, which is clearly not religious instruction but the celebratory, almost Dionysian release that accompanies making a communal "joyful noise unto the Lord." The main and enduring appeal of Fifth Sunday sings to the people who attend them season after season is the opportunity they provide for a day of unadulterated fellowship.

Gardner (1969:14) argues that the Los Angeles Christian Indian church subculture represents cultural and behavioral changes in response to the novel urban environment. Pan-Indian churches, he suggests, "offer the American Indian an urban substitute for the close-knit supportive structure of the reservation environment" (1969:24). His point of reference is the large, urban-born, syncretic, and highly successful Indian Revival Center. Gardner's position, though well taken with regard to his case study, is narrowly focused. Rather than being substitutes for familiar social structures, Los Angeles Christian Indian churches with large Eastern Oklahoman memberships are re-creations of traditional social forms in the urban setting. In these congregations, the emphasis is on cultural continuity and maintenance of valued social forms, not innovation.

Cultural continuity is maintained in Los Angeles Christian Indian churches through the re-creation of familiar and valued architectural, behavioral, ideational, and expressive cultural forms in novel environments. Figure 9.1 provides the physical plan of the First Southern Baptist Indian Mission on Clara Street in Bell Gardens, one of four Los Angeles Indian churches in which the congregations are largely from eastern Oklahoma. Two of the other three

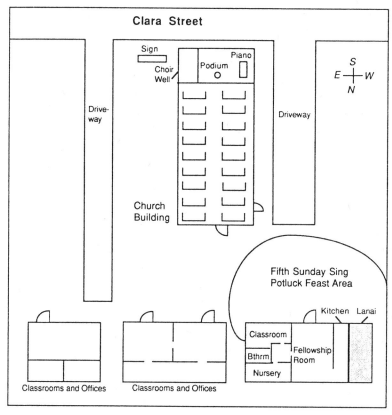

Figure 9.1 First Southern Baptist Indian Mission, Clara Street, Bell Gardens, California

churches, the Brighter Day Indian Mission in south Los Angeles and the First Baptist Indian Church in South Gate, have remarkably similar physical plans.

Even the Muskogee Mission, a tiny and predominantly Creek splinter group in the city of Bell, attempted with its slender resources to transcend its meeting room architectural limitations. Its parishioners deliberately transformed their archetypal urban storefront church (a rented twenty by forty feet of commercial space) into a microcosm of Christian Indian ceremonial space. An area measuring approximately fifty square feet at the back of the store is partitioned and outfitted as a kitchen. The rest of the space can quickly be transformed from a place of worship, complete with the ubiquitous upright piano, lectern, and stack of hymnals, to a place of communal dining.

The Muskogean church ground plan consists of a church building, a cookhouse, outbuildings for use either as classrooms for Bible instruction or emergency living space for members of the congregation, and a large, open area in which feasts and games can be held. In 1984 and 1985, I had the occasion to recontact several Creek and Choctaw former members of the Los Angeles Eastern Oklahoman churches who had, in the intervening years, returned to their Oklahoma hometowns. I accompanied these friends on their weekly rounds of church sings, eventually visiting fifteen Eastern Oklahoman church grounds. Whether in Bethel, Rocky Hill, Broken Bow, Wewoka, Jesse, or Antlers, Oklahoma, I was struck by the similarity of the grounds' physical configurations; indeed, they were virtually carbon copies of each other. A comparison of figures 9.1 and 9.2 underscores the parallel between the rural Oklahoma church ground design and that of the Eastern Oklahoman churches in Los Angeles. The configurations of the church grounds in Los Angeles represent a cultural continuity of at least one hundred fifty years.[10]

Early ethnographic reports suggest that the historical roots of such continuities in Southeast Indian ceremonial space may in fact antedate the introduction of the Christian mission campground complex in 1817 (McKee and Schlenker 1980:54). Swanton (1931: 221), relying on early French accounts of pre-Christian Southeastern Indian settlements, states that "every Choctaw town of any size had an open place or square with cabins about it constructed like those in the Creek towns." Spoehr (1968[1947]: 211) argues for the superimposition of the nineteenth-century Christian church community configuration on preexisting parallel village forms:

> Among the Creeks, Cherokee, and Choctaw, the Christianization of the Indians resulted in the formation of a new local unit—the church community—that exists today in similar form in all three tribes. The Creek church has either superseded the old ceremonial square ground or exists side by side with it, the two being separated by only a mile or two. The important thing is that the town organization has tended to hang on; its ceremonial center is simply changing from the square ground to the church. The same thing holds true of the Cherokee and Choctaw. Among these two tribes the old town organization has gone. Its place has been partly taken by the church community, the only local grouping that is essentially Indian outside of the household. Each church community consists of a dozen or two families living within two or three miles of a church house. Although all the mem-

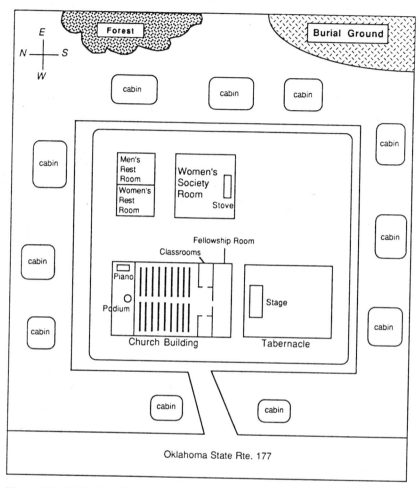

Figure 9.2 Kullichito (Big Well) Presbyterian Church, Bethel, Oklahoma

bers of the church community may not be regular church goers, they are still considered members of the community, if for no other reason than that they will be buried in the church cemetery. It is the cemetery, as much as the church house, that expresses the unity of the group.

Spoehr is adamant about the absence of clan or kin structures in the social organization of the Christian Indian church communities. He notes: "There is one difference, however, well worth emphasizing. It is that in the church organization the clan and kinship play no important role, or at most only an incidental one" (1968[1947]: 211). He attributes the absence of clan as an organizing principle in the church community to the introduction of Christianity among the Choctaw, saying, "The decline in the social importance of the clan in Oklahoma is related to the dispersion of its principal functions to other groups. . . . The ceremonial functions of the clan have disappeared, as native religion and ceremony gave way before mission teaching and the establishment of Indians churches" (1968[1947]: 209).

There is, however, intriguing ethnolinguistic evidence to the contrary. The Choctaw term *iksa*, which historically has meant "moiety" or "clan," is said to have been used interchangeably in reference to clan, territorial group, and church sect (Swanton 1931:78). The multiple referents of *iksa* suggest either semantic drift or historical sociostructural syncretism and encryption. It is possible that the meaning or semantic content of *iksa* has shifted and expanded over time, its semantic range perhaps eventually including all three concepts under the larger, more generic semantic category "residential group." More likely, however, the multiple definitions of the term represent the continuing existence of older and now-encrypted indigenous sociostructural forms. Original clan structures may, in fact, underlie the church community organization. Masked by an overlay of Christian church congregational structure recognized by and acceptable to the missionaries who worked to bring the Choctaws into the Christian fold, the older social structure of the clan towns may thereby have been preserved.

Although most ethnohistorians suggest that the *iksa*, or clan system, was on its way to extinction by the time the Choctaw were removed to Oklahoma in 1830, Debo (1961[1934]: 76) contends that older group loyalties often persisted into the twentieth century. Thompson and Peterson (1975:188) lend further support to Debo's findings: "Choctaw communities today, and to an even greater extent in the past, are not just locality groups, but to a large extent also kin groups."

Eastern Oklahoman Christian community life today is as synonymous with Muskogean ethnic identity as are family and locational group loyalties. Friends of mine who had returned to Oklahoma after twenty or more years in Los Angeles travel thirty or forty miles from their in-town homes to their home churches for singings, even though another church of their denomination may be within a few minutes of their current residences. The explanation for their willingness to drive such distances is typified by the statement of Rachael Battiest, a fifty-six-year-old Choctaw woman I visited in Broken Bow, Oklahoma, in August 1985: "All my kin go to the home church. I just feel more comfortable worshiping there." Clan structure may still exist and, in fact, dictate Eastern Oklahoman home church membership and attendance. Clearly, more systematic genealogical documentation is called for in order to substantiate this supposition.

The pre-Christian village configuration and importance of kinship as a principle of social organization are not the only indigenous culture traits to have survived and, indeed, to have been perpetuated by Christian Indian church community membership. The communal feast and ceremonial foods that mark the midway point in any sing were equally imperative features of pre-Christian Choctaw ceremonial life. According to Swanton (1931:221), "What they lacked in ceremonialism they seem to have made up for in social dances and feasts. . . . Our principal French authority states that they held most of the feasts when the corn was green . . . or at harvest festivals lasting five days."

A Christian mission to the Choctaws was established in 1818 (Debo 1961[1934]: 42). In the first decades of Christian missionary work among the Choctaw, the occasion of a visit by an itinerant New England preacher prompted Choctaw feasting that in several respects parallels features of the contemporary sing feast. Henry C. Benson, A.M., recounts in *Life among the Choctaw Indians* (1970[1860]: 126):[11]

> Our accommodations during the progress of the meeting were not luxurious, but plain and substantial. There had been no great temptation to an excessive indulgence of the appetite; the food, however, was abundant and healthful, consisting principally of boiled beef and yams, corn bread, coffee, and the never-failing *tom-ful-la*.[12] It was all prepared by the Indian women, or their colored servants, and served out in bountiful quantities and in a style of primitive simplicity.

Group singing is another aspect of the Choctaw's indigenous culture perpetuated yet transformed by the Christian sing phenomenon. Cushman (1972[1899]: 108) states: "Many of the ancient Choctaws were adepts in the art of singing their native airs, of which they had many." Swanton (1931:221–23), relying on eighteenth-century French accounts of pre-Christian Muskogean ritual, observes:

> Some of [the Creeks'] most favourite songs and dances, they have from their enemies, the Chactaws; for it seems these people are very eminent for poetry and music. . . .

The ancient Choctaws were as susceptible to all the pleasing emotions produced by the sweet concords of sound as any other people. . . .

Yet the ancient Choctaw, in all his solemn ceremonies, as well as amusements and merry-makings, did not depend so much upon the jarring tones of the diminutive drum as he did upon his own voice; which in concert with the monotonous tones of the drum, to the cultivated and sensitive ear a mere jargon of sound—was to the Indian ear the most exciting music, and soon wrought him to the highest state of excitement.

Even the Choctaw language was to have its salvation in and perpetuation through service to the Lord. One of the first priorities of the Choctaw Indian missionaries was the establishment of literacy among their parishioners (Debo 1962[1934]: 62). Within ten years of the arrival of the first missionary among the Choctaw, the Bible and a hymnal had been translated into Choctaw and printed for public use (Peterson 1979:147). These were widely and enthusiastically studied and used in congregational singings. By the 1830s, when Benson (1970[1860]: 40–41) preached among the Choctaw, he could report: "When adults have been converted and received into the Church, they have been urged to study the alphabet and learn to read in their own language; and I do not remember one native Christian man who was not able to read the Choctaw Testament." Today, the Choctaw Bible and hymnal are the only exposure most urban Choctaw have to written Choctaw literature and language. The Choctaw class members to which sing speaker Buck Jones alluded earlier used these examples of written Choctaw in their attempts to recapture their tribal language.

There is perhaps no clearer parallel between pre-Christian and contemporary Choctaw social forms than in the comparison of eighteenth-century indigenous ceremonial roles of bandleaders and speakers at feasts and the masters of ceremonies and speakers at Fifth Sunday sings.

The band captain now called out the name of each family in turn and the members of it then marched up to the table and seated themselves. . . . While they were eating they preserved perfect order and the captains addressed them all that time. . . . After all had had enough, the head chief would call them to order again and make a speech in which he recounted the facts regarding their race and told them what they ought to do and what they should refrain from doing. (Swanton 1931:225)

Several indigenous pre-Christian Southeastern Indian ceremonial forms, statuses, and roles survive and are perpetuated by the contemporary Christian Indian church community and, particularly, by their sing ceremonies. Given the zeal with which the Christian missionaries fought to abolish dancing, "heathen" ceremonial practices, matrilineal descent structures, and women's roles in the communal gardens (Spoehr 1968[1947]: 209), it is no wonder that the valued sacred ritual and vital sociostructural elements that delineated and sustained the Choctaw awareness of themselves as a corporate people went underground. Old social and ritual forms were masked by a thin veneer of Christian community structure and ceremonialism. Christian Indian church members practiced a semblance of correct Christian church behavior and embraced a certain, though superficial, amount of Christian iconography.

The underlying social and processual structures of the contemporary sing and the church grounds continue to reflect an earlier, tenacious, and still-operant indigenous community form and ceremonial structure. The sing and the church ground configuration are two aspects of ceremonial and organizational tradition that traveled with the Muskogeans on their 1830 trek to Oklahoma as well as to Los Angeles 125 years later. The persistent and essentially conservative nature of the underlying earlier social forms, as well as the sociostructural model of ideal Muskogean community, is illustrated by these phenomena. Fifth Sunday sings, the physical configuration of the church grounds, and the tribe-specific character of congregation membership provide a microcosmic model for and nexus of contemporary Christian Indian community, whether in Bethel, Oklahoma, or Bell Gardens, California.

NOTES

1. A longtime member of this congregation informed me that the mission became the First Southern Baptist Indian Church in 1975. Since this chapter describes an event that occurred in 1973, I have chosen to refer to the congregation by its original name.

2. The incorporated cities of Bell, Bell Gardens, and Cudahy used to house the slaughterhouses and feeding yards of the Cudahy Meat Packing Corporation. The oversized city blocks that still exist in these subsequently incorporated municipalities reflect their former use as fattening pens.

3. A special is a performance by a soloist, an instrumental group, or an entire church choir for the benefit of the assembled congregation. Specials

are distinguished from congregational singing by their performance quality. They make audiences of congregations, while singings ensure the participation of the entire congregation for ritual completeness. Sing emcees attempt to keep specials to a minimum as the incorporative function of sings is mitigated if individual recognition overshadows the integrative effect of congregational singing.

4. I overheard the comments quoted here as I walked out of the morning services and during the lunch break. I recorded them in my field notes, but because I had so recently become acquainted with the community, I could not at that time identify the speakers.

5. "Victory in Jesus" is one of fifty or more favorite gospel hymns included in the several Protestant interdenominational hymnals that the Christian Indians use in their church services. Most of the hymns and hymnals are used across ethnic and racial congregations throughout the South. No sing is ritually complete without a congregational rendition of these favorites.

6. The Stamps Quartet was a gospel singing group well known throughout the South since the 1930s for their up-beat, four-part harmonizations of Southern gospel hymn favorites. Their fame was succeeded and sustained by several published collections of their gospel hymn arrangements. The Stamps-Baxter Publishing Company in Dallas, Texas, also published a number of instruction books for pianists wishing to develop the Stamps piano style. Although many Southeastern Indians learned to play gospel hymns "by ear," some received piano lessons while attending Christian boarding schools. The Stamps Quartet hymnals and teaching courses were often the pedagogical mainstays of such instruction. These attempts to bring Christian culture to American Indian children have had the effect of providing a much-valued skill and role that have been incorporated into sacred and secular ritual. Christian Indians now assume gospel piano playing as an Indian activity.

7. The concepts "white man's time" and "Indian time" are pantribal and, among non-Indians who have had dealings with American Indians, probably panethnic. The terms allude to the relative weight that whites place on punctuality, particularly in work situations, and ritual performance. "Indian time" refers to the propensity with which Indians ignore advertised office hours or starting times of ritual events. Indians are said to prefer to "let things happen when they are ready to happen" and to "go with the flow." Deviations from the formal schedule can be anywhere from a half hour to four hours, depending on the particular situational and logistical difficulties attached to any given event.

8. The Los Angeles Indian chapter of the Church of the Latter-day Saints, for example, is composed largely of Navajos and Hopis. Originating from Salt Lake City, Utah, Mormon missionaries saw proselytizing their Indian neighbors as their sacred and Scripture-mandated mission. The Navajo and Hopi to the south were among the first American Indians targeted for inclusion in the Mormon fold. Similarly, Episcopal, Methodist, Presbyterian, and

Baptist missionaries were the most active religious forces among the South-eastern Indian communities. The core memberships of the two Indian Baptist churches in Los Angeles are predominantly from the Five Civilized Tribes of eastern Oklahoma.

9. Aside from committed membership in Alcoholics Anonymous, conversion and personal commitment to and participation in a religious community has proved to be one of the most successful substitutes for alcohol and drug addiction among American Indians in Los Angeles (Weibel-Orlando 1984).

10. When the Creeks and Choctaws were removed from their ancestral lands in Mississippi and Georgia in the 1820s and 1830s, the Baptist, Methodist, and Presbyterian missionaries who had been working among them since 1817 accompanied them to their new homes in Oklahoma Indian Territory (Berkhofer 1972:105). Church campgrounds were among the earliest settlement patterns in the new Creek and Choctaw territories (Cushman 1972[1899]: 412).

11. Written in 1860, Benson's *Life among the Choctaw Indians* chronicles his missionary work with the Choctaws during the 1830s and 1840s.

12. *Tom-fu-la* is a variant of *tash-lubona*, or hominy corn stew.

10

The Los Angeles City-County Native American Indian Commission: Political Forum at the Ethnic Frontier

> The Indian Commission has developed a close-knit spirit of coordination and cooperation with many of the major Indian services agencies in Los Angeles County. The Commission works closely with these agencies in planning and developing programs, services, activities, and events and serves as an effective liaison between the Los Angeles Indian community, elected officials, and government agencies for the benefit of the Indian community. (LACCNAIC 1987b:2–3)

IN 1986 THE Los Angeles City-County Native American Indian Commission (LACCNAIC), or the Indian Commission, as it is more commonly known among active Los Angeles Indian community members, celebrated its first decade of service to its constituents. In a full-page *Talking Leaf* article, the multipurpose institution was hailed as having initiated "a new era of self-determination for urban Indians" (Pierce 1985:6).

The concept of an Indian commission was developed in the early 1970s by a consortium of Los Angeles Indian self-help project directors.[1] Commission advocates argued that "the absence of an Indian governmental entity in urban areas as well as lack of urban Indian input into the legislation, rules, and regulations governing the allocation of funds and services had dramatically diminished the availability and accessibility of these resources to urban Indians." Further, an Indian commission was needed because "many local government jurisdictions misunderstand the special relationship between the federal government and Indian people and erroneously assume that all of the Indian needs will be provided for by federal government resources [which thereby] leads to Indian people being deprived of funds and services available to all disadvantaged citizens" (LACCNAIC 1981:4). By 1976, through active promotion of the idea at the mayoral and county supervisory levels, Indian commission advocates were able to convince city and county officials of the necessity of their proposed political innovation.

A joint city-county effort initiated in May 1976 and adopted as Ordinance 11409 of the Administrative Code of the County of Los Angeles on September 7, 1976, created the legal framework for the LACCNAIC. Effective October 8, 1976, the ordinance provides Indians in Los Angeles a uniquely legislated sociopolitical position and negotiatory mechanism vis-à-vis the city and county governments. The Indian Commission is the first of its kind, representing official recognition of an urban Indian community by local governments (Pierce 1985:6). No other ethnic group in Los Angeles has had similar recognition or political status.

The charter by which the LACCNAIC was initiated and under which it still operates includes guidelines for the development of recruitment criteria, organizational parameters, membership selection mechanisms, and executive staffing. The commission has fifteen members, all of whom serve three-year terms. Five commissioners are appointed through a review system executed by staff in the Los Angeles mayor's office. Each supervisor from Los Angeles County's five supervisory districts also appoints a qualified district member to the commission. The five remaining seats are filled through Indian communitywide elections.

The process of seating the LACCNAIC's ten appointed commissioners was initiated in October 1976 and carried to completion during the next four months. This ten-member commission convened for the first time in February 1977. The first task of the new commissioners was to administer the election of the five community representatives. Five voting districts were established and polling sites were assigned. The task of administering the first popular election of commissioners was contracted to the United American Indian Council (UAIC), a nonprofit private corporation established in the early 1970s for the development of Indian-run service programs and research projects.

The first community election of Indian commissioners was held in May 1977, and the complete fifteen-member commission panel sat for the first time the following month. It was a historic occasion. Charged to "improve and expand program services to enhance the socioeconomic well-being of Indian citizens of the City and County of Los Angeles and to increase Indian participation in all aspects of community life" (LACCNAIC 1987b:i), the commission spent the next year defining its status and roles vis-à-vis the community it was mandated to represent.

The Indian Commission, in its first annual report, describes itself as having taken "an initial step in the development of a participative government in which Indian people can have an impact on decisions and programs which affect their lives." The commission goes on to assert that "Indians [in Los Angeles] now have the opportunity to identify their own circumstances and aspirations and to develop plans and programs which will address the problems and needs of Indians living in the Los Angeles urban environment" (LACCNAIC 1981:5).

Commission Membership

Although there is no formal statement about Indian ancestry as a requisite for appointment to the commission by the mayoral and county supervisory offices, the informal and tacit rule is that people interested in membership should be recognizably Indian. In fact, since 1978 only two acknowledged non-Indians have ever sat on the commission. They earned their appointments to the LACCNAIC through their singular contributions to the Indian community as recognized by the city and/or county officials who appointed them. Because Indian Commission appointments are made by city and county government officials, strict rules of nondiscrimination must be followed. However, the popular election of the five community representatives on the commission is not governed by the same strictures. Community-elected commissioners must be able to prove that they are at least one-quarter American Indian, members of a recognized tribal group, and residents of the district they represent.

During the first election, the UAIC facilitators developed an Indian population-by-area formula that divided Los Angeles County into five geographical units with approximately equal numbers of Indian residents. Candidates ran for office in the districts in which they resided. Only residents of a district could vote for that area's representative.

Election to the Indian Commission is perhaps the highest community honor an Indian can achieve in Los Angeles. The recruitment criteria include active participation in Indian community public life, acknowledged support and understanding of Indian cultural activities and causes, and enough of a following to ensure a majority of votes in one's district. People who run for the commission are usually well-known core participants in Indian community life. A typical commission member's career includes a decade or more of employment or volunteerism within the network of Los Angeles Indian social services programs. So it is that a recent commission panel included the president of a highly successful, Indian-run entrepreneurial advisory corporation, the editor of *Talking Leaf*, a University of California at Los Angeles student counselor, the acting director of the Job Training Partnership Act program, the president of the Los Angeles Indian Council on Aging, and the pastor of one of the largest Indian Christian churches in Los Angeles.

There have been delightful and telling exceptions to an insistence on high community prestige and respectability as prerequisites of commission membership. Chester Big Hand (Cheyenne), one of the most colorful characters of the Los Angeles Indian community, was one such exception. His credentials for a seat on the commission included his wide reputation in the powwow subcommunity as a clown dancer. His appearance at a Saturday night powwow in his bedraggled, homemade caricature of a fancy dance outfit was a welcome event. I encountered Chester Big Hand for the first time in 1973. By that time his fancy dance bustle, emblazoned with his self-appointed, penciled, misspelled title "CHEIF," had already lost most of its turkey feathers to the ravages of his vagabond life. His dance style could be characterized as *commedia buffa alla Cheyenne*. In operatically overdrawn gestures, he flirted outrageously with all the women and invited the prettiest girls to dance. His antics evoked shrieks of embarrassed laughter from his comely and unsuspecting victims and guffaws of approval from their amused dates.

Chester Big Hand perpetuated a clowning tradition that has roots in the old men's and women's participation in the Cheyenne scalp dance and the Contrary Dancers' eccentricities in the Cheyenne *massaum* ceremony (Grinnell 1972:329; Hoebel 1978:24). The quintessential marginal, Chester Big Hand was rewarded by his community for making a career of publicly doing the undoable. Through ribald ritual, he regularly, and at the behest of his coethnics, turned structure into antistructure, thereby underscoring the continuing saliency of the established order.

Aside from getting out the vote of the powwow people, Chester Big Hand credited his election to the Indian Commission to his large and highly supportive skid row Indian constituency.[2] His wanderlust, which set in early in his youth, eventually brought him to Los Angeles. From 1968 until his untimely death in 1981, he lived by his wits on the city streets, successfully exploiting the subsistence possibilities of downtown Los Angeles's seediest streets, back alleys, flophouses, missions, and the Winston Street sanctuary of the United American Indian Involvement (UAII). His inner city street life-style was interrupted only by occasional, short recuperative respites in the homes of relatives, friends, and various substance abuse treatment centers in southern California. The self-proclaimed "mayor of Indian skid row," he also, and with wickedly disarming and self-deprecating humor, admitted to being a "serious drinker" and a "wino."

On several occasions, Chester Big Hand explained to me that even though he was, at times, unable to make it to commission meetings, the other commission members had steadfastly refused to accept his resignation.

> I tried to resign [from the commission] but they wouldn't let me. "Your people need you as their representative on the commission," they said. "You have a duty to speak for the people who can't speak for themselves. Your people voted you onto the commission for a reason. They are the people that most need our help. And you are the one person they trust to really know what their problems are and to be unafraid to speak up for them to the commission." (September 15, 1979)

The LACCNAIC's executive director assured me that, although Chester Big Hand's self-aggrandizing rendition of this group's concerns may have been tinged with hyperbole, it largely represented the sentiments of the commission at the time: "To tell you the truth, I don't think anybody thought he had a chance. [We thought,] 'Well, knowing him, he's just fooling around.' But he knew all the people down at UAII, one of our voting sites. He got a very high turnout and he had his powwow friends. He got out and got the vote. He was a politician" (Bill Fredricks, November 30, 1988).

Chester Big Hand did have certain claims to respectability within the Indian community, the most obvious being that he was a full-blood Cheyenne. He was not only a descendant of one of the most prestigious families in American Indian history[3] but also spoke his tribal language. He knew all the powwow songs, including the

"49ers."[4] He performed his clown dances to perfection and for the delighted amusement of pantribal and panethnic audiences. He was a much-loved figure whose constituency crosscut several segments of the Indian community.

Chester Big Hand had won the hearts and votes of his skid row constituency because he could be expected to share with them his bottle and his hard-won panhandling earnings. When challenged, he could also be counted on to back up his "bros" with his considerable physical bulk and boxing acumen—an important factor considering the number of street fights that broke out with regularity among the various skid row factions. Because he spoke with authority for a constituency with whom most Indian Commission members felt great sympathy, his inclusion on the LACCNAIC was assured. Indeed, it superseded any concerns about continuing to seat a commissioner who, when he remembered the monthly meeting time and place, could not be depended on to be sober when he arrived to take his place at the council table.

The skid row constituency that voted Chester Big Hand onto the commission was a desperately needy if numerically small segment of the Los Angeles Indian population. The other Indian commissioners at the time realized his considerable and intimate knowledge of the issues confronting the downtown Indian subculture and his general acceptance by that population as their spokesperson. He was a critical link for the dissemination of information from the downtown frontline human services organizations to the commission and from the commission to those agencies charged with the provision of services to the inner-city population. Chester Big Hand retained his seat on the Indian Commission for almost a full three-year term. His career as a commissioner underscores a general tendency within Indian communities for tolerance, willingness to include the cultural marginal in community activities, and culture-specific ranking and recruitment criteria.

Commission Statuses and Roles

The LACCNAIC's official hierarchy includes a chairperson, vice chairperson, recording secretary, and treasurer. These positions are filled by yearly internal, often hotly contested elections. It is the chairperson's prerogative to form standing and ad hoc committees as issues are raised and monitoring of their resolution by the commission is felt necessary. The committees usually have no more than three members and include seated commissioners as well as other Indian community members and non-Indians with expertise in the area of concern. Care is taken to avoid conflicts of interest between individual commissioners and the issue, program, or proposed project under review. A commissioner who is also an employee of the Indian Centers, Inc., for example, would defer membership on any committee formed to oversee the administration of an ICI project.

From its initiation, the Indian Commission was budgeted for an administrative staff of two full-time employees—an executive assistant to the commission (since 1981 an executive director) and a supporting administrative/secretarial assistant. In 1977 when the executive assistant position was announced, it was the first county-funded position of its kind. As such, it served as a model for all future, pivotal administrative positions designed to facilitate the flow of information and services between the Indian community and the various government agencies with which Indian program directors and petitioning Indian individuals must interact. The political and economic possibilities of the Indian Commission's executive assistantship were not lost on the upwardly mobile administrators and academically trained Indians in Los Angeles. The initial list of applicants included the names of several of the community's best-known program directors and grants writers. Personal campaigns were waged, and constituencies were pressed into vocal support of individual candidacies.

Bill Fredricks, the Blackfeet man chosen to fill the position in 1977, continued as LACCNAIC executive director until May 1990. This impressive service record to the Indian community says as much about his executive competence as it does about his consummate political acumen. He has become skilled at mediating the demands of a watchful Indian constituency and the complexities of not only city and county bureaucracies but also the multiple labyrinths of state, federal, and private funding and policy development agencies.

Commission Functions

The Indian Commission continues to be funded yearly by Los Angeles County, even though similarly structured institutions have not due to budget cutbacks. Its ability to survive the budgetary knife for the last twelve years is testament to its vital role as the Los Angeles Indian community's paramount pantribal council and forum.

The LACCNAIC is a primary disseminator of information about funding sources for Indian social services programs. As such, it functions as a broker between individuals or social services organizations within the Los Angeles Indian community and the program funding sources. For example, the commission "was instrumental in procuring the State Office of Economic Opportunity (OEO) Community Service Block Grant (CSBG) Indian set-aside programs currently administered by the Los Angeles County Department of Community and Senior Citizens Services and subcontracted to local Indian organizations to provide emergency shelter, health, and food programs to disadvantaged members of the community" (LACCNAIC 1987b:4).

Often asked to review and endorse Indian organizations' grant proposals, the commission, in some instances, has acted as an employment screening panel for such projects. Commission members are asked to sit on advisory committees of projects that range from the development of an Indian culture site in the Santa Monica mountains to the Urban Indian Senior Citizens Outreach and Needs Assessment Project. In other cases, the commission has taken the responsibility for not only advocating certain social services but also deciding which agencies receive funds to provide those services.

Information-gathering projects have occupied the Indian Commission on a number of occasions. Chief among these efforts was the special census count in 1986. The commission has been vociferous in its claim that figures from the 1980 U.S. Census for the Los Angeles County Indian population represented an undercount that could seriously impact continuing Indians social services programs. In 1986 the commission established the Indian Census Committee to "develop effective strategies to assure an accurate count of American Indians in both the 1986 special census and the 1990 census" (LACCNAIC 1987b:6). Other commission information-gathering projects have included a broad range of research and analysis for identifying and assessing those conditions that adversely affect the welfare and socioeconomic status of urban American Indians.

Indian rights advocacy by the LACCNAIC has taken the form of regular review of governmental policies, legislation, and rules and regulations to determine their impact on the Los Angeles Indian community. These legislative reviews often prompt position papers. Commissioners appear at conferences and hearings at all levels of government to address the issues under discussion and to inform policymakers as to the possible impact of the proposed legislation on the Los Angeles Indian community. The commission's occasional emergency press conference appearances and the distribution of press releases are additional vehicles by which Indians are assured a voice in policy development and public opinion management.

Crisis management, particularly when community members or organizations are experiencing difficulty in dealing with government agencies, is another commission function. Acting as a catalyst rather than a direct participant, the LACCNAIC sees as its charter the third-party facilitation of discussion, debate, information sharing, and consensus development between an aggrieved or petitioning party and the appropriate service delivery agency. Advocacy of Indian affirmative action programs in the workplace and encouraging Indians who need affirmative action assistance to use the existing mechanisms are other forms of crisis management in which the commission has taken a facilitative role.

The Indian Commission also functions as a dispute mediator and network facilitator. This was particularly clear, for example, when, during excavation of a San Fernando roadbed, a prehistoric Indian village site was uncovered. The discovery was brought to the attention of the commission, which then facilitated communication between the excavators and environmental impact specialists, archaeologists, ethnologists, three affected area tribes, the California Native American Heritage Commission, and State Senator Alan Robbins. Commissioner Zoie Dungee was quoted in a 1985 issue of *Talking Leaf* as saying, "Much of what we [the commissioners] do keeps everyone from stepping on each other's toes" (Pierce 1985:6)

Information dissemination initiated or invited by government agencies (including tribal governments) vis-à-vis the Los Angeles Indians is often channeled through the commission. In 1985, for example, the Navajo Board of Election Supervisors and the Navajo Election Administration asked the commission to help conduct public hearings in Los Angeles for the purpose of soliciting information from the local Navajo people on five proposed Navajo Tribal Council reapportionment plans. The subsequent public hearings conducted by the Indian Commission represented the first attempt by a tribal government to communicate with its relocated tribal people in urban centers.

Cultural awareness among Indians and non-Indians is fostered through commission-sponsored formal presentations in schools and museums, training seminars, and workshops. The commission sponsors or cosponsors many cultural, social, and recreational events and assists in mobilizing facilities, equipment, or other resources to conduct such events (LACCNAIC 1987b:3–4).

In its first decade of service to the Los Angeles Indian community, the commission had no problem identifying an agenda. In fact, quite the opposite was true: there was so much to do that it had to prioritize its agenda. During that first decade, the LACCNAIC functioned as an ombudsman, a public forum, a spokesman, a censor, an initiator of scores of position papers and policy statements, and an advocate of government action on the part of the far-flung Los Angeles Indian community.

A Commission Meeting: Democratic Debate and Consensus Development Processes

The LACCNAIC meets on the third Tuesday of each month. On March 17, 1987,[5] I attended a commission meeting, in part because I was concerned about a research and intervention project within the Los Angeles Indian community that was under consideration by the county's Department of Community and Senior Citizens Services, the Los Angeles Indian Council on Aging, and the University of Southern California.[6] Nothing about the circa 1960 county office building at Sixth and Vermont or its commodious tenth-floor boardroom in which the Indian Commission met suggested the ethnic orientation of its inhabitants. The large council table that dominated the room easily accommodated the commission's fifteen members and its two paid administrators. Two rows of folding chairs had been set up for the benefit of any visitors who might attend the open meeting.

Anxious not to miss any of the proceedings, I arrived approximately ten minutes ahead of the scheduled gavel time of six o'clock. I should not have fretted. It would be some time before the meeting formally came to order. The executive director and his assistant were placing packets of information for the members of the commission on the table. The current chairman of the LACCNAIC had also arrived early. He was talking with the executive director about some needed last-minute adjustments of that evening's agenda. Four of the fifteen commissioners were present and were variously doing some last-minute caucusing in anticipation of that evening's election of officers or drawing themselves a cup of industrial-strength coffee from the thirty-cup urn that had just been carried into the room.

Commission meetings are public affairs, and community members as well as government officials and students of Indian affairs are made welcome. Visitors are asked to sign the meeting roster and, when doing so, to provide their mailing addresses and information about their representative affiliations. Meetings on officer election night usually bring out a crowd. Eventually, perhaps ten other guests would come and go during the two-hour meeting. However, at six o'clock I was the only visitor present.

When I entered the boardroom, the administrative assistant handed me an agenda and urged me to sign in. Commission member Roy Flandreau had invited me to attend the meeting, and he took it on himself to introduce me to the few members already assembled whom, he reckoned, I did not know. He made a point of introducing me as Dr. Weibel-Orlando, a professor from the University of Southern California, thereby establishing both my credentials and the degree of formality with which he thought the other commissioners and I should interact.

Since the passage of a binding motion requires the majority vote of at least eight commissioners, we waited for a quorum to assemble. At 6:05 P.M., the punctual but busy and overcommitted commissioners present began checking their watches. One of them remarked that someone ought to make a few phone calls to see if anyone else was planning to attend that evening's meeting.

The LACCNAIC tries not to run on Indian time,[7] since the members who regularly attend monthly meetings need to be assured that the two hours they block out of their busy schedules for commission business will be sufficient. Sessions scheduled for 6:00 P.M. should not start at 7:00 P.M. and run until 10:00 or 11:00 at night. Nonetheless, in the absence of a quorum, we continued to wait. At ten minutes after six, the eighth commissioner, Rev. John Goodman, entered the room. Offering the obligatory apologies and the standard explanation about Los Angeles rush-hour traffic, he cursorily reviewed the agenda materials as he settled into his appointed place at the council table.

At 6:15 the chairman called the meeting to order and asked the secretary to call the roll and thereby establish that a quorum was present. The commission meeting then began in earnest with *Robert's Rules of Order* structuring the general business, special presentations, and subsequent discussions. An agenda had been placed at the disposal of each commissioner, and extra copies of it were distributed to the invited speakers and to welcomed spectators as they arrived.

Each place at the council table was marked by an impressive portfolio of commission documents. Included among the official papers were the minutes of the last commission meeting, the evening's first order of business. Review and approval of the minutes of the last meeting were serious agenda items that engendered lengthy discussions of remembered differences between the original discourse and its reportage in the minutes. At the onset of the discussion, parliamentary procedures were strictly enforced. Impulsive remarks were ruled out of order. Acceptance of a motion and its seconding were asked routinely at the appropriate moment. After about fifteen minutes of general discussion, a group consensus was eventually reached, reported discrepancies and typographical errors corrected, omissions inserted, and the minutes accepted as revised.

The next order of business was the administrative report. The responsibility of the executive director, this report was essentially a summary of his activities of the previous month on behalf of the LACCNAIC and as a result of decisions made at earlier commission meetings. Bill Fredricks's report was the catalyst for much detailed scrutiny, evaluative discussion about the relative effectiveness of his efforts on the commission's behalf, and a litany of admonishments about greater effort, faster turnaround between policy development and outcomes, and concerns about full disclosure.

Of particular concern was a letter in support of a resolution by U.S. Senator Daniel Inouye (then chairman of the Senate Select Committee on Indian Affairs) to include American Samoans under the rubric "Native Americans" in future legislative and agency funding actions. Mr. Fredricks had drafted the letter that week and was about to send it to Senator Inouye on behalf of the commission. Much, often-heated debate ensued. Operating from a perspective of limited good (Foster 1965a), Mr. Flandreau, among others, was concerned that agreeing to call Samoans Native Americans would be cutting the Native Americans' already skimpy slice of the public funding pie even more slimly.

The issue went back and forth. Mr. Flandreau suggested an amendment to the letter, which was then discussed and further amended. There was a call for a community hearing on the issue and that possibility was also discussed. Throughout the proceedings, one commissioner or another would ask to be apprised of where, in correct parliamentary procedure, the issue was at that particular time. The chairman struggled gamely to keep the meeting operating at some level of parliamentary order. However, the issue of the political and economic consequences of ethnic boundary definition and maintenance was keenly felt. Debate quickly devolved from procedural correctness into emotional and impulsive personal position statements and abandonment of any recognizable form of codified procedural order.

After about ten minutes of continuous and unstructured debate, John Lewis, the respected president of the long-lived Indian entrepreneurial assistance program, an accomplished congressional networker, and the about-to-be-elected commission chairman, interjected his perspective as a Washington, D.C., "insider." He noted: "Inouye is a strong Indian supporter. He is not out to split the funding pot one more time. He simply sees the reasonableness of calling Samoans Native Americans so that they can have a claim to a separate funding base of their own. Inouye's asked for our support on this issue. Let's not alienate his good will by turning down his request for support."[8] Chastened by Mr. Lewis's temperate words, the commissioners debated the issue for another ten minutes before reaching a consensus. The letter from the Indian Commission would not be a blanket endorsement of Inouye's resolution but would recognize Samoans, and particularly those who had immigrated to the mainland, as indigenous people in need of special community services funds. However, those funds should not be extracted from funds already earmarked for American Indian programs.

In his role as executive director of the commission, Bill Fredricks noted the commissioners' comments. With diplomatic aplomb, he responded to what he determined were unworkable directives with reasoned explanations as to why impulsive requests or suggestions for action were not bureaucratically feasible. The process of representative democracy, consensus development, and the definition and maintenance of the parameters of an ethnic frontier had been given full and dynamic sway.

At 6:40 P.M. the final acceptance (with amendments) of the administrative report was followed by a series of committee reports. Depending on a committee's level of activity in the previous month and the topicality of the issues each committee addressed, the reports ranged from cursory announcements of no further progress or an inability to find a mutually acceptable time to meet to lengthy discussions of works in progress.

In accordance with standard business meeting proceedings, the committee reports were followed by a very brief report on old business. At around seven o'clock, the new business segment of the meeting began with the annual election of commission officers. Election night polemics and the overt manifestations of factional alignments that marked previous elections did not surface on this particular evening. Perhaps the presence of several spectators who had arrived by the time the elections started dampened the political machinations that, my source assured me, usually occur on election night. In any event, the elections proceeded with orderly and parliamentary correctness. People who, during their premeeting caucuses, had realized they would not command a majority of the votes discretely declined further consideration when nominated for office. The secret ballot was just that; a dead heat prompted a second, equally secret ballot. The elections were over within a half hour. The orderly succession of executive authority had proceeded for another year with due speed.

At 7:30 the LACCNAIC took up a second order of new business. Scheduled speakers listed in this section of the formal agenda proceeded to present their cases to the commission. Each presentation engendered considerable heated discussion and pointed inquiry. The formal rules for inclusion on a commission meeting agenda stipulate that the executive director must have at least two weeks' notice in order to include an issue on the next month's meeting agenda. Under situations of extreme urgency, however, new business agenda rules can been relaxed to include a hearing of late-developing issues within the Los Angeles Indian community. Scheduled speakers are expected to make formal, informational presentations to the Indian Commission. Issues brought before the commissioners should not be personal or trivial but of general Indian community interest. Supporting documentation of a particular position is expected, and corroborating witnesses, especially if they are commission members, are always positive contributions to any petition for help or moral support.

This particular evening's presentations and petitions for commission support were wide-ranging. Letters of support for about-to-be-submitted social services funding proposals were respectfully requested of the commission by a number of Indian-run social services agencies. Requests for memoranda of understanding between non-Indian social services agencies about to submit a proposal for funding of programs that would impact Indian individuals were prefaced by careful summaries of the programs' objectives. The funding proposals written by non-Indians were particularly scrutinized by the more wary commissioners, who harbored and voiced their concerns about the viability of such agencies acting as sponsors of programs impacting Indian constituents. Commissioners challenged the petitioners to demonstrate how their proposed projects would benefit

American Indians. Then, satisfied that their concerns had been adequately addressed, the commissioners usually agreed that some documented form of LACCNAIC approval for the project would be forthcoming. Such promises were usually tempered by admonishments to try harder to recruit "qualifiable" Indian staff.

A third genre of Indian Commission new business consisted of a wide range of informational presentations. These reports included summary evaluations of new bills that either created funding sources or else curtailed or canceled existing, familiar sources of social services funding; first- and secondhand accounts of state and federal Indian Affairs committee meetings; and comments on the meaning and impact of new state and federal policy decisions on Los Angeles Indians.

A fourth type of presentation included information about ongoing Indian-related projects and requests for formal, written support of them. For example, a team of four graduate architectural students at UCLA had been asked by a conservation consortium to design a small museum complex for the Santa Monica Mountains Indian Cultural Center. Their cooperative project, complete with architectural renderings, diorama, ground plan, elevations, and estimations of cost, was presented to the Indian Commission for its information, comment, and eventual approval.

A catchall final announcements segment of the meeting allowed for the presentation of less-comprehensive, more-personal issues (the illness of a treasured member of the community, an impromptu powwow at a local community college, the appointment of a community member to a position with the potential for providing a platform from which Indian issues might be given a wider hearing, an Indian who had been singled out for recognition by his or her peers, and the need for Indian extras in a proposed film). Essentially ceremonial and symbolic gestures, responses to the announcements ranged from decisions to send flowers or a card from the commission to the ailing community member to ordering a city or county proclamation struck to commemorate an Indian individual's singular achievements during the past year.

In this final phase of the meeting, larger issues that had arisen subsequent to the cutoff date for placement on the formal agenda were presented to the commission for immediate discussion and action. Issues such as the governor's decision to cut funds for Indian health services were given a hearing and judged worthy of placement on the following month's formal agenda. Had the issue been critical, that is, a decision by outside governing bodies was imminent and its outcome clear, collective action would have been taken at the time of informal presentation. The meeting continued in this vein for another half hour. Procedurally, it was a fascinating blend of parliamentary rigor and pragmatic expediency. Issues ranging from personal and ceremonial gestures of goodwill and recognition to matters of national political urgency and the maintenance of ethnic group boundaries received equal public hearing in a representative forum. Every issue engendered a cycle of debate, discussion, and inquiry. As in historic Indian tribal councils, the process of consensus development truly ran on Indian time, with the debate continuing until group consensus was reached. Commissioners waiting to be recognized by the chairman so as to express their opinions on a particular subject felt tricked by the parliamentary pundit who, tiring of the debate, would use his or her prerogative to call the question. What mattered, after all, was debate and consensus development, having one's voice heard in the community's formal political arena. Some impassioned speakers chose to ignore *Robert's Rules of Order* and speak even though the question had been called, ensuring themselves a voice in the decision-making process. It took another half hour before the discussion was exhausted and a consensus was reached. Satisfied that all issues of a general nature had been given a forum, the chairman gaveled the meeting into adjournment at the reasonable non-Indian hour of 8:30 P.M.

Discussion

In certain aspects, the Los Angeles City-County Native American Indian Commission parallels the councils of elders that dominated the political structure of several North American tribal societies during the nineteenth century. LACCNAIC commissioners, however, are not predominantly older members of the Los Angeles Indian community. In fact, the age range of the commissioners is quite wide. In 1987 a thirty-year-old urban-born Navajo man was a member of a commission panel that also included a Cherokee/Cree man in his late seventies. Rather than biological age, longevity, recognition in and contribution to Los Angeles Indian community affairs, and demonstrated sagacity are the sociopsychological determinants of community elderhood. Commission membership represents the pacific and mediating ideals of the corporate group, which, historically, were thought to be embodied in the older, sagest members of the tribe. Community elderhood, then, has become a social rather than a chronological cultural category.

Membership on the Indian Commission parallels the traditional bases of tribal council leadership. For instance, Driver (1975:446) notes that among the Iroquois, "ideally, chiefs were even-tempered, mild-mannered men who neither engaged in nor paid attention to gossip. Their internal rule was by persuasion and reason." Political firebrands, people with personal agendas to promote, and Indians with records of divisive and self-aggrandizing behavior when participating in community activities are suspect as LACCNAIC appointees. Rather, the reasoned, politic person adept at cross-cultural communication who does not personally or publicly seek out the honor but is promoted by acclamation of a recognized constituency becomes a member of the Indian Commission.

People wishing to serve on the LACCNAIC must initiate and sustain among their constituencies a careful campaign of intimation. Their personal interest in serving on the commission should be couched in terms of "seeing a need to help my people." Having said this, the campaign hopefuls must rely on the zeal of trusted friends to get out the vote or to successfully convince a city or county officer that their candidate's appointment to the commission would constitute a positive service to the Indian community. Lobbying on one's own behalf would be seen as immodest, aggressive self-aggrandizement, and "not the Indian way of doing things."

The Indian Commission parallels, both in structure and some functions, the historic peace councils that presided over the supra-band convocations of the Cheyenne (Grinnell 1972) and Sioux (Powers 1977), as well as the supratribal League of the Iroquois (Wallace 1972). The commission is proudly and publicly a pantribal organization. Newspaper articles and formal commission documents that list the names of its fifteen members also list the commissioners' tribal affiliations and current employment or community status. In 1986, when the president of the Los Angeles Indian Council on Aging and I began to confer with the commission about our proposed senior citizens outreach project, the fifteen commissioners claimed heritage in eighteen discrete tribes or bands.

In the nineteenth century, the purview of tribal councils and pantribal leagues included political frontier issues such as rights of territorial usage, the development of extratribal alliances, and coalitions vis-à-vis traditional enemies, as well as negotiations with the encroaching white settlers and colonizing political forces. The parallels between these historic tribal council responsibilities and those with which the LACCNAIC concerns itself are obvious. Historically, tribal councils were also responsible for the orderly execution of subsistence activities and the general physical and psychic well-being of their people. The Indian Commission, by contrast, does not assume the responsibility of ordering, sanctioning, and controlling intracommunity relations. In fact, the commission has steadfastly and purposely refrained from taking on the role of a community tribunal, even though its charter allows and provides the mechanisms for doing so. The comments of the first LACCNAIC executive director on this subject are revealing:

> There was a misconception of the commission by many commissioners as well as the community. They looked at us in terms of the tribal government, as the ultimate agency to do everything. In fact, one of the first things we did was to adopt a policy of noninterference with Indian organizations. We felt right from the beginning that our first job was to build a working relationship between us [the commission] and all of the Indian organizations in the community. We didn't want them to feel we were there to butt into their business but [rather] to help them improve and expand their services to the Indian community. It was a matter of building trust. That's why, if anyone in the community asked us to investigate another Indian organization (and they sure did in the beginning), we just said that wasn't our job. . . . The last thing we wanted to be was a policing agency. That would have destroyed the commission faster than anything else. (Bill Fredricks, November 30, 1988)

The significance of this pantribal, quasi-political liaison structure has been debated in all quarters of the Los Angeles Indian community since the commission's inception. Tribal factionalism among the commissioners seems not to have ever been the divisive, counterproductive force it has been in the development stages of other, earlier Los Angeles pan-Indian organizations. Rather, the commission's pointedly pantribal makeup is offered as evidence of not only the heterogeneity, complexity, and size of the Los Angeles Indian population but also its ability to transcend tribal and regional differences. The commission proves to its Indian and non-Indian monitors that Indians can work together as a cohesive political body in certain circumstances. The Indian Commission is the microcosmic representative at the ethnic frontier of its presumed equally cohesive supratribal ethnic constituency.

The LACCNAIC is viewed by Indian and non-Indian individuals and organizations as the forum in which to make known one's presence in and meaning for the Los Angeles Indian community. This perspective is underscored by the regularity with which innovations and initiatives that have the potential for affecting the Indian community are placed on the commission's monthly agenda. The underlying assumption of such presentations is that the commission is a representative body for the larger Indian community. Commission approval is held to be synonymous with community approval of impacting projects and activities.

The Indian Commission was chartered to act as an information retrieval and dissemination center. That function has been thwarted largely by the absence of an apparatus for the dissemination of information. Few people besides those who regularly attend the commission's monthly meetings receive a summary of that body's decisions and subsequent actions. *Talking Leaf*'s monthly issues rarely carried anything but the most superficial accounts of commission activities.[9] The commission's operating budget allows only for a monthly mailing of the executive secretary's notes of the meeting to the commission members.[10]

The inability to disseminate widely the information it is charged to assemble, analyze, and share has also limited the commission's ability to sustain general interest in its activities either by spectators or by principal actors. The time, money, and energy spent in running communitywide election campaigns that brought out no more than six or seven hundred voters at any election quickly proved cost-ineffective. Seating new community representatives on the commission is now handled by a vote among the seated commissioners.

Although the LACCNAIC has the authority and infrastructure to seek out and administer social services grants and contracts, it has refrained, except under rare and extraordinary circumstances, from doing so. The commission's rationale has been that it does not wish to create an atmosphere of competition with the established Indian-run social services agencies in Los Angeles whose existence depends on successful grant applications. Rather, the commission sees its role as the funding facilitator for Indian community organizations, a role it has performed through letters of support, lobbying efforts, and the dissemination of information about funding availability to the appropriate parties in the Indian community.

How, then, is the first decade of the Indian Commission to be assessed? As illustrated in section VI, the commission's political impact can be considerable. The well-placed position paper, a well-timed letter of recommendation or its pointed absence, can initiate a chain of actions, both intended and unanticipated, that reverberate throughout the Indian community's economic, political, service delivery, and social structures. When the commission reaches consensus on a proposed course of action, it can function in ways that parallel the internal policing and extraterritorial political mechanisms of historic tribal councils. It does so only reluctantly, however.

The official presence of pantribal accord vis-à-vis the non-Indian establishment within which the Indian Commission is structurally embedded and which it must approach with budget and policy requests is an extremely important political innovation and vehicle. In many ways, the commission's very initiation and continued existence is its major accomplishment. The LACCNAIC ensures the far-flung and increasingly heterogeneous Los Angeles Indian population a mechanism by which a stance to be construed as ethnic solidarity and strength can be symbolically demonstrated. The commission emblematically displays Indian solidarity to an audience that otherwise would dismiss its petitions for public social services as simply the self-serving interests of a few small special interest groups and not the consensus and will of a significant ethnic constituency.

As Bill Fredricks incisively pointed out, although the Indian Commission initially made the decision to take on, selectively, the traditional status and roles that historic tribal councils, contemporary tribal governments, and the Bureau of Indian Affairs have played in Indian life, it has the potential to do so. There is reason to believe that in its second decade, having solidified its role as the mechanism by which ethnic frontiers are defined, crossed, and maintained, the Indian Commission may turn its attention to the important work of establishing intracommunity cohesion. The commission, in its maturity, may take on the role and receive general recognition as the Los Angeles American Indian community's final and encompassing moral authority.

NOTES

1. The presidents of the United American Indian Council and the United Indian Development Association were chief among the developers and advocates of the Indian commission concept. The idea of an Indian commission was first advanced publicly in an August 22, 1974, article in the *Los Angeles Times*.

2. In 1978 and 1979, I spent approximately six months doing fieldwork among American Indians who lived in and around the Los Angeles skid row

district. Chester Big Hand was my key informant. During that time, we identified no more than one hundred fifty Indians who lived on skid row.

3. Chester Big Hand's real name has been obscured to protect the privacy of his surviving family members. However, students of American Indian and particularly Cheyenne history will immediately recognize the name and thereby his direct descent from one of the great leaders of the Cheyenne Dog Soldiers who, during the 1860s and until his death during the Beecher Island fight in 1868, led many daring and successful forays against the U.S. cavalry (Grinnell 1972:119–21).

4. The term "49ers" refers to highly secular and occasionally ribald songs usually sung "at the drum" after the final public powwow dances and at some distance from the center of the formal dance ring.

5. The commission meeting described here is based largely on the March 17, 1987, session I attended. Certain issues discussed at that session have been omitted and others have been taken from the minutes of either previous or subsequent meetings to illustrate the range of issues with which the commissioners deal on a regular basis. However, all incidents described were actual public events.

6. In December 1986, Roy Flandreau, the president of the Los Angeles Indian Council on Aging, Robert Ryans, a senior officer of the Los Angeles County Department of Community and Senior Citizens Services, and I collaborated on the development of an Indian senior citizens outreach and needs assessment research project that eventually was awarded federal funding. At the time, Mr. Flandreau was also an Indian Commission member and had been instrumental in obtaining the endorsement of the commission for our collaborative project. The Urban Indian Senior Citizens Community Services System project was funded eventually by Grant 0090AM0273 from the Office of Human Development Services in the U.S. Department of Health and Human Resources. A seventeen-month granting period was initiated in September 1987. The county-administered project enjoyed a memorandum of understanding with the Indian Commission.

7. "Indian time" is defined in note 5, chapter 9.

8. All the quotes from the March 17, 1987, meeting are taken from my field notes, which I recorded in situ.

9. Between 1978 and 1986, the commission was featured in only three articles in *Talking Leaf*, though its monthly meetings and executive offices had been consistently listed in that publication's community directory since 1981.

10. In January 1990, I received my first copy of the American Indian Activity Calendar. Disseminated by the commission, this thirteen-page photocopied document listed day by day over one hundred Los Angeles Indian community activities in the month of January. Bill Fredricks and the commissioners had been well aware of the need to fill the information gap left by the demise of *Talking Leaf*. They had been working to establish the calendar as a vehicle for the dissemination of community information for over a year before its first mailing.

V

Status, Role, and Individuals as Facilitators of Community Process

> The community is not only a territorial unit and a table of
> organization; it is also an enduring temporal pattern of
> coexistences, an ordered time-progress of individuals . . .
> through roles and relationships. (Arensberg and Kimball
> 1965:17)

ULTIMATELY, THE impetus for community resides in the decision of individuals to interact in regular, patterned, repetitive activities. In doing so, individuals take on roles that, though they can be created by individuals, are defined and validated by community consensus. A particular activity or social arena may embody a number of roles which necessitate that individuals interact on a regular basis in relation to the roles they assume. Additionally, individuals can take on multiple roles that dictate interaction across community sectors.

The city is, like other human communities, a collection of individuals who exist as social beings primarily through their roles, which structure their relations with others. Urban lives, then, are shaped as people join a number of roles together in a role repertoire and adjust them to each other to some degree. The social structure of the city consists of the relationships by which people are linked through components of their role repertoires (Hannerz 1980:249).

In a city and ethnic configuration as complex as the Los Angeles American Indian community, an individual can access a diversity of roles and their validating contexts. By doing so, the individual can construct a constellation of setting-specific selves (Hannerz 1980: 224). The city, in other words, is an environment in which there are many and varied ways of making oneself known to others and in which considerable manipulation of personal history and image management is possible. The opportunities are there, in the social structure. What people do with their role inventories, and how consciously they seize on them, can vary considerably (Hannerz 1980:232).

Where role repertoires are varied, more or less original combinations of experiences and resources offer scope for innovative adaptations and strategies. In such contexts, individuals are also more likely to face new and unrehearsed strains and conflicts, a lack of fit between the individual competencies and the various roles the individual attempts to enact. Thus, there are risks as well as rewards involved in role innovation and the assumption of unfamiliar statuses and roles available in the urban context (Firth 1955:2).

Life histories of exemplar community members provide a longitudinal perspective of the fluidity of an individual's constellation of roles within and across social scenes and time. Fluidity is not just change between roles, it is also change in relationships and networks. Understanding the full diversity of urban life entails being aware of the varied ways in which an individual's role repertoire changes as time passes. The key concept in an examination of fluidity in social life is "career," not in the everyday sense of the word, but in the sequential organization of life situations (Hannerz 1980:270).

The three exemplary community figures presented in chapters 11–13 were chosen because they represent a range of life careers characterized by considerable role density. Their role repertoires encompass several dimensions of the Los Angeles Indian community role inventory.

Joe Whitecloud,[1] the culture conservator described in chapter 11, is a full-blood Tewa traditionalist. He grew up in his family's pueblo, speaks his people's language, and knows the ceremonial dance cycles. Nevertheless, he has successfully sustained employment in the mainstream urban-industrial setting. For this reason, he could also be considered a biculturalist. Trudy Whitecloud, his British-born wife, exemplifies another set of statuses and social processes within the pantheon of Los Angeles American Indian community types, namely, non-Indian affines and their relative incorporation into urban Indian life.

Community incorporation of non-Indians is a negotiated process.

Non-Indians who marry American Indians can elect to distance themselves completely from the ethnic group, selectively participate in Indian activities, or, through public performance, demonstrate their right to full community incorporation. The decision to include or exclude individuals from full incorporation ultimately belongs to the community. In Trudy Whitecloud's case, she has, through her demonstrated forty-year devotion to her Indian family and a commitment to the preservation of the powwow tradition, proved herself to be not a "wannabee" or a hobbyist but a person with "an Indian heart."[2]

By their essentially exclusive involvement with the Many Trails Indian Club, the Whiteclouds exemplify selective ethnic community participation and membership. Within their chosen, narrow segment of ethnic activity, however, they experience considerable role density. They are executive heads of an institution, fund-raisers, public relations experts, arbiters and perpetuators of other selective community statuses and roles, and culture conservators.

The exclusivity of the Whiteclouds' ethnic community participation contrasts sharply with Sophie Wade's multiple community involvements described in chapter 12. Mrs. Wade's total immersion in Los Angeles Indian life exemplifies core community membership. She too has rightful claim to the prestige associated with full-blood membership in her tribal group and a traditional upbringing and cognitive orientation in adult life.

Curiously, Mrs. Wade's culturally conservative early life experience (she grew up in rural Oklahoma among other Choctaws, spoke only Choctaw until she went to school at age thirteen, and was educated in Indian schools) did not deter her from acquiring several competencies (dressmaking, fashion design, and formal Methodist ritual) that allowed her to participate successfully in non-Indian social spheres in adult life. These competencies, plus the skillful use of her ethnic identity vis-à-vis her chosen non-Indian peer groups, ensure Mrs. Wade a number of special and created social niches within Indian and non-Indian social spheres. Her late-in-life career trajectory exemplifies another form of bicultural competence. The self-created cultural brokerage between her Christian Indian and Anglo-Christian communities has provided her high status and prestige within a narrow segment of the urban Indian community or selective Indian community participation.

Serendipity, available time, a personal ethic of Christian charity, and a self-perception of herself as "someone who can get things done" pulled Mrs. Wade, late in life, into full-core participation in the Los Angeles Indian community. In the 1980s, she not only retained her high status as a moral authority within a sacrosocial segment of the Indian community but also assumed total immersion in, identification with, and leadership of Indian secular, economic, and political spheres.

Mrs. Wade's increasing role repertoire and involvements in multiple urban Indian institutions place several analytic issues in sharp relief. Her life career trajectory illustrates the limits to which status, prestige, and cultural competencies accrued in one community sphere can be transferred to another. It also demonstrates the relative license with which individuals fashion their own life career trajectories and ethnic personae. Finally, Mrs. Wade's life career trajectory underscores how individuals consciously create, modify, and use their ethnic identity vis-à-vis chosen peer groups for personal benefit.

Bill Fredricks's life experience and ethnic career trajectory, described in chapter 13, exemplifies a third constellation of community types. He too grew up within a culturally conservative community. However, his Anglo father and Indian mother provided an alternative, bicultural enculturation experience that had both positive and negative effects on his developing sense of self. The explanatory power of Mr. Fredricks's life history lies in its illustration of the psychological ramifications of growing up as a half-breed, or mixed-blood, in a reservation community that clearly ranked fullbloods, white people, and half-breeds in that order.

Mr. Fredricks's initial response to the particular ascribed ethnic category to which he was assigned at birth could be considered negative overcompensation. His youthful attempts (heavy drinking, barroom brawling, and challenging legal authority) to prove himself worthy of being stereotyped as the supermacho Indian man were less than personally advantageous. After moving to the city and acquiring certain marketable skills in Indian and non-Indian political and economic spheres, Bill Fredricks, in mid-life, was able to fashion a career uniquely suited to a man who, genetically and cognitively, straddled two worlds. The exemplar bicultural specialist, he has maximized his ethnic marginality. His ability to encode and decode the cultural tenets of his two worlds and to translate those codes for both cultural spheres has been an essential factor in his rise to administrative and political Indian leadership in Los Angeles.

Bill Fredricks is a highly visible, full-time core participant in the Los Angeles Indian community. His right to assume this status is unquestioned. Yet he does not embody obvious markers of ethnic group membership: he is not phenotypically Indian; his memory of the Blackfeet language is faulty; and he does not announce his ethnicity through easily recognized emblems such as Indian jewelry, clothing, or public displays of himself in stereotypic Indian activities. His inclusion in the Los Angeles Indian community underscores the relative importance of biology, cognitive orientation, and active contribution to group process in structuring an ethnic identity. He considers himself inherently Indian. His mother's tribal origin provides the biological prerequisite for his inclusion in his chosen ethnic peer group. His conspicuous and self-selected cognitive orientation, rather than his documented genetic inheritance, is the dominant factor in his construction of ethnic self.

Because of his early enculturation into Blackfeet community life, Mr. Fredricks knows he is Indian. Importantly, he knows that he thinks and acts Indian and that, through demonstrated advocacy, he contributes meaningfully to the preservation of the Los Angeles American Indian community ethos. That Bill Fredricks, in mid-life, has been able to sustain leadership roles in the political and human services sectors of the Los Angeles Indian community illustrates his assumption and his community's acceptance of him not as "an apple," a "damned Progressive sellout," or a "wannabee" but as a "sycamore" or a "white Indian."[3]

In analyzing these three life trajectories as they relate to the Los Angeles Indian community structure, I explore how individuals use, create, and think about social roles, as well as how roles shape individual experience. A second focus is the fluidity with which individuals cross and manipulate, rather than merely accept, institutional and role boundaries. Community structure and cohesion are manifested by individuals' abilities to take on multiple roles and their willingness to become involved in collective action across institutional settings.

Importantly, all three individuals described here represent significant age, sex, socioeconomic, and tribal segments of the Los Angeles Indian community. They also are all aware of each other and their respective community statuses. Finally, they all felt a responsibility to respond to and take an active part in the resolution of the community crisis discussed in section VI. By describing the career paths and community events that brought Joe and Trudy Whitecloud, Sophie Wade, and Bill Fredricks into active conjunction, community as social process is revealed.

NOTES

1. Grandpa Whitecloud, who is mentioned in chapter 8, is no relation to Joe Whitecloud. Although both families are Pueblo, they come from two distinct communities. Grandpa Whitecloud and his family are from the Laguna pueblo, located west of Albuquerque and one of the most westerly of the Rio Grande pueblos. The Santa Clara pueblo in which Joe Whitecloud grew up is a forty-five-minute drive north of Santa Fe and one of the most easterly of the Rio Grande pueblos.

2. A person described as having "an Indian heart" has been paid a high compliment, whether that person is non-Indian or Indian. The term is meant to convey the perception that the person both adheres philosophically to a constellation of the most positively valued mores of Indian community life and behaves accordingly. The terms "wannabee" and "hobbyist" are discussed in some detail in chapter 8.

3. The term "sycamore" is another Indian social category. Sycamore trees have silvery white bark and reddish cores. Like the term "white Indian," "sycamore" refers to people who, though they are part-Indian, do not have stereotypical Indian features. They are, however, culturally Indian. The terms are sometimes used to refer to non-Indians who have "an Indian heart." However, having "an Indian heart" is a more positively toned label than either "sycamore" or "white Indian." The difference is associated with the level of adherence to an Indian ethos rather than an accident of birthright and early enculturation.

11

The Powwow Patron
as Culture Conservator

JOE WHITECLOUD grew up fancy dancing. A member of the Santa
Clara, New Mexico, pueblo Winter clan, Joe's first exposure to the
dancing style usually associated with Plains expressive culture was
at Indian dance demonstrations performed for tourists. Local pueblo
groups are paid to perform these dances at the cliff dwellings and
Anasazi ruins that dot the north-central New Mexico high desert
landscape. Each of the eighteen pueblos that straddle the north-
ernmost source of the Rio Grande system has a richly developed
yearly cycle of indigenous ceremonial and social dances. They nevertheless have borrowed freely from the dance styles of their Plains
neighbors to the east in the twentieth-century development and
expansion of their secular social and exhibition dance complexes.

Taos, the easternmost of the Rio Grande pueblos, was already
practicing a version of the Plains warrior and fancy dances when Joe
was a boy. Taos and Santa Clara are an easy forty-five-mile ride from
each other. Communication, trade, and cultural exchange between
the two pueblo groups have been constants for as long as they have
occupied that high desert river basin. Joe remembers vividly his first
exposure to powwow dancing: "See, the Taos Indians don't have
powwows. But they do do the powwow dances. And my Dad and I
would go up there. By watching them, I got to learn how to do it.
And then sometimes we'd have guests coming from mostly the
Kiowa tribe. They'd come to our village. And they'd put on not a
powwow but an exhibition—round dance, two-step. And I learned it
that way, too" (May 20, 1988). Accompanied by his uncles and cousins, Joe learned the secularized versions of Pueblo plaza dances as

well. From the time he was "so high," his family was well known for their exhibitions of eagle, hoop, and warrior dances at the various tourist attractions around Santa Fe.

Joe was baptized into the Roman Catholic faith, but he also adhered to the Tewa belief system, which fostered his participation in his agricultural community's annual ceremonial cycle of green corn, rainbow, and buffalo dances. The son of a clan elder, his early years were spent within the ordered and protective embrace of pueblo life and its encompassing network of classificatory and fictive clan relatives. He was taught and speaks both Tewa and English. He learned his village and clan song and dance cycles. He was trained to follow his father's example as a model of Pueblo spiritual leadership. He also adhered to his father's model of bicultural competency—namely, Joe's father combined membership in the pueblo's clown society with a career as a chief electrical engineer for the Army Engineer Corps in the Santa Fe–Los Alamos region.

World War II and the draft changed forever what was to have been Joe's classically Pueblo life career trajectory. Joe served with the armed forces in Europe, and while in England, he met, fell in love with, and married an English girl not yet out of her teens. Trudy Whitecloud's arrival at Santa Clara is one of her favorite stories about her introduction to pueblo life and the palpable culture shock it engendered.

> When I came from England to the reservation, [it seemed] way out . . . nowhere. They dropped me off in Lamy, New Mexico. It's a little tiny thing in the middle of the railroad [line]. It's nothing. I mean nothing. And [Joe] was waiting for me on the bus. They had a bus that was going to take us to Santa Fe. [It had] wicker basket seats. . . . I thought, "My goodness, what have I got myself into. . . ." And on that rickety old bus, we got to Santa Fe. His mother and father were waiting there. We got into their car to go down to the reservation. . . .
>
> They butchered a cow and had this big feast. It smelled so good in the house. I was hungry, so I sat down. And they put this red hot chili [in front of me]. The hottest thing I had ever eaten was curry. I sat there and [took] one mouthful and didn't know what to do. It was so hot I was about dying. Anyway, I finally got it down. . . . (May 20, 1988)

After her appreciative husband offered that Trudy is now the family's chili specialist and their powwow club friends confirmed that the transplanted Londoner makes "the best chili in the whole world," Trudy continued her personal chronicle.

> I was getting so homesick . . . so the next day, [Joe] said, "I'm going to take you on a nice ride." You know, I'm a city girl. . . . We got in the

car and we [went] up the Rio Grande . . . where there's nothing but mountains. I was waiting to see the big buildings . . . to see the ocean [like] where I was from. Then he pulled the car to the side and said, "Isn't this beautiful?" And I said, "Yes" [Trudy mimicked a very tentative agreement]. I couldn't see anything. And then he said, "I'm going to sing you an Indian love song." I thought, "Oh, great, this is going to be nice!" (I had never heard an Indian song before.) And I sat back. And all of a sudden . . . [Trudy imitates Joe's explosive, high-pitched, Tewa love chant] I jumped up and said, "That's it, I'm going home!" (May 20, 1988)

In the eight years that the Whiteclouds lived at Santa Clara before relocating to Los Angeles, Trudy grew to love the sage, pine, table-lands, and mountains of the Santa Fe area as fervently as did her full-blood Tewa husband. Three of their five children were born on the reservation. Enchanted by the physical beauty and *communitas* of pueblo life, the lure of a remembered urban life-style grew fainter with each year.

As with thousands of other non-Indians who marry into close-knit Indian families or who have had the opportunity to live in Indian residential communities, Trudy consciously observed and took on as her own her husband's people's folkways. To American Indians, the essentially derogatory social label and category "apple" is a metaphor for someone who is phenotypically Indian but thinks and acts in ways associated with the dominant culture. There is no clear conceptual opposite of this social category. Rather, American Indians make qualitative and semantic distinctions between Anglos who are "wannabees" and those who have "Indian hearts." A "wannabee" is someone who self-consciously emulates Indian behavior and dress, who conspicuously avows all things and causes Indian. Placement in this social category denotes that a person has incorporated only a superficial understanding and appreciation of the subtleties of Indian worldview, interactional style, and public presentation of self. The person with "an Indian heart" is thought to have incorporated valued culture traits either through empathetic osmosis or from being inherently predisposed to such goodness of spirit. Most people in Trudy's circle of Indian friends and relatives would agree that she has "an Indian heart."

Trudy may have initially pined for Piccadilly, but urban relocation had always been the farthest thing from Joe's mind. When he returned to Santa Clara after the war, he secured steady and relatively well paid employment as an operations engineer at the Los Alamos atomic research facility, which at the time was under military jurisdiction. In the early 1950s, however, the facility reverted to a civilian administration and became unionized. Although Joe joined the operating engineers' union, that fraternal membership did not provide the hoped-for job security. According to Trudy and Joe, the new civilian administration imported large numbers of Anglo employees from Texas and elsewhere. The New Mexican Indians and Hispanic-Americans originally employed at Los Alamos were systematically released from their duties.

In the 1950s, Los Alamos was one of the largest, year-round, full-time employers in north-central New Mexico. A man with Joe's specialized training and work experience had few other employment alternatives in the area. When Joe was released from his position at Los Alamos, urban relocation seemed to be his only economic alternative. In 1955, with their three sons and the few personal belongings the Bureau of Indian Affairs (BIA) relocation officer had suggested could be taken with them, the Whiteclouds boarded the train to Los Angeles. Their relocation experience echoes that of thousands of other American Indians whose decisions to relocate to urban-industrial centers were born of economic necessity (push) rather than sociocultural appeal (pull).

> We were [in Los Angeles] a week and we were about ready to go back to the reservation. . . . They put us in that dump down there right off the Harbor Freeway . . . roach bugs all over the place. . . . They took us to this one-bedroom place. . . . They had those Murphy beds in the wall. . . . Imagine it, with three boys. We were losing one of them all the time. They were playing with [the Murphy bed], you know. (Trudy Whitecloud, May 20, 1988)

Joe was lucky. With BIA assistance, he found work in Los Angeles almost immediately. His early placement, however, was not the best of all possible employment situations. Trained as an aircraft mechanic before World War II, Joe had developed and perfected those skills all through the war. He had hoped to find work at an air base. But those positions were heavily unionized in Los Angeles, so Joe settled for assembly line work in an aircraft research unit. In 1955, at thirty-three years of age, he was literally starting over.

Both Joe and Trudy have mixed emotions about what they viewed as the demeaning paternalism with which the BIA field office in Los Angeles handled their transition to city life. Happy to have been given the names of other Indians in Los Angeles with whom to associate, the Whiteclouds nevertheless bristled at the BIA field officer's assumption that all Indian families were "just off the buckboard" and totally unprepared to handle any of their own living arrangements. Horrified by the accommodations provided for them by the BIA Relocation Program and confident that they could find a more acceptable place to live, the Whiteclouds struck out on their own.

> The first place we headed for was the beach. It was a hot October. . . . The smog was so bad we were literally crying. It was terrible. . . . We saw a little place that said "rentals" . . . and we went in. And we rented a place at Hermosa Beach. . . . I think it was $62 a month. It was beautiful. Three bedrooms, big closets. . . . The next thing we went back to report to the BIA. Oh . . . they were mad at us. Because, when you come, they tell you [what you can do]. You were told. You were supposed to visit [the beaches], not live there. . . . You were supposed to live where they put you—in that dump down out there [in] downtown L.A. And I said, "If we can afford to live there, we'll live there." So on our report, they put we were "uncooperative." (Trudy Whitecloud, May 20, 1988)

Since the Whiteclouds moved to Los Angeles in 1956, they have established a remarkable record of stability, perseverance, and cultural continuity. At sixty-six years of age in 1988, Joe was still working a full shift for the electronics company that has been his employer for over twenty years. As a result of Joe's exemplary work record, the Whiteclouds were able to purchase the comfortable Hermosa Beach home in which they raised their five children. Their circle of closest friends continue to be other American Indians, as has been the case from the time they arrived in Los Angeles. Their leisure-time pursuits have persistently focused on performance and perpetuation of pan-Indian expressive culture.

By 1960 the Whiteclouds had joined and were extremely active in the Federated Indian Tribes (FIT), one of the earliest Los Angeles social clubs devoted to the perpetuation of Indian expressive culture. In its heyday, the FIT required members to dress in Indian ceremonial regalia when they attended any of the association's cultural activities. The Indian dance practice and costume-making classes held twice a week were well attended by fully outfitted devotees of Indian arts and crafts. Those members trained in Indian folk crafts taught untrained members. Joe was one of the powwow dance and song instructors. In full Plains ceremonial regalia, including an elaborate war bonnet, he shared his specialties—the eagle, hoop, and war dances—as well as the powwow social dances he had learned as a child from the traveling Kiowa dance troops. His students were scores of relocated Iroquois, Navajos, Cherokees, and even one or two Kiowa powwow dance enthusiasts. Trudy faithfully attended the weekly costume design and construction classes. As the mother of four Indian boys, she was expected to construct their powwow dance regalia when they were old enough to take to the dance floor.

Buttressed by ties of a shared history of urban migration and ethnic intention, FIT members provided a wide, pantribal circle of blood relatives (both near and distant), fictive kin, and pantribal friends for the transplanted Indians. Although attenuated a quarter of a century later by the return migration of a significant number of old-timers, the affectional, expressive, and instrumental ties initiated by those early attempts at cultural conservation and perpetuation continue to sustain a viable and dynamic social network and subcommunity. This network is what is meant when people refer to a certain subgroup within the Los Angeles Indian population as "the powwow people."

In the early 1960s, several members of the FIT decided that the skills learned in the weekly Indian culture classes needed an arena. From this impetus, the Many Trails Indian Club was born. For its first few years, the club was a loosely assembled group of Indian dance and music enthusiasts who hosted a number of increasingly successful and well-attended powwows. In contrast to the decidedly Southern Plains[1] character of the Drum and Feather Club powwows (the first Indian club to host powwows in Los Angeles), Many Trails, as its name suggests, is intentionally intertribal. Many Trails was instrumental in introducing Northern Plains–style powwow dance traditions to the Los Angeles area.

The Many Trails Indian Club, incorporated in 1966, was instituted "to perpetuate the song and dance of the Indian people" (George Beaverstail, May 20, 1988). In May 1988, I attended a lively session of the Many Trails monthly club meeting for the purpose of recording the club's history. Several of the current powwow club patrons who attended that meeting had been members since its inception. Three of the families were, in fact, among the club's originators.

When asked why they started the powwow club, the members offered rationales that can be categorized by three sociocultural themes. The primary intent clearly had been, and continues to be, conservation and enculturation of a cultural ideal to succeeding generations of urban-born American Indians. "To keep the culture alive" and "so that the children can perpetuate the culture" were generally agreed upon as the club's most highly valued goals.

A second theme suggests a generic impulse, a human requirement for association that crosscuts and supersedes familial and generational ties. The club members assume that intergenerational interaction is best expressed and sustained in meaningful participation in a shared ethnic community activity. They variously told me: the monthly powwow helps "to keep the Indian people together"; powwows are places "to get acquainted, to meet new friends"; and powwows are places "to be, not just with children, but with the grandparents, parents, brothers, sisters, aunts, uncles . . . so that everybody could be together."

Beyond the perpetuation of one's inherent or adopted expressive culture, and in addition to providing the sociopsychological satisfaction that interaction with other members of one's ethnic group engenders, powwows are also stages on which cultural values, community structures, and the behavior appropriate to such worldviews and social structures are modeled for succeeding generations to emulate.

Our children never got into the problems that many of the children did get into [in the city] because they were involved with their Indian culture and heritage. And it still keeps the same respect that they have on the reservation. Like on Joe's reservation . . . people used to come to the door and say that they came to see their aunt or uncle or grandpa. . . . But it was just their respectful way of saying everybody was an aunt or uncle. . . . It was a form of respect. Even today, the Bissonette's little girls, they call me Aunt Trudy. They never call me anything else. It's so nice to hear children talk that way. (Trudy Whitecloud, May 20, 1988)

Twenty-two years after its incorporation, the Many Trails Indian Club can point proudly to its success in accomplishing its goals. In the late 1960s and into the 1970s, the club boasted over two hundred active members. Monthly activities included powwows, holiday potluck dinners, and softball games pitting the "young kids against the adults" in which "everybody laughed till their sides gave out." Each month the club members scheduled a special event or developed a syncretic theme for the powwow. In October, for example, shocks of corn and some pumpkins would be brought in on powwow night to adorn the stage of Burbank's Olive Street Recreation Center. "Just down the street from NBC Studios," this public facility was the scene of the Many Trails monthly powwows for over a decade before the club moved its powwow venue to Long Beach. In February the club always bought candy and distributed it to everyone who attended the Valentine powwow. At Easter the club members ensured that each child attending that month's powwow got a present from the Easter bunny. For Mother's Day the women of the club would get together and make corsages to be handed out to all of the mothers who attended the May powwow. Trudy Whitecloud and George Beaverstail agreed that, "for the important occasions, we always tried to [make] . . . a theme for that month's powwow" (May 20, 1988).

Under the creative and innovative patronage of the Whiteclouds, Beaverstails, Cruthers, Big Elks, and a core group of about a dozen other families, the Many Trails Indian Club initiated many of the activities and ritual structures that are now associated with Los Angeles powwows. The Many Trails old-timers proudly assert that their cultural innovations have been emulated by the other Indian social groups who sponsor Los Angeles powwows.

Although Joe concedes that powwow princess contests[2] have been held in Oklahoma since the 1940s, it was Many Trails that initiated the annual event in Los Angeles. Selection as the Many Trails powwow princess was a widely sought honor to which many young women aspired. Trudy explains: "In the 'old days,' so many young women competed in the Many Trails powwow princess contest that the judges awarded not only a top prize but also selected four runners-up to act as the powwow princess's attendants"[3] (May 20, 1988).

The Indian arts and crafts powwow trading area is also a Many Trails innovation. Sales booths of local craftspeople are now staples at all the powwows. According to George Beaverstail, "It just seems that whatever Many Trails does, the other clubs pick up on. We set the trend" (May 20, 1988).

The powwow guest celebrity of the month was yet another Many Trails innovation. In the 1960s and 1970s, several Many Trails members worked as bit players, extras, or technical advisors in the then-flourishing cowboys-and-Indians genre of the Los Angeles film and television industry. George Beaverstail, one of the original members of Many Trails, was one of the "Hollywood Indians." In the old days, his invitations to celebrity friends and workmates would ensure the appearance of one or two film stars at the monthly powwows. This served as another drawing card for the increasingly popular social event. At one powwow, he recalled, "Barry Goldwater, Jr., came out. He was running for an office up in San Fernando Valley and he'd just married a Miss America or one of those beauty queens. And at that time we had Slim Pickens, Bob Fuller—he used to play the young doctor on *Emergency*—and Burt Reynolds was there . . . he's half Indian, you know. . . . One time even Marlon Brando showed up" (May 20, 1988).

The Many Trails Indian Club, as a corporate entity, was often hired to do film segments, television ads, and even housing development promotions when scripts called for large groups of Indians on camera. The evening I spent talking about club history with Many Trails members was regularly punctuated with knee-slap, belly-laugh remembrances of the club's checkered film career. Ruined takes, skittery horses, slithering rattlesnakes, and latter-day Indians who could not or would not ride horses, play dead, or say "how" for the general public's entertainment were remembered with as much glee as were the very occasional opportunities for Indians to speak a line of dialogue on camera.

Many Trails has always made a point of not assuming a political posture. The club's avoidance of controversial issues contrasts sharply with the political activism of the Concerned Community Indian Movement (CCIM), a relatively new Los Angeles Indian association and the current sponsor of Los Angeles's third-Saturday-of-the-month powwows. George Beaverstail, the Many Trails vice president, offered this assessment: "There is a difference . . . [between us and] CCIM. They believe in dealing with political issues. We don't. We're strictly social. We are nonpolitical. We might take a stand on Indian issues [vis-à-vis a non-Indian perspective]. But we are strictly social . . . for the perpetuation of the song and dance" (May 20, 1988).

During the 1988–89 powwow season and after a quarter century of promoting the development and preservation of pantribal Indian expressive culture, the Many Trails Indian Club continued to have a loyal following. Its card-carrying membership roster, although reduced from its 1960s peak of more than two hundred, was still impressive. Its monthly powwows were among the best-attended social events of the Los Angeles Indian community. Every second Saturday of the month, three to four hundred people, mostly Indians, would show up at the Cecil B. De Mille Junior High School in Long Beach to observe, enjoy, and participate in four hours of Indian song, dance, and socializing.

The powwow social arena is not the only context in which Many Trails Indian Club members exhibit their cultural competencies and roles as culture conservators. Joe Whitecloud, his sons, and his grandchildren regularly perform as a dance group for schools, museums, and other public programs. In 1988 they traveled to Indonesia to perform their "traditional" Indian dance program as a part of the newly reconstituted Buffalo Bill Wild West Show.

In an earlier interview, Joe provided some insight into his lifelong dedication to "the perpetuation of Indian song and dance." When asked what ideas or values had remained meaningful to him over the years, he offered:

> It was important for me to teach my children as well as other Indian children the best of both [Indian and non-Indian] worlds. I tried to give my kids the best education and home environment possible. And I also taught them the best of the Indian ways. . . . I knew I lost a lot when I left the reservation. Whenever I go back [to visit] my folks at Santa Clara, I ask about the ceremonies and procedures. I do that so I can teach my kids and grandchildren about those things. I learn these things so that I can be a better elder—someone who will be able to pass on our traditions to the kids coming up. (September 9, 1985)

Discussion

Joe Whitecloud, the soft-spoken president of the Many Trails Indian Club, continues to share concerns about cultural conservation with most of his Los Angeles Indian powwow peers. He is fully cognizant and accepting of his children's and grandchildren's need to function with cultural competence in their world of personal computers, space satellite communication, and postindustrial robotization of the workplace. He is nonetheless mindful of the cultural trade-offs inherent in rapid and complete linear assimilation of the predominant, superethnic sociocultural trends. The trade-offs are perceived as spiritual losses. He is convinced of the sociopsychological benefits of being in community that he experiences in his mother's village, in his father's clan kiva, and in the easy, pantribal camaraderie of the Los Angeles powwow.

Joe's powwow patronage is his response to the conviction that community, as expressed in the acknowledgment of and participation in a shared ethnicity, is a positive human experience. In the act of conserving and sharing his *bricolage*[4] of inherited, adopted, and invented expressive American Indian culture, Joe ensures his children's and their children's continuing experience of the unifying and enriching *Gemütlichkeit* of community consciousness, participation, and inclusion.

Participation in the synthetic urban powwow provides for the experience of *communitas* that others have variously labeled "pan-tribalism" or "pan-Indianism." I refer to Victor Turner's (1974) use and definition of *communitas* for specific reasons. Joe and Trudy Whitecloud spoke repeatedly about the closeness and integrative nature of pueblo community life. A social environment in which classificatory social categories make all community members aunts, uncles, grandparents, and grandchildren and certain shared, if time-limited, activities make all participants social and cultural equivalents is, I suggest, what Turner (1974:45), citing Florian Znaniecki, meant when he defined *communitas* as "a bond uniting people over and above their formal bonds."

One has to experience only once the incorporating and homogenizing effect of the Green Corn Dance as it is practiced at the Santa Clara pueblo to understand the unifying effects of such shared experience and its generation of *communitas*. Two hundred multigenerational pueblo members in identical dance regalia moving in slow, stately, and uniform rhythmic columns across the pueblo ceremonial plaza in full view of the entire community is the behavioral expression of group unity and collective consciousness. Being one of a hundred-strong, shoulder-to-shoulder phalanx of dancers in synthetic, pantribal powwow regalia ritually replicates, in the urban social sphere, the Whiteclouds' cherished Pueblo expressions of experiential oneness. Whether the powwow dancer is Pueblo, Sioux, Navajo, or Iroquois, the experience of shared ritual participation dissolves such social categories. The resulting supratribal Indian consciousness is the antistructural bond that allows for the development of a new sociostructural form—the urban Indian community.

NOTES

1. There are two distinct powwow dance and song styles. The Southern Plains style, with its origins in the dance traditions of the Plains cultures (e.g., Cheyenne, Kiowa, Arapaho), who were relocated to the western sections of Oklahoma territory in the 1870s, features the more flamboyant double-bustle dance regalia and fancy dance steps. The Northern Plains style (e.g., Sioux, Crow, Blackfeet) tends to perpetuate earlier, more subdued forms of dance regalia, slower and more stately dance steps that often mimic animal movements and men at the hunt, and a riveting high falsetto signature chant style. For a full discussion of these dance style differences, see Young (1981).

2. See Weibel-Orlando (1988b) for a detailed discussion of the powwow princess crowning ceremony and the iconic import of this community role model.

3. In the 1980s, the Many Trails Indian Club sponsored a senior and junior powwow princess. In 1989 seven teenagers and five adolescent girls competed in the respective contests. This was to be the last Many Trails powwow princess contest.

4. See note 6 of the Introduction for a discussion of *bricolage*.

12

Church Elder as Moral Authority

I am now 76 years old and still feel that I should do something to help our Indian community. [If] I can contribute
in a small way, some one thing, that will help them, then I
feel my time has been well spent. (Sophie Wade, personal
correspondence, October 1, 1986)

SOPHIE WADE and I met for the first time on a hazy Sunday afternoon, on July 29, 1973. It was the occasion of my second Fifth
Sunday Sing. I arrived at the Brighter Day Mission, that month's
sing host, around ten in the morning. Consistent with the sing ritual
schedule, the Sunday school classes were ending and the formal
church service was about to begin as I entered the modest meeting
hall at Broadway and 119th Street, where the church has been located almost from its inception in 1959. The church's interdenominational congregation has watched its once-integrated neighborhood become increasingly annexed by the principal Los Angeles
low-income black community.

The morning's congregational singing ended, as it always does,
around noon. After the mandatory introductions and explanations
about my reasons for coming to a singing, I followed the congregation out into the enclosed courtyard that separated the sanctuary
from the cookhouse. As I was standing in the food line trying, without success, to choose among the fried, baked, fricasseed, and
stewed chicken offerings and the seven varieties of apple pie, Sophie
Wade made her entrance. Filled with purpose, exuding self-
confidence, and possessing the authoritative stride of an officiating
matriarch, Mrs. Wade commanded the courtyard. Pausing in the
doorway before taking her place at the end of the food line, Sophie

scanned the gathering and waited, fully expecting the respectful acknowledgment and deference with which the Fifth Sunday Sing picnickers greeted her.

Slowly making the rounds of the tables of picnickers, Sophie claimed her place as church community elder. The picnickers recoiled in laughter at her witheringly caustic greetings and indelicate observations. Attempted repartees ended in Sophie besting her less-skilled joking partners. The courtyard had dissolved into hooting laughter at her clever, outrageous caricatures, more often than not in Choctaw, of her friendly, if diminished, verbal adversaries.

Sophie Wade had presence and my undivided attention. She was fashionably color-coordinated in a prim, handmade, turquoise blue polyester dress correctly accessorized for the season with summer white heels, pop beads, white straw hat, white handbag, and white gloves. She was dressed as befitted a high-status community elder and leader of her people's church. I made a mental note to discover where and under what circumstances this sprightly Indian elder had acquired such social grace and authority.

One of the host parishioners introduced me to Sophie as a UCLA student and fiddle player. We immediately established the joking relationship that characterizes our interactions to this day. Our first exchange included some fun about how she was going to remember my name.

> Joan: Weibel—it rhymes with Bible.
> Sophie: Well, if you all are not careful I may just end up a-calling you Jo-anne of the Bible.

Unskilled in the stylistics of Indian joking exchanges, I laughed self-consciously and quickly conceded her superior skill at the game. Pleased with her witticisms and my easily won submission, she sat down with me to talk.

Sophie seemed concerned that I understand she had a perfectly acceptable reason for arriving so late in the day.

> You see, I'm not a member of this congregation. And most people who belong to other churches go to their own church Sunday school on the morning of a singing to help support their congregation. And then, after their church service is over, they go to the church that won the right to have the singing at their place this time for lunch and the afternoon singing. I usually get to the host church in time for lunch, but this Sunday, after my church's services were over, I had to attend a woman's auxiliary meeting. You see, I'm the past president of the group and I had to be there to show the new president how to do

things the right way. . . . So that's why I was kind of late today. (July 29, 1973)

She was already telling me about how she wished to be viewed by her community and me. Being busy with important work, in demand, competent, and conscientious are all career themes Sophie was to reiterate to me in the course of our ongoing relationship. Her initial presentation of self was designed to inform me, from the onset, that I was dealing with a figure to be reckoned with within the Los Angeles Indian community.

Another early and continuing theme of Sophie's self-disclosure is her extensive network of friendships and associations both within and beyond her ethnic group. She quickly let it be known that she did not belong to a Christian Indian church. A staunch Methodist for more than thirty years, her primary allegiance in 1973 was to the overwhelmingly non-Indian Pacific Southwest Methodist Conference. Forthrightly, she explained: "I belong to the white people's Methodist church over in Maywood. You see, when you're a Christian, it doesn't matter if you are white, red, green, yellow, or blue. You're a Christian. Jesus loves everyone the same. He doesn't care about the color of the person's skin" (July 29, 1973).

Sophie self-identified as a Christian first and an Indian second. That is not to say, however, that she was not aware of her ethnicity and its potential as a personal resource. Indeed, she used it to great advantage. She continuously lobbied for more Indian programs and missions in her local church, at the annual meetings of the Pacific Southwest Methodist Conference, and at national and international Methodist convocations.

> I feel that I can do a better service for my people there than I can by joining one of the Indian churches here. I bring the Choctaw children's choir to sing "specials" for the white folks at my church. I get the white people to donate food, clothes, and money to poor Indian families. I get them to make donations to the Indian mission building funds. I get them to do a lot of things for the Indians by being there and knowing what they have to offer that could help Indians. Besides, I am a Methodist and there aren't any Indian Methodist churches I could belong to in Los Angeles. (July 29, 1973)

Membership in an all-Anglo Christian church did not mean that Sophie had been relegated to a marginal position by her ethnic group. A full-blood Choctaw, the ethnic ancestry of this short, wiry, brown-skinned woman cannot be denied. Her pralines-and-cream, smooth contralto drawl and easy laughter are stylistically pure eastern Oklahoma back hills "chucklin' Choctaw" (Lafferty 1972). She speaks fluent Choctaw and is quick to let you know it. She is, without argument, one of the most recognized and honored members of the Los Angeles Christian Indian subcommunity. Her membership rights in that subcommunity are unquestioned.

In 1973 Sophie's marginality to the Christian Indian subcommunity was self-imposed. She had chosen to exercise her Indian identity in the larger and obviously more politically powerful all-Anglo church setting for complex reasons. Her stated motive—to help secure more programs and assistance from the mother church—is certainly one of them. Her status as a token Indian in the Methodist church hierarchy, however, also had provided much personal satisfaction and prestige. In that context, her authority in Indian matters went unchallenged. She could take on, without community constraint, the statuses and roles of cultural interpreter and model Christian Indian women—roles she performed with relish.

Marginal membership in the Christian Indian church subcommunity was enhanced by the roles Sophie played in her "white people's" church. She was seen as a kind of culture broker who was able, through her connections with the Indian church community, to arrange for groups of Indian singers and musicians to present Indian Christian music programs at her church. Her cultural brokerage provided the Indian groups with extraethnic community exposure and occasionally a "love donation" to their church from an appreciative and grateful Anglo congregation. Being the cultural liaison between her Indian people and her church people was an enviable social position. Sophie knew it and promoted it.

Sophie and I were late to the singing that afternoon; in fact, we talked long past the third verse of "I Saw the Light" as well as the kitchen cleanup. Fascinated by her energy and personal style, I continued to observe her interaction with the other sing participants for the rest of the afternoon.

Her Fifth Sunday Sing roles were clear. She was expected to lead the congregation in the singing of Choctaw hymns. Graciously sharing her Choctaw hymnal with me, she grinned, chuckled, and inevitably convulsed into uncontrollable and conspicuous giggling at my sorry attempts to mimic both unfamiliar chord progressions and absolutely foreign Choctaw lyrics. She was expected to give a report about the Methodist activities on the part of American Indians during the announcement section of the program. This she did with obvious pride and authority. Throughout the sing, Sophie teased and joked with the men, laughed and gossiped with the women, and

admonished and directed the restless children, the not fully prepared kitchen staff, the disorganized sing officials, and the nonpar-
ticipating congregation members. Her comportment on this day was
appropriate to the roles of Christian Indian elder and Choctaw matriarch. In a gathering of church folk who, she can reasonably assume, are not as well informed as she is on "how to run a singing," it
is her duty as the church matriarch to "set a good example" and
"show her people the way Choctaws do it back home."

I would see Sophie at every Fifth Sunday Sing I ever attended. Her
sing roles have remained fairly constant over the years. I have never
seen her at a powwow, however. She once explained, "You see, there
are powwow folks and there are church folks. And you are either one
or the other. You can't be both. Powwow singing is the old way of
thinking and singing. It's not Christian. They worship other things
there and not in the Christian way. I've never been to a powwow
and, from what I hear about what goes on there, I never will" (June
16, 1978).

Sophie's world is clearly divided into good and bad domains—
Christian and pagan belief systems, spiritual and secular realms,
sacred and profane arenas. She identifies with and places herself in
the good, Christian, spiritual, sacred sector of her social field. Not
having experienced the Plains ceremonial traditions in her youth,
she equates the unfamiliar powwow activities and Plains culture
ethos with darker human and spiritual fields and forces.

In all the years I have known Sophie, I have never seen her at an
Indian bar. She is a teetotaler and has been all her life. Her absten-
tion is in part a function of her Southern Methodism, for prohibition
and temperance are mainstays of the Methodist ethos. Her aversion
to the consumption of alcoholic beverages is also the result of a
childhood during which she witnessed devastating bouts of drunkenness among the relatives who occasionally took her, her brothers,
and her sisters in after the death of their parents.

> When I was about six years old my grandpa used to go to town. And
> he'd drink there. And he'd come home and all us kids would run out
> to the woods to hide because if he caught us there's no telling what he
> might have done with us when he was in that condition. One time I
> said to my grandma, "Grandma, why don't me and you run off?" And
> she said, "No, Baby, we can't do that. It's not your grandpa that does
> things like that. . . . Your grandpa is a fine man. He sees that we have
> something to eat. He sees that we have clothes to wear. He sees that
> we have a place to live. He's good to us. But when he goes to town and
> gets those strong drinks from white people, that's what makes him do

that." And I thought to myself, If that's what causes that, I'll never drink. And I never have. And neither have my kids. Every one of them promised me they would never drink. And they never have. I am very proud of them for that. (January 23, 1984)

Sophie Wade was very sure of her place and roles in the Los Angeles Indian community when I met her in 1973. She was a church elder, a cultural specialist, a culture broker. Being Choctaw and Christian were synonymous cultural and personal dimensions. Her ethnic range included pan-Indianism only in that she saw herself as spiritual kin to all other Christian Indians. For that matter, she could have been considered panethnic with regard to all those people she considered her Christian brothers and sisters. She was not a powwow person, animist, or Indian politico. Hers was a life ordered by the dictates of earning a living, keeping tabs on her family, and doing the work of her Lord.

About two years after our first meeting, at yet another Fifth Sunday Sing, Sophie shared with me some excellent, self-generated news. The Pacific Southwest Methodist Conference had finally agreed to provide Indian Methodists in Los Angeles with their own pastor and church. Sophie was "fair to bursting" with excitement.

I've been working on this for years. This has been my dream—to have an Indian Methodist church in Los Angeles. You see, I may feel comfortable worshiping with white people, but I know lots of Choctaws and other Indian Methodists don't. That's why I'm the only Indian in my church. Indians want to be with their own people. They're just more comfortable that way. They don't have to dress fancy. They can take their kids to the service. They can have potlucks and serve their Indian food. They can sing their own songs. And Indians love singing. They can sing until midnight—all night if they want to—in their own churches. They can't do that in the white churches. It just works out better for them having their own church to go to. (August 31, 1975)

Sophie had been instrumental in the Methodist conference's decision to fund an American Indian initiative in Los Angeles. On her insistence and the church administration's interest in reaching out to minority groups in general, the First Native American and United Methodist Mission[1] was established under the auspices of an essentially all-white Huntington Park Methodist congregation in 1975. It was a political and social coup. Not only was Sophie now a member of a formal church organization that fostered an Indian congregation, she was its founding mother.

Sophie was also directly involved in the choice of the fledgling group's initial, formal leader. The Reverend Richard Price was an older, full-blood Chickasaw and an ordained Methodist minister. Sophie had met him some years earlier at one of the innumerable national church conventions she regularly attends on behalf of her home church. Because Chickasaws and Choctaws share territorial and linguistic ties, Sophie felt a special and immediate bond between Reverend Price and herself.

Reverend Price had come up through the church ranks the hard way. He and his Cherokee wife had spent the better parts of their adult lives ministering to small, dwindling rural Oklahoma Indian church communities. Those congregations offered a young, ambitious pastor few prospects for proving his organizational, fundraising, and congregation development abilities. A mix of antebellum chivalrousness, perseverance, and relentless outreach, however, carried Reverend Price to one of the largest Methodist urban Oklahoma congregations by the mid–1970s. Building a Methodist Indian congregation literally from the ground floor up in the largest concentration of urban Indians in the country had been presented to him as a growth opportunity by the Methodist conference leaders— a challenge he and his ministerial helpmate wife eagerly accepted.

The work of building a Los Angeles Indian Methodist congregation began in midsummer 1975. Reverend Price's ecclesiastical scholarship and southern gentlemanliness and Sophie's nononsense assertiveness and knowledge of the Los Angeles Indian church community were complementary, synergistic resources. Originally housed in a predominantly Anglo Huntington Park Methodist church, the Native American Ministries had fifty-four Indians on its membership rolls and its own church building in the Pico-Union area of central Los Angeles by the end of its first year.

Sophie's role as community expert and Reverend Price's right-hand person in the fledgling church provided her even higher prestige among the Los Angeles Christian Indians than had her status as token Christian Indian in her former Anglo home church. She became highly visible within both the Methodist lay worker hierarchy and the Christian Indian subcommunity. Unlike her unchallenged claim to the ascribed status of Christian Indian elder in the Anglo church, her new status as church group initiator and recruiter was achieved. She in fact had created her own life career path. Her relationship vis-à-vis the Los Angeles Christian Indians had been redefined. The boundary between other Christian Indians and herself had become blurred. She was no longer the marginal "negative instance"—that one full-blood Indian who felt comfortable—

indeed, duty-bound—worshiping with non-Indians. Still, it was only in 1982 that Sophie asked to be released from membership in her all-Anglo Maywood home church and submitted her name for inclusion on the membership roster of the Native American Ministries because "I was needed there." By this symbolic act, she announced her full incorporation into the Los Angeles Christian Indian subcommunity.

Along with Reverend Price, his family, and a cadre of other Indians who had "grown up going to Methodist church meetings back in Oklahoma," Sophie worked steadily to develop the ministry's membership and its annual calendar of ceremonial and social events. Tragedy struck the project in 1977. Reverend Price suffered a series of massive heart attacks from which he never fully recovered. He was forced to limit his missionary activities and died the following year.

Convinced of its Indian mission's success and its future growth potential, the Southwest Methodist Conference conducted a nationwide search for Reverend Price's replacement. Reverend John Goodman was the ultimate choice for the position. Young, commanding of stature, a full-blood Seneca, a seminarian, and a veteran of the inner workings of the Methodist conference hierarchy, his arrival from New York was a much-heralded event. People expected great things to happen to the fledgling church under his energetic stewardship. In 1988 the First Native American and United Methodist Church celebrated Reverend Goodman's ten-year pastorate with an honoring banquet. His is one of the most long-lived and productive ministries in the history of Indian church leadership in Los Angeles.

Sophie Wade continued to be instrumental in the work of the ministry she had conceived, enthusiastically supporting the new pastor and his shopping list of innovative, progressive programs. Initially, however, she was not totally comfortable with the social activism that characterized Reverend Goodman's mission. As a Southern Methodist, Sophie viewed the Christian mission as being more circumspect and traditional than the young pastor did. Bible study, singing, preaching, and saving souls were, to her mind, preacher's work. Spiritual healing—not emergency housing for indigents, clothing for the poor, and day care for the children of working mothers—is the work of the Lord. Nevertheless, she supported these programs and even worked part-time in the emergency care office of the downtown church, because she "saw the need was there."

Over the ensuing years, Sophie assumed most statuses available to church lay leaders. She has, at various times in her Native American Ministries career, been a lay speaker, cluster prayer leader, Fifth Sunday Sing emcee, kitchen detail coordinator, Christmas bazaar chairwoman, and representative to the National Council of Methodist Ministries. She continues to be the Native American Ministries' moral authority, admonishing matriarch, exemplar traditionalist, and executive whip.

In 1975 I formally interviewed Sophie in the neat, two-bedroom, 1920s stucco-and-red-tile neo–Spanish Colonial bungalow she now owns in a modest, still predominantly Anglo and Hispanic Los Angeles suburb. This full-blood Choctaw woman, who was orphaned after only one month of life, has obviously come a long way from her humble Choctaw Territory beginnings.[2] Today she is surrounded by three generations of her children, grandchildren, and great-grandchildren, who "do for her"—which, she assures them, is the Choctaw way. Fiercely independent, Sophie prefers to live alone, although three of her children live only a few minutes away, and her sons and grandsons occasionally live with her for short periods. Her sons are expected to (and do) supplement her modest Social Security payments, and unexpected expenses are submitted to and absorbed by one or more of her five adult children. Visiting grandsons mow the lawn, pull weeds, wash windows, and carry out the garbage. Concerned for their mother's safety, her sons dutifully keep the upscale Oldsmobile they bought her in excellent repair and running condition.

In contrast, Sophie never knew her parents or her maternal grandparents. She lived with her paternal grandparents for a while before they died. From that point on, she and her brothers and sisters were shuttled among various sets of relatives. For major portions of their childhood, they literally raised themselves. Sophie does not talk much about this period of her life. When asked who raised her, she was suddenly and uncharacteristically silent. The pain of harsh memory clearly registering in her eyes, she allowed only a moment of unmanaged recall before obscuring my witness of it. Collecting her thoughts, and with lowered eyelids, she shrugged and tossed off an obligatory, purposely vague answer: "Oh, we lived here and there, for a bit with one relative, and then we'd go to another relative's house for a while . . . but mostly we just kind of raised up ourselves."

Sophie did not go to school until she was thirteen and then stayed for only as long as she was forced to. She had studied some English by the time she entered the Indian Orphans Home in Goodland,

Oklahoma, but was more comfortable conversing in Choctaw. Corporally punished for speaking Choctaw in the Christian boarding school, she pointedly did not teach her children to be fluent in Choctaw.

> My husband and I decided we didn't want our children to learn to speak it [Choctaw] till they got older. . . . It was difficult for me to learn how to speak English. I had a hard time learning. And I've noticed so many children that's learned how to talk English after they learned to talk Choctaw, they talk very broken. And I told my husband, "Let's teach our children how to speak English 'cause they have to go to English schools so they won't have a difficult time." So we never did teach them how to talk our language. (January 23, 1984)

At sixteen, with only four years of formal education, Sophie left the church-administered Indian boarding school to get married. She spent her early adulthood raising other people's children as well as her own. The 1920s and early 1930s were the glory days of the Oklahoma oil industry. Wildcatters moved onto Indian lands in droves, and most Indians leased their oil-rich lands for a pittance to non-Indian oil speculators who had the technology to exploit the underground reserves. Many Anglo wildcatters got lucky and made great fortunes.[3] Even a few Indians who still held lands over the great Oklahoma oil reservoirs got good legal advice and made their own fortunes. Money was easily made in Oklahoma in the 1920s if one simply was willing to work for it.

At eighteen, Sophie went to work for "some rich folks" who had "a houseful of children." The lady of the house needed help with the cooking and cleaning and took Sophie in to do it. Although she stayed with that family for less than a year, the memory of that first paid employment and positive relationship with Anglos remains clear and orienting. Sophie speaks with great affection for and admiration of her Anglo benefactress. It was under the tutelage of that kind, strong, and accomplished woman that Sophie perfected her social graces. She learned to cook "white people's food," set a formal dinner table, sew, assemble a wardrobe, talk to the hired help, and host a party. Her benefactress's word was unquestioned authority. Sophie readily and happily emulated that firm but genteel matriarchal style.

Thirty years, two marriages, and five children later, Sophie Wade moved to Los Angeles to live with an unmarried adult son who "needed her." The dressmaking she learned in the sewing room of her first benefactress provided her with a marketable skill. In her mid-fifties, she found employment in a series of light industries that required someone who knew how to use a sewing machine. She eventually worked her way up to sample maker for a famous leather goods manufacturer, where, thanks to her productivity and "like family" relationship with the owners of the firm, she continued to be employed long past the regular retirement age.

Sophie finally retired at age seventy, but it was hardly to the proverbial rocking chair. Her busy schedule of prayer meetings, church services, Methodist Conference conventions, Methodist women's auxiliary planning sessions, and Indian Centers, Inc. (ICI), board meetings precluded the more traditional roles of caretaker grandmother. She was also heavily involved in volunteer human services work for the Native American Ministries. She still designed and made her own fashion-dictated outfits. In addition, her handiwork includes more traditional forms such as patchwork quilting. One of her quilts is, in fact, usually offered as the grand prize in her church's annual Christmas bazaar raffle.

Within a year of her retirement, Sophie again found regular work as a seamstress. Conveniently, her new employer's facility was in central Los Angeles, just blocks from her church in the Pico-Union area and from the main administrative offices of the ICI on Washington Boulevard. Propinquity and her recent community outreach involvement on behalf of her church's social services programs pressed Sophie into association with the staff at the Indian Center. In effect, she assumed a liaison position between her church's social services programs and those offered by the ICI. Without premeditation, her social network was expanding. She began to interact on a regular basis with Indians in Los Angeles to whom she would have "paid no mind" a decade earlier.

In 1981 Sophie was approached to put her name in nomination for membership on the ICI Board of Directors. She recalled: "I started working at the church downtown. We were close to the women's alcoholic house and the men's alcoholic [treatment center]. Seeing all those people and their need and feeling that the Indian Center was there and they said that they needed someone to be on the board who cares and who would look after their interests, the Indian community interests. So that's when I run for the board" (January 23, 1984). She was elected handily, and in 1984, when I began recording her life history, she was beginning her second three-year term. She had added a secular and core ethnic community honor to her already considerable accolades.

The ICI was an entirely new social arena for Sophie. In 1981 close to a hundred people were employed at the downtown facilities and the satellite operations in Culver City and Bell Gardens. Most of the ICI staff were Indians Sophie never would have had the opportunity to meet before, given the narrowly defined boundaries of her Christian Indian community. A few ICI employees were churchgoing people, but most were not. Rather, the ICI staff personnel were predominantly powwow people whose company Sophie, just a few years earlier, would have eschewed. As approximately 98 percent of its funding was from public sources, partisan and sectarian views had to be suppressed in deference to an ostensibly operant legal/rational bureaucratic ethic—making the ICI a totally, and pointedly, secular arena. Additionally, the staff's after-work and Friday night drinking parties at Rusty's, The Factory, or The Hut are legend in Los Angeles Indian folklore. They were not only not negatively sanctioned but were elevated to secular ritual. What role could a teetotaler, a Christian Indian lady, have in such a social context?

Why she would get involved in ICI activities was not a question Sophie asked herself. She understood the process as transference of her already proven church leadership skills to a secular Indian arena. Responding to the appeal for help at the Indian Center was consistent with other previous callings that, in the purest expression of Christian charity, she had answered during her lifetime. She explained: "I'm working with them [the ICI] more closer now than I used to because I see the need for them lot more than I did. They need me there to help keep things going. When I see my people in need, then I've just got to do whatever I can to help" (February 21, 1984).

In 1982 Sophie was petitioned by the ICI's executive director to become the organization's treasurer:

> [The executive director] took me aside and begged me to think about being treasurer of the board. He said to me, "Sophie, I need someone I can trust, someone who is honest and strong, someone who won't be persuaded by other people and the things they say. I know everyone in the Indian community respects you and will trust you to be fair and honest. I need your help. You are one of the few people I can trust to bring this board around. Please say you'll help. Please let me put your name in nomination for treasurer of the board." (November, 11, 1984)

What heady things to be said of an Indian elder who, only a few years earlier, had thought of herself simply as a "good Christian woman" and a tireless church worker. Although she had never held such a position before and had no previous experience with administering the funding portfolio of a major social services facility, Sophie believed she was the right person for the job. She considered moral authority and personal integrity, the traditional markers of Choctaw church leadership, to be appropriate—indeed, requisite—skills for secular community leadership. Sophie had left much "to the wisdom of the Lord" in her lifetime, and she had faith that God would provide in his own manner and send signs to "show her the way."

Sophie served as treasurer of the ICI Board of Directors for two and a half years, stepping down from those duties in 1984. At that time, she was also serving as the chairwoman of the board's Committee on the Budget and Finance and its Committee on the Legislature. She even admitted to attending a powwow or two each year, when "forced to go on ICI business," a true expression of loyalty to duty. She was determined to be a model board member and set an example of pan-Indian comportment for the rest of the ICI directors.

Discussion

Consistent with Simić's (1987) model of fluctuating ethnic involvement across the life span, Sophie Wade's complete and unavoidable immersion in Choctaw life in childhood, her reduced involvement in core ethnic activities in early and middle adulthood, and her increasing involvement in pan-Indian activities in old age produces a clearly parabolic life career trajectory. At the private level of family, friends, and informal associations, Sophie maintained a high ethnic contexture throughout her life. She sought out and associated with other Indians wherever she lived. Both of her husbands were Indian. She visits family in Oklahoma once or twice a year. At the public level of work and formal organizations, however, she clearly had sought out and interacted in mostly Anglo social contexts until late in life. Through a set of circumstances, both self-created and serendipitous, Sophie Wade was drawn in her postretirement years into almost complete immersion in core ethnic activities.

Is this perfectly demonstrated instance of Simić's ethnic life career model an inherent social process universally intensified in old age? In Sophie's case, her late-in-life involvement in secular Indian community matters was heavily imbued with the elements of chance. If the Pacific Southwest Methodist Conference had not been committed to greater outreach to ethnic minority groups, the Native American Ministries would not have been realized. In that case, Sophie might well have lived out her life as the emblematic "token Indian" in an all-white Methodist congregation. If she had not accepted postretirement employment two blocks from the Indian Centers, Inc., or if the Native American Ministries had not moved its facility to downtown Los Angeles, she probably never would have "seen the need" for her involvement in social services programs for the broader Indian community. She no doubt would have continued to find fulfillment and prestige as "a good Christian lay leader" in her Indian church.

Even as an octogenarian, Sophie Wade is one of the most visible women in the Los Angeles Indian community. Honored for her volunteer outreach work for the Los Angeles County Community and Senior Citizens Program, a winner of the County Employee of the Month Award, and feted at elders' dinners by the Indian community, Sophie commands the deference and affection of a wide range of her Indian and non-Indian associates.

Sophie understands that her rapid rise within the political hierarchy of the Los Angeles Indian community owes much to the prerogatives of Indian old age. A traditionalist, she has assumed leadership roles due morally upright senior members of an Indian community who wish to counsel their less-experienced members. To Sophie, membership on the ICI Board of Directors was an ascribed as well as an achieved status, an honorific. In that spirit, and despite her relative lack of administrative training, experience in social services, and prior political involvement, she subsequently accepted the posts of treasurer, vice chairwoman, and eventually chairwoman of the ICI board.

Fully believing that her "goodness of purpose" and its exemplification would raise the machinations of the ICI Board of Directors and the center staff above potential petty infighting and fiscal wrongdoing for personal gain, she placed her trust in the executive director to heed her counsel and "do the right thing for the good of the community." Her primary mission in the new social field was not executive directive but the embodiment of moral authority. As a "good Christian woman," it was her role to set an example. She assumed that her membership on the ICI board lent legitimacy, prestige, and a model of moral comportment to that institution. Her association with the Indian Center would raise that institution above community criticism, innuendo, and challenge. These honorific functions are traditionally conferred on and performed by older community members who most clearly embody recognized attributes of moral authority (long, healthy, productive lives, spiritual strength, and sagacity)—attributes Sophie clearly saw in herself. It was obvious to her that a life of Christian good works was her preparation for and legitimation of her new community role as a moral authority in secular matters. Board membership validated her well-spent life and also the center as a community institution worthy of association with her good name and reputation.

NOTES

1. The First Native American and United Methodist Mission is the precursor of the First Native American and United Methodist Church in Norwalk. Since its inception in 1975, the organization has had a number of name changes. The mission, within a year of its inception, became the Native American Ministries. With the move to the church grounds in Norwalk and merger with the Anglo congregation already established there, the congregation assumed its current title. In May 1990, the church began to experiment with separate services for the Native American and Anglo members of the congregation. A Choctaw lay leader explained that the Indian members of the congregation had, for some time, not felt comfortable worshiping with the elderly Anglo host members. Having a service of their own meant that Indian Methodists could relax, be more informal, and sing in their own tribal languages without feeling self-conscious.

2. Sophie Wade was born in her parents' eastern Oklahoma Choctaw back-hills cabin in 1910. Her mother died giving birth to her; her tubercular father died a month later.

3. Angie Debo's several ethnohistories of the Oklahoma Indians—*The Rise and Fall of the Choctaw Republic* (1961[1934]), *And Still the Waters Run* (1940), *The Road to Disappearance: A History of the Creek Indians* (1941), and *The Five Civilized Tribes of Oklahoma: Report on Social and Economic Conditions* (1951)—provide excellent documentation of and insight into this period of American history.

13

The Bicultural Specialist: "Making It" in Both Worlds

My grandmother, in her wisdom, had the foresight to see that if you were going to be Indian, you're going to be *nothing.*[1] And she just said, "Well, you don't have to suffer like I did. You don't have to be Indian. You're half white. You're half Indian. So you're going to be given a choice. And I'm going to make that choice for you. You won't have to go through the indignities of having to learn English for the first time when you go to school and in front of all those white kids like I did." So one day she just quit [speaking the tribal language to her grandchildren]. (Bill Fredricks, February 24, 1979)

THIS DRAMATIC matriarchal edict echoes the early enculturation experience of thousands of "breeds" who, because of their mixed racial heritage and phenotypically Caucasian appearance, were viewed by their parents and grandparents as having cultural and ethnic identity options. Bill is, by tribal enrollment, three-eighths Blackfeet. Legally, he is considered Indian and is eligible for all the community services that ethnic designation engenders. Over his lifetime, he has been the recipient of many federally mandated entitlements due his people.

Aside from a slightly ruddy complexion and the telltale rolling gait that a lifetime of walking in cowboy boots produces in so many Indian men, even the experienced observer would be hard-pressed to identify Bill Fredricks as an American Indian. Since assuming the position of executive assistant (and later executive director) of the Los Angeles City-County Native American Indian Commission, he has taken to wearing conservative three-piece business suits that, no matter how well tailored, always seem to constrain his six-foot-two-inch wrangler's frame. He is rarely seen in public during the workweek without his attaché case. Looking more like an Oklahoma wildcatter or a Texas cattleman forced off his horse and into town for a business meeting than a descendant of a buffalo-hunting nation of High Plains warriors, his public persona is clearly not among the more commonly recognized contemporary American Indian stereotypes.

Bill could pass as an Anglo. Indeed, his grandmother's drastic decision not to teach him, his siblings, and assorted cousins the Blackfeet language was meant to prepare him and them for that eventuality. However, he consciously, to the point of stubbornness and in the face of considerable opposition, has chosen not to pass. This early decision shaped his social experience and reverberates throughout his life history.

In February 1979, Bill and I began to organize his life history. At the end of a five-hour interview marked by his remarkably clear personal insights and candidness, I felt confident enough about the rapport we had established to ask him about the issue of passing.

"Bill, you're three-eighths Blackfeet but five-eighths Caucasian. And you look about as Indian as I do. You could pass . . ." With my pregnant pause, he shifted uncomfortably in his chair, as if by doing so he could elude an unanticipated flash of difficult memory.

"Um-hum. And it bothers me," he offered.

"Have you ever identified with white people?" I pressed.

"No. [If] a white person calls me a dirty Indian, it don't bother me one bit. But Indians that call me a white man, I get *pissed* off. I always got more of it from the Indian community."

Emboldened by his frankness, I continued to probe: "Why is it so important for you to be considered an Indian?" He responded:

> Because that's what I *am*. I want to be accepted for what I feel I am. In front of a whole group of Indians one time I said, "How many of you guys, of you so-called Indians, been born on a reservation and know your culture, know your background, know your ceremonies? You call me not a native because I look white and have green or blue eyes. Yes, I don't have the characteristics that you prescribe as Indian. How many of you have been to an Indian boarding school? How many know your language and can speak it? How many know your traditions or your history? I've done a complete history study on our reservation and tribe." So I said, "To me, I'm far more Indian than you'll ever be. But you're throwing me out and calling me not an Indian

because I'm not the right color." It *really* used to bother me . . . trying to be accepted for what I want to be accepted for. And I've told them this: "A person, a 'breed,' has the opportunity. You don't. You *have* to be Indian. I'm an Indian by *choice*. It has a lot more meaning."

Bill was certainly right in assuming he had a choice of public ethnic stances at some point in young adulthood. His early years, however, left him little personal choice. Born in the midst of World War II in Browning, Montana, on the Blackfeet Reservation, his earliest associations were with other Indians and "breeds." At that time, aside from a small cadre of Bureau of Indian Affairs (BIA) employees, shop owners, and ranchers, few Anglos lived in the small Indian agency town. Bill grew up in a large extended family in which his maternal grandmother, a true and absolute matriarch, and grandfather were in the home or in close proximity to the natal home during most of his childhood, as were scores of his Indian aunts, uncles, and cousins.

Although the family was bilingual, they usually spoke Blackfeet in the home. Because of his grandmother's insistence that the children learn English, Bill was fluent in both languages by the time he went to school. He attended a public elementary school on the reservation for the first six years of his formal education and Indian boarding schools for the next six years of junior and senior high school. At the urging of his grandmother, a staunch supporter of the Catholic church, he also attended summer sessions at the reservation's Catholic mission school.

Except when he accompanied his father on two short job-hunting forays into suburban areas in the state of Washington, Bill spent his childhood on a rural reservation and in quite traditional Blackfeet context. He remembers with great satisfaction and some longing the easy friendships and social warmth of Indian community life, his grandmother's poultices, the talk of buffalo hunts and range wars by the tribal elders who daily waxed nostalgic on the town hall benches, and the annual summer encampments he and his family joined. "In the old days . . . every year, the elders of the tribe would go out and set up camp right west of Browning. They had a traditional place. And they just lived there. There were no special ceremonies and gatherings. They just went there just like the old days. Particularly the elders. Then they'd have their dances, their ceremonies. I lived up there [during the summer]. Those are some of the most enjoyable [memories] of my life" (February 24, 1979).

Bill's concerns about maintaining tribal traditions in what are assumed to be the purest expressions of earlier cultural forms, as well as his rejection of attempts to synthesize traditional Indian ceremony with contemporary, secular, and non-Indian activities, are representative of both the conservative perspectives of archtraditionalists and those of the ethnic marginal whose Indian identity is bolstered through "super-Indian" protestations and presentations of self.

> Every time I'd go back [to Montana], I'd try to schedule it around Indian Days. It's part of you, you know. I used to go back almost every year. I was so disappointed when I went back after it finally became commercialized. Now they call it Browning Indian Days. And [they] added a parade and organized it. This used to be more or less an encampment. Then it came to be more or less of an organized ceremonial. It kind of deteriorated the whole situation. The last time I went back, I was just very dismayed with the fact that it was so commercial . . . gambling stands, hot dog stands. It took away from the whole atmosphere. It's been four of five years since I've been back home. (February 24, 1979)

As with so many reservation Indian youths and particularly the children of mixed parentage, Bill was exposed early to the excesses of reservation binge drinking, which led to his adolescent experimentation with alcoholic beverages and identification with and membership in the young male Indian heavy-drinking party cliques.

> It's an acceptable thing. Everybody else does it. And there's nothing else to do [on reservation]. Peer pressure is the biggest thing. Especially [for "breeds"]. Because I know that identity crisis [is associated with the] degree of Indian blood and acceptance. A strong Indian man is one that can "hold his liquor." [And he's also] a good fighter. The peer pressure to drink is *tremendous*. [A "breed"] has to prove that [he's an] Indian by drinking and getting around . . . [because] that's what Indians *do*. . . . I'd probably say that the highest percentage of drinkers are "breeds."[2] (February 24, 1979)

By the time he graduated from high school, Bill considered himself a "professional drinker." At eighteen, when he left for Los Angeles for the first of four attempts to "get off the res," he drank every day he had the money to do so and in amounts that would be considered unhealthy on any scale of alcohol consumption.

The tentative nature of Bill's first attempts at urban relocation is typical of the migration pattern of thousands of young, unmarried Indian men who, wishing desperately to improve the quality of their lives, accepted the BIA's offer to help them relocate to an urban city.

> I knew before I got into it [that] it was [going to be] lousy. [I used it] as an escape. There was just no opportunity [on the reservation]. You get

older and you realize that. . . . So I chose relocation. [It] really didn't have what I wanted. The best thing they had to offer was computer programming. That wasn't really my goal, but my sister had been down here and [she told me] that the educational system down here was so much better than in Montana. I could get a job and I could get into the educational system easily. . . . And so that's why I used the BIA to get to school down here. (February 24, 1979)

Relocation to Los Angeles was not an easy transition. Unaccustomed to an urban life-style, Bill experienced anomie and alienation.

I had a very difficult time adjusting. Typical Indian. It wasn't so much an Indian cultural adjustment as it was a rural/urban culture adjustment. I couldn't stand the coldness, the size, just a whole different atmosphere socially. The first time lasted about three months. I got a job, made enough for a train ticket home, and that was it. That time I stayed [on the reservation] about six months. When it began to get cold, I realized that I had made a mistake. I did that about three or four times. (February 24, 1979)

On his second and third tries at urban life, Bill gradually, and with the assistance of other relatives already in the city, began to build a social network of other Los Angeles Indians. For many of the relocatees, the so-called Indian bars provided the initial context in which they could find each other and commune. He recalled: "The second time [I came to Los Angeles], I asked, 'Where's the Indians at?' My brother, he knew where to find Indians in L.A. So we went to the Indian bars to find them. I was too young to get served. Every time I walked in, they'd throw me out. And I kept coming back. We weren't there for drinking. We were just there to find some Indians" (February 24, 1979).

Those initial contacts quickly led to Bill's involvement in Los Angeles Indian athletics. Tall, powerful, aggressive, a competitor, Bill was welcomed to the Indian bowling, basketball, and baseball leagues. His weekends took on an established pattern. The Saturday league match was followed by a night of partying and making the rounds of the Indian bars with his league mates. Basketball in the fall and winter, baseball in the spring and summer, and a steady regimen of bowling meets provided year-round recreation, social life, and the mechanism for the development of a shared sense of community among the young Los Angeles Indian relocatees.

By the mid-1960s, Bill had settled into the Los Angeles scene. He studied accounting at Sawyer Business College for approximately eighteen months. He met and married a part-Sioux woman, and they started a family. He enrolled at UCLA, where he majored in public service administration. Consistent with the idealism of the times, he fully intended to put his newly acquired skills to good purpose back on the reservation. In fact, he returned one year to introduce some of his development ideas to the tribal officers, only to discover that the skills he had acquired in the city and his good intentions were not necessarily appreciated or wanted back home.

> When I first came out here, I planned on getting an education and going back [to the Blackfeet Reservation] and helping my people. My original goal was to get a B.A. or an M.A. in business administration or public service administration with the intention of going back and becoming a superintendent on my reservation. . . . But I got down here and I got involved in local Indian affairs. And [when] I went back home, a lot of things I planned on doing [I realized weren't going to happen because] of the whole social change that had been going on in this country. . . . And, you know, you change, you get older, a little maturity. . . . You realize you ain't going to change the whole world. So I just told my wife, "I'm going to work five years . . . and then I have plans to go back on my reservation and open a small business on an economic development bill." But I don't know. I said five years, but that was ten years ago. And I'm just getting in deeper here all the time. (February 24, 1979)

Bill was approximately one year away from graduation at UCLA when major federal funding was secured by the Los Angeles Indian Center for the development of a training and employment outreach project. He applied for and was awarded one of several middle and top management positions made available to members of the Indian community by this funding. His original intention was to complete his studies at UCLA while working part-time at the center. But, much to Bill's regret, that career path never eventuated.

> I've always planned on [going back to college]. But you know how it goes. . . . I just never have had the time. The fact is that when I first took the job at the Indian Center and left UCLA, I took a lower job than was offered to me [i.e., the developer's job] because I explained [to the center director] that I wanted to continue my education. Then when I got down there, they never hired anybody else. So I more or less ended up doing the supervisor's job. So I eventually said, "If I'm going to do it, I might as well get paid for it." And . . . I got so involved in Indian affairs that I never did go back to finish my education. (February 24, 1979)

In the ensuing years, Bill competed for and assumed a number of increasingly responsible positions in the social services sectors of both the Los Angeles Indian and county bureaucracies. When I began my fieldwork in 1973, he was the Indian affairs specialist for the Greater Los Angeles Community Action Agency, a human services delivery organization. He had also formed the United American Indian Council, a nonprofit organization designed to provide technical assistance to Indian and non-Indian research and social services organizations.

As the director of the UAIC, Bill wrote the proposals for and administered a number of landmark research and community services projects. Among the most visible and effective of his grantsmanship efforts were the UAIC's successful collaboration with a research team from UCLA in the first comprehensive survey of the drinking practices of the Los Angeles Indian population (Burns, Daily, and Moskowitz 1974) and the supervision of the first communitywide election of members to the Los Angeles City-County Native American Indian Commission (LACCNAIC) in 1977.

By the mid-1970s, Bill was increasingly recognized and called on by the Los Angeles Indian community for his proven skills as a grantsman, program facilitator, and social services administrator. When people spoke of Los Angeles Indian leaders, his name was usually included in the list of a dozen or so young men and women whose careerist activities and commitment to the development of urban Indian community services paralleling those available to Indians on reservations earned them a place in the developing Los Angeles Indian political oligarchy. Bill, by paying his dues, was clearly one of the up-and-coming young-bloods among the Indians in Los Angeles.

The availability of set-aside funds for social services delivery in ethnic minority communities led the administrative leaders of the Los Angeles Indian community in the early 1970s to consider developing an institutional mechanism by which a united Indian voice could be articulated to funding and service agencies at all levels of government. In August 1974, Leonard Rivers, then the president of the United Indian Development Association (UIDA), wrote an editorial that was printed in the *Los Angeles Times*. In it he outlined both the need for such a structure and the proposed bureaucratic structure by which it could be realized. The concept fired Bill Fredricks's imagination. "He [Rivers] talked about . . . the need to establish some kind of an agency to interface with all levels of government to meet the needs of Indians. . . . I knew Leonard [so] we got to talking. . . . And we talked with the elected officials about the concept of the commission [the LACCNAIC]. . . . They basically agreed to it. And that's how it started" (November 30, 1988).

For the next two and a half years, Bill and a cohort of other Indian community leaders committed themselves to the establishment of such a liaison organization. The concept was not without its detractors in both the Indian and non-Indian camps.

> [The] Los Angeles County Human Relations Commission said we were "undermining [its] work of trying to create a whole united community rather than separating communities by different ethnicities." So we had to meet with them first to explain the uniqueness of Indians and their relationship to the federal government. [We explained to them] how our funds are set aside, [how the federal government] doesn't have a Bureau of Caucasian Affairs or Black Affairs or Mexican Affairs . . . and that there's funds available that we're missing out on because we weren't organized. . . . So they [the Los Angeles County Human Relations Commission] turned around. (November 30, 1988)

After convincing Los Angeles city and county officials of the need and rationale for an American Indian commission, the advocates had the monumental job of creating a support base for the concept among the active members of the Los Angeles Indian community. For two years Bill attended Indian organization meetings, made formal and informal presentations of the Indian commission concept, and lobbied known leaders of particular constituencies for their support. (In the process, he also fashioned a new community status and role for himself.) Much community resistance focused on the question of who would make up the proposed commission. Initially, "all of the commissioners were to be appointed. Nobody in the community liked that much. 'We need a guarantee that there [were] going to be Indians on the commission. . . .' Some of the community fear[ed that] 'some of the larger groups are going to gobble us up or get five people on there. And they're going to run the commission'" (November 30, 1988).

Through all the debates and several redrafts, amendments, and personal guarantees that the formulation of an Indian commission would not eventuate in a granting, jurisdictional, and service providers' turf war, commission advocates saw their concept come to fruition on February 24, 1977. The original Indian commission budget provided for two full-time staff positions, an executive assistant to the commissioners and administrative/secretarial assistance, which the county had the authority to fill by appointment. To satisfy concerns of the Indian community and still comply with a hiring freeze then in place, the county government named an interim executive assistant who was one of the few American Indian county employees at the time. No one harbored any serious reservations about this particular person's capabilities; however, several community members did take exception to the manner in which the position was filled, even if temporarily. They demanded a say as to how and to whom it would be permanently assigned. "We had to go and get it opened up for Indians," Bill recalled. "So we had to go back and draft up a job description, get a waiver from the Board [of Supervisors], and go through the whole county hiring process. [It is] a very stringent hiring process that the county has, and they adhered to it precisely. . . . It prolonged the hiring of staff for six months or so" (November 30, 1988).

Bill applied for the executive assistant position, as did several other American Indians and county employees. In July 1978, largely because of his proven administrative, liaison, and grantsmanship skills, as well as his tireless efforts in the creation of the commission itself, Bill was hired as the first executive assistant (now executive director) of the Los Angeles City-County Native American Indian Commission. He confided: "After working so hard on it for two or three years, I began to say, 'It's something that you created, you worked on. . . .' You can't help but feel that, 'I put it together, I think I'll be the best guy to do it, make it work. . . .' Maybe it's true. Maybe it's not. But after a while I really did believe that" (February 24, 1979).

Bill's commitment to the Indian commission project was complete. As he explained: "I turned down many good job offers in the private sector. I was unemployed. In fact, [I was] waiting for this position [in which] I could feel that I was doing my thing rather than going out and working in some other area" (February 24, 1979). The appointment was a peak experience and critical turning point in his administrative and ethnic careers. He viewed it as the position for which he had worked, studied, and hoped all his adult life. He was not about to tempt the fates.

Although his early, nonstop weekend athletics and drinking party social pattern had been tempered by marriage, family, and career responsibilities, in 1977 Bill was still a member in good standing of the Los Angeles Indian bar scene—albeit a somewhat more upscale, uptown bar scene than had been his earlier downtown haunts. The Hut,[3] a cozy bar within easy walking distance of the Indian Centers, Inc., and the LACCNAIC offices, was the de facto club of the Los Angeles Indian administrators and Bill's unofficial office.

There's an important thing about Indian leadership in the early days. Some people [would] come out and sit there [in a community meeting] all night long and not say a word. [Back then] people [were] fearful of speaking out, of being put down. I [used to] feel that way a lot of times. . . . That's what made the get-together [at the Hut] after the commission meeting so valuable. We [would] analyze [what went on in the formal meeting] and then those people [would] speak up where they wouldn't have [in the formal meeting]. A lot of people had good ideas . . . but maybe it's inhibitions, maybe they didn't feel so [self-conscious] in a less high-pressure situation. More Indian business got done in Indian bars than in any workshops or meetings that they [the commission] had. (January 24, 1989)

As indicated earlier, and as Bill made clear in my most recent talks with him, most Indians who appear at the commission meetings are much more self-confident and no longer afraid to speak up for themselves.

Appointed LACCNAIC executive assistant in July 1978, Bill, two months later and without benefit of treatment or a support group, "went on the wagon." "Maybe it's because I finally felt that I had achieved that Indian status (a matter of personal pride) that I didn't need to drink to prove it to myself. I feel that I'm accepted and that I'm now recognized as that by the community. Funny thing, after I stopped, well, Buddy, Henry, and Ritchie [his drinking partners among the Indian community leadership] really cut down too. Maybe I'm exerting a kind of reverse peer pressure on them to conform"[4] (February 24, 1979).

Discussion

Something of a history buff, Bill Fredricks clearly understood the ethnohistorical significance of his new position and role in the Los Angeles Indian community. No other ethnic minority commission had ever been established in Los Angeles. Thinking of it as his own creation, Bill meant for the LACCNAIC to be a success. He was aware that some of the Indian organizations initiated in the mid-1970s had already atrophied and that some no longer existed. These attempts at self-determinacy were short lived due in large part to inexperienced, inept, or careless grass roots administrations. It would not happen to the Indian Commission if he could help it.

A decade later, Bill still regarded his charge to execute the directives of the commission with the utmost seriousness. He saw himself as a vital liaison between his ethnic constituencies and his county employers. A bicultural specialist, Bill is uniquely qualified for and performs an important function in his continuing role as a translator of two cultural codes. His mixed Anglo and Indian heritage reflects the multiracial background that is a reality for a significant and growing number of people who identify as American Indians. His inherent potential for ethnic duality is also the analogue of multiple cognitive orientations that are the acquired and requisite social competencies of contemporary American Indian life.

It is still widely held that enforced exposure to two or more competing cultural perspectives (Indian, Anglo, and urban Indian), which characterized the enculturation experience of Indians who found their way into urban centers during the last fifty years, was essentially an alienating, stressful life experience. Numerous early studies of Indian urban migration and urban and rural Indian drinking patterns point to the ultimately debilitating social marginality that such cultural overload engenders (Ferguson 1968; Graves 1971; Levy 1985). My own studies of the correspondences between certain sociocultural, biological, and demographic antecedents (among them, degree of Indian ancestry) underscore the association between heavy drinking and mixed racial heritage (Weisner, Weibel-Orlando, and Long 1984).

A growing body of literature, however, reassesses the notion that mixed heritage and/or the mixed enculturation experience (traditional family life, the enforced acculturation within the context of BIA schools, and the intrusion of the host culture via the mass media into Indian life), which characterizes the life experiences of contemporary American Indians regardless of blood quantum, necessitates cultural marginality and universally negative psychological outcomes (Spradley 1969; Oetting, Edwards, Goldstein, and Garcia-Mason 1980; Garcia-Mason 1985; Weibel-Orlando 1988a). Rather than a confusion of competing stimuli, bicultural or multicultural enculturation can be an additive, expanding, empowering life experience.

The individual who has achieved multiple cultural competencies and has learned to read the latent content of social interaction that cues culturally appropriate behavior in a given social setting has a decided cognitive advantage over the monocultural competent who is forced to interact at an ethnic frontier. The skillful practitioner of multiple cultural codes must be, in effect, a supple and empathetic student of semantic translation. Sensitive to the subtle, often nonverbal cues that define a particular social context and its cultural content, the successful bicultural specialist is able to shift tone, affect, interactional style, speech pattern, and lexicon at will in order to fit in and function persuasively on the ethnic frontier.

Positive biculturality is a hard-won competency. Bill Fredricks's life history is a case in point. For the first twenty years of his life, Bill invested considerable energy in denying his status as a person with "a foot in both worlds." His early preoccupation with "fitting in" with his Indian peers and denying his Anglo heritage is apparent in his dogged emulation of the stereotypical supermacho, hard-drinking, young male Indian. Recognizing the inevitability of his grandmother's earlier pronouncements about the fate of traditional Indian life and cultural isolationism in the twentieth century, Bill, in young adulthood, prepared himself for competency in the white world. A college education and on-the-job training in grantsmanship and social services delivery were the contexts in which he developed his bicultural competencies. His decade as the executive director of the Los Angeles City-County Native American Indian Commission clearly indicates these competencies.

At the nexus of several code-specific social arenas, Bill's multicultural experiences have provided him with the ability to translate the cultural codes of his two worlds to and for each other. Bicultural competency has personal and social rewards. For Bill, the personal rewards are high community recognition, self-actualization, and a sense of being allowed "to do his own Indian thing." For the community, his translational skills have facilitated a needed liaison between governmental structures and a people who do not know about, understand, or, often, respect the cultural codes and sociostructural mechanisms by which their social needs are transformed into political policy and action.

Placed at the center of a complex network of information sources of which he is the conduit and disseminator, Bill is also an educator and an explicator. As the LACCNAIC executive director, he functioned as an Indian rights advocate, a facilitator of the collective will of the commission, and, importantly, a role model for a community in which exemplary administrative leadership and bureaucratic expertise are in short supply.

> Indians, probably more than any other group, have an inferiority complex, because we have been brainwashed into doing what the white people expected. Now Indians have come to expect it of ourselves. I [used to] feel very insecure when I'd get a new job. [I'd] think, Am I capable? Do I have the qualities? I can't help think that maybe it's because I have Indian in my background. . . . [Indians are told that

they] can't do these things—become doctors or become lawyers or do highly technical academic-related activities. . . . Everybody's telling you, "You can't do it. Indians can't do that." [But] you get one or two role models . . . I think that's really been our problem. We never had people who would say, "I made [it] this way. I can do it [and so can you]." I think we are just beginning to develop the role models and we can realize we *can* do it. (February 24, 1979)

For Bill Fredricks, life has come full circle. His lifelong attempts to "be accepted for what I am" and "to do something for my people" have paid off in multiple cultural sensitivities. He optimizes a dynamic marginality that, rather than being personally detrimental and psychologically limiting, has allowed him to operate with competence in Indian and non-Indian worlds.

Importantly for Bill, his personal growth can be measured by Indian markers of success. Like the nineteenth-century Blackfeet peace chief who, having grown weary of raiding and the freewheeling exuberance of the bachelor warrior society life, took up the robe and pipe of sagacious counsel,[5] Bill Fredricks has been able to direct his hard-won bicultural capacities in ways that benefit his intended community. His work of facilitating communication across ethnic frontiers for the good of the Los Angeles Indian community is consistent with his earliest model of ideal mature male Indian comportment. The Indian elder as arbiter, sage, and facilitator of the common good during the great annual tribal encampments and councils was the ultimate status to which High Plains men could aspire in later life. Listening to the Blackfeet ancients who gathered in front of the Browning Town Hall to reminisce in the crystalline Montana sunshine, Bill accepted their depiction of Blackfeet elderhood as the template from which his own life career trajectory would be fashioned. True to his American Indian traditions, Bill Fredricks has "never forgotten where he comes from."[6]

NOTES

1. To give the reader a sense of Bill Fredricks's delivery style and strength of conviction, I have italicized the words and phrases he emphasized in his conversations with me. The quotations are from a life history interview on February 24, 1979, and a series of discussions from November 1988 through January 1989.

2. Bill Fredricks's personal insight into the psychological conflicts that lead to disproportionately heavy drinking among "breeds" was subsequently born out by my Indian drinking-patterns research (Weisner, Weibel-Orlando, and Long 1984).

3. When Bill Fredricks and I edited a draft of this chapter on January 22, 1989, he informed me that the Indian bar was a dying institution in Los Angeles. In his opinion, "Indian bars had their purpose in the beginning. But other social institutions have taken their place. And few bars can be considered Indian social centers anymore." This view of institutional shift is shared by Price (1975). Since a few of the bars remain favorite sites for Indian recreational drinking, I have obscured their identity to ensure the partygoers' privacy.

4. Bill Fredricks was thirty-six years old when he stopped drinking. His decision to lower his alcohol consumption at approximately mid-life is consistent with a trend I and my colleagues at the UCLA-NPI Alcohol Research Center subsequently identified (Weisner, Weibel-Orlando, and Long 1984). His reasons for not drinking are remarkably consistent with the stake-in-society theory as developed by Ferguson (1976) in her work with Navajos in Gallup, New Mexico.

5. Ewers (1982:142) describes this status passage.

6. Sanctions urban Indians place on other members of their community parallel those employed in reservation settings. Gossip, shaming, and shunning continue to be powerful social control mechanisms. On several occasions I have heard Indians say of others whom the English would label as being "full of themselves" that "they don't remember where they came from." This phrase suggests that self-aggrandizing public displays are "not the Indian way" and that Indians who are not modest about their successes in either the Indian or non-Indian world, or who do not participate in or minimize the importance of Indian community life and cultural traditions, have forgotten their cultural tenets and ethos. An even more pointedly negative and personally directed comment is, "They've forgotten that *I* *know* where they came from."

VI

Community as Expressed in Institutional Crisis

A MAJOR THEORETICAL and methodological issue remains: Can "viable community" be demonstrated in the collection of ethnic organizations, cultural arenas, and institutional roles that Indians in Los Angeles have created and sustained over the last fifty years? Or, in the final analysis, is the regular use of the term "community" by Indian activists simply the kind of practiced political ploy, manipulative metaphor, or conceptual convenience about which Cohen (1980) and Jones (1987) caution us? What social phenomenon is so encompassing that ethnic community structure—Arensberg and Kimball's (1965) "functional interdependencies" or Guldin's (1980) "ethnic interactional intensities"—is demonstrated by its occurrence? Arensberg and Kimball (1965:110) provide a clue when they suggest that "special interest groups as well as communities gain strength through the solution of problems."

Crisis event analysis as developed by Schensul, Nieves, and Martinez (1982) is useful when one is confronted by the magnitude of the community rupture described in the final section of this book. A crisis event, the point at which ordinary and traditional means of assistance break down and the individual (or community) is forced to seek alternative means of problem solving (Schensul et al. 1982:101), can provide Werner and Schoepfle's (1987, I:57) "epistemological window." The threatened loss of a provider of a constellation of community services Los Angeles Indians had come to expect as entitlements, first on the reservation and then in the city, was that naturally occurring anomaly, that rip in the sociocultural cloth. By documenting the aftermath of the 1986 closing of the oldest Indian community services organization in Los Angeles, I have been able to discover and observe cultural rules and regularities that govern dynamic collective action and thereby community structure.

14

Indian Self-Determination: Institutional and Devolutional Processes

Institutionalization of Community Services

Claiming the Lowansa Tipi[1] as its forerunner, the Indian Centers, Inc. (ICI), in 1984 looked forward to hosting a series of public events the following year to celebrate its fifty years of service to the Los Angeles Indian community (Anonymous 1985). At that time, the ICI was the single largest Indian social services agency in Los Angeles. Since the mid-1970s, its portfolio of provider contracts and grants had become increasingly diversified. Emergency food and shelter, preschool child care and training, alternative high school and Graduate Equivalency Diploma (GED) preparation, job training, and foster child care programs were among the comprehensive social services programs the Indian Center offered the Los Angeles Indian community. The ICI hosted monthly honoring dinners, pow-wows, workshops, public hearings, and its own board of directors meetings to which every Indian in Los Angeles was welcome. More than any other Los Angeles American Indian institution, the ICI was the arena in which political, economic, social, and ceremonial cohesion occurred. Its presence and the constituency it served legitimized claims of a viable Indian community in Los Angeles.

Monitoring the administrative processes of the Indian Center's services programs was the critical responsibility of a select board of directors. The nine members of the board were responsible and accountable for all the fiscal, policy, and staffing decisions. Board membership, which constituted a major community administrative and policy-making function and was considered a particularly prestigious honor, had been determined, until 1982, by community election.

In 1984 Roy Flandreau, a member of the Los Angeles City-County Native American Indian Commission, and Sophie Wade, the Christian Indian elder, in addition to their other high-profile community roles, were also community-elected members of the ICI Board of Directors.[2] They took their board work seriously. Their directorship duties included regular attendance at monthly board meetings and a voice in all decision-making processes; in addition, as elected vice chairwoman, Sophie was expected to preside over meetings the chairman was unable to attend. Board directorship also required some remarkably heroic efforts over the years on the part of both Mrs. Wade and Mr. Flandreau. From its inception in 1935, the Indian Centers, Inc., had had a hand-to-mouth existence, only barely weathering several fiscal crises. Mr. Flandreau described a number of times, in the course of his life history interviews,[3] during which he had personally underwritten the costs of such ICI business as the monthly distribution of *Talking Leaf* or the filing of nonprofit status papers with the appropriate state agencies.

The year 1984 was no exception. In 1982 the Indian Centers, Inc., had been named the Los Angeles Indian services provider for a major federally funded job training and employment program.[4] By the end of the 1983–84 fiscal year, however, there was some danger that the U.S. Department of Labor would not re-fund the Job Training Partnership Act program at the center until discrepancies in the contract's last audit could be justified. The JTPA grant was then the ICI's largest individual source of income. Without those funds, the ICI would have had to seriously retrench.

Steadfast in her belief that the center must be saved no matter what the personal cost, Sophie Wade flew to Washington, D.C., to defend the ICI's administration of the JTPA grant to the Labor Department. Pulling out all of her moral authority stops, she played the forthright Indian community elder and advocate of a wrongly accused and greatly needed Indian social services institution to a fascinated and impressed audience of Labor Department bureaucrats. It worked, just as the conscious use of her ascribed status as Indian elder vis-à-vis Christian Anglos had worked at Methodist national conferences for the past twenty years. The defunding process was stopped. It appeared that she had saved the day.

Rumors and intimations were always circulating within the Los Angeles Indian community about impending funding or personnel crises at the ICI, so I was unsure how much of Mrs. Wade's recounting dealt with real fiscal crisis and how much was the Homeric narrative of a woman unused to dealing with federal bureaucracies and their at times labyrinthine fiscal procedures. At the time, I did not view her saving-the-center-from-defunding saga as an omen of things to come. Nevertheless, I arranged to attend the monthly ICI board meetings in order to observe Mrs. Wade in her new community role, to study the center's continuing importance as a community arena, and to discover the basis for the latest rumors of fiscal crisis.

The ICI board meetings followed a familiar agenda. As with the Indian Commission meetings (see the discussion in chapter 10) and the board meetings of scores of other Indian social services agencies I have attended over the years, calls to order were followed by an obligatory introduction of the people in attendance. A roll call of the directors was often followed by a delay until the requisite five directors were in attendance and a quorum was thereby established. Then the meetings began in earnest. Copies of the minutes of the last board meeting were read and accepted with minor revisions and discussion. Directors would then turn their attention to the executive director's monthly comprehensive reports. Robert Daniels, the ICI's executive director since October 1981, would talk the board members through his report as well as various other program and fiscal reports.

As of the October 1984 meeting, the ICI appeared to be in remarkably sound fiscal and administrative shape. It was, at the time, administering five ongoing social services programs subcontracted by the county of Los Angeles and had, only three months earlier, secured a sixth county contract to provide counseling and sanctuary in cases of Indian domestic violence. Among the contracted social services were a modestly funded youth diversion project, an emergency shelter program, an Indian child welfare service, day care centers in areas of marked Indian residence, and a catchall program entitled "Basic Survival," which was designed to help Indian people develop better coping strategies vis-à-vis urban social and economic networks.

A large ($400,000) city omnibus grant had also been awarded to the Indian Center that summer, although various bureaucratic impediments the executive director was at a loss to explain had delayed the release of funds. (Mr. Daniels minimized the issue, attributing the delay to a "cash flow problem" and "nothing for the board to be concerned about.") Finally, a $1.7 million JTPA grant for fiscal year 1984 from the U.S. Department of Labor, the largest such grant ever awarded the ICI, not only solidified the center's institutional prominence in the community but also consolidated the executive director's control of the Indian Center. With that grant, the ICI had become the chief provider of job training and employment services for unemployed and underemployed American Indians in Los Angeles.

The official operating budget of the Indian Centers, Inc., as of October 1984 was $2,914,212 (ICI 1984). Mr. Daniels was looking forward to 1985 with confidence. In his report, he asserted that the JTPA project should ultimately be funded at $2.5 million a year and that the ICI's yearly operating budget would top $3 million in the next funding cycle. Board members voiced their approval of his fiscal projections and his handling of the funds by enthusiastically and unanimously accepting the executive director's report without discussion or revision.

Committee reports, customarily the next agenda item, were usually short affairs. New business included such concerns as filling key committee positions left vacant by recent resignations and board approval of executive decisions. Board subcommittees were chronically without chairpersons or were understaffed. Several minutes of discussion would usually lead to the appropriately reluctant acceptance by one of the attending board members of yet another committee membership "for the good of the community." The presentation of resolutions needing board review and approval were equally perfunctory processes. Usually drawn up by the executive director or his legal counsel, these resolutions generated little discussion and received quick approval by enough directors to ensure their swift execution.

Board meetings called at 7:00 and formally begun at 7:30 usually ended within an hour. Although there had been some indication that systemic and procedural difficulties were plaguing the center and impeding its orderly flow of funds, at the meetings I attended the executive officer confidently assured the board and interested onlookers that he was "on top of things" and that the "cash flow problem" was temporary. The official word on the state of the Indian Center assured one and all of its continuing fiscal solvency, expanding services to the community, and administrative confidence.

The executive director's comments notwithstanding, I left the October meeting with an uneasy sense that things were not quite right. The ICI board meetings had a reputation for, and a colorful history of, fractious community debate. In fact, I had participated in such dynamic dialogue on several occasions. In 1979 I sat on the ICI Emergency Housing Advisory Board, and its marathon monthly meetings had been marked by spirited exchanges among committee members who held clearly differing points of view and agenda and were not averse to expressing them in public.

Dialectical process had not characterized the ICI board meetings in the fall of 1984. Among other things, the spontaneity of earlier Indian consensus development was missing. The board publicly displayed procedural correctness, complete trust in the executive director, and a general lack of individual dissent or agenda. Even the Indian community's perennial gadfly, Roy Flandreau, had seemed muted and detached. His usual pithy objections, lengthy orations, and avuncular admonitions had been reduced to carefully worded, if pointed, requests for information, sardonic double entendres, and stagy asides. Something was amiss. The board's orderly consideration of issues had been too orchestrated, too pat. I missed, and wondered what had happened to, the freewheeling candor and angst of earlier community debate.

Fiscal Accountability and Deinstitutionalization

The first tangible evidence of the underlying stresses about to undo the Indian Centers, Inc., surfaced in January 1985. Roy Flandreau and I were recording his life history at the time. Although he was officially still a member of the ICI Board of Directors as well as an officer of OCEOLA, Inc., the real estate holding company that managed the old Indian Center site on Washington Boulevard, he had not been to a board meeting since October 1984.

During that afternoon's three-hour interview, Mr. Flandreau's home phone rang four times. On each occasion he announced to me that it was probably someone from the ICI, and that he was not going to take the call. He explained that his signature was needed on a document he did not wish to authorize. With relation to the center, he was voluntarily and steadfastly incommunicado.

Mr. Flandreau's behavior was a clear demonstration of an American Indian interactional and political strategy: conflict avoidance through nonconfrontation. Rather than publicly voice his refusal to condone an executive decision with which he disagreed, he made himself unavailable to peer pressure. Notwithstanding its cultural antecedents, this was highly unusual behavior for the irrascible Roy Flandreau. I guessed the confrontation he was resolutely avoiding concerned something major, an issue that surpassed the usual internecine skirmishes of Indian community politics in which he had previously participated with considerable relish.

With each unrequited and unsettling ring of the phone, Mr. Flandreau offered additional information about the ICI's recent fiscal history and current institutional crisis. According to him, the problems had begun several years earlier. A letter, to which I later became privy, from the general manager of the city's Community Development Department to the mayor's office, with a carbon copy to the city attorney, confirmed that the "Indian Centers, Inc. [had] been experiencing both administrative and fiscal problems since 1981" (Ford 1985a).[5]

Sophie Wade and Rev. John Goodman of the Native American Ministries were both members of the ICI Board of Directors in early 1981 when its director resigned to accept employment elsewhere. An acting director, appointed from among the center's administrative staff, was to oversee the day-to-day operations of the center while the board instituted a national search for a new director. Mrs. Wade described the board's attempt to establish a legal-rational hiring process at that time: "When we [were] looking for the director, we said we wanted a director here, yes . . . a qualified person. [He didn't] particularly have to be an Indian, but Indians were our first choice. But we [did] want them to be qualified, not somebody just because [he] was an Indian . . ." (January 23, 1989).

As it happened, one of the job candidates embodied all the preferred employment qualifications. Robert Daniels, a Seneca with graduate degrees in education and the philosophy of religion and years of grantsmanship and social services administration experience, was the board's choice to fill the position. In October 1981, he arrived from the East Coast. With no local constituency, Mr. Daniels entered the highest paid and most prestigious office in the Los Angeles Indian community—a position that historically had gone to well-respected members of the Los Angeles Indian community who over the years "had paid their dues"—as an unknown, untried outsider.

It was generally agreed among the core members of the Indian community that Robert Daniels bore considerable watching before approval and cooperation would be extended to him. Sophie Wade, however, was one of his consistently staunch supporters. She commented: "He's a go-getter. He told us that when he was looking for a job. He said that if he can't get us, the Indian Center, a million dollars by the end of that year, that he wouldn't ask to be here any longer, but if he made a million dollars for the Indian Center, that he would expect to have a 10 percent raise for . . . [the] coming year. So that's the kind of contract he got. And he did [it]. . . . He hit two million for the Indian Center" (January 23, 1984). Through skilled grantsmanship and expert use of his many and nationwide contacts in grants administration offices, Mr. Daniels managed to reach his fiscal goals in his first year. It appeared that he was truly the go-getter he had promised the ICI board he would be. As a result, his title was changed from director to executive director of the ICI in February 1982.

Mr. Daniels's initial flush of success was far from complete. The first sign of erosion of community support for his directorship occurred at the ballot box. To operate with authority, the executive director of the Indian Center needed, according to the center's legal and corporate guidelines, a quorum of unimpeachable and representative community members willing to serve with consistency on the board. Historically, highly visible and respected members of the Indian community had always been elected; over the years, however, attempts to run communitywide elections for new board members had become logistical nightmares. By 1982 the center's board election outcomes largely did not represent a community mandate. With each year, progressively smaller numbers of people voted, let alone ran, for the once-coveted honorific positions.

Board elections were deemed too costly and time consuming and were therefore discontinued. Instead, the executive director decided to nominate people with whom he had established rapport and he asked current board members also to make nominations. Candidates' names were submitted to the board, along with nominating petitions that carried the requisite number of community member signatures. Directors who retained their seats on the board and attended the monthly meetings voted among themselves for inclusion or exclusion of the nominees. Concurrently, seasoned, administratively experienced board members began to mail in their resignations.

Within two years, the erosion of community support for Mr. Daniels's directorship was such that seats on the ICI board remained unfilled for months at a time. As a result, on occasion it was impossible to obtain a quorum at the monthly board meetings. Mr. Daniels sorely needed a full board and elected officers whose prestige and reputations placed them and his executive directorship above community suspicion. Sophie Wade, the embodiment of moral authority, was particularly suited for the honor, and Mr. Daniels pressed her to continue her board service. In 1982 she was elected board treasurer.

In 1983, when Mrs. Wade took on the further responsibility of treasurer of OCEOLA, Inc., at Robert Daniels's suggestion, he was about to complete his second year as executive director of the Indian Centers, Inc. His touted grantsmanship skills were well supported, as he had continued to increase dramatically the gross dollar value of the ICI contract and grants portfolio. The number of services, employees, and people served by the center's programs had also increased substantially with each year. Although Mr. Daniels lacked a clear community mandate, from all appearances his leadership was sound and his stewardship of the center firm.

While rumor and innuendo about how the ICI administered its wealth of contracts and grants had existed for as long as it had received public funds for the delivery of social services, there had been little public documentation of alleged fiscal improprieties. Based largely on anecdotal reports by disgruntled employees, the possibility of fiscal laxness at the Indian Center had been easily dismissed as idle gossip. Until mid-1984, discontent with the administration had been confined to intramural protestation and community speculation.

In July 1984, with the onset of a new fiscal year and a new funding cycle, the problems could no longer be contained in-house. At that time, the California Department of Education elected not to re-fund the center's youth programs for fiscal year 1985. The first tear in the ICI's weave of local, state, and federal contracts and grants, it set in motion a series of parallel and associated funding decisions that eventually unraveled the center's entire fiscal matrix.

On October 5, 1984, the director of the Training and Job Development Division of the Community Development Department (CDD) of the city of Los Angeles sent a letter to Robert Daniels stating that, "during the past two (2) years, the ICI has had a traditional problem of not maintaining a fiscal system that could be audited in a manner to adequately protect funds from potential fraud and/or abuse as defined by the federal guidelines." The city's JTPA officer further advised Mr. Daniels that, because of the accounting irregularities that had been brought to his attention, "at this time, we do not feel comfortable in releasing advance funds for October" until satisfactory explanations for such irregularities could be supplied (Bruce 1984).

With this written request for additional fiscal information from the center's administrative staff, the city grants manager had begun to establish a paper trail. Copies of the cautionary letter were distributed to the general manager of the city's JTPA division, the chief accountant of the CDD and its program monitor, the councilman of the city district in which the ICI was located, the Los Angeles deputy mayor and chief liaison with the Indian community, and the mayor of Los Angeles. At this point, the ICI administration was no longer in control of its own image management. First the state and now city funding agencies had sounded alarms that would reverberate throughout the center's supralocal funding and support network.

On October 31, 1984, the Special Investigations Unit (SIU) of the CDD conducted a fiscal review of the grants it had awarded to the Indian Centers, Inc. The review resulted in the funding agency questioning approximately $119,000 in expenditures. After several meetings with the ICI management, the city investigating officer, on November 16, 1984, filed an eight-page report with the city's CDD general manager. That report outlined eleven areas of questionable costs and accounting procedures, four possible remediations, and recommended changes in the ICI fiscal system. The CDD general manager's decision to cast the fiscal review findings far afield was to have a devastating effect on the Indian Center's integrity as a public administration institution. By notifying the California Department of Education of the city's intent, he underscored his concurrence with both the state's earlier findings and the city's present policy of withholding funds from the center. This action served to support the state's final decision to defund all of its contracts with the ICI.

The city special investigator also systematically distributed copies of his report to higher-ranking members of the city's bureaucracy. The concurrence of his administrative superiors with his recommendations was swift. By November 21, 1984, the SIU officer in charge of the ICI investigation had obtained the authorizing signatures of the city's director of job training programs, the director of the Health and Human Services Agency, two assistants to the general manager of the CDD, and the general manager himself. This consensus with the investigator's findings and recommendations made remedial action mandatory. Too many people in strategic decision-making positions in the city government now knew about the fiscal problems at the ICI. There was no way to negotiate, sub rosa, a mutually acceptable means of continuing to fund the Indian Center.

A three-page summary of the SIU officer's findings and recommendations was sent to the ICI on November 27, 1984. That letter put the center on notice that, "pursuant to the aforementioned findings, . . . the City of Los Angeles shall not release any additional JTPA funds until such time ICI submits to the city the [written response and all supporting documents] requested in the four recommendations" (Ford 1984:3). Mr. Daniels and his support staff (consisting of a lawyer, the financial director of the ICI, and an outside accounting consultant) dutifully tried to satisfy the funding agency's informational requests. They met with a city representative on December 11, 1984, and in subsequent discussions agreed that the SIU would (1) review the ICI's new fiscal plan, and (2) review (on an ongoing basis) the implementation of the system, after which the city would submit its written approval. In a follow-up memo to his department chief, the SIU investigator described the proposed plan as "a courtesy to ICI," since the first fiscal plan submitted to the SIU by the ICI "was totally unacceptable and same was returned to ICI without action" (Hughley 1985).

On December 20, 1984, the Indian Center transmitted two letters to its city granting agency. One letter specified the corrected fiscal system it would implement; the other contained responses to the $119,000 in questioned costs. During subsequent meetings, the ICI advised the city's fiscal investigators that it would need an appropriate amount of time to implement the system. The CDD agreed to the center's request and also offered to provide any technical assistance and/or review required for such implementation. The investigatory climate had cooled. It seemed that compromise and remediation could, after all, be reached and that the center's viability as a social services provider could be sustained.

During the last week of January 1985, a series of meetings between a CDD representative, the ICI financial officer, and an outside accounting consultant, to be held at the center's offices on Sixth Street, were scheduled, postponed, rescheduled, and missed. At those times, the ICI was to have provided "(1) verification that it had implemented its 'new' fiscal system and (2) . . . documentation pursuant to the $119,000 in questioned costs" (Hughley 1985). On Friday, February 1, 1985, the ICI hand-delivered a letter from its executive director to the CDD stating that the center was suspending its city-funded Cable TV Training Program because of the city's refusal to live up to its contractual commitments to the center (Daniels 1985a). This correspondence included an eleven-page opinion from the ICI's legal counsel alleging numerous improprieties by the SIU officer during his January 29, 1985, investigation. Apparently, the center's administrators had decided that the best defense was a strong offense.

The ICI executive director also disseminated widely his and the center's legal counsel's position papers. The director of the city's JTPA program, the deputy mayor, the ICI's district councilman, two officers of the U.S. Department of Labor, and the ICI lawyer all received copies of these documents. Importantly, except for those sent to the ICI lawyer, the documents were distributed to administrators within the funding hierarchy superior in rank to those individuals who had initiated the investigation of the center's fiscal policies. Theoretically, the recipients of the ICI documents had the authority to mitigate the investigation if they so desired.

The SIU officer's response to the ICI suspension of services funded by contract no. 62606 was to attempt to postpone for a day a scheduled meeting with the ICI so that he would have time to confer with the CDD general manager about the consequences of the center's February 1, 1985, pronouncements. Calls to the ICI to that effect went unacknowledged by ICI officers. The next day, the Indian Center hand-delivered a second written complaint against the city's SIU officer to the CDD general manager. Mr. Daniels claimed to be "dismayed that [the SIU officer] cancelled the meeting that day," and he admonished that the cancellation only "further delayed the too often delayed resolution of the city's 'questioned costs' and thereby delayed resumption of services to the Indian community [and necessitated] needless costs for services from its outside attorney and auditor—a repetition of similar needless waste caused by his [the city auditor's] one and a half hour tardiness for an appointment on January 29, 1985" (Daniels 1985b).

The city responded rapidly to this second set of complaints and countermoves. In a letter dated February 12, 1985, addressed to the executive director of the Indian Centers, Inc., the general manager of the Community Development Department announced the city's intent to issue a thirty-day contract termination notice. The letter also suspended program operations for contract no. 63072 (the emergency housing funds) based on "concerns with regard to the agency's overall fiscal adequacy" (Ford 1985a). In the harshest language yet, the CDD general manager declared:

> You have been found to be in noncompliance with Sections 505 and 506 of your contract, and as such, you are requested, per the provision of Section 703.c, to submit a corrective action plan within five (5) working days, setting forth the corrective actions to be taken, subject to City approval, in writing, and pending resolution of this matter, any cash requests submitted will not be honored by the City. Be further advised that per Section 706, you are to immediately notify employees and other parties contracted under the terms of agreement of the suspension status of your agency within five (5) working days. (Ford 1985a)

In addition to the chairman of the ICI Board of Directors, the chief of the California Department of Education and the chief of the Labor Department's Division of Indian and Native American Programs were also sent copies of the city's notice of intent to defund the Indian Center, thereby making the fiscal accountability of the center a national issue. According to trusted community sources, relevant Los Angeles County officers were also contacted at this time about the city's intent to defund the ICI. There is, however, no clear record of written correspondence between the city and county officials at this point in the defunding process.

On February 19, 1985, the CDD general manager, in a four-page memo, asked the mayor's office for a special hearing of the ICI case at the Grants, Housing, and Community Development Committee meeting scheduled for that same day. The rationale was that a speedy review was needed "in order to prevent any further possible misuse of federal funds" (Ford 1985b). The memo went on to outline the city's basic concerns about fiscal accountability at the center and to recommend that action be taken subsequent to the proposed defunding. The city's fiscal officer suggested that alternative "existing service deliverers who can provide a similar service to current participants of the ICI" be located and that a "process for transferring current participants to the agency selected" be developed (Ford 1985b). The CDD also recommended that the defunding take place no later than thirty days after notifying the Indian Center of the decision to defund.

A photocopy of this memo was forwarded to the city attorney, further extending the network of public administrators now involved in the ICI funding crisis. Executive authority in the matter had been relegated to the city's top legal official. The city's posture was no longer one of information seeking and offers of technical assistance. Its goal had become how best to "safeguard federal funds" (Ford 1985b). Unfortunate references (in four places in the February 19 letter) to the "termination" and "closeout" of the ICI, rather than the termination and closeout of the city's two contracts with the ICI, foreshadowed the ultimate effects of the city's intended and eventual action.

Building Community Support in Times of Crisis

By the end of February 1985, the executive director of the Indian Centers, Inc., and his fiscal and legal advisors were no longer able to keep the defunding crisis from coming to the attention of ICI employees, its board of directors, or the Indian community. Luckily for the center, the city's Board of Grants Committee postponed its hearing of the CDD request for termination of its ICI contracts for one week. It was not much time, but ICI employees and board members moved quickly to develop a ground swell of community support. In a flurry of telephone calls and emergency meetings, ICI administrators attempted to mobilize their contacts within the Indian community to assist the beleaguered center.

Los Angeles City-County Native American Indian Commission support was critical. Despite three years of community discontent about the current ICI administration, the LACCNAIC had been true to its policy of laissez-faire with regard to the intramural affairs of Indian community organizations. Even though certain members of the Indian Commission now knew about the funding crisis at the center and had made regular but informal reports to the commission since August 1984, the LACCNAIC as a body had steadfastly refused to intervene. "We took a 'hands-off' policy," Bill Fredricks insisted. "[We were] not to meddle in [the] internal affairs of an organization unless it becomes [an] overriding factor . . . a detriment to the community. Like the Indian Center . . . we had all kinds of complaints. . . . 'Hey, do something about it.' [We told them,] 'We can't do anything about it until you come up with some documentation'" (November 30, 1988).

On February 19, 1985, Pete Chessman, an ICI employee and staff representative, attended an Indian Commission meeting and asked for a place on that evening's agenda. In an impassioned narrative, he told of the treatment of the Indian Center by the city investigators and the current circumstances at the center because of the city's investigation. He requested commission support of the ICI's attempt to prevent the city's proposed defunding of Indian Center contracts. The commission requested that its executive director, Bill Fredricks, arrange a fact-finding meeting with the ICI executive director (LACCNAIC 1985).

During the next month, Mr. Fredricks and the executive committee of the Indian Commission held a series of meetings with the ICI and city personnel about the community crisis. The city's final decision to defund the center continued to be postponed. This hiatus gave the commission's executive committee time in which to meet and attempt to negotiate on behalf of the Indian Center with the city's CDD officer and a representative from the city council. By that time, however, city officers in all quarters were in agreement that there were "very serious problems with the Indian Center's fiscal management" and "in all probability the City would defund the Indian Center" (LACCNAIC 1987b). Faced with a seemingly inevitable circumstance, the commission's executive committee offered city officials suggestions for the orderly transfer of grants money to other appropriate, existing Los Angeles Indian organizations.

By mid-March 1985, the ICI had had all it would take from what its administrators labeled a harassing city bureaucracy. Robert Daniels sent a letter to the Community Development Department declining the $400,000 JTPA grant that had funded the Institute for Career and Vocational Training employment programs. Unfortunately, bureaucratic processes had been set in motion that could not be stopped by a dramatic rejection of a troublesome, but relatively small, slice of the ICI grants pie. Investigations into the integrity of the fiscal management of all other ICI grants were already underway at county and national levels. John Lewis and Bill Fredricks, as representatives of the LACCNAIC, met with the director of the JTPA program in the city's Community Development Department on April 19, 1985, to discuss the possibility of keeping the now-declined JTPA funds within the Los Angeles Indian community. In the course of those discussions, the commission representatives were informed that it was distinctly possible the Indian Centers, Inc., would lose its other city grants as well. Stunned, the commissioners asked for a full, documented report. The CDD forwarded the requested documentation to the Indian Commission on April 29, 1985.

The commission's executive committee took only one day to review the documents the CDD had provided before deciding that the matter was so serious it had to be brought before the ICI's board of directors:

> We happened to get that documentation because the city called us and asked us, "What's going down?" So they [the city officials] brought [us] all this information regarding the ICI investigation, and how they had lost funds, and information that the other agencies were considering having some sort of sanctions against them [the ICI]. So, it was imperative . . . we [had] to do something. We [couldn't] just let this agency go down and lose that many programs, especially when, behind the scenes, we had helped [the ICI] get a lot of those programs. So we [had to] go to bat for them. (Bill Fredricks, November 30, 1988)

On May 9, 1985, the executive director of the Indian Commission received the county's fiscal review reports from its ICI investigations. To its credit, the ICI fared better in the county reports. The county investigators had been considerably more positive in their assessment of the center's management of county-generated funds even though, as early as November 16, 1984, the county had questioned costs on all five of its grants to the ICI. In terms of its performance, the ICI "qualitatively and quantitatively . . . continues to perform satisfactorily. It consistently is meeting or exceeding program goals under its CSBG and JSSP contracts" (Tunks 1985). ICI management and operations also posed no problem for the county investigator, who felt that "current agency staff are good, performing satisfactorily, professionally, and with a discernible degree of personal commitment to doing quality work. Reports, etc., are generally good and on time" (Tunks 1985).

As with the city, the county's concern was essentially the lack of efficient fiscal management at the ICI. But even that, the report suggested, was expected to improve. The county's "fiscal monitor is continuing to work extensively with the agency in its efforts to take necessary corrective action. This satisfactory resolution to major and minor deficiencies can be achieved" (Tunks 1985). However, the county officer did not give the ICI a clean bill of fiscal health. His report included three suggestions about remedial steps that needed to be taken by the Indian Center to avoid a probation effective April 1, 1985, a suspension effective June 1, 1985, and termination of county contracts by June 30, 1985. The center was clearly not out of the woods vis-à-vis their commitments to the county. Loss of a second, major slice of its funding pie seemed imminent unless immediate and drastic corrective steps were taken.

Shaken by the prospect that the county might also elect to withdraw funds from the center, Mary Waters, John Lewis, and Bill Fredricks, as the executive committee of the Indian Commission, attempted to make a presentation of the accumulated documents to the Indian Center's board. The meeting resulted in heated confrontations between members of the commission legation and the center's legal counsel and board chairman. Both center officials refused to acknowledge the right of the commission's representatives to question ICI administrative procedures.

The next day, the center's lawyer presided over a second special ICI board meeting. In a letter the lawyer had drafted for board approval and signature, the Indian Commission chairman and executive director were roundly attacked for instigating the previous night's meeting. Roy Flandreau, having been apprised of a move to oust him from the board for nonattendance, and having sensed an impending resolution of the center's administrative crisis, decided to attend that day's board meeting. Unable to contain himself, he told the center's lawyer, in no uncertain terms, what he thought of a letter that besmirched the reputations of two of the most respected members of the Indian community (June 5, 1985). Charges and countercharges of libel were hurled. Dissension was now rife among the ICI board members and between the board and the administration it was charged to monitor.

In an extraordinary display of patience, community loyalty, and due diligence, the Indian Commission's executive committee continued to investigate and mediate between the city, county, and state funding agencies on behalf of the center. The LACCNAIC waited over a year to take a public stand. It did, however, make recommendations to the ICI for corrective actions—suggestions that the center's executive director largely ignored.

Losing the Community Mandate

Resolutely, the Indian Centers, Inc., toughed it out alone for another seventeen months. During that time, the center staff delivered those social services that remained funded. *Talking Leaf* was published, if somewhat more sporadically than it had been in the past. To celebrate its fifty years of operation, the ICI hosted the announced National JTPA Conference in the summer of 1985. That same year, Jimmy McElvey, the ICI board chairman, and Roy Flandreau handed in their resignations. Sophie Wade, still loyal—if not to Robert Daniels, then at least to the idea of a Los Angeles Indian center—agreed to serve as chairperson of the board as of December 1985, when Mr. McElvey stepped down. She canvassed friends in her church and county administrative networks to join her on the ICI Board of Directors.

The Indian Center's last year was a period of slow attrition. One by one, service contracts and grants reached expiration and were not re-funded. The executive director struggled to develop alternative funding sources. The city, county, state, and federal funding agencies continued to ask for accountability on two- and three-year-old contracts that still had not been properly closed out.

The Indian Commission continued to seek alternative solutions to the center's fiscal accountability crisis. According to its 1986–87 annual report, before issuing a public position paper on the matter, the commission had conducted thirteen months of extensive negotiations with the ICI board and its administration.

Nobody wanted to see the center close down. Nobody. The city didn't. The county didn't. The commission certainly didn't. We all worked for thirteen months to try do stop it from happening. But Daniels and his cronies wouldn't work with us. And by the time we were asked by the city and county for advice, the center was beyond help. There was no way we could have continued to support it as it then existed. To do so would have damaged our own credibility. The writing was on the wall. (Bill Fredricks, March 10, 1989)

The language of a June 16, 1986, commission letter, proposed for dissemination to all funding agencies that had contracts and/or grants with the Indian Centers, Inc., suggests the advocacy group's frustration with its errant protégé:

> The LACCNAIC has long been aware of a continuing history of se- rious fiscal management problems within the fiscal administration of Los Angeles Indian Centers Incorporated Grant Programs. Our Com- mission has made an extended good faith effort to work with the ICI Board of Directors and its Administration in a concerted effort to resolve these problems.
>
> Although the Board Chairperson and several members of the ICI Board have made sincere efforts to implement corrective measures, they have been continually overruled by actions of the majority of the Board and Administration. . . . As of this date, all of our efforts have been in vain, as the majority of the ICI Board of Directors and Admin- istration have failed to take any substantive corrective measures to improve their fiscal management system. In addition they have failed to adequately account for program funds received on behalf of the Los Angeles Indian Community.
>
> These failures and the cavalier attitude of the majority of the Board and its Administration regarding these serious problems has led our Commission to lose all confidence in the fiscal integrity and fiscal management capability of [the] ICI Administration.
>
> Because of these adverse circumstances, the Commission has been reluctantly forced to withdraw its support for continuing grant fund- ing for Indian Center programming. . . .
>
> This was an extremely distasteful and difficult decision for our Commission, as we usually try to the best of our ability to promote and support all Indian organizations. (LACCNAIC 1986)

The commission's letter went on to outline the devastating effects the dismantling of the Indian Center would have on the Los Angeles Indian community. It expressed the commission's willingness to work with the funding agencies to find alternative solutions to de- funding.

By the time the LACCNAIC had made its position public, the die already had been cast in Washington, D.C. On August 15, 1986, Sophie Wade, as chairwoman of the ICI Board of Directors, received notice from the U.S. assistant secretary of labor that, "pursuant to Section 164(f) of the Job Training Partnership Act (JTPA) and the Implementing Regulations of 20 CFR 632.23 (a), Emergency Termination, as of this date the Department of Labor is terminating the Indian Centers, Inc. of Los Angeles Grant No. 99–4–0085–55–055–02 funded under Section 401 of JTPA" (Semerad 1986).

The death blow had been struck. With the loss of its major source of funds, the Indian Center had only five small service grants from the county left to administer. Their combined administrative budget lines would not meet the center's considerable overhead without dramatic retrenchment. The county acted swiftly to cut its losses. On September 12, 1986, the Los Angeles County Area Agency on Aging's Community and Senior Citizens Services Department asked its board of supervisors for permission to terminate its contracts with the ICI.

One month later, with the resignations of every other member of the ICI Board of Directors and the executive director in hand, Sophie Wade put pen to paper. In a letter addressed and distributed to the U.S. secretary of labor, the secretary of state of California, the attorney general of California, the Internal Revenue Service, the mayor of Los Angeles, the board of supervisors of the county of Los Angeles, the U.S. Bureau of Indian Affairs, and the Los Angeles American Indian community, Mrs. Wade, in her last official act as chairwoman of the ICI Board of Directors, announced that "for all official and practical purposes the Indian Centers, Incorporated, ceases to exist" (Wade 1986).

NOTES

1. The Lowansa Tipi was the original American Indian meeting place in Los Angeles. It was established in 1935 by Mira Frye Bartlett, a Kickapoo Indian from Oklahoma, with the help of the Society of Friends (Anonymous 1985:1).

2. Roy Flandreau has filled many community leadership positions since his arrival in Los Angeles in the early 1970s. From 1974 until 1977, he was the director of the Indian Centers, Inc. In that capacity, he was instrumental in the standardization of the production and distribution of *Talking Leaf* and in securing the first ICI-administered, federally funded temporary employment and training grant for Indians in Los Angeles. Ill health forced his retirement in 1977, although he later served on the ICI Board of Directors, from which he resigned in 1985. Since that time he has devoted his energies to the development of social services programs for the urban Indian elderly. He currently acts as an advocacy planner for the Los Angeles County De-

partment of Community and Senior Citizens Services and is the organizer and president of the Los Angeles American Indian Counsel on Aging.

3. Roy Flandreau and I recorded his life history during a series of interviews that was initiated in November 1984 and culminated in June 1985.

4. The Job Training Partnership Act (JTPA) was an initiative of the Reagan administration and the 1980s alternative to the Comprehensive Employment and Training Act (CETA) programs instituted by federal administrations in the 1970s.

5. All letters cited in section VI and dated through May 10, 1985, are located in an untitled report the LACCNAIC compiled and presented to the ICI Board of Directors on that date. A complete copy of the untitled report, along with photocopies of letters dealing with the closing of the ICI that had been generated subsequent to May 10, 1985, were given to me in November 1988 by the executive director of the Indian Commission. Letters dated subsequent to May 10, 1985, had been added as addenda to the original report.

15

Community Response
to Institutional Crisis

> Indian people are long accustomed to tragedies and adversity, but have always demonstrated the ability to overcome and persevere. Now more than ever is the time for the Commission, Indian community organizations, and the entire Indian community to unite in a spirit of coordination and cooperation with elected officials to reestablish local Indian programs and to advocate the full rights and funding of federal urban Indian programs in an atmosphere of local autonomy and Indian self determination. (LACCNAIC 1987b:iv)

THE U.S. DEPARTMENT OF LABOR, on August 14, 1986, formally announced its intent to terminate its Job Training Partnership Act (JTPA) grant with the Indian Centers, Inc. (ICI). This national-level funding decision set in motion a flurry of at once cooperative and competing responses to the impending institutional vacuum within the Los Angeles Indian community. Some community responses were highly successful; others, for a variety of structural reasons, were doomed to failure. All attempts at institutional reconstruction, however, provide insights into the mechanics and guiding principles that structure community processes.

Sophie Wade, long since abandoned by the four other people who were still formally members of the ICI Board of Directors when she was elevated to chairwoman of the board, spent the next six months trying to reconstitute an Indian Center support group. While Los Angeles City-County Native American Indian Commission (LAC-CNAIC) members, the directors of the Orange County Indian Cen-

ter, the Los Angeles Indian Health Center, the American Indian Free
Clinic in Compton, and the ministers of the various Indian churches
with whom she had had long personal associations were sympathetic and willing to defend her role in the crisis, few were interested in
working with her toward resuscitating the ICI.

Sophie and I were in communication fairly regularly throughout
the ICI crisis. After the center closed, we talked at length about
reorganizing the center around a more modest mix of limited social
services funding and volunteer efforts. Attempting to learn from
past errors, Sophie was adamant that more community control in
the center's day-to-day operations was needed. She was equally convinced that the criteria for center employment or directorship established at the time the ICI had hired Robert Daniels were still sound:
"I want the best people I can find for the new board. I want people I
can work with and can trust to do the right thing. It doesn't matter if
they are Indian or not, as long as they will do what's right for the
Indian community" (February 26, 1987).

Sophie had strict criteria for board membership. In fact, except for
the editor of *Talking Leaf,* a Cherokee county employee she had
convinced to join the old ICI board the year before, John Lewis (who,
besides being a member of the LACCNAIC and the longtime president of the United Indian Development Association, was also a
member of Sophie's church), and me, the only other person she
could think of with whom she could work successfully was her
middle-aged son Roger. All of us may, in fact, have had the requisite
skills for and experience working with a service center and with
administrative bureaucracies. However, it was clear that Sophie's
choice of teammates was based on social and emotional, not legal-
rational, criteria (whether or not she liked the people, how well she
knew them, how they had treated her during the past two tu-
multuous years, her traditional right as a community elder to hand-
pick her support team, and the extent to which she was still con-
nected to certain social networks within the Indian community).

By March 1987, the reality of Sophie's spent community coin was
clear. She had called a meeting at her home to which she invited
three people from her list of prospective developers to plan the res-
urrection of the Indian Center. On the appointed evening, she and I
sat and talked for an hour over coffee and doughnuts, waiting for her
two other supporters to arrive. They never did. Both people had
elected to do other things that evening. There was to be no ground
swell of community support for her dream of reviving the center.

Sophie's inability to create a caucus revealed important elements of Indian community process. She had been imbued with ceremonial prominence, which she had mistaken for political power. The moral authority she had achieved and practiced so effectively in one social arena had not been wholly transferrable to another. Individuals become the embodiments of the institutions they create and foster. The center's taint was also Sophie's stain. Structural and institutional changes do not occur in cyclical surges and ebbs; nor do they manifest themselves in phoenixlike resurrections of older institutional forms from the ashes of their recent immolation. Rather, older structures and the people associated with them, having lost their community mandates, are abandoned. Alternative institutional forms and new personal leadership are allowed to surface in their wake.

The LACCNAIC, having abandoned its policy of laissez-faire in internal Indian community matters in March 1985, took an active role in the attempts to reconstitute the Los Angeles Indian social services delivery system. Its rationale for doing so was that mediation between local Indian organizations and their extramural funding agencies had traditionally been a commission function. During its thirteen months of investigation, the commission made a concerted effort to sustain the services of the Indian job training and employment programs (Fredricks 1986). Commission representatives tried to convince the U.S. Department of Labor to place its JTPA Indian grant either under the direct administration of the commission or with one of the other well-established Los Angeles Indian organizations. Several were suggested.

The American Indian Health Center on Pizzaro Street in the central city and its parent organization, the American Indian Free Clinic in Compton, had become increasingly eclectic in their health and human services offerings. Their record of ten years of relatively trouble-free administration of public funds made them strong candidates for task at hand. If no existing local Indian organization satisfied the administrative prerequisites of the Department of Labor, the commission suggested that the funds be granted directly to appropriate city or county agencies, which would then hire qualified American Indians to administer the program.

The Department of Labor had another agenda and other funding criteria. It was willing to continue to fund programs that provided job training and employment services to Indians, even through another Indian organization. However, it wanted assurances that the Indian organization eventually chosen had both a proven track record of fiscal responsibility and success in the administration of a

JTPA program. It was a catch-22 situation: the only Los Angeles Indian organization that met the second criterion was the Indian Centers, Inc., which the Labor Department had just elected to defund. Only the Orange County Indian Center, located approximately forty miles to the southeast of downtown Los Angeles, met both criteria. In fact, the OCIC had been administering JTPA funds responsibly for at least as long as the ICI had.

One week after its letter of termination to the ICI, the Department of Labor notified the Indian Commission that the unused portion of the center's JTPA contract would be turned over to the OCIC as a stopgap measure. Not meant as a permanent arrangement, the action was an expediency in the best interests of the Indians who benefitted from the delivery of the training program. Described as "the nearest existing Indian JTPA grantee," the Orange County Indian Center hastily found a Los Angeles location just a few blocks from the old ICI facility. It hired many of the people who had manned the ICI's JTPA program and opened its doors to the community within a month. The OCIC was authorized to operate as the interim administrative agency only "until the end of the current funding cycle, June 30, 1987" (Fredricks 1986).

In September 1986, the LACCNAIC chairman and its executive director flew to Washington, D.C., to meet with key officials of federal Indian funding agencies. The commission representatives had a dual mission. The first was to advocate on behalf of the Los Angeles Indian community for general increases in urban Indian social services program funds. Second, the commission representatives hoped to talk to officials in charge of the funding and defunding processes about the loss of much-needed programs and services in the Los Angeles Indian community resulting from the closing of the Indian Center.

The commission representatives met on September 3, 1986, with Bureau of Indian Affairs personnel from the Indian Child Welfare Act program to discuss potential ways of retaining that program in Los Angeles. Several alternatives for keeping these funds within the Los Angeles Indian community were discussed. Although negotiations with funding officers in both Washington and Sacramento continued for the rest of the year, the LACCNAIC, due to "unfavorable legal restrictions, rules, and regulations," was unable to secure those funds for the Los Angeles Indian community (LACCNAIC 1987b:9).

On September 4, 1986, the Indian Commission legation met with two representatives of the Labor Department's Division of Indian and Native American Programs (DINAP). Daylong negotiations produced no immediate shift of funds from the OCIC to an existing Los Angeles County Indian institution. Unwilling to rescind the department's decision of August 14, 1986, the federal representatives agreed only that "the most feasible solution was to have local Los Angeles Indian groups apply for prime sponsorship for the 1987 fiscal year beginning July 1, 1987" (LACCNAIC 1987b:9).

The decision to open up the next federal funding cycle to competitive bid within the Los Angeles Indian network of community organizations initiated a series of events that continues to reverberate throughout that institutional network. Letters of intent to apply for Department of Labor JTPA funds for fiscal year 1987 were due October 5, 1986, less than a month after the Indian Commission's initial meeting with DINAP officials. It was not very much time to write a grant proposal, much less convince a local institution to take on the service delivery responsibilities the grant would mandate. The LACCNAIC legation, in its assumed role as community developer, had to act quickly.

The commission canvassed the local incorporated Indian organizations that had some experience in human services program administration. The well-funded and administratively strong American Indian Free Clinic in Compton and the American Indian Health Center were encouraged to apply. In fact, their administrators had already made plans to do so. The Indian churches were also canvassed. Reverend Goodman's group (FNAUMC) was particularly targeted since it already had experience administering social services such as its caring and crisis centers. Even groups as diverse as the incipient and essentially volunteer organizations (e.g., the Long Beach Indian Center, the powwow clubs, the Indian Council on Aging, and an activist group called Concerned Community Indian Movement, which had been the ICI's most vociferous critic) were polled as to their interest in accepting the responsibility of administering one or more of the now-defunded social services programs.

Although interest in being the Los Angeles Indian JTPA service provider ran high, not every Indian organization was equipped to accept that responsibility. Smaller, largely volunteer groups such as the powwow clubs and the Christian Indian missions elected to restrict their activities to their original organizational intent. The Many Trails Indian Club's response to the crisis typifies the smaller groups' conflicting goals of community cooperation and institutional integrity:

[We] were asked to take it over because we were the only ones [who] had the right credentials, charter, the bylaws. In fact, we were going to. . . . And then we realized how few of us we were and the stress it would have on us, the responsibility, how much work [it would be]. . . . And we would not any longer be social. We really wanted to help out, we really did. We went as far as to offer to sign any papers they needed to have signed. I really think we could have gotten the funds because . . . we have a state charter, an IRS revenue number, . . . and everything we've ever done has been above board. But we felt that we could just absolutely not handle it. And we always try to keep politics out of what we do. (various Many Trials members, May 20, 1988)

Importantly, though Many Trails eventually decided it could not take on the responsibility of delivering social services, it did not question other concerned community members' rights to ask them to do so. As participants in Los Angeles Indian community life and structure, every local grass roots Indian organization assumed both the right and the responsibility to respond in some way to the community crisis.

Five Indian organizations with social services delivery or grants administration experience expressed interest in becoming the JTPA service provider for Los Angeles Indians and, by October 5, 1986, had filed letters of intent to apply for federal JTPA funds in the next funding cycle. Three of the five were local Indian organizations; the other two were located in areas other than Los Angeles County. At the suggestion of the Department of Labor, members of the LAC-CNAIC (one of the three local applicants) met with representatives of the other two local applicants. This meeting eventuated in a consortium agreement among the community administrations, the Indian Commission, and the county Department of Community and Senior Citizens Services whereby the latter two jointly would apply for the JTPA fund set-asides for urban Indians. Those funds, once procured, would then be contracted out to the Indian organization members of the consortium according to the recommendations of the Indian Commission. In this way, a system of checks and balances would be developed among the administrative support and expertise of the county bureaucracy, the monitoring and policy development functions of the commission, and the service delivery capabilities of the established local organizations.

At the appointed time, the LACCNAIC, the Department of Community and Senior Citizens Services, and the Indian community consortium submitted a joint advance notice of intent to apply for the next year of Los Angeles Indian JTPA funds. By January 1987, the commission's executive committee had convinced the two local Indian organizations to join in support of the county-commission proposal and to withdraw their individual proposals from consideration by the Labor Department. A memorandum of agreement was proposed among all the affected parties and was forwarded, along with the letter of intent, to the Department of Labor. Bill Fredricks was particularly proud of the consortium concept: "It meant that we would have had the checks and balances that were missing with the ICI. We [the commission] would have monitored what went on at the service agency to whom we subcontracted the services. And we would have had the county's administrative support and expertise to back us up. It would have worked" (November 30, 1988).

DINAP contracts and grants officers at the Department of Labor were less convinced. Additionally, the Orange County Indian Center had been delivering JTPA services to the Los Angeles Indian community for eight months when the final funding decision was made for fiscal year 1987. In that time, the OCIC had built an impressive record of administrative competency. It had not only taken over the central city JTPA operation but also had opened satellite offices in the south-central and south bay areas. The consortium application was therefore denied, and the OCIC was awarded a second year of JTPA funding.

The LACCNAIC, on behalf of the newly formed consortium, appealed the decision. Bill Fredricks explained the commission's position:

> We had no quarrel with the way the Orange County Indian Center came in at the last minute and took over the JTPA program. They do a good job and probably saved the program for Indians in Los Angeles. There's no doubt about that. We didn't contest the decision. We contested the Department of Labor's right to make that decision. The legislation [Indian Self-Determination Act of 1975] clearly mandates self-determination and local community autonomy. We don't think they have the right to come in and decide who is going to administer programs for the Los Angeles Indians. That goes against the spirit of Indian self-determination. The community is supposed to determine who they want to serve them. The commission, as the representative body of the community, is in the best position to do that. We challenged DOL's right to decide what Indian organization was going to handle the JTPA funds for Los Angeles because they didn't consult with us about our preference. That kind of paternalism violates the terms and intent of the Indian self-determination legislation. (March 15, 1989)

Holding that proven fiscal integrity and prior administrative experience, not territorial prerogative and community preference, are the criteria by which Labor Department funding decisions are made, the department dismissed the commission's appeal. Significantly, in its second year of operation, the Los Angeles division of the Orange County Indian Center's JTPA program changed its name to the Southern California Indian Centers, to reflect its regional, inclusive, and thereby legitimate presence in Los Angeles.

The Indian Commission's consortium concept fared better as an administrative and executive work plan when presented to state, city, and county government funding agencies. At its executive committee meeting on Tuesday, August 26, 1986, the commission wholeheartedly endorsed Los Angeles County plans to extend the Indian Community Service Block Grant (CSBG)[1] contracting cycle to a two-year period beginning with the 1987 allocation of revenue. In addition the executive committee approved the plan for Indian Commission participation in the CSBG funding process. The commission agreed to make an assessment of the Indian community to determine needs and to establish program priorities for CSBG funds. It agreed to review and evaluate Indian-targeted CSBG proposals for the city and county, to develop recommendations for funding allocations for Indian grantee agencies, to assist in monitoring and evaluating program effectiveness of Indian grantee agencies, and to interface with and assist Indian grantee agencies (LACCNAIC 1987a).

Because of these assurances, the commission was instrumental in procuring the CSBG Indian set-aside funds of the state's Office of Economic Opportunity for another year. In 1987 the program was administered by the Los Angeles County Department of Community and Senior Citizens Services and monitored by the Indian Commission. The provision of emergency shelter, health, and food programs to the disadvantaged Indians in Los Angeles was subcontracted to appropriate local Indian organizations. On the commission's recommendations, the Los Angeles County Board of Supervisors provided CSBG grants to the First Native American and United Methodist Church's Native American Caring Center for emergency food, clothing, and household supplies; the American Indian Free Clinic in Compton, for health services delivery; and the skid row sanctuary run by the United American Indian Involvement, for emergency food and housing provisions. When no Indian organization with an established relationship with the city and county social services networks could be located to administer grants such as the city emergency housing program and the county domestic violence program, the funds, Indian staff, and program model were transferred, relatively intact, to respective existing city and county host agencies.

Certain human services the Indian Centers, Inc., had provided the Los Angeles Indian community did not survive the institution's defunding. Pete Chessman, the editor of *Talking Leaf*, with an occasional assist (informational and monetary) from Roy Flandreau, continued to print quarterly issues of the community newspaper for another two years before it was discontinued. The Indian Child Welfare Program was lost due, the 1987 Indian Commission report states, "to a host of legal entanglements." Those impediments included the lack of provision for the transfer of funds to any organization other than the original funding source within the city or county (LACCNAIC 1987a:8). Since 1988, however, the Southern California Indian Center has provided similar services (advocacy, counseling, parent education, and foster home development) under an Indian Child and Family Services program (*Peace Pipe Line* 1989).

Discussion

What had gone so quickly and irreparably wrong? How could an institution of such longevity, programmatic diversity, and obvious contributions to the Los Angeles American Indian community have been felled with such finality? Could the process of devolution and loss of community support have been stayed at some point? What lessons can be learned from a processual analysis of institutional crisis?

Superstructural Antecedents of Deinstitutionalization

By 1986 political and economic forces both within and external to the Los Angeles Indian community were instrumental in affecting a general contraction of urban Indian social services delivery systems. At the national level, the economic policies of the Reagan administration, the block grant funding system, and a generally low level of interest in continuing to fund ethnic minority social services programs substantially reduced the ease with which urban Indians had been able to secure funding sources for needed human services programs.

Additionally, the influx of new ethnic groups (Southeast Asians, Samoans, and Central and South American political and economic refugees) in significant numbers, who were eligible and in competition for social services program monies from a retracting resource pool, further reduced the funding potential for future Indian human services programs. Given the block grant system and its emphasis on equitable distribution of funds based on population figures, the relatively small Los Angeles Indian community realistically recognized the threat these new funding rules posed to continued support of the parallel urban Indian social services programs. Concepts of need and the precedent of Indian set-aside funds versus population size became the Indian social services lobbyists' powerful and largely effective rallying points.

Restructuring the national social services funding process into the block grant system had a number of consequences for the Los Angeles Indian community. First, it introduced a new set of variables and buffer agencies in what had traditionally been a direct, one-on-one relationship between federal funding agencies and Indian social services delivery institutions. At least three new sets of structural relationships—Indian program administrators and state funding agencies, Indian program administrators and county funding agencies, and Indian program administrators and city funding agencies—had to be cultivated. Second, various and often contradictory application processes, application of funds stipulations, monitoring requisites, and reporting procedures of the new funding sources had to be mastered. Third and most important, applicant Indian organizations had to assimilate a new philosophy of administration and adopt a new sociopolitical ethos.

In the social services funding heyday of the 1970s, the one-on-one relationships between federal funding sources and the Indian services delivery representatives, unmitigated by the administrative demands of mid-range bureaucracies, allowed for greater flexibility, interpretation, and improvisation in the day-to-day operations of the local services delivery institutions and the annual dispensation of funds. Decision making and execution of those decisions were facilitated with relative ease and rapidity. Having administered Indian programs for over a hundred years, the Bureau of Indian Affairs understood, made allowances for, and exercised restraint when dealing with the occasional unorthodox accounting procedures of grass roots administrations. There were no third-party monitors; rather, the services delivery institution was accountable directly and only to its funding source. The climate of this sociopolitical structure (the federal government vis-à-vis Indian self-help programs) was characterized by an easy, laissez-faire liberalism that was perhaps a response to increasingly confident Indian demands for self-determination. The moral weight of the concept of Indian autonomy and the Indian Self-Determination Act of 1975 became the rationale for a largely hands-off approach to Indian program administration on the part of their federal monitors.

With the advent of the block grant funding structure and its second, third, and occasionally fourth levels of administrative authority, the issue of accountability had become attenuated. Importantly, city, county, and state funding agencies, because of the novelty of working with urban Indian social services delivery organizations, felt themselves particularly vulnerable to public and federal scrutiny. Sensitive to the issues of fiscal accountability to their federal block grant funding agencies and the federal administration's concerns with establishing cost-efficient local operations and cost-effective services, intervening state, county, and city funding administrative structures became increasingly formulaic about their funding policies, monitoring procedures, and documentation requirements. Notions of fiscal rigor and literal interpretation of contractual agreements supplanted an earlier ethos of minimally questioned dissemination of expected entitlements as needs arose and from whatever funding source had currently available monies equal to the immediate costs of needed services. Self-conscious in their new roles as Indian program fund administrators, mid-level agencies imposed their models of fiscal accountability on grass roots programs used to the more relaxed fiscal demands of their former federal protectorates.

Infrastructural Antecedents of Deinstitutionalization

Urban Indian social services delivery program administrators, anxious to perpetuate their operations, struggled to assimilate new application and reporting procedures. Emphases on fiscal accountability, the development of "standardized fiscal procedures," and "comprehensive fiscal system plans" were noted. Indian programs (the ICI is a classic example of this) were caught in a double-bind situation. For funding to occur, a posture of a priori fiscal competence had to be assumed. After giving convincing presentations of themselves as fiscal competents, Indian program administrators were then self-consciously reluctant to ask for help or clarification when fiscal procedures and requirements were imperfectly understood. Clear stipulations that technical assistance in fiscal and administrative matters was available from the funding sources often were not heeded until the fiscal crisis had grown so large that easy, internal remediation was no longer possible.

Countervailing forces were also at work in the Los Angeles Indian community. The general pattern of residential dispersal of families active in Indian community affairs away from the inner city to outlying Los Angeles County residential areas—as discussed in chapter 2 (see also map 2.1)—further dissipated the sense of community that ongoing, face-to-face interaction among a core group of actors provides. Consequently, Indian social services institutions became increasingly more geographically dispersed and specialized in the programs they offered. Those still located in the inner city either served a particularly select group of locals (the sanctuary on skid row and the alcoholism intervention programs within a few miles of skid row) or became increasingly geographically removed from the targeted clientele. The Indian Centers, Inc., in the central city area and the American Indian Free Clinic in Compton are examples of such dislocations (see also map A.1 and table A.2 in the Appendix).

In addition to increasing geographic dispersal within the Los Angeles Basin, discernable out-migration from Los Angeles was gathering momentum. Increasing numbers of people who had migrated as young adults to Los Angeles in the 1950s were approaching retirement age in the 1980s. After thirty years of industry and careful money management, many urban Indians looked forward to financially secure retirements. Release from the urban employment sector and reduced incomes fostered a number of life career choices. Chief among them was the decision to stay in or leave the city. Almost half of the people I had interviewed since 1973 who would have been fifty-five or older in 1983, when I began a study of aging in the Indian community, were no longer in Los Angeles. They had gone home (Weibel-Orlando 1988a); that is, they had returned to their ancestral lands to live, in old age, among ethnic and age cohorts. Consequently, several of the most active and involved Los Angeles Indians were no longer available to fill the symbolically important community roles of revered elder and moral authority. Boards of directors lost people whose history of community service and personal integrity validated the organizations to which they had lent their names.

In the case of the Indian Center, a dispersed Los Angeles Indian residential pattern and the move of many successful community members to still more distant suburbs meant that increasingly fewer people were taking the time or were motivated to trek to the center's downtown location for monthly board meetings. Nomination to a seat on the ICI Board of Directors, which as recently as the late 1970s was a highly prized and hotly contested status, went begging in the 1980s. The center's role as the informal social and spiritual center of the Los Angeles Indian community, which had characterized its early climate of volunteerism, had gotten lost in blizzards of bureaucratic paperwork, data management, and legal-rational social services delivery. Old-timers impressed by the center's computers, word processors, conference call capabilities, and executive travel accounts nevertheless felt alienated from their own creation. The state-of-the-art social services delivery facility that the ICI had become was no longer "our Indian thing" to its founders. The coincidence of these forces resulted in a vacuum of validating institutional leadership, a crisis of institutional integrity, the opportunity for multiple fissions among formerly cooperating social services organizations, and the development of individualized and isolated social services fiefdoms.

Core administrative elites, having solidified their positions in the Los Angeles Indian social services delivery system's power hierarchy, became increasingly insular and removed from wide community scrutiny. The ICI executive directorship is a prime example of this process. Having demonstrated his right to rule by making good on his claims of successful grantsmanship, Robert Daniels consolidated his personal power with his elevation to the executive directorship. He increasingly buffered his personal interaction with community members and the ICI funding agencies with time-limited and essentially ceremonial public appearances as well as the construction of ramparts of protective personnel around an increasingly remote directorship. These intervening structures further removed him from direct public scrutiny and community accountability.

Mr. Daniels's actions, easily interpreted as classic avoidance behavior, fanned the already smoldering and ultimately destructive fires of suspicion with which his original appointment had been greeted. The community reacted by withdrawing its initial tentative support of the center's new executive director. Because he had become synonymous with the ICI, his disassociation from the community also meant the community's estrangement from the center. Therefore, withdrawal of both psychological support and use of its facilities and services by the group it was mandated to serve was inevitable.

Cultural Antecedents of Deinstitutionalization

One other obvious infrastructural failing is that the ICI's executive director should have functioned as a bicultural specialist and liaison but did not. Robert Daniels appeared to be just the sort of

Indian administrator the center needed to operate effectively in the new funding climate. Highly educated, a proven grantsman, and an experienced Indian program administrator, he could also speak the language of his Indian constituency. Importantly, he was conversant as well in the languages of Washington, D.C., lobbyists, federal funds administrators, and national Indian caucuses. Trained as an educator, he should have been uniquely socialized to translate the cultural codes of his various constituencies to one another. That he apparently failed to do so contributed to his and the center's downfall.

Mr. Daniels appears to have had a less than holistic perspective of his status vis-à-vis the funding agencies and the Indian community he served. Proficient at satisfying short-term goals (contracts and grants acquisition), the executive director appeared unable or unwilling to deal with long-term goals, for example, convincing his constituency of the rationale for and the need to comply with funding source procedural requirements and providing the center staff with the requisite administrative skills to effect an orderly flow of administrative documentation and services. In fact, he may have been incompletely enculturated. His administrative style suggested that he had learned the technique and form by which one interacts with the host society's human services funding sources but had little understanding of or appreciation for the underlying philosophy and operating principles of the legal-rational bureaucracy that managed those resources. He appears to have been operating under an older and rather more traditional form and philosophy of patrimonial rule and resource administration.

Within nineteenth-century tribal organizations, loved relatives, friends, and persons with whom one had economic and political ties were those who people in positions of authority elevated to political power. These ties would, at times, take precedence over the use of more rational selection criteria such as skill and talent or the democratic process of community election by majority vote or through group consensus. If Indian leaders operated from this more traditional perspective of workmate selection, it would have been perfectly sensible to nominate trusted relatives and friends to their institution's board of directors. Issues of nepotism and conflict of interest that would prevent such appointments in city, county, state, and national governments were not salient concerns in establishing early Indian community political and administrative hierarchies.

Robert Daniels's and the ICI's bookkeeping styles suggest the continuing model of generalized reciprocity that characterizes the distribution of resources among Indians to this day. Families, informal social networks, and tribal entities are expected to respond to individual requests for financial assistance when needs arise. Monies are pooled. Loans are not formalized. There is a general consensus that a gift or loan will eventually be repaid when the need to do so arises and that everyone has equal rights of participation in the communal resource pool. The concept of budget line-item integrity, the sanctity of separate funding sources for individual programs, and the importance of the expenditure of funds in a prescribed time period for a previously specified purpose as opposed to when the need arises for a range of purposes were, in part, the reasons why the funding agency auditors described the ICI's accounting system as "chaotic" and "undocumented."

Further, the center's bookkeeping laxity and its executive director's refusal to accept the legitimacy of the funding agents' criticisms reflect earlier assumptions that funding of Indian programs is analogous to entitlements. As such, the expenditure of the funds should not be judged by the same rules that govern the dispensation of public funds to non-Indian organizations. Mr. Daniels's charge of harassment and ethnic discrimination on the part of the funding agencies reflects an ethnopolitical stance and a diversionary ploy, colorfully described by Wolfe (1970) as "mau-mauing." As a political strategy, "mau-mauing" was particularly effective in the 1960s and 1970s vis-à-vis a relatively sensitive, empathetic, and liberal federal government. In 1985, however, its psychological impact was lost on a government bent on the decentralization of human services delivery and convinced that Indian self-determination meant grass roots volunteerism, freedom from government interference, and, by extension, freedom from public funding support.

The final Indian Center administration constituted a negative mirror image of bicultural competency. Rather than comprehending and translating the cultural codes of two intersecting segments of the complex society and generating the positive accommodations that such understandings can facilitate, the center's actions in failing to comply with the fiscal demands of its funding agencies suggest a clash or manipulation of conflicting and mutually unintelligible codes, culture perspectives, and goals. The ICI administrator's avoidance of and hostility toward outside inquiry are examples of the counterproductive behaviors associated with such anomic conditions. The confusion that prompted the ICI crisis exemplifies what has been been described previously as negative cultural marginality or anomie among urban Indians (Ablon 1971a; Garbarino 1971; Graves 1974; Olson 1971).

The Heuristic Power of Crisis

> This is important information to get out to the community. . . . If we can learn from our mistakes in the past, then that's good. The old system was designed for failure. The government's monitoring system left a lot to be desired. The Indian programs did not get the technical assistance they needed to keep their books the way the funding agencies wanted them to. And no one really monitored what was going on at the center until they absolutely had to. And by that time, it was too late to do anything about it. . . . Now is the perfect time for the Indian community to pull together to build a comprehensive governance system like we've laid out here. So [it is] a good thing to be doing this at this time. (Bill Fredricks, March 23, 1989)

This indigenous analysis of the community crisis provides a number of lessons. The frontiers at which two culture-specific administrative styles converge can be the locus for positive creative innovation and synergistic growth and for negative exploitation of ambiguity. The selection of the person who is to effect the liaison between the two cultural systems becomes critical to the perpetuation of the linkage of local and supralocal institutions. Bicultural competencies are not sufficient to the task. Personal integrity and identification with and loyalty to one's constituency are other critical criteria that must be considered when awarding community leadership.

The work of sustaining community institutions is at once the right and responsibility of every community member. There is danger in its delegation. The fiscal laxity and communicative errors that brought the Indian Centers, Inc., to its knees might not have occurred or gone unquestioned for as long as they did if the administration had had to answer to an informed, independent, and authoritative board of directors. Community strength is directly related to the vigor with which its members participate in, contribute to, and monitor its institutional integrity.

Fiske (1979) insists that the evolution of urban Indian organizations can only be understood within the context of their supralocal associations. As a case in point, the demise of the wealthiest Indian organization in Los Angeles (as opposed to the continued vitality of the churches and powwow clubs) underscores the fragility of the associations between core community institutions and their supralocal support agencies. The Indian Center's primacy in the Los Angeles Indian community for two decades was the direct result of national social services funding policies. The sweeping changes in human services funding priorities and administrative requirements introduced by the Reagan administration and the center's inability to respond appropriately to those changes directly affected the organization's ability to function and, eventually, to exist in the community. In contrast, the ongoing Indian churches, powwow clubs, and athletic leagues have never relied on public funding and external agendas to structure and sustain their organizations. Their focused activities are supported through personal donations, tithes, and various small-scale fund-raising events.

Institutional longevity is dependent on a group's control of its own resources. Certain grass roots organizations now advocate for complete separation of Indian organizations from supralocal dependencies as the answer to the instabilities of contemporary American Indian political and institutional life. The vulnerability of an organization dependent on external resources for its survival mirrors the ephemerality of core community experience and continuity. Ensuring a sustained core community, the experience of daily, purposeful, cooperative, and locally controlled economic and social activity is an emerging urban Indian issue of the 1990s.

New Directions in the Structure of Community Cohesion

Several sociostructural shifts have been proposed to promote urban Indian community cohesion. In 1988 the executive director of the LACCNAIC was convinced that the commission will have an increasingly important role in sustaining cohesiveness.

> The commission has never realized its potential. In the beginning, we didn't want it to be a community tribunal. I don't think the community was ready for it at the time. But that's a service we could really perform for the community. After the center went down, I saw the need for a change in the political structure and our role in the community. If we had played that role of a traditional tribal council with the Indian Center sooner, maybe we could have saved it. . . . If the commission had had some "teeth," we might have been able to step in and turn things around. But we didn't have the authority to do it. It was so frustrating. Our hands were tied. (Bill Fredricks, November 30, 1988)

Bill Fredricks's ideas about giving the commission "some teeth" include providing the institution with the authority to address and

resolve Indian community problems, to develop policy, and to oversee and monitor the execution of its policy recommendations by
Indian organizations. This authority would have to be mandated by
the federal funding agencies and the Los Angeles County government. Importantly, such supralocal mandates would have to be acknowledged by the Los Angeles Indian organizations and the Indian
community at large. Mr. Fredricks hopes the LACCNAIC will be
given these mandates and thereby successfully broaden its current
liaison and advisory relationship to the Indian community and the
supralocal public funding bureaucracies.

> We were given the mechanism for securing and administering grants
> and contracts. But we never did go for them because we didn't want to
> compete with the Indian community organizations. But with the way
> things are with block grant funding, you've got to be connected to the
> city and county governments in some way or else you're out. Indians
> have got to learn to work from within the system. And that's where
> the commission comes in. We've done it for ten years now—
> successfully. We've lasted because we have the checks and balances of
> the county structure to fall back on. You just can't get rid of a com-
> missioner or employee you don't like. You have to go through a whole
> procedure. We know these things. . . . That's why, if we could just get
> enough of the commissioners to agree to go in this direction, we could
> be a real force in the Indian community. (November 30, 1988)

Convinced that the future of urban Indian social services delivery
lies in the development of a two-pronged, integrative approach, Mr.
Fredricks maintains, first, that Indians must be part of the system in
order to bring about systemic change. Placement of qualified Indians
in key positions within the existing supralocal service delivery
system—a benevolent ethnic infiltration—is an immediately applicable political strategy (and is already practiced with some success).

Mr. Fredricks's second approach is more revolutionary. By March
1989, he had developed, with input from core members, an omnibus
governance plan for the Los Angeles Indian community. The plan
included integrating the activities and resources of four institutional sectors: the county government social services agencies and funding resource centers; the LACCNAIC or an urban Indian agency
structured much like the commission that would develop policy for,
oversee, and monitor all Indian social services delivery programs in
Los Angeles; the Indian social services delivery organizations; and
the Indian community at large. He explained:

> There is a need to separate policy development and oversight from
> administration and execution. Tribal governments have tried both to

make and execute social services delivery policy decisions. It hasn't worked as well as it should because there are no checks and balances. Once agencies get their funds, they tend to lose sight of their long-term goals. They concentrate on short-term goals—maintaining their own organizational entity—rather than providing the best service to the most people.

In the consortium system and governance plan I am proposing, the commission or the new urban Indian umbrella oversight agency would serve as a conduit for social services funds from granting agencies to the local Indian organizations who would deliver the services. The agency would set policy and service delivery priorities, evaluate and make recommendations to the resource agencies about who in the Indian community is most qualified to provide those services, and monitor and evaluate the quality of those services. (March 15, 1989)

Although it would be guaranteed autonomous decision-making powers, the urban Indian oversight agency Mr. Fredricks envisions would be placed within the framework and have to adhere to the administrative tenets of its supporting county agency. The county would provide administrative expertise and structure to the Indian oversight agency and the Indian social services delivery organizations to which it, on the advice of the new urban Indian agency, would subcontract for services. The fourth sector, the Los Angeles Indian community, would have direct access both to the local Indian social services organizations and to the LACCNAIC or the new Indian governance agency. According to this plan, either the existing commission or the new agency would hold regular open forums in which people could voice their opinions and suggestions for improved community services.

This integrated division of labor and bureaucratic structure, Bill Fredricks assumes, would maintain a reasonably objective system of checks and balances. In this way, institutional isolation, which fosters deviant, self-protective, and counterproductive administrations, as in the case of the Indian Centers, Inc., could be avoided and continuity of services to the community ensured. He would, in fact, like to see every city with a significant Indian population set up this sort of urban Indian commission or oversight agency "with teeth."

Figure 15.1 is Mr. Fredricks's structural conceptualization of the new governance plan. As he carefully outlined his model to me over three interview sessions, I felt sure I understood the structure of the model until he began to draw it. I had not expected a circle; rather, I had envisioned the hierarchical structure of Figure 15.2. We therefore discussed our conceptual differences at some length.

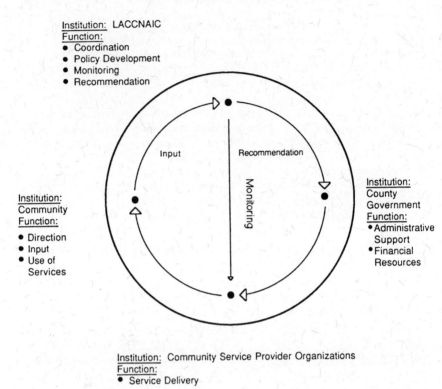

Institution: LACCNAIC
Function:
• Coordination
• Policy Development
• Monitoring
• Recommendation

Institution:
Community
Function:
• Direction
• Input
• Use of
Services

Institution:
County
Government
Function:
•Administrative
Support
•Financial
Resources

Input   Recommendation

Monitoring

Institution: Community Service Provider Organizations
Function:
• Service Delivery

Figure 15.1 Urban Indian Governance Plan: Community-generated Model

While Mr. Fredricks's model might be construed to depict the primacy of the commission or the new urban Indian oversight agency and a diamond-shaped hierarchy of community sectors, he means to depict a different community configuration. The circle, he argues, emphasizes cooperation, incorporation, and the recognition of the structural equivalency of the four sectors; and it deemphasizes notions of hierarchical levels of increasingly superior political authority and power. His model recognizes each sector's set of particular skills and expertise. Additionally, the nonhierarchical circle underscores the importance of coordinating the cooperative efforts of all four sectors.

With this governance structure, information would flow clockwise from the community to the LACCNAIC or its to-be-developed structural equivalent to the supralocal funding agencies to the Indian social services delivery agencies and back to the community, in unending and continuous streams, generating appropriate alloca-

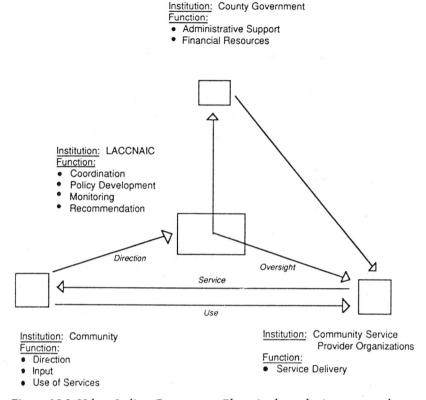

Figure 15.2 Urban Indian Governance Plan: Anthropologist-generated Model

tion, production, and use of needed services. Information could transect the circle; that is, each sector could interact with all the others and, with relative ease, also disseminate information to all other sectors. The success of this plan depends, of course, on universal acceptance of the premise that the system can work optimally only when each sector is treated as an equal and its own specialized contribution is integrated into the cooperative effort. Omission or noncompliance of any one of the sectors would put the entire system into jeopardy.

Bill Fredricks's community circle is at once inclusive, fragile, and traditionally Indian. The integrative, harmonic, and healing potential of the circle is a core concept in many American Indian cultures. It is the orienting structure of such diverse phenomena as the tribal village, the Sun Dance, the powwow arena, the sweat lodge, the

Native American church ritual ground, and the medicine wheel. Significantly, supralocal institutions are treated not as overarching and subsuming political structures but as environmental resources. Their potential is expressed only in community action. The relationship between the supralocal resource centers and community, then, is symbiotic interdependency rather than unilateral dependency.

The Indian biculturalist becomes a critical community facilitator in Bill Fredricks's indigenous models. People who competently straddle and are able to encode and decode messages from both the supralocal administrative institutions and the ethnic collectivity they serve will be indispensable to the development of these models of ethnic community continuity in complex society.

NOTE

1. The block grant system, introduced by the Reagan administration in 1981, constituted a radical restructuring of the federal distribution of public services funds. Rather than at the federal level, the decision as to who would deliver human services for which federal funds were available was delegated to state-, county-, and municipal-level public administrations. These administrations were provided with large blocks of public federal funds which they had the authority to allocate according to regionally developed distribution formulas.

16

Toward a Definition of Indian Community in Los Angeles

Marred by human tragedy and the agonizing loss of the oldest and largest Indian community institution, 1986 was an extremely troubled year for the Los Angeles Indian community. (LACCNAIC 1987:iii)

T HE LOS ANGELES City-County Native American Indian Commission, as a function of its original charge, presents an annual report on Indian affairs and commission activities to the Los Angeles County Board of Supervisors. The forbidding assessment of "the state of the Los Angeles Indian community" that begins this chapter is the opening statement of the commission's 1986–87 report. The document continues, for eight more paragraphs, to list and describe the several tragedies that had befallen the Indian community in the past year. The untimely death of several prominent and beloved core Indian community members, a horrifying plane crash that destroyed the Cerritos home of a former Indian commission member and took his life as well as those of five members of his family, and the closing of the Indian Centers, Inc., were all mourned as irreparable losses that had touched and diminished the entire Los Angeles Indian community. The official document is a Greek chorus of lament and oracular portent.

Natural, unforetold, and inexplicable disasters, earthquakes, floods, plagues, drought, crop failures, and wars were signs, during two thousand years of Chinese dynastic history, that all was not well with the gods and their earthly representatives. Such disasters were omens that current temporal (dynastic) power was out of balance and therefore had lost its "mandate of Heaven" (De Bary, Chan, and Watson 1966:170–71). Although American Indians do not hold worldviews that incorporate the concept of a "mandate of Heaven," most American Indian societies do sustain beliefs that personal and community well-being are functions of social and spiritual balance. Additionally, many contemporary American Indians acknowledge the existence of, look for, read, and act in response to extraordinary environmental signs.

In 1986 the signs of social and spiritual imbalance in Los Angeles Indian community affairs were there for all to see and read. The unrelenting series of disasters listed in the commission's annual report were tangible, undeniable proof that something was terribly wrong. The imbalance was such that only a collective response of epic proportions could restore the community's psychic and social harmony.

The Ritual Processes of Community Reintegration

Psychological wounds caused by the deaths of several prominent core members slowly healed in a year of public and ritually structured mourning. Family members and close friends refrained from powwow dancing and other forms of secular ethnic displays and recreational pursuits. Privately, devastated family members and friends sought solace in the ministrations and prayers of trusted pastors and spiritual guides. The end of the year of mourning was marked by a number of spectacular memorial powwows and feasts. These communal rituals were meant to reincorporate mourning individuals into, and to reintensify the shared values of, the Los Angeles Indian community. The Yackytooahnipah family memorial powwow in October 1987 was described as Los Angeles's largest public outpouring of community sentiment and respect ever.[1]

The rent in the Los Angeles Indian community's institutional structure caused by the closing of the Indian Centers, Inc., has taken longer to mend. Accusations of wrongdoing, the need to affix blame, acrimonious and exaggerated rumors of exploitation of public funds for personal gain, premeditation, and conspiracy still circulate and divide the community. In 1989 the sociostructural tear had not fully closed and the healing process had left considerable psychosocial scar tissue. The rupture caused by the closing of the center and the subsequent attempts to bring the community's institutional structure back into balance continue to provide an epistemological opportunity, or "window" (Werner and Schoepfle 1987), for the understanding of community processes.

In 1989 the Los Angeles Indian community was poised between resolution of old internecine struggles, fending off emerging pretenders to authority, and a new steady state (Wallace 1956) or reintegration (Turner 1974). The offending protagonist and the institution that, by association, was sullied have been expelled and expunged. A mutually acceptable resolution of the divisive struggles between various in-place and interloping organizations for institutional recognition by supralocal funding sources and the Indian community was yet to be accomplished. It appeared, however, that rapprochement was underway.

In early 1988, the LACCNAIC, the Los Angeles Indian community's only formal representative council, and the Southern California Indian Center stood in political opposition to each other. Less than a year later, the SCIC petitioned the Indian Commission to support its planned expansion of social services programs. Subsequent to considerable discussion, the commission voted to write a letter of reference on behalf of the SCIC. Cooperation between the two former adversaries appeared possible.

Incorporating rituals facilitate the process of reestablishing a new societal steady state. Within a year of its inception, the SCIC regularly sponsored well-attended powwows in the Los Angeles area. In 1988 the SCIC satellite office in Commerce sponsored successful elders' lunches at Thanksgiving and Christmas in cooperation with Roy Flandreau and the Los Angeles Indian Council on Aging. Plans were made to make the elders' luncheons monthly affairs. The granddaughter of a prominent SCIC officer and longtime Orange County resident was chosen as the 1989 Many Trails Indian Club's junior powwow princess. Her grandfather spoke for her to a receptive Los Angeles crowd of five hundred or more powwow-goers who had packed into the Cecil B. De Mille Junior High School gym on February 11, 1989. Women in the crowd trilled[2] their approval of the crowning of "an Orange County girl." Friends from Orange County and Los Angeles participated wholeheartedly in her ritual giveaway.

Flyers describing the SCIC's continuing and expanded community services were passed about the gym.[3] Throughout the evening, SCIC officers and staff held court. Their lawn chairs prominently placed at the edge of the powwow dance arena, the "Orange County people" sat and conversed comfortably with friends and relatives. The SCIC drum group's Southern Plains–style music inspired scores of dancers to take to the floor in one of the most spectacular displays of movement and color of the 1988–89 Los Angeles pow-wow season. The mood was cordial and conciliatory. A Los Angeles Indian community new steady state seemed not only possible but imminent.

Community as Collective Rights and Responsibilities

In the two years following the demise of the Indian Centers, Inc., core community members, acting as representatives of their various Indian organizations, worked collectively and competitively to bring the community back into balance. Through those acts, the Los Angeles Indian community structure, process, and ethos revealed themselves. An impressive and wide-ranging number of people responded to the institutional crisis. Importantly, Indian community members saw their responses as not only appropriate but also their responsibilities. Community, then, is a field, resource, and arena for social action defined by individual and collective rights of participation and responsibilities for its continuance.

Community as Institutional Integrity

During its period of turmoil, the Los Angeles Indian community was sustained by a number of institutions that continued to provide their services relatively unaffected by the political fires all about them. Although the American Indian Free Clinic in Compton and the Indian skid row sanctuary had agreed to join the county-Indian Commission consortium in their abortive attempt to have job training and employment funds placed with Los Angeles–based Indian organizations, they also minded their own shops. Both organizations continued to secure funds for and provide the kinds of human services for which they were originally chartered and have developed expertise. Their continuity is ensured by their concentration of effort in areas of proven effectiveness and community need.

The Los Angeles City-County Native American Indian Commission is still the most widely recognized formal community forum and liaison between the Indian community and non-Indian sectors of the larger society. The United Indian Development Association (UIDA) has provided two decades of counsel and service because, as Bill Fredricks put it, "they're interested in ends, not short term gains" (November 30, 1988). This service organization, too, has kept its original focus: to provide technical advice to aspiring Indian entrepreneurs, which is as viable a community service today as when it was first offered in 1969.

The church groups and powwow clubs also survived the upheaval of 1986 by steadfastly adhering to their original charters and traditional pursuits. Although the Many Trails Indian Club members recognized the appropriateness of having been asked to help out in what was perceived as a Indian community crisis, they elected not to take on the administrative duties of the orphaned human services projects. The powwow club members determined that their integrity as a community group would be maintained by continuing to do what they do best. They avoided the lures of organizational growth, increased political power, heightened community prestige, and complete, daily immersion in core community activities. Instead, the Many Trials Indian Club's board of directors elected to maintain its role as culture conservator and thereby sustain its original direction. Community as a collection of complementary, indigenous institutions and interactive organizations with specific agenda and personnel, the vitality of which transcends individual institutional involvements, describes in large measure the overarching social structure of the Los Angeles Indian community.

Community as Cultural Continuity

The Los Angeles Indian institutional configuration is far from stable or static. Rather, it is characterized by major structural flux. The relative stability of a particular organization is subject to a number of internal and external forces. The longevity of a particular organization is directly correlated to its cultural integrity. The longest-lived Los Angeles Indian organizations foster cultural themes that transcend urban migration and urbanism. The Los Angeles Indian church and powwow groups, for example, continue social institutions and practices that have been integral to Indian social life for at least one hundred fifty years. Identification with and the opportunity to contribute to familiar, focused activities are powerful motivators that contribute to the continuing vitality of these community institutions.

Community as Cultural Calendar and Public Ritual

An annual calendar of social events, rituals, and stages on which cultural dramas are played out for their symbolic content and enculturational properties provides other venues for the expression of

community among American Indian in Los Angeles. The cultural
arenas are the contexts in which community statuses and roles are
enacted and empowered. These social positions can be conventional
statuses (powwow club officer), individually created roles within
traditional social forms (Christian moral authority), and novel innovations in response to urban Indian life (bicultural liaison). Importantly, these statuses and roles succeed individuals who inherit or
achieve them and are validated and sustained only in the community context.

The Los Angeles Indian community, then, is characterized by
nodes of interaction and ethnically toned activities in which Indians
from across the Southland can come together for specified periods of
time "to be with other Indians" and "to do things the Indian way."
With the end of such reincorporating events, members of the ethnic
collectivity disassemble and return to their widely dispersed homes,
the better for having participated in the collective exercise of ethnic
community.

Community as Communications Network

Vital to community continuity, in view of Los Angeles's dispersed residential and decentralized institutional pattern, is an
ongoing, widely cast communications network. Telephone contact
teams, a steady stream of one-page informational handouts, face-to-
face communications at community events, and gossip are all effective, if limited, "moccasin telegraph" communications strategies.
Talking Leaf, the monthly Los Angeles Indian newspaper, provided
the vital informational link between core, selective, and peripheral
community members until its demise in 1988. The former editor of
Talking Leaf, the Indian Commission, the SCIC, the Alliance of
Native Americans (ANA), the Concerned Community Indian Movement (CCIM), and the county's Indian Senior Citizens Outreach
Program all agree that it is essential to develop some vehicle for the
timely and widespread dissemination of information to Los Angeles
Indians. All five organizations now include some provision for dissemination of Indian community information in their already tight
operating budgets.

Community as a communications system may be one measure by
which the vitality and density of a given collectivity can be assessed. If the proliferation of and standing-room-only crowds at recent powwows and church events are indications of community
response to information dissemination, then it is apparent that such
an intelligence system does exist and that the impulse for participa-

tion in advertised social events—that is, community—is still strong among the Indians living in Los Angeles.

Community as Longevity and Shared History

Certain conventional markers of community can still be applied when defining the Los Angeles Indian collectivity. Longevity and shared history, two standard criteria of community, clearly apply to the Indians in Los Angeles. An overwhelming majority of them migrated to the urban center from rural and reservation homelands. Migration, participation in the development of urban Indian institutions, and the continuous interaction with other American Indians in Los Angeles constitute a constellation of social processes spanning fifty years.

Even extreme tribal heterogeneity and the social distance such social categories foster and sustain are supplanted by overarching and inclusive, rather than exclusive, social categories. Indian social services staff, powwow club members and dancers, Christian Indians, and athletic league participants in Los Angeles are group memberships in which common ideological bonds or team goals override tribal differences. The development of a pan-Indian political stance vis-à-vis the non-Indians in Los Angeles is another novel and transcending social category. The idea that some causes, needs, and activities are so profound or all-encompassing that tribal cooperation, rather than animosity, is the only reasonable response has effectively provided Indians in Los Angeles with another rationale for collective action.

The perceived need to demonstrate community agreement and consensus when dealing with powerful and insensitive supralocal agencies that control needed resources is yet another factor in the development of pantribal cooperation as a highly positive value and goal in the Los Angeles Indian community. The collective response to the Indian Center's funding crisis and the attempt to construct a community consortium approach to problem solving are examples of the power of perceived external threat to arouse the community spirit or common interest of diverse Indian organizations in Los Angeles.

Community as Locality

The geographically dispersed configuration of the Los Angeles Indian population and its institutional facilities is quite different from my earliest, personal experience of community and from the classic community study models of isolated, nucleated, rural communities and ethnic urban neighborhoods. Even so, the dispersed Los Angeles Indian community does have geopolitical boundaries, albeit extremely attenuated and fluid ones. With respect to administrative authority (political institutions) and rights to valued community resources (economic institutions), clear us/them boundaries are drawn between Orange County Indians and those who are members of the Los Angeles Indian community. There is evidence, however, that this territorial dichotomy is becoming blurred. By 1990 the combined Los Angeles County and Orange County Indian populations should have exceeded 100,000. Politically, this population statistic would carry considerably more weight than the separate county figures. As a matter of political pragmatism, the regionalization of Indian Country, L.A., and its publicly funded social services programs makes considerable economic sense.

Although some of the city, county, state, and federal funding and social services delivery agencies are located within the legal boundaries of Los Angeles County, they have never been considered Indian community institutions. Rather, they are resources in the supracommunity environmental field to be exploited for the communal good. If Bill Fredricks's community governance plan is instituted, however, this us/them dichotomy may also become blurred. As illustrated by figure 15.1, supralocal resources become an integral fourth sector of Fredricks's cohesive total community concept.

Geopolitical boundaries are arbitrary, imposed, mutable, and, in the end, superficial parameters of community. In fact, Indian community boundaries contract and expand with individual involvements and intent. People who travel to and from their reservation family homes with regularity can be considered members of the Los Angeles Indian community although they live in Arizona, South Dakota, or Oklahoma for major portions of the year. The same is true of people who have lived most of their adult lives in Los Angeles and, on retirement, decide to go back home. Although these people no longer live in the Los Angeles area, their children and grandchildren do. Regular visits continue to connect "returnee" grandparents with their urban families, friends, and activities. Indians who live in Barstow, San Bernardino, Riverside, or San Diego but are regular participants in the weekly Los Angeles Indian powwow circuit, church, or athletic activities, are also considered members of the Los Angeles Indian community. The obvious geopolitical marker, the county line, is therefore not useful in determining who is and who is not a member of the Los Angeles Indian community.

Community as Ethnic Group Membership

Other, more salient and indigenous markers must be used in conjunction with locality to determine membership in the Los Angeles Indian community. Ethnicity is obviously one of them. At first measure it can be assumed that all 48,000 people who self-identified as Indian in the 1980 census count in Los Angeles have Indian community membership prerogatives. Additionally, Indians who migrated to Los Angeles since the last census, Indian children born in Los Angeles since 1980, and all of the non-Indians who married into or were enculturated into Los Angeles Indian homes also have the right to claim Los Angeles Indian community membership prerogatives if they so choose.

Categories of Community Participation

Core Membership

All Indians in Los Angeles are free to participate in most Indian organizations and activities, but they in fact exercise their community membership prerogatives selectively. Core community members such as Bill Fredricks, Sophie Wade, Rev. John Goodman, and Roy Flandreau have established life careers that include daily, face-to-face, total immersion in Indian community activities. This level of community experience includes involvement in multiple, cross-cutting ethnic organizations and the assumption of community-defined statuses. Core ethnic community memberships allow individuals to integrate their political, economic, religious, and social activities within one cultural context. Total immersion in ethnic community life mitigates compartmentalization and fragmentation of life experience, a condition the classic urbanization literature equates with urban life and of which it is highly critical.[4]

Selective Membership

Other Indians in Los Angeles (e.g., members of the Many Trails Indian Club, parishioners of the Indian churches, and members of the Indian athletic leagues) experience community selectively. Activities and institutions integral to the cultural life of the rural or reservation home communities are reconstructed in the urban field. The Saturday night powwow described in chapter 8 and the

Oklahoma Christian Indian church community traditions described in chapter 9 are clear examples of such sociocultural continuities.

Focused involvement in one urban Indian subgroup's activities does not necessarily mean a less intensively experienced community membership. Church membership can mean face-to-face interaction with the same people three or four times a week. Choir practice, Wednesday prayer meetings, and daylong Sunday services bind small groups of Indians into powerful, pantribal Christian brotherhoods and sisterhoods. References to membership in the Christian family, and all of the rights and responsibilities that metaphor implies, provide individuals with a sense of close-knit, supportive interdependencies (community). The same can be said of the powwow circuit members. Fringing parties, the weekly powwow, dance lessons, outfit-making sessions, and the manufacture and collection of giveaway gifts bring individuals into frequent and continuing association with each other. As with the annual tribal convocations for purposes of the great collective hunt, one's continuing sense of community is intensified and made real by regular, ritualized, and continuing interaction with people who mirror one's own delight in "doing some Indian."

Peripheral Membership

Other Indians in Los Angeles tend to express their ethnic community membership symbolically, through occasional, emblematic participation in some cultural event or activity. The powwow participants who go to powwows "to have a good time" but who "don't stay around to help out with the dirty work" are nonetheless peripheral members of the Los Angeles Indian community. People who maintain their subscriptions to monthly community newsletters in order to be kept informed about "Indian Country" happenings but are not active in any Indian organization also have the birthright, if they choose to exercise it, to opt for selective or total community immersion.

Nonassociated Indians

The large majority of American Indians who live and work in Los Angeles rarely, if ever, publicly display their ethnic group membership. For them, ethnic identity has become internalized, private; it is expressed most freely only in the home or when visiting the rural homelands. Little is known about these nonparticipants in Los Angeles Indian community life. They are, however, thought to be the community's largest untapped resource.

To me, [the Indian] community means everybody. I guess in the true sense of the term, [community] would consist of just those active participants, the organizations, and their memberships. But there is a much larger unknown to me that I refer to as "community"—those that have no need for contact. They're probably the great majority [and] the people [who] probably have the most potential to help us. They have isolated themselves because they don't have the need. Our community has been based on those who are in need and those who can offer assistance. We have to identify those people in our community who have had personal successes or who have certain skills and bring them into the helping and assistance end of our community. (Bill Fredricks, March 23, 1989)

The Changing Parameters of Community

Bill Fredricks makes an important point. The Los Angeles Indians' self- and externally imposed definition of themselves as a community is changing. Early notions of Indians in Los Angeles as economic refugees in need of help were fostered by the Bureau of Indian Affairs, well-intentioned non-Indian church and philanthropic groups, and the Los Angeles Indians themselves. Collective activity and institutions were created for and structured by the need to help out "those poor relocated Indians." The wealth of public funds in the 1960s and 1970s for self-help social services programs within impoverished ethnic minority groups further defined urban Indians as a "community of need."

In the 1980s, however, successful urban careers have lifted many American Indian families above the poverty line and into solid working- and middle-class life-styles. The dispersed residential patterns illustrated by map 2.1 graphically demonstrate this mobility. There indeed may now be a critical mass of upwardly mobile urban American Indians who can effect the kind of intraethnic group philanthropy that characterizes certain ethnic minority groups in Los Angeles (e.g., the Jewish, Asian, and Armenian communities). Core community members intent on perpetuating and incorporating currently nonassociated candidates into their ethnic associations will have to create new strategies of incorporation to do so.

Indians peripheral to or not associated with Los Angeles core ethnic activities are in the majority. Does this mean that the Los Angeles Indian community is losing its vitality? Is it doomed to symbolic and superficial ethnic pursuits and performance in another generation? I do not think this will be the case. I refer to my early and continuing personal community experience to defend this position.

Although the selection of and intensity with which I became involved in my hometown community activities were based on idiosyncratic, individual interests and talents, I knew that I had the option of participating in most community activities at any point in my life if I chose to do so. Relatively unlimited rights to its resources was assured simply because of my location in and continuing identity with that community.

As I matured and began to shift reference groups, personal pursuits, and locations, my involvement in the community life of Bethel, Connecticut, became increasingly peripheral. That small New England town, however, is no less community to me because of my marginal participation in its ongoing activities or my move, in 1972, to California. My sense of community membership is sustained by the comforting certainty that, having been born and reared in Bethel, I have a birthright to its resources and capacities for incorporative social interaction. Yearly holiday visits to the family homestead allow the expression of certain community member prerogatives. Visiting family, classmates, my first church congregation, neighbors, and old after-school haunts are appropriate, familiar, and anticipated social rituals of community reincorporation. Easily won expected embraces, the familiarity of the greeting ritual, and the recognized patterning of information exchanges are sought out, relished, and returned. They provide the interactional fix that validates continued membership in a valued reference group for all the individuals involved in such exchanges.

My experience of community, I contend, is shared by most of the residents of the small town in which I was raised. Community as a continuing social field, personal resource, and sociocultural potential is, I further suggest, how most Indians in Los Angeles experience their urban community. The existence of identifiable Indian organizations across time provides Indian individuals with a field of potential resources to which they have inherent rights of participation. Occasional, gratuitous involvement in Los Angeles Indian activities are expressions of peripheral community members' birthrights. Being identified and recognized by the reference group as Indian or a person with "an Indian heart" are sufficient for initial and unquestioned acceptance into a social arena in which individuals can display certain valued and life-enhancing cultural competencies.

In the final analysis, the peripheral community members' emblematic expressions of ethnic identity illustrate the driving sociopsychological forces that eventuate in the construction and continuing viability of community. Ethnic institutions and the statuses and roles they validate over time are the products of the human will to community. They are the evidence of the human propensity for community, not its essential definition. Recognition of a collective interest, or, as Bill Fredricks put it, "our common bonds," sustains and defines community whether or not individuals actively participate in its group activities. The psychological high of joint participation in some shared and leveling activity, if only rarely, and the camaraderie that being with one's own people produces provide the opportunity and fulfill the human predisposition for *communitas*. In the practice of community (familiar, patterned, consensual, collective interaction, and ritual, both secular and sacred), we are comforted by the knowledge that we are not alone; we demonstrate who we are and who we are not; and we remember (or construct) and experience the unifying common source from which we, as community members, all come and to which we all belong.

NOTES

1. One of the last issues of *Talking Leaf* (vol. 53, no. 1; see Anonymous 1988) was devoted to a pictorial and editorial essay of the Cerritos memorial powwow. The memorial powwow was also covered by the *Los Angeles Times* (see Baker 1987).

2. Clapping is not the customary manner in which approval is exhibited at Indian events. Excitement, joy, or approval, particularly among the women, can be demonstrated by a piercing, high-pitched trilled call.

3. In dynastic China, a ruler's right to rule, or a "mandate of Heaven," was not bestowed unconditionally on unproven pretenders. Rather, it was demonstrated by a history of heroic good works. Since August 1986, the SCIC has persevered in its good works, that is, delivery of social services to its constituency. In this way, SCIC demonstrated its institutional and administrative mandate. I am indebted to my University of Southern California colleague Eugene Cooper for an explanation of the criteria by which "mandate of Heaven" was determined.

4. Most urban anthropology readers include a reprint of Wirth's (1938) landmark article. In "Urbanism as a Way of Life," he describes the tendency in urban society toward fewer "primary" associations, greater reliance on "secondary" associations, and a general compartmentalization of activities and associations.

Appendix

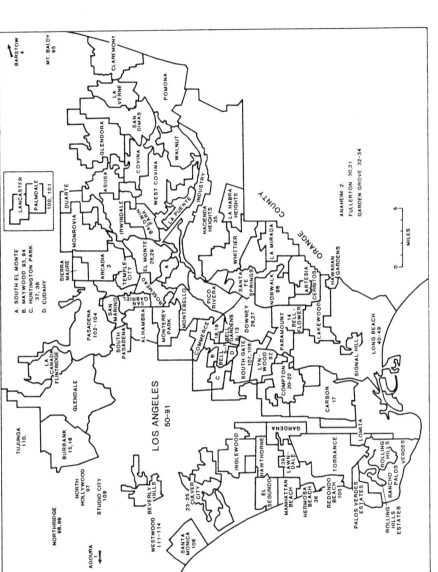

Map A.1 Location of American Indian Organizations in Los Angeles County, 1978–88

Table A.1 A Comparison of Native American Tribal Representation in Los Angeles, 1966–86: A Numerical Summary

Sources Persons reported	*Talking Leaf* (12/77–6/86) n = 481	Burns et al. (1974) n = 518	Price (1966) n = 2,945
1. Abenaki	1	0	0
2. Alaskan	1	0	0
3. Apache	8	14	92
4. San Carlos¹	5	0	0
5. Sonoran	1	0	0
6. Apache/Navajo	1	0	0
7. Arapaho	1	4	25
8. Arikara	2	6	35
9. Arikara/Gros Ventre	1	0	0
10. Assinibone	4	0	18
11. Blackfeet	6	4	47
12. Caddo/Osage	2	0	0
13. California, unspecified	7	0	0
14. Chumash	7	0	0
15. Cahuilla	1	0	0
16. Chumash/Choctaw	1	0	0
17. Cupeño/Luiseño/Diegueño	1	0	0
18. Diegueño	1	0	0
19. Fernandeño	1	0	0
20. Gabrielino	5	0	0
21. Hupa	1	0	0
22. Juaneño	1	0	0
23. Luiseño	4	0	0
24. Luiseño/Ponca/Haida/Tlingit	1	0	0
25. Miwok/Mission	1	0	0
26. Mono	1	0	0
27. Morongo	1	0	0
28. Pomo	3	5	3
29. Quechan	3	2	0
30. Shasta	1	0	1
31. Yurok	1	0	0
32. Yokut/Chichansi	1	0	0
33. Carrier	1	0	0
34. Cheyenne	10	13	97
35. Cheyenne/Arapaho	4	0	0
36. Cheyenne/Kickapoo	4	0	0
37. Chickahominy/Pamunkey	1	0	0
38. Colville	1	0	14

(*continued*)

Table A.1 (*Continued*)

Sources Persons reported	*Talking Leaf* (12/77–6/86) n = 481	Burns et al. (1974) n = 518	Price (1966) n = 2,945
39. Comanche	5	4	59
40. Coushatta	2	1	0
41. Cree	2	0	6
42. Crow	1	2	19
43. Crow/German	1	0	0
44. Delaware/Cherokee	1	0	0
45. Eskimo/Coeur D'Alene	1	0	0
FIVE CIVILIZED TRIBES			
46. Cherokee	24	18	185
47. Cherokee/Chippewa	1	0	0
48. Cherokee/Creek	1	0	0
49. Cherokee/Creek/Hawaiian	1	0	0
50. Cherokee/Irish	1	0	0
51. Chickasaw	1	4	14
52. Chickasaw/Cherokee	1	0	0
53. Choctaw	32	33	134
54. Choctaw/Blackfeet	1	0	0
55. Choctaw/Cherokee	1	0	0
56. Choctaw/Chinese	1	0	0
57. Choctaw/Sioux	1	0	0
58. Creek	24	33	183
59. Creek/Chippewa	4	0	0
60. Creek/Laguna	1	0	0
61. Creek/Osage	1	0	0
62. Creek/Seminole	1	0	0
63. Creek/Shawnee	1	0	0
64. Hidasta	2	1	0
65. Hidatsa/Mandan	1	0	0
IROQUOIS	0	1	142
66. Mohawk	3	0	0
67. Onondaga	1	0	0
68. Oneida	3	2	0
69. Oneida/Creek	1	0	0
70. Oneida/Mohawk	1	0	0
71. Seneca	12	3	0
72. Seneca/Cherokee	1	0	0

(continued)

Table A.1 (*Continued*)

Sources Persons reported	*Talking Leaf* (12/77–6/86) $n = 481$	Burns et al. (1974) $n = 518$	Price (1966) $n = 2,945$
73. Iroquois/Chippewa	1	0	0
74. Kickapoo	4	3	64
75. Kiowa	17	7	85
76. Kiowa/Cherokee	1	0	0
77. Kiowa/Comanche	1	0	0
78. Kiowa/Comanche/Cherokee	2	0	0
79. Kiowa/Delaware	1	0	0
80. Kiowa/Pawnee	1	0	0
81. Lumi	1	0	0
82. Mandan/Hidatsa	3	0	0
83. Maricopa	0	0	1
Maricopa/Hopi	1	0	0
84. Mattaponi	1	0	0
85. Menominee	1	1	0
MEXICAN INDIAN	0	1	45
86. Aztec/Taraxcan	1	0	0
87. Huichol/Otomi	1	0	0
88. Tarahumara	1	0	0
89. Navajo (Dineh)	48	90	417
90. Navajo/Seminole	1	0	0
91. Nez Percé	3	0	31
92. Nez Percé/Winnebago	1	0	0
93. Ojibwa	1	0	0
94. Chippewa	11	21	92
95. Chippewa/Cayuga	1	0	0
96. Chippewa/Sioux	1	0	0
97. Omaha	1	5	23
98. Omaha/Sioux	1	0	0
99. Osage	3	0	18
100. Osage/Cherokee	1	0	0
101. Ottawa	2	0	1
102. Paiute	2	7	33
103. Pyramid Lake	1	0	0
104. Southern	1	0	0
105. Paiute/Shoshone	2	0	0
106. Papago	9	16	74
107. Papago/Cahuilla	1	0	0
108. Piegan/Blackfeet	2	1	0

(*continued*)

Table A.1 *(Continued)*

Sources Persons reported	*Talking Leaf* (12/77–6/86) $n = 481$	Burns et al. (1974) $n = 518$	Price (1966) $n = 2,945$
109. Pima	1	17	55
110. Pima/Choctaw	1	0	0
111. Pima/Papago/Chumash	1	0	0
112. Ponca/Haida/Tlingit	1	0	0
113. Potawatomi	2	0	7
114. Pueblo	3	13	151
115. Acoma	2	1	0
116. Hopi	8	8	0
117. Hopi/Cherokee	4	0	0
118. Hopi/Cherokee/Mexican American	1	0	0
119. Hopi/Choctaw	1	0	0
120. Hopi/Papago	2	0	0
121. Hopi/Pima	2	0	0
122. Isleta	2	0	0
123. Laguna	5	4	0
124. Pueblo/Diegueño	2	0	0
125. San Juan	2	0	0
126. Santa Clara	2	0	0
127. Tewa	1	4	0
128. Sac and Fox	4	4	6
129. Sac and Fox/Creek	1	0	0
130. Shawnee	3	3	9
131. Shoshone/Paiute	4	0	0
132. Shoshone/Paiute/Mono	1	0	0
133. Sioux *(See also* Sioux/Lakota)	26	63	354
134. Cheyenne River	1	0	0
135. Oglala	3	0	0
136. Rosebud	2	0	0
137. Santee	1	0	0
138. Sisseton	3	0	0
139. Standing Rock	1	0	0
140. Yankton	3	0	0
141. Sioux/Arikara	1	0	0
142. Sioux/Creek	1	0	0
143. Sioux/Laguna	1	0	0
144. Sioux/Lakota	1	0	0
145. Sioux/Mandan/Hidatsa	2	0	0
146. Sioux/Winnebago	1	0	0
147. Skagit/Snohomish	1	0	0

(continued)

Table A.1 (*Continued*)

Sources Persons reported	*Talking Leaf* (12/77–6/86) n = 481	Burns et al. (1974) n = 518	Price (1966) n = 2,945
148. Ute	1	2	13
149. Wak/Chumi	1	0	0
150. Winnebago	5	0	42
151. Winnebago/Omaha	1	0	0
152. Winnebago/Pueblo	3	0	0
153. Yaqui/Apache	1	2	0
154. Yuki	1	0	0

The following tribes were not cited in any description of a Los Angeles American Indian resident in *Talking Leaf* articles from December 1977 to June 1986 but were mentioned in either or both the Burns et al. (1974) and Price (1966) studies.

Aleut	0	0	2
Algonquin	0	1	0
Athabascan	0	1	3
Band of Snakes[2]	0	1	0
Bannock	0	1	0
Caddo	0	1	2
Chemehuevi	0	1	0
Chickahominy	0	0	2
Chukchansi	0	1	0
Clallam	0	1	0
Cocopa	0	0	4
Coeur D'Alene	0	1	2
Delaware	0	0	31
Eskimo	0	0	4
Euchee (Creek)	0	2	0
Flathead	0	1	7
Gros Ventre	0	5	65
Haida	0	1	1
Havasupai	0	1	0
Huron	0	0	1
Iowa	0	2	0
Jemez	0	4	0
Karok	0	4	0
Klamath	0	1	3
Kutenai	0	0	3
Lillooet	0	0	1
Maidu	0	4	0

(*continued*)

Table A.1 *(Continued)*

Sources Persons reported	*Talking Leaf* (12/77–6/86) $n = 481$	Burns et al. (1974) $n = 518$	Price (1966) $n = 2,945$
Mandan	0	2	8
Maricopa	0	1	1
Mission	0	5	38
Mohave	0	3	10
Mohican	0	0	4
Nanticoke	0	0	10
Nomlaki	0	1	0
Ottawa	0	0	1
Oto	0	3	7
Pawnee	0	2	8
Peoria	0	0	1
Ponca	0	4	19
Powhatan	0	0	2
Quapaw	0	1	2
Quechua	0	0	2
Quillayute	0	1	0
Santa Rosa	0	1	0
Salish	0	0	1
Santo Domingo (Pueblo)	0	2	0
Seminole	0	0	108
Serrano	0	1	0
Sherwood[2]	0	1	0
Shoshone	0	6	19
Spokane	0	0	1
Tejitas[2]	0	1	0
Tlingit	0	1	8
Tolowa	0	1	0
Umatilla	0	1	1
Umpqua	0	0	1
Washo	0	1	1
Wintu	0	3	0
Wiyot	0	6	0
Yakima	0	0	18
Yavapai	0	1	9
Yuma	0	0	34
Wea	0	0	6
Zuni	0	1	0
Unknown	0	2	0
Subtotal	481	518	2,945

(continued)

Table A.1 *(Continued)*

Sources Persons reported	*Talking Leaf* (12/77–6/86) *n* = 481	Burns et al. (1974) *n* = 518	Price (1966) *n* = 2,945
Other ethnic categories mentioned in *Talking Leaf*			
Tribe not mentioned	521		
Caucasian	22		
Mexican American	5		
Black	1		
Filipino	2		
Total number in subsamples	1,032	518	2,945

1. Indented tribal designations are: (a) place-specific variants of the larger, more generic tribal name, as in the case of the Apaches and the San Carlos Apaches; (b) place- and subculture-specific variants of a larger culture area, as in the case of the California Indians and the Five Civilized Tribes; or (c) individuals affiliated with more than one tribe, in which case the individuals are listed under the first tribe mentioned.

2. Tribe is reported by respondent but does not appear on BIA census list of tribes.

Table A.2 Indian Organizations in Los Angeles County and Vicinity, 1978–88

Organization, by location	Type	Active in 1988[1]
Agoura		
1. Four Directions (formerly in L.A.)	education/religion	yes
Anaheim		
2. Haskell Institute Alumni Association of Southern California	recreation	unknown
Arcadia		
3. California Indian Education Association	education	no (1978)
Barstow		
4. Whitecloud Drummers	recreation	yes
Bell		
5. Indian Center South	social services	no (3/84)
5a. Adult Education	education	no (8/84)
5b. Child Development	social services	no (6/84)
6. Indian Help Line	alcoholism treatment	yes
7. Muscogee Mission	religion	yes
Bell Gardens		
8. Church of Latter-day Saints, Indian Mission	religion	yes
9. First Southern Baptist Indian Church	religion	yes
10. The Grassy Shores (Indian Bar)	recreation	yes
11. Indian Center Service Branch	social services	no
11a. Day Care	social services	no
11b. Preschool	education	no
12. Indian Revival Center	religion	yes
13. Tribal American Consulting Corporation	education	no (1978)
Bellflower		
14. A Universe of Metaphysics Universal Church	religion	yes
Burbank		
15. "Our American Heritage" (KLAC radio show)	communications	no (1984)
16. Indian Lodge, Inc.	alcoholism treatment	no (1985)
Carson		
17. Southern California Indian Centers, Inc.	social services	yes

(continued)

Table A.2 *(Continued)*

Organization, by location	Type	Active in 1988[1]
Commerce		
18. Indian Center South	social services	no (5/86)
18a. Graphic Arts Program	education	no (11/84)
19. Southern California Indian Centers, Inc.	social services	yes
Compton		
20. American Indian Athletic Association	recreation	yes
21. American Indian Free Clinic	medical	yes
22. Main Artery	alcoholism treatment	yes
22a. Native American Treatment	alcoholism treatment	yes
Culver City		
23. Billy Mills Indian Youth Leadership	education	unknown
24. California Winnebago Club	recreation	no
25. Indian Centers, Inc., West	social services	no (8/86)
25a. Elders Services	social services	no (8/86)
25b. Preschool	education	no (8/86)
Downey		
26. American Indian Women on the Move	social services	yes
27. L.A. County Education Center	education	yes
El Monte		
28. ICI San Gabriel Valley Center	social services	no (1983)
29. Urban Indian Development Association	economic	yes
Fullerton		
30. American Indian Bowling Association	recreation	yes
31. Inter-Tribal Student Council, California State University at Fullerton	education	yes
Garden Grove		
32. American Indian Unity Church	social services	yes
33. Orange County Indian Center	social services	yes
33a. Senior Citizens' Program	social services	yes
34. Soaring Eagles	alcoholism treatment	yes
Hacienda Heights		
35. Red Tepee	recreation	yes

(continued)

able A.2 *(Continued)*

Organization, by location	Type	Active in 1988[1]
Hermosa Beach		
36. Many Trails Indian Club	recreation	yes
Huntington Park		
37. American Indian Library Service	education	yes
38. Huntington Park Indian Free Clinic	medical	no (3/83)
Lawndale		
39. Indian Educational Enrichment Program	education	yes
Long Beach		
40. Alaskan Natives of Los Angeles	recreation	no
41. American Indian Studies Program, California State University at Long Beach	education	yes
42. Crossroads Inn (Indian bar)	recreation	yes
43. Eagle Lodge	alcoholism treatment	yes
43a. Alumni	alcoholism treatment	yes
44. The Elders' Circle	alcoholism treatment	no
45. Indian Center, Inc., Long Beach	social services	no (8/86)
46. Indian Child Welfare Program	social services	no (8/86)
47. Iroquois Social Dance Group	recreation	yes
48. Long Beach Unified School System, Educational Opportunity for Native Americans	education	yes
49. South Bay Indian Services, Inc.	social services	no (1982)
Los Angeles		
50. Alliance of Native Americans	political	yes
51. American Indian Community Coalition	political	yes
52. American Indian Council on Aging	social services	yes
53. American Indian Drum and Feather Club	recreation	yes
54. American Indian Education Commission	education	yes
55. "American Indian Hour" (radio show)	communications	yes
56. American Indian Men's Club	recreation	no (1985)
57. American Indian Registry for the Performing Arts	recreation	yes
58. American Indian Student Alliance	education	yes
59. Brighter Day Indian Church	religion	yes

(continued)

Table A.2 (*Continued*)

Organization, by location		Type	Active in 1988[1]
60.	California Urban Indian Health Council	medical	yes
61.	Concerned Community Indian Movement	political	yes
62.	Disabled American Indian Veterans Services	social services	yes
63.	Eagle Spirit Productions	recreation	yes
64.	Equal Employment Opportunity (county; Native American programs officer)	social services	yes
65.	The First American Indian Church	religion	yes
66.	Indian Actors Workshop	recreation	no
67.	Indian Alcoholism Commission of California	alcoholism treatment	yes
68.	Indian bars	recreation	
	Columbine	skid row	no
	The Astor	skid row	yes
	Rusty's	central city	no
	The Hut	mid-Wilshire	yes
	Moulin Rouge	mid-Wilshire	no
	Pretty Girl	mid-Wilshire	no
	The Irish Pub	central city	no
	The Shrimp Boat	skid row	no
69.	Indian Centers, Inc.	social services	no (10/86)
69a.	American Indian Local Merchants Group	economic	no (1984)
69b.	Central High School	education	no (1983)
69c.	Central High School Parent Committee	education	no (1983)
69d.	Foster Parent Program	social services	no (8/86)
69e.	Graphic Arts Program	education	no (12/84)
69f.	Indian Child and Family Resource Center	social services	no (8/86)
69g.	Job Training and Employment Program	social services	no (8/86)
69h.	Legal and Counseling Services	social services	no (8/86)
69i.	College Motivation Program	education	no (8/86)
69j.	Women's Group	social services	no
69k.	*Talking Leaf* (newspaper)	communications	no (1988)
69l.	Tutorial Program	education	no (8/86)

(*continued*)

Table A.2 *(Continued)*

Organization, by location	Type	Active in 1988[1]
70. Indian Guardian Angels	social services	unknown
71. Indian Men's Lodge	alcoholism treatment	no (1983)
71a. Indian Lodge, Inc., Detox	alcoholism treatment	no (1983)
71b. Women's Lodge	alcoholism treatment	no (1983)
72. Intertribal Communications Commission	communications	unknown
73. Jim Thorpe Powwow Committee	recreation	no (1984)
74. L.A. American Indian Bowling Association	recreation	yes
75. L.A. American Indian Concerned Citizens	political	yes
76. L.A. American Indian Women's Coalition	political	no
77. L.A. City-County Native American Indian Commission	political	yes
78. L.A. City-County American Indian Employees Association	economic	yes
79. L.A. County Affirmative Action Indian Community Liaison	political	yes
80. L.A. County Department of Public Social Services, American Indian Liaison	social services	yes
81. L.A. County Human Rights Commission	social services	yes
82. L.A. Indian Health Center	medical	no (1986)
82a. Family Life Information and Education Program	social services	no (1986)
82b. Family Resource Center	social services	no (1986)
83. First Native American and United Methodist Church Urban Outreach Project (Caring Center)	social services	yes
84. L.A. Unified School District, Educational Opportunities for Native Americans, Title IV Program	education	yes
84a. Parents' Committee	education	yes
85. L.A. City Mayor's Office, Native American Indian Liaison	political	yes
86. Little Big Horn Association	recreation	yes
87. Native American Fine Arts Society	recreation	no

(continued)

Table A.2 (*Continued*)

Organization, by location	Type	Active in 1988[1]
88. Parents' Anonymous	alcoholism treatment	no (198
89. Southern California Indian Center	social services	yes
90. United American Indian Involvement	social services	yes
91. U.S. Senatorial American Indian Liaison	political	yes
Lynwood		
92. Indian Centers, Inc., Indian Housing Assistance Center	social services	no (198
Maywood		
93. Indian Centers, Inc., Indian Preschool	education	no (198
93a. Daycare and Child Development	education	no (8/8
94. Tribal American Preschool	education	no (197
Mt. Baldy		
95. Mother Earth Drug Rehabilitation Program	alcohol and drug treatment	no (198
Norwalk		
96. First Native American and United Methodist Church (formerly in Los Angeles)	religion	yes
North Hollywood		
97. Tri-Valley Council of North Hollywood	political	unknov
Northridge		
98. American Indian Student Council, California State University at Northridge	education	yes
99. American Indian Studies Program, California State University at Northridge	education	yes
Palmdale		
100. Advancement of the American Indian	political	no (198
101. Intertribal Mission for Native Americans	religion	yes
Pasadena		
102. "American Indian Hour" (KPCC radio show)	communications	yes
103. Continuous Journey to the Sun	recreation	no (198
104. First American Media Experience	recreation	no
Redondo Beach		
105. Ebb Tide (Indian bar)	recreation	unkno'

(continue

ble A.2 *(Continued)*

Organization, by location	Type	Active in 1988[1]
Santa Monica		
6. Native American Culture Center in the Santa Monica Mountains	recreation	yes
South Gate		
7. American Indian Bible Church	religion	yes
8. First Indian Baptist Church	religion	yes
Studio City		
9. "American Indian Airwaves" (KPFK radio show)	communications	yes
Tujunga		
0. Indian Center North	social services	no (1982)
Westwood		
1. American Indian Law Students Association, University of California at Los Angeles	education	yes
2. American Indian Studies Program, University of California at Los Angeles	education	yes
3. Native American Student Association, University of California at Los Angeles	education	yes
4. Native American Studies Faculty Association, University of California at Los Angeles	education	yes
Unknown		
5. All Nations Drummers	recreation	yes
6. American Indian Community Service	social services	unknown
7. American Indian Movement	political	yes
8. Big Mountain Support Group	political	yes
9. The California Indian Legal Services	social services	unknown
0. The Gourd Society	recreation	yes
1. Indians for Reagan-Bush	political	no (1984)
2. International Treaty Council Support Group	political	yes
3. Leonard Peltier Defense Fund	political	unknown
4. Longest Walk Committee	political	no (1978)
5. Medicine Wheel Group	medical	unknown
6. Melvin Deer Singers	recreation	no
7. Nighthorse Campbell Campaign	political	no (1986)

(continued)

Table A.2 *(Continued)*

Organization, by location	Type	Active 1988[1]
128. Northern Paiute Language Class	education	unknow
129. Silverheels Evangelistic Ministry	religion	unknow
130. Standing Arrow Singers	recreation	unknow
131. Steward Headley Drum	recreation	unknow
132. Two Snakes Dance Ensemble	recreation	unknow
133. Two Valley Drummers	recreation	yes
134. Tribal Education Workers Association	social services	unknow
135. Yellowthunder Camp Support Group	political	unknow

1. Date of organization's demise, if known, is in parentheses.

References Cited

Ablon, Joan. 1964. "Relocated American Indians in the San Francisco Bay Area: Social Interaction and Indian Identity." *Human Organization* 23:296–304.

———. 1971a. "Cultural Conflict in Urban Indians." *Mental Hygiene* 55:199–205.

———. 1971b. "Retention of Cultural Values and Differential Urban Adaptation: Samoans and American Indians in a West Coast City." *Social Forces* 49(3): 385–92.

Abu-Lughod, Janet. 1961. "Migration Adjustment to City Life: The Egyptian Case." *American Journal of Sociology* 67(1): 22–32.

Adair, James. 1968. *The History of the American Indians.* 1775. New York: Johnson Reprint Corp.

Aikens, C. Melvin. 1983. "The Far West." In *Ancient North Americans.* J. D. Jennings, ed. pp. 149–202. San Francisco: W. H. Freeman and Co.

Anonymous. 1984. "'Let Peltier Go,' Say Soviets." *Talking Leaf* 49(6): 13.

Anonymous. 1985. "Indian Centers Celebrates 50th Year by Hosting National JTPA Conference." *Talking Leaf* 50(4): 1,6–7.

Anonymous. 1988. "Cerritos Memorial Pow Wow." *Talking Leaf* 53(1): 1, 7–11.

Anonymous. 1989. "Indian Child and Family Service." *Peace Pipe Line* (Norwalk, Calif.: First Native American and United Methodist Church) 8(1): 6.

Ansari, Ghaus, and Peter J. Nas, eds. 1983. *Town-Talk: The Dynamics of Urban Anthropology.* Leiden: E. J. Brill.

Arensberg, Conrad M. 1968. *The Irish Countryman.* 1937. Reprint. Garden City, N.Y.: Natural History Press.

Arensberg, Conrad M., and Solon T. Kimball. 1965. *Culture and Community.* New York: Harcourt, Brace and World.

Bahr, Howard M., Bruce A. Chadwick, and Robert C. Day, eds. 1972. *Native*

Americans Today: Sociological Perspectives. New York: Harper and Row.

Baker, Bob. 1987. "Powwow of Dream Is Taking Form as Tribute to Cerritos Air Crash Victims." *Los Angeles Times,* October 9, 1987, sec. 2, p. 1, col. 1.

Barnes, J. A. 1954. "Class and Committees in a Norwegian Island Parish." *Human Relations* 7(1): 39–58.

Barth, F. 1969. *Ethnic Groups and Boundaries: The Social Organization of Culture Difference.* Bergen, Norway: Universitets Fortaget.

Bell, James R. 1979. "The Rules and Regulations of Aggression and Violence among the American Indian Men of Skid Row, Los Angeles." *California Anthropologist* 9(1): 1–28.

Benson, Henry C. 1970. *Life among the Choctaw Indians and Sketches of the South-west.* 1860. New York: Johnson Reprint Corp.

Berkhofer, Robert F. 1972. *Salvation and the Savage: An Analysis of Protestant Missions and American Indian Response, 1787–1862.* New York: Atheneum.

Bowden, Henry Warner. 1981. *American Indians and Christian Missions: Studies in Cultural Conflict.* Chicago: University of Chicago Press.

Bramstedt, Wayne G. 1977. "Corporate Adaptations of Urban Migrants: American Indian Voluntary Associations in the Los Angeles Metropolitan Area." Ph.D. dissertation. University of California at Los Angeles.

Brandon, William. 1974. *The Last Americans.* New York: McGraw-Hill.

Bruce, D. 1984. Letter to R. Daniels, dated October 5, 1984. In LACCNAIC (1985).

Bureau of Indian Affairs (BIA). 1977. *Summary of Arrivals, Adult Vocation Training, and Direct Employment Service in Los Angeles.* Report. Los Angeles: BIA Los Angeles Field Office.

Burns, Marceline, John M. Daily, and Herbert Moskowitz. 1974. *Drinking Practices and Problems of Urban American Indians in Los Angeles.* Report PB 251727/4GI. Los Angeles: National Technical Information Service.

Chapple, Eliot Dismore, and Carleton Stevens Coon. 1942. *Principles of Anthropology.* New York: Henry Holt and Co.

Cohen, Abner. 1980. "The Lesson of Ethnicity." In Gmelch and Zenner, pp. 207–17.

Coleman, Michael C. 1985. *Presbyterian Missionary Attitudes toward American Indians, 1837–93.* Jackson: University Press of Mississippi.

Connell, John. 1973. "Social Networks in Urban Society." In *Social Patterns in Cities.* Institutions of British Geographers, Special Publication No. 5. B. D. Clark and M. B. Gleave, comps. pp. 41–52. Oxford: Alden Press.

Cook, Sherbourne F. 1943. *The Conflict between the California Indian and the White Civilization.* Vol. 1, *The Indian versus the Spanish Mission.*

Ibero-Americana, No. 21. Berkeley and Los Angeles: University of California Press.

―――. 1967. "Conflict between the California Indian and White Civilization." In *The California Indians: A Source Book*. R. F. Heizer and M. A. Whipple, eds. pp. 465–74. Berkeley and Los Angeles: University of California Press.

Craven, Paul, and Barry Wellman. 1973. "The Network City." *Sociological Inquiry* 43(3–4): 57–88.

Cushman, Horatio Bardwell. 1972. *History of the Choctaw, Chickasaw, and Natchez Indians*. 1899. Reprint. New York: Russell and Russell.

Daniels, R. 1985a. Letter to D. Ford, dated February 1, 1985. In LACCNAIC (1985).

―――. 1985b. Letter to D. Ford, dated February 4, 1985. In LACCNAIC (1985).

De Bary, William, Wing-Tsit Chan, and Burton Watson. 1966. *Sources of Chinese Tradition*. Vol. 1. New York: Columbia University Press.

Debo, Angie. 1940. *And Still the Waters Run*. Princeton: Princton University Press.

―――. 1941. *The Road to Disappearance: A History of the Creek Indians*. Norman: University of Oklahoma Press.

―――. 1951. *The Five Civilized Tribes of Oklahoma: Report on Social and Economic Conditions*. Philadelphia: Indian Rights Association.

―――. 1961. *The Rise and Fall of the Choctaw Republic*. 1934. Reprint. Norman: University of Oklahoma Press.

Doughty, Paul L. 1970. "Behind the Back of the City: Provincial Life in Lima, Peru." In *Peasants in Cities*. W. Mangin, ed. pp. 30–46. Boston: Houghton Mifflin Co.

Driver, Harold E. 1975. *Indians of North America*. Chicago: University of Chicago Press.

Epstein, David. 1972. "The Genesis and Function of Squatter Settlements in Brasilia." In Weaver and White, pp. 51–58.

Evans-Pritchard, E. E. 1940. *The Nuer*. New York: W. W. Norton and Co.

Ewers, John C. 1964. *The Emergence of the Plains Indian as the Symbol of the North American Indian*. Annual Report of the Board of Regents of the Smithsonian Institution. Publication No. 4613. Washington, D.C.: Smithsonian Institutiton.

―――. 1982. *The Blackfeet: Raiders on the Northwestern Plains*. Norman: University of Oklahoma Press.

Ferguson, Frances N. 1968. "Navajo Drinking: Some Tentative Hypotheses." *Human Organization* 27:159–67.

―――. 1976. "Stake Theory as an Explanatory Device in Navajo Alcoholism Treatment Response." *Human Organization* 35:65–78.

Firth, Raymond. 1955. "Some Principles of Social Organization." *Journal of the Royal Anthropological Institute* 85:1–18.

Fiske, Shirley J. 1975. "Navajo Cognition in the Urban Milieu: An Investigation of Social Categories and Use of Address Terms." Ph.D. dissertation. Stanford University.

———. 1977. "Intertribal Perceptions: Navajo and Pan-Indianism." *Ethos* 5(3): 358–75.

———. 1979. "Urban Ethnic Institutions: A Reappraisal from Los Angeles." *Urban Anthropology* 8(2): 149–71.

Fiske, Shirley J., and Joan Weibel. 1980. "Navajo Social Interactions in an Urban Environment: An Investigation of Cognition and Behavior." *Bulletin of the Southern California Academy of Sciences* 79(1): 19–37.

Ford, D. 1984. Letter to R. Daniels, dated November 27, 1984. In LAC-CNAIC (1985).

———. 1985a. Letter to R. Daniels, dated February 12, 1985. In LACCNAIC (1985).

———. 1985b. Letter to T. Bradley, dated February 19, 1985. In LACCNAIC (1985).

Foreman, Grant. 1934. *The Five Civilized Tribes.* Norman: University of Oklahoma Press.

Foster, George M. 1948. *Empire's Children: The People of Tzintzuntzan.* Mexico, D. F.: Smithsonian Institutions, Institute of Social Anthropology, Publication No. 6; Washington, D.C.: Smithsonian Press.

———. 1965. "Peasant Society and the Image of a Limited Good." *American Anthropologist* 67:293–315.

———. 1969. *Applied Anthropology.* Boston: Little, Brown and Co.

Fredricks, Bill. 1986. Letter to R. Medina, dated August 27, 1986. In LAC-CNAIC (1985).

Gans, Herbert. 1962. *The Urban Villagers.* New York: Free Press.

Garbarino, Merwyn S. 1971. "Life in the City: Chicago." In Waddell and Watson, pp. 168–205.

Garcia-Mason, V. 1985. "Relationship of Drug Use and Self-Concept among American Indian Youth." Ph.D. dissertation. University of New Mexico.

Gardner, Richard E. 1969. "The Role of a Pan-Indian Church in Urban Indian Life." *Anthropology UCLA* 1(1): 14–26.

Gmelch, George, and Walter P. Zenner, eds. 1980. *Urban Life: Readings in Urban Anthropology.* New York: St. Martin's Press.

Goffman, Erving. 1959. *The Presentation of Self in Everyday Life.* Garden City, N.Y.: Doubleday/Anchor Books.

———. 1963. *Behavior in Public Places.* New York: Free Press.

Gordon, Milton. 1964. *Assimilation in American Life.* New York: Oxford University Press.

Graves, Theodore D. 1971. "Drinking and Drunkenness among Urban Indians." In Waddell and Watson, pp. 275–311.

———. 1972. "The Personal Adjustment of Navajo Indian Migrants to Denver, CO." In Bahr, Chadwick, and Day, pp. 440–66.

———. 1974. "Urban Indian Personality and the 'Culture of Poverty.'" *American Ethnologist* 1(1): 65–86.

Grinnell, George Bird. 1972. *The Cheyenne Indians*. Vol. 2. Lincoln: University of Nebraska Press.

Guillemin, Jeanne. 1975. *Urban Renegades: The Cultural Strategy of American Indians*. New York: Columbia University Press.

Guilmet, George M. 1976. "The Nonverbal American Indian Child in the Urban Classroom." Ph.D. dissertation. University of California at Los Angeles; Ann Arbor, Mich.: University Microfilms.

Guldin, Gregory. 1980. "Whose Neighborhood Is This? Ethnicity and Community in Hong Kong." *Urban Anthropology* 9(2): 243–63.

Hannerz, Ulf. 1980. *Exploring the City: Inquiries toward an Urban Anthropology*. New York: Columbia University Press.

Heer, David M., and Herman Pini. 1990. *A Human Mosaic: An Atlas of Ethnicity in Los Angeles County, 1980–1986*. Panorama City, Calif.: Western Economic Research.

Hertzberg, Hazel W. 1971. *The Search for an American Indian Identity: Modern Pan-Indian Movements*. Syracuse: Syracuse University Press.

Hirabayashi, James, William Willard, and Luis Kemnitzer. 1972. "Pan-Indianism in the Urban Setting." In Weaver and White, pp. 77–87.

Hoebel, E. Adamson. 1978. *The Cheyenne*. New York: Holt, Rinehart and Winston.

Holzberg, C. S. 1982. "Ethnicity and Aging: Anthropological Perspectives on More Than Just the Minority Elderly." *The Gerontologist* 22(6): 249–257.

Hughley, G. 1985. Memorandum to S. Porter, dated March 14, 1985. In LACCNAIC (1985).

Indian Centers, Inc. (ICI). 1984. *Director's Fiscal Reports*. Board of Director's Meeting Agenda Addenda, October 11, 1984. Los Angeles: ICI.

James, Bernard J. 1961. "Social-Psychological Dimensions of Ojibwa Acculturation." *American Anthropologist* 63:721–46.

Janowitz, Morris. 1952. *The Community Press in an Urban Setting*. Chicago: University of Chicago Press.

Jones, Delmos J. 1987. "The 'Community' and Organizations in the Community." In Mullings, pp. 99–122.

Jorgensen, Joseph G. 1971. "Indian and the Metropolis." In Waddell and Watson, pp. 66–113.

Keefe, Susan Emley. 1980. "Personal Communities in the City: Support Networks among Mexican-Americans and Anglo-Americans." *Urban Anthropology* 9(1): 51–74.

Keller, Robert H. 1983. *American Protestantism and United States Indian Policy, 1869–82*. Lincoln: University of Nebraska Press.

Kimball, Solon T., and William L. Partridge. 1979. *The Craft of Community Study: Fieldwork Dialogues*. Gainesville: University Presses of Florida.

Kroeber, Alfred L. 1967. "The Native Population of California." In *The California Indians: A Source Book*. R. F. Heizer and M. A. Whipple, eds. pp. 68–81. Berkeley and Los Angeles: University of California Press.

Kurath, G. 1966. *Michigan Indian Festivals*. Ann Arbor, Mich.: Ann Arbor Publishers.

Lafferty, R. A. 1972. *Okla Hannali*. Garden City, N.Y.: Doubleday and Co.

Langness, Louis L., and Gelya Frank. 1981. *Lives: An Anthropological Approach to Biography*. Novato, Calif.: Chandler and Sharp.

Leeds, Anthony. 1973. "Locality Power in Relation to Supralocal Power Institutions." In *Urban Anthropology: Cross-cultural Studies of Urbanization*. A. Southall, ed. pp. 15–41. New York: Oxford University Press.

Lévi-Strauss, Claude. 1963. *Structural Anthropology*. Claire Jacobson and Brooke Grundfest Schoepf, trans. New York: Basic Books.

––––––. 1966. *The Savage Mind*. Chicago: University of Chicago Press.

Levy, Jerrold. 1985. "An Alcohol and Suicide Prevention Program for Hopi Youth." Paper presented during the session "Illness Prevention and Health Promotion in North American: Medical Anthropology in Action" at the 84th Annual Meeting of the American Anthropological Association, Washington, D.C.

Lewis, Oscar. 1967. "Further Observations on the Folk-Urban Continuum and Urbanization with Special Reference to Mexico City." In *The Study of Urbanization*. P. M. Hauser and L. F. Schore, eds. pp. 491–502. New York: John Wiley and Sons.

Long, John, Lena Canyon, and David Churchman. 1973. "Tribal American Preschool: A Descriptive Account of Education for Urban American Indians." *Journal of American Indian Education* 13(1): 7–13.

Los Angeles City-County Native American Indian Commission (LAC-CNAIC). 1981. *Report on Los Angeles Urban Indian Affairs, February 10, 1977 to December 31, 1980*. Los Angeles: LACCNAIC.

––––––. 1985. Untitled report, circa May 10, 1985. Los Angeles: LAC-CNAIC.

––––––. 1986. Letter to "All Agencies including Mr. Medina," dated June 16, 1986. Los Angeles: LACCNAIC.

––––––. 1987a. Minutes of the January 1987 Commission Meeting. Los Angeles: LACCNAIC.

––––––. 1987b. *1986–87 Report on Indian Affairs of Los Angeles City and County*. To the L. A. County Board of Supervisors and the Mayor of the City of Los Angeles. Los Angeles: LACCNAIC.

Los Angeles County Community Development Department (LACCDD). 1982. *1980 Census: Hispanics by Race, by Age, by City and Census Designated Place, Universe, All Persons*. Report STF1. March 19, 1982. Tables 12–13. Los Angeles: LACCDD.

Los Angeles County Department of Regional Planning (LACDRP). 1981. *1980 Census Reports: 1980 Population (Five Racial Groups and Hispanics) for Eighty-one Cities in Los Angeles County*. Report NC80–1. December 9, 1981. Los Angeles: Affiliate Census Data Center, Research Section, LACDRP.

———. 1982. *1980 Census Reports: Los Angeles County Population.* Report NC80–9. June 16, 1982. Los Angeles: Affiliate Census Data Center, Research Section, LACDRP.

———. 1983a. *1980 Census Reports: 1980 Census: Asians and Pacific Islanders by Place Shown as a Percent of Total Population.* Report NC80–22. January 5, 1983. Los Angeles: Affiliate Census Data Center, Research Section, LACDRP.

———. 1983b. *1980 Census Reports: 1980 Census: Total Unemployed Racial Groups and Hispanics by City and Census Designated Place.* Report NC80–25. July 12, 1983. Los Angeles: Affiliate Census Data Center, Research Section, LACDRP.

Lowie, Robert H. 1917. *Notes on the Social Organization and Customs of the Mandan, Hidatsa, and Crow Indians.* APAMNH, vol. 21, pt. 1. New York: Natural History Press.

———. 1954. *Indians of the Plains.* New York: McGraw-Hill.

Lynch, Owen. 1980. "Political Mobilization and Ethnicity among the Adi-Dravidas in a Bombay Slum." In Gmelch and Zenner, pp. 229–37.

———, ed. 1984. *Culture and Community in Europe: Essays in Honor of Conrad M. Arensberg.* Delhi: Hindustan Publishing.

Margolies, S. 1973. "Powwows and Peyote Help Indians Adjust to Life in the Big City." *Wall Street Journal,* June 5, 1973, pp. 1, 31.

Mayer, Philip. 1962. "Migrancy and the Study of Africans in Towns." *American Anthropologist* 64:576–92.

MB. 1985. "Community Strength Shines through Clouds of Doubt; Programs Continue." *Talking Leaf* 50(4): 8.

McKee, Jess O., and Jon A. Schlenker. 1980. *The Choctaws: Cultural Evolution of a Native American Tribe.* Jackson: University Press of Mississippi.

Mead, George Herbert. 1967. *Mind, Self, and Society.* Chicago: University of Chicago Press.

Mead, Margaret. 1966. *New Lives for Old: Cultural Transformation—Manus, 1928–53.* New York: Dell.

Mitchell, J. Clyde. 1969. *Social Networks in Urban Situations.* Manchester: University of Manchester Press.

Moore, Sally Falk. 1978. "Old Age in Life-Term Social Arena: Some Chagga of Kilimanjaro in 1974." In *Life's Career—Aging: Cultural Variations on Growing Old.* B. G. Myerhoff and A. Simić, eds. pp. 23–76. Beverly Hills, Calif.: Sage Publications.

Morgan, Lewis Henry. 1858. "Laws of Descent of the Iroquois." *Proceedings of the Eleventh Meeting of the American Association for the Advancement of Science.* August 1957. Pt. 2. Cambridge, Mass.: AAAS.

———. 1871. *Systems of Consanguinity and Affinity of the Human Family.* Smithsonian Contributions of Knowledge, vol. 17. Washington, D.C.: Smithsonian Institution.

———. 1904[1851]. *The League of the Iroquois.* New York: Dodd, Mead and Co.

Morinis, E. Alan. 1982. "'Getting Straight': Behavioral Patterns in a Skid Row Indian Community." *Urban Anthropology* 11(2): 193–212.

Mucha, Janusz. 1983. "From Prairie to the City: Transformation of Chicago's American Indian Community." *Urban Anthropology* 12(3–4): 337–71.

Mullings, Leith, ed. 1987. *Cities of the United States: Studies in Urban Anthropology*. New York: Columbia University Press.

Murdock, George Peter. 1949. *Social Structure*. New York: MacMillan.

Myerhoff, Barbara. 1980a. *Number Our Days*. New York: E. P. Dutton.

———. 1980b. "Re-membered Lives." *Parabola: Myth and the Quest for Meaning* 5(1): 74–77.

Nanda, Serena. 1980. *Cultural Anthropology*. New York: Van Nostrand.

Oetting, E. R., G. S. Edwards, G. S. Goldstein, and V. Garcia-Mason. 1980. "Drug Use among Adolescents of Five Southwestern Native American Tribes." *International Journal of the Addictions* 15(3): 439–45.

Officer, James E. 1971. "The American Indian and Federal Policy." In Waddell and Watson, pp. 8–65.

Olson, James S., and Raymond Wilson. 1984. *Native Americans in the Twentieth Century*. Urbana: University of Illinois Press.

Olson, John W. 1971. "Epilogue: The Urban Indian as Viewed by an Indian Caseworker." In Waddell and Watson, pp. 398–407.

Oswalt, Wendell. 1988. *This Land Was Theirs: A Study of North American Indians*. Mountain View, Calif.: Mayfield.

Park, Robert E., Ernest W. Burgess, and Roderick D. MacKenzie. 1925. *The City*. Chicago: University of Chicago Press.

Paul, Doris. 1973. *The Navajo Code Talkers*. Philadelphia: Dorrance and Co.

Pelto, Pertti J. 1972. "Research Strategies in the Study of Complex Societies: The 'Ciudad Industrial' Project." In Weaver and White, pp. 5–20.

Peterson, John H. 1979. "Three Efforts at Development among the Choctaws of Mississippi." In *Southeastern Indians since the Removal Era*. W. L. Williams, ed. pp. 142–53. Athens: University of Georgia Press.

Pierce, Chris. 1985. "A New Era for Urban Indians: Los Angeles City[-County] Native American Indian Commission, 1976–1986." *Talking Leaf* 50(10): 6.

Plotnicov, Leonard. 1983. "Urban Anthropology in the U.S.A." In Ansari and Peter, pp. 140–57.

Powell, John Wesley. 1880. "Sketch of Lewis H. Morgan." *Popular Science Monthly* 18:115.

Powers, William. 1977. *Oglala Religion*. Lincoln: University of Nebraska Press.

Press, Irwin, and Estellie M. Smith. 1980. *Urban Place and Process: Readings in the Anthropology of Cities*. New York: MacMillan.

Price, John A. 1966. "American Indians in Los Angeles: A Study of Adaptation to a City." Ms. Department of Anthropology, University of California at Los Angeles.

――――. 1968. "The Migration and Adaptation of American Indians to Los Angeles." *Human Organization* 27:168–75.

――――. 1975. "U.S. and Canadian Indian Urban Ethnic Institutions." *Urban Anthropology* 4(1): 35–52.

――――. 1978. *Native Studies: American and Canadian Indians.* Toronto: McGraw Hill Ryerson.

Prucha, Francis P. 1979. *The Churches and the Indian Schools, 1888–1912.* Lincoln: University of Nebraska Press.

Radin, Paul. 1949. "The Culture of the Winnebago as Described by Themselves." *Special Publications of the Bollingen Foundation* 1:38.

Redfield, Robert. 1955. *The Little Community.* Chicago: University of Chicago Press.

Rose, Phyllis, and George Howell. 1986. "Pro-Khadafy Stand Upsets Several Community Leaders." *Talking Leaf* 51(6): 4.1.

Salisbury, Richard F., and Mary E. Salisbury. 1972. "The Rural-oriented Strategy of Urban Adaptation: Siane Migrants in Port Moresby." In Weaver and White, pp. 58–68.

Schensul, Jean J., Iris Nieves, and Maria D. Martinez. 1982. "The Crisis Event in the Puerto Rican Community: Research and Intervention in the Community/Institution Interface." *Urban Anthropology* 11(1): 101–28.

Scheper-Hughes, Nancy. 1979. *Saints, Scholars, and Schizophrenics: Mental Illness in Rural Ireland.* Berkeley and Los Angeles: University of California Press.

Semerad, R. 1986. Letter to S. Wade, dated August 14, 1986. In LACCNAIC (1985).

Shaw, Bruce. 1980. "Life History Writing in Anthropology: A Methodological Review." *Mankind* 12(3): 226–33.

Simić, Andrei. 1987. "Ethnicity as a Career for the Elderly: The Serbian-American Case." *The Journal of Applied Gerontology* 6(1): 113–26.

Snyder, Peter Z. 1971. "The Social Environment of the Urban Indian." In Waddell and Watson, pp. 206–43.

――――. 1973. "Social Interaction Patterns and Relative Urban Success: The Denver Navajo." *Urban Anthropology* 2(1): 1–24.

Southall, Aidan. 1973. "The Density of Role-Relationships as a Universal Index of Urbanization." In *Urban Anthropology: Cross-cultural Studies of Urbanization.* A. Southall, ed. pp. 71–106. New York: Oxford University Press.

Spier, Leslie. 1925. *The Distribution of Kinship Systems in North America.* University of Washington Publications in Anthropology, 1(2). Seattle.

Spoehr, Alexander. 1968. "Changing Kinship Systems: A Study in the Acculturation of the Creeks, Cherokee, and Choctaw." In *The Seminole.* A. Spoehr, ed. pp. 150–233. Field Museum Anthropological Series, Publication No. 583. 1947. Reprint. Chicago: Field Museum of Natural History.

Spradley, James P. 1969. *Guests Never Leave Hungry: The Autobiography of James Sewid, a Kwakiutl Indian.* New Haven: Yale University Press.

———. 1972. "Adaptive Strategies of Urban Nomads: The Ethnoscience of Tramp Culture." In Weaver and White, pp. 21–38.

Swanton, John R. 1918. *An Early Account of the Choctaw Indians.* Memoirs of the American Anthropological Association. Vol. 5, no. 2. Lancaster, Pa.

———. 1928. *Social Organization and Social Usages of the Indians of the Creek Confederacy.* Forty-second Annual Report of the Bureau of American Ethnology. Washington, D.C., pp. 25–472.

———. 1931. *Source Material for the Social and Ceremonial Life of the Choctaw Indians.* Smithsonian Institution, Bureau of American Ethnology, Bulletin 103. Washington, D.C.: Government Printing Office.

Talai, Vered Amit. 1988. "When Ethnic Identity Is a Mixed Blessing: Armenians in London." *Ethnos* 53(I-II): 52–62.

Taylor, Theodore W. 1986. *American Indian Policy.* Mount Airy, Md.: Lomond Publications.

Thompson, Bobby, and John H. Peterson, Jr. 1975. "Mississippi Choctaw Identity: Genesis and Change." In *The New Ethnicity: Perspectives from Ethnology.* J. W. Bennett, ed. pp. 179–96. St. Paul: West Publishing Co.

Tunks, B. 1985. Memorandum to G. Flores, dated March 11, 1985. In LAC-CNAIC (1985).

Turner, Victor. 1974. *Dramas, Fields, and Metaphors: Symbolic Action in Human Society.* Ithaca: Cornell University Press.

U.S. Department of Commerce, Bureau of the Census. 1973a. *Census of Population.* Vol. 1, *Characteristics of the Population.* Pt. 1, *United States Summary.* Sect. 1. Table 1, "Indian Population by Sex and Urban and Rural Residence: 1970." p. 1. Washington, D.C.: Government Printing Office.

———. 1973b. *General Population Characteristics.* Table 23, "Race by Sex, for Areas and Places: 1970." pp. 6–100. Washington, D.C.: Government Printing Office.

———. 1982a. *Population and Housing: Advanced Estimates of Social, Economic, and Housing Characteristics.* Report PC 80–1-B, *California.* Table 50, "General Characteristics for Selected Racial Groups for Counties: 1980." pp. 6–678. Washington, D.C.: Government Printing Office.

———. 1982b. *Population and Housing: Advanced Estimates of Social, Economic, and Housing Characteristics.* Supplementary Report PHC 80–82. Pt. 6, *California.* Table P–5, "General, Social, and Economic Characteristics by Race and Spanish Origin: 1980." pp. 6–162. Washington, D.C.: Government Printing Office.

————. 1983a. *General Population Characteristics: California.* Table 15, "Persons by Race: 1980." pp. 6–19. Washington, D.C.: Government Printing Office.

————. 1983b. *Twentieth Census, 1980: Characteristics of the Population.* Vol. 1, *General Population Characteristics.* Chap. B, Pt. 1, *United States Summary.* PC80–1-B1. Table 38, "Persons by Race and Sex: 1980." Washington, D.C.: Government Printing Office.

Vanderwagen, Craig, Russell D. Mason, and Tom Choken Owan. 1986. *Background, Plenary Session, and Action Plan: Indian Health Service (IHS) Alcoholism/Substance Abuse Prevention Initiative.* Washington, D.C.: U.S. Department of Health and Human Services.

van Gennep, Arnold. 1960. *The Rites of Passage.* London: Routledge and Kegan Paul.

van Willigen, John. 1986. *Applied Anthropology.* South Hadley, Mass.: Bergin and Garvey.

Waddell, Jack O., and O. Michael Watson, eds. 1971. *The American Indian in Urban Society.* Boston: Little, Brown and Co.

Wade, Sophie. 1986. Letter to the "Native American Indian Community," dated October 13, 1986. In LACCNAIC (1985).

Wallace, Anthony F. C. 1956. "Revitalization Movements." *American Anthropologist* 58:264–81.

————. 1972. *The Death and Rebirth of the Seneca.* New York: Random House.

Weaver, Thomas, and Douglas White. 1972a. "Anthropological Approaches to Urban and Complex Society." In Weaver and White, pp. 109–35.

————, eds. 1972b. *The Anthropology of Urban Environments.* Monograph Series No. 11. Washington, D.C.: Society for Applied Anthropology.

Weibel, Joan. 1977. "Native Americans in Los Angeles: A Cross-cultural Comparison of Assistance Patterns in an Urban Environment." Ph.D. dissertation. University of California at Los Angeles.

————. 1978. "Native Americans in Los Angeles: A Cross-cultural Comparison of Assistance Patterns in an Urban Environment." *Anthropology UCLA* 9(1–2): 81–98.

————. 1981. "There's a Place for Everything and Everything in Its Place: Environmental Influences on Urban Indian Drinking Patterns." In *Social Drinking Contexts.* Research Monograph No. 7. T. C. Harford and L. S. Gaines, eds. pp. 206–27. DHHS Publications No. (ADM)81–1097. Washington, D.C.: National Institute on Alcohol Abuse and Alcoholism.

Weibel, Joan, and Thomas Weisner. 1980. *An Ethnography of Urban Indian Drinking Patterns in California.* Report prepared for the California State Department of Alcohol and Drug Programs, Sacramento. Los Angeles: Alcohol Research Center, University of California at Los Angeles.

Weibel-Orlando, Joan. 1984. "Alcoholism Treatment Centers as Flawed Rites of Passage." *Medical Anthropology Quarterly* 15(3): 62–67.

———. 1988a. "Indians, Ethnicity as a Resource, and Aging: You Can Go Home Again." *The Journal of Cross-cultural Gerontology* 3:323–48.

———. 1988b. "Miss America and Powwow Princess: Icons of Womanhood." *Urban Resources* 4(3): LA 1–8.

———. 1989. *Urban American Indian Elders Outreach Project.* Final report to the Administration on Aging, Washington, D.C. Los Angeles: Los Angeles County Area Agency on Aging, Department of Community and Senior Citizens Services.

Weisner, Thomas, Joan Weibel-Orlando, and John Long. 1984. "Serious Drinking, White Man's Drinking, and Teetotaling: Drinking Levels and Styles in an Urban American Indian Population." *Journal of Studies on Alcohol* 45(3): 313–35.

Werner, Oswald, and Mark G. Schoepfle. 1987. *Systematic Fieldwork: Foundations of Ethnography and Interviewing.* 2 vols. Newbury Park, Calif.: Sage Publications.

West, James. 1945. *Plainville, U.S.A.* New York: Columbia University Press.

Wilder, Thornton. 1977. *The Bridge of San Luis Rey.* Harmondsworth, U.K.: Penguin Books.

Wirth, Louis. 1938. "Urbanism as a Way of Life." *American Journal of Sociology* 44:3–24.

Wissler, Clark. 1916. "General Discussion of Shamanistic and Dancing Societies." *American Museum of Natural History Anthropological Papers* 11(2): 853–76.

Wolf, Eric R. 1966. "Kinship, Friendship, and Patron-Client Relations in Complex Societies." In *The Social Anthropology of Complex Societies.* M. Banton, ed. pp. 1–22. New York: F. A. Praeger.

Wolfe, Tom. 1970. *Radical Chic and Mau-mauing the Flak Catchers.* New York: Farrar, Straus and Giroux.

Wulff, Robert M., and Shirley J. Fiske. 1987. *Anthropological Praxis: Translating Knowledge into Action.* Boulder, Colo.: Westview Press.

Young, Gloria. 1981. "Powwow Power: Perspectives on Historical and Contemporary Intertribalism." Ph.D. dissertation, Indiana University; Ann Arbor, Mich.: University Microfilms.

Zenner, Walter P. 1980. "Ethnicity and Class in the City." In Gmelch and Zenner, pp. 201–6.

Index

Calif. State University (*cont.*)
gram, 137; at North Ridge, American
Indian studies program, 137
Campgrounds, Christian church: con-
tinuity, 170, 175; in Oklahoma, 87,
131, 168, 170–73, 175, 177n.10; in
the Southeast, 170–71, 175
Canyon, Lena, 105
Caring Center. *See* FNAUMC
Carson, Calif., 27
Case history, as research method, 39
Caucasians. *See* Anglos; Choctaws, re-
lations with whites; Population figures (1980), in Los Angeles, whites;
Residential patterns, whites; Time,
white man's; Whites
Cecil B. De Mille Junior High School,
86, 137, 139, 151n.6, 213, 291
Census, population: and the Indian
Complete Count Committee, 19–20;
and the Los Angeles Special Census,
19–20; undercount of, 8n.1, 19–21
—American Indians: 1890, 13; 1910,
12; 1950, 13; 1970, 24–31; 1980,
8n.1, 19, 21, 23–32, 108, 297; 1990,
19, 21, 296
Central High School, ICI, 104, 118
Ceremonies, 131, 132, 143, 152n.15;
calendar of, 131, 133, 137, 224;
Cheyenne, 181; Choctaw, 173–75;
church, 153; continuity of, 153, 173–
75; healing, 110–14; traditional, 132,
143. *See also* Rites
Cerritos, Calif., 28, 289, 301n.1
Chadwick, Bruce A., 63n.8
Chan, Wing-Tsit, 290
Chapple, Eliot Dismore, 125, 126
Cherokees, 35, 37, 123, 134, 140, 149n,
150n.2, 161, 223; Christianization of,
170–72; church community, 170–72;
language, use of, 159, 167; in Los Angeles, 193, 209, 268; in the Southeast,
170–72
Chessman, Pete, 261, 275
Cheyenne-Arapaho Nation of California, 89
Cheyennes, 35, 37, 123, 126n.3, 181,
182, 198n.3; clown dancers, 181, 183;
contrary dancers, 181; Dog Soldiers,
198n.3; kinship terms, 123; *massaum*

ceremonies, 181; peace councils, 194;
scalp dances, 181
Chicago urban studies, 31
Chickasaws, 35, 37, 134, 161, 223; and
Choctaws, 223
Chippewas, 35, 37
Choctaws, 35, 37, 87, 88, 89, 114, 131,
134, 150n.2, 155, 157, 161, 164, 165,
173, 218, 219–20, 225–26, 229; band
leaders, 174; and Baptists, 177nn.8,
10; Bible, 174; ceremonies, 173–75;
and Chickasaws, 223; Christianization of, 170–75; church community,
170–73, 175, 177n.10, 222; clans,
172–73; clan towns, 172, 173;
dances, 173, 175; feasting, 173, 174;
foods, 173; harvest festivals, 173;
head chiefs, 174; hymnal, 174, 220;
hymns, 220; *iksa*, 172; kinship reckoning, 172–73; language classes, 165,
174; language, use of, 159, 165, 167,
174, 220, 226; literacy among, 174;
matriarchs, 220; matrilines, 175; and
Methodism, 177n.10, 218–19; mission work among, 173, 174, 175,
177nn.8, 10, 11; in Mississippi,
177n.11; in Oklahoma, 170, 172,
177nn.8, 10, 221, 231nn.2, 3; 225–26,
231n.2; oratory, 174; pre-Christians,
170, 172, 173–75; and Presbyterians,
177n.10; removal of, 177n.10; return
migration, 170, 172–73; roles, 173,
174, 175; song traditions, 172–73,
175; in the Southeast, 170; statuses,
174, 175; towns, 170–72; urban, 174;
relations with whites, 222; women's
roles, 173, 175
Choctaw Territory, 177n.10, 225–26
Christianity, 12, 41, 87, 153–77 passim,
221, 222; and boarding schools,
176n.6, 234; in eastern Oklahoma,
153, 155, 156, 161, 168, 170–73, 175,
177nn.8, 10; and healing, 156; in Los
Angeles, 168–70, 181, 218–19, 220;
and Roman Catholicism, 206, 234; in
the Southeast, 157, 170–71, 175,
176nn.6, 8, 177nn.8, 10; and Indians,
41, 87, 134, 150n.2, 153–77 passim,
201, 219
Chumash, 140; sit-ins, 36

A Note on the Author

JOAN WEIBEL-ORLANDO, a member of the anthropology faculty at the University of Southern California, is the author or co-author of numerous articles in such journals as *Medical Anthropology Quarterly*, *Human Organization*, and the *Journal of Alcohol Studies*; she also wrote and directed the video presentation *Going Home: A Grandmother's Story*, which chronicles a Lakota woman's return to the Pine Ridge Reservation in South Dakota after living for twenty-six years in Los Angeles. Weibel-Orlando is currently writing a book, with Andrei Simić and others, based on research among aging members of three ethnic communities in California. She is also at work on a film about the Los Angeles American Indian community, which will be a permanent exhibit in the Times Mirror Hall of Native American Cultures in the Los Angeles County Natural History Museum.

DATE DUE